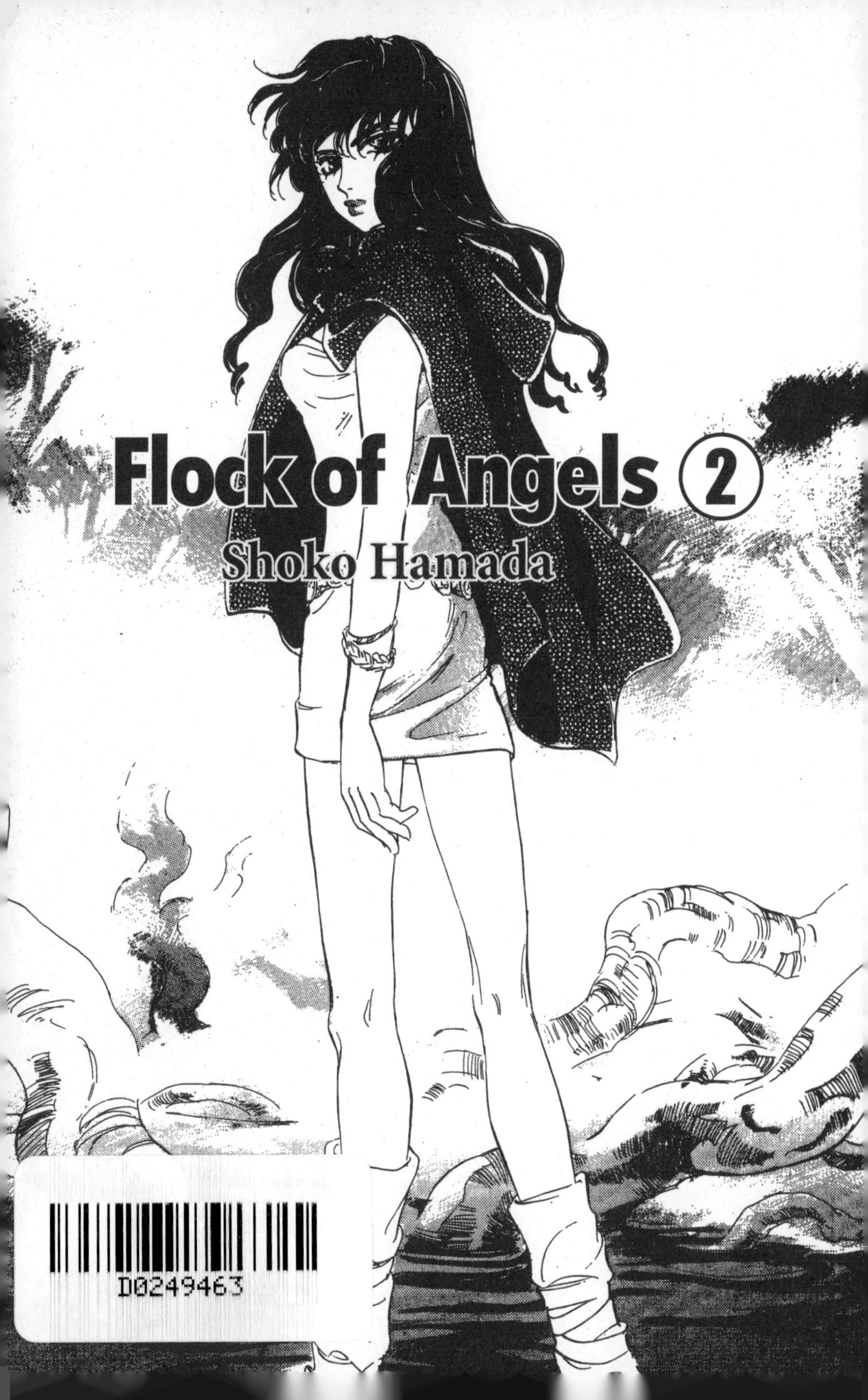

Flock of Angels ②

Shoko Hamada

Flock of Angels

Contents

Chapter 6

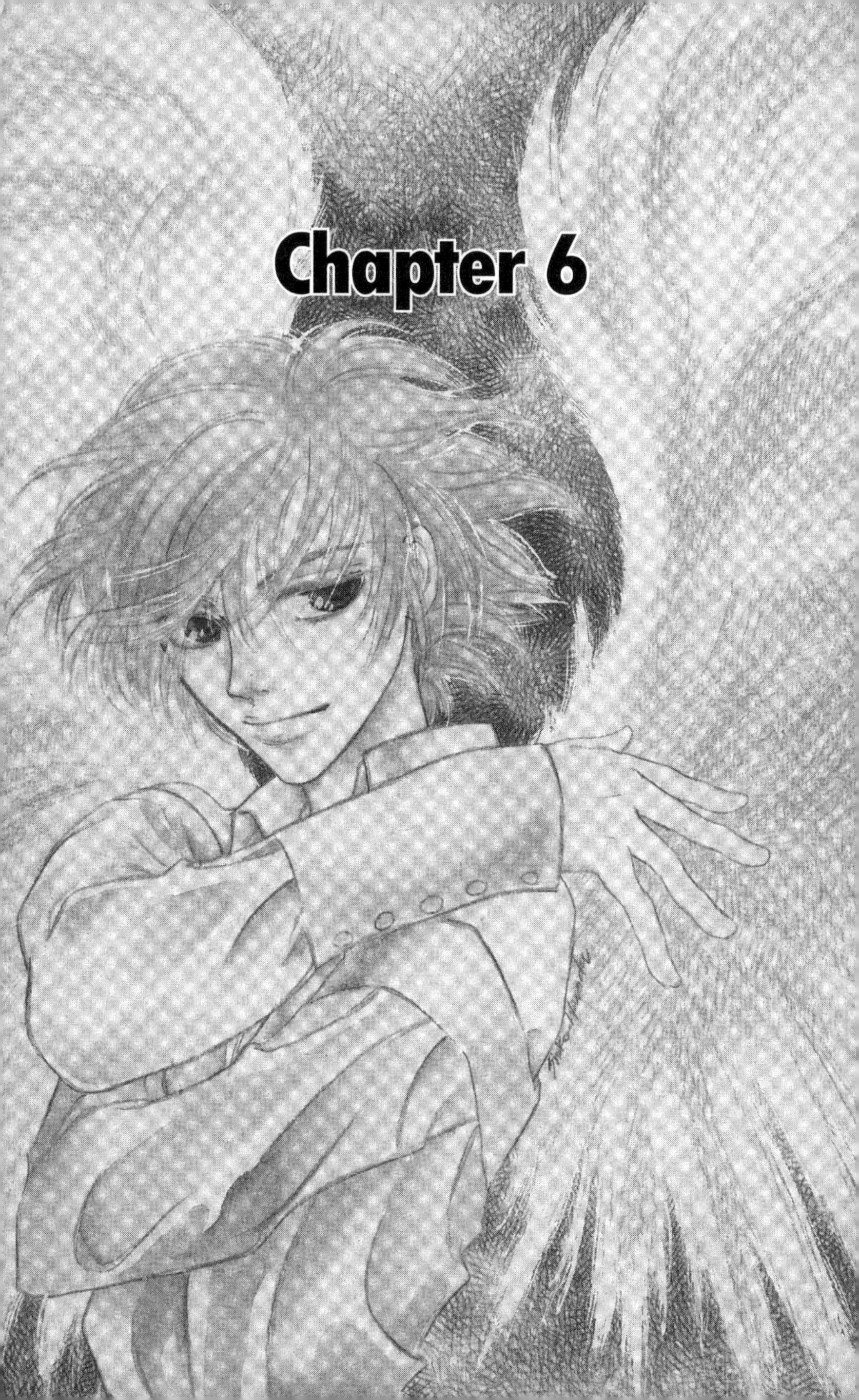

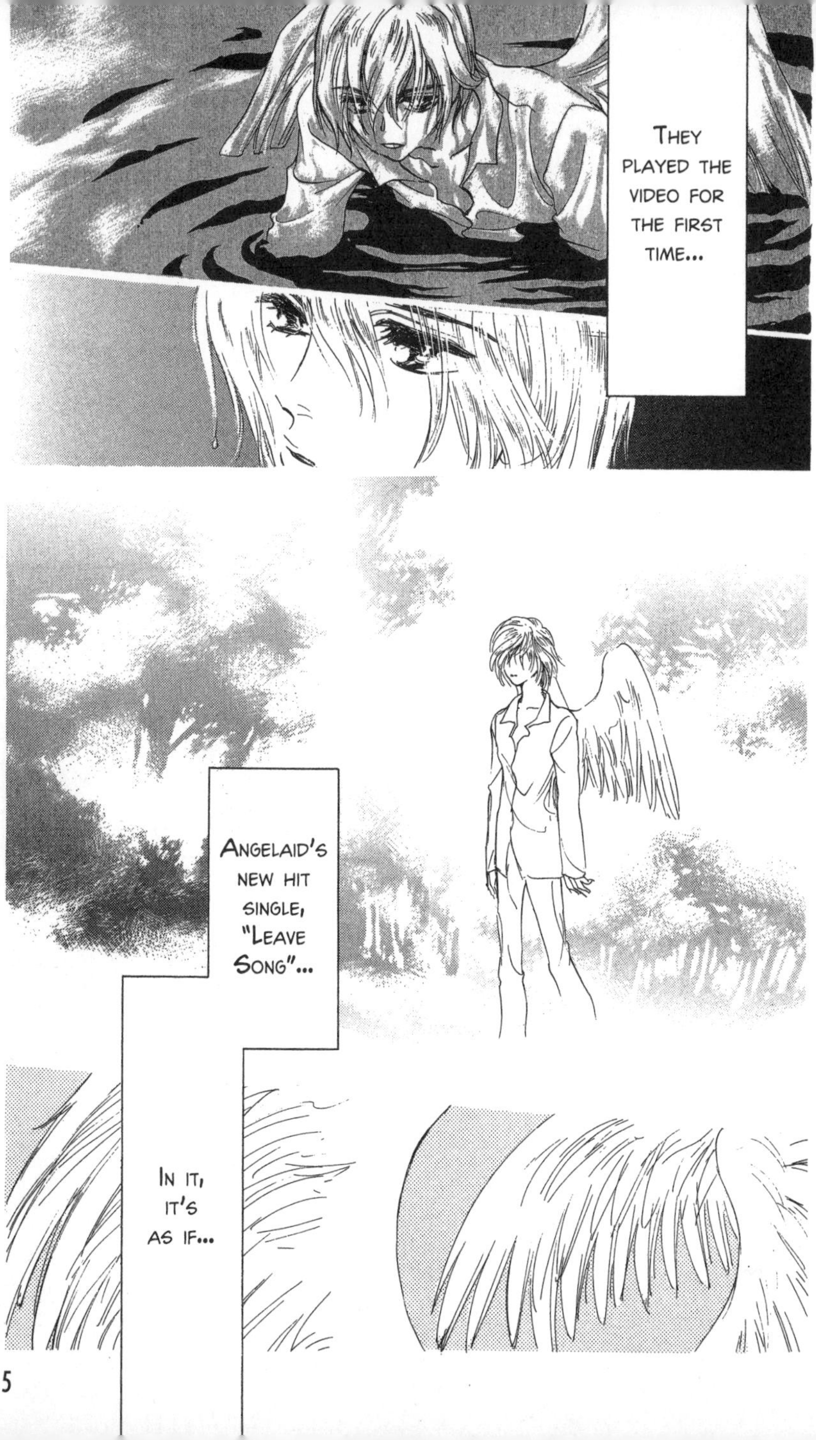
They played the video for the first time...
Angelaid's new hit single, "Leave Song"...
In it, it's as if...

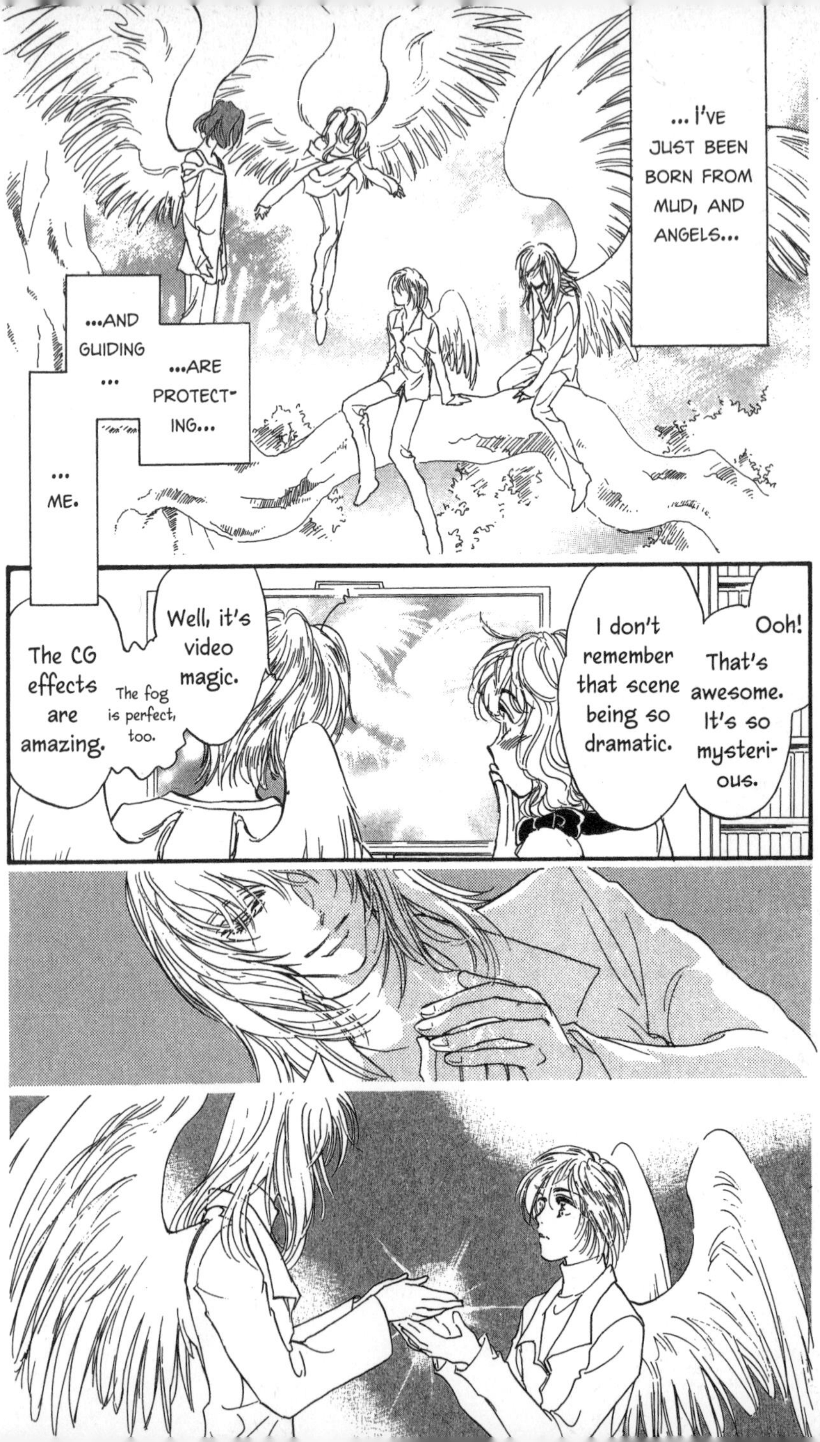
...I'VE JUST BEEN BORN FROM MUD, AND ANGELS...
...ARE PROTECTING...
...AND GUIDING...
...ME.
Ooh! That's awesome. It's so mysterious.
I don't remember that scene being so dramatic.
Well, it's video magic.
The fog is perfect, too.
The CG effects are amazing.

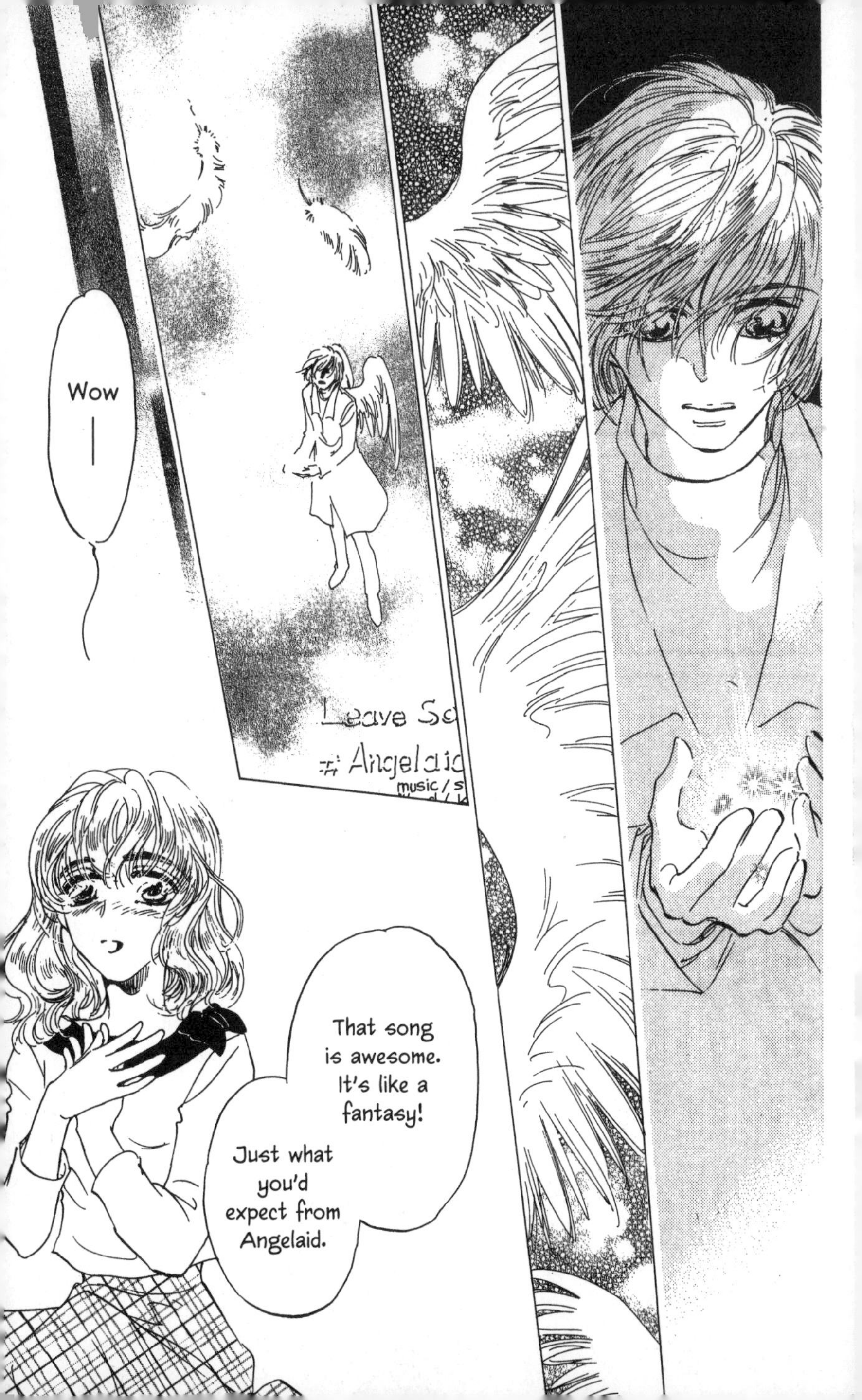
Wow —
That song is awesome. It's like a fantasy!
Just what you'd expect from Angelaid.

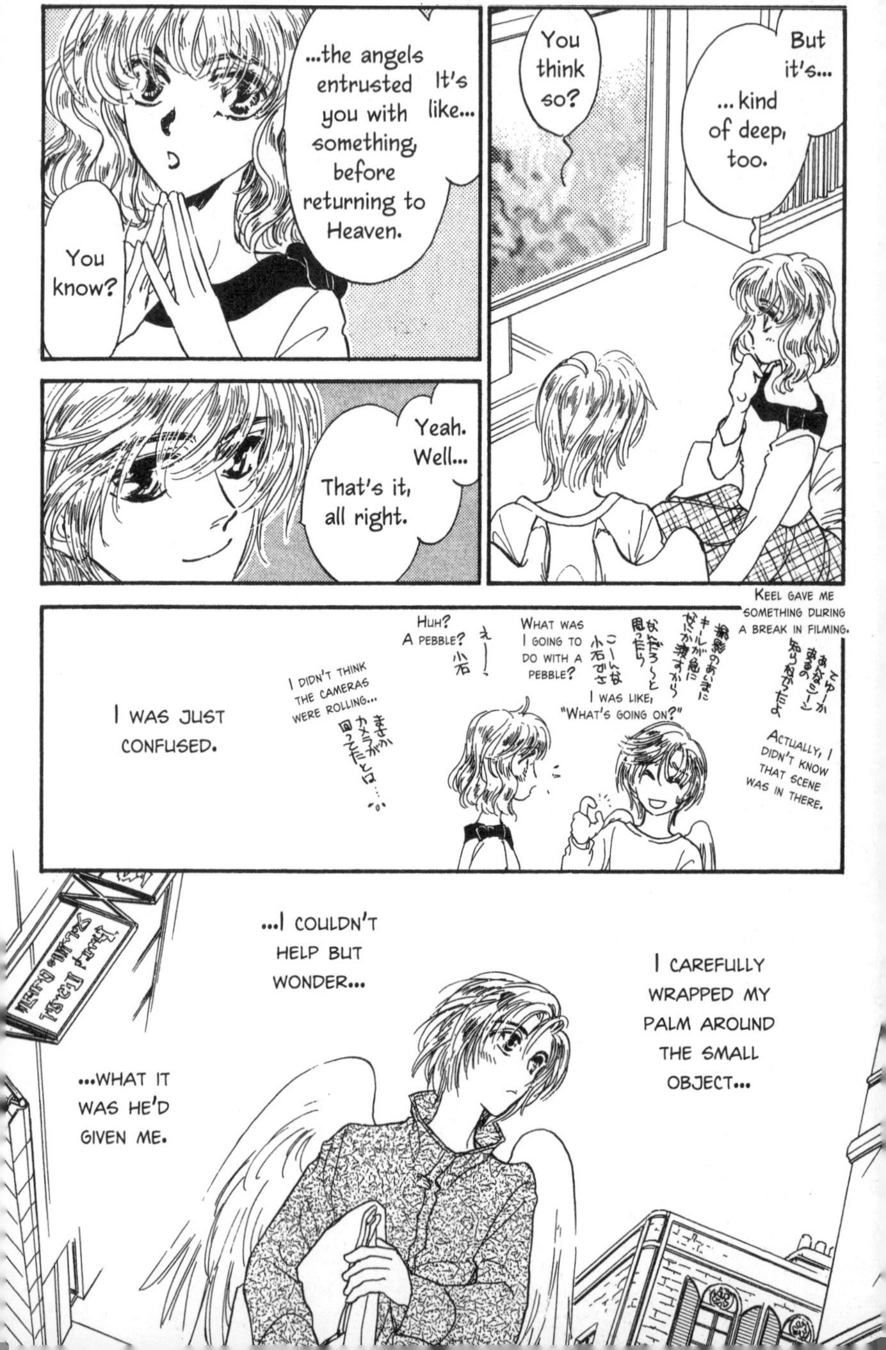
But it's...
...kind of deep, too.
You think so?
It's like...
...the angels entrusted you with something, before returning to Heaven.
You know?
Yeah. Well...
That's it, all right.
Keel gave me something during a break in filming.
そやーかあんなシーンあるの知らなかったよ
Actually, I didn't know that scene was in there.
撮影のあいまにキールが急になにか渡すからなんだろ～と思ったら
I was like, "What's going on?"
こーんな小石でさ
What was I going to do with a pebble?
えー！小石
Huh? A pebble?
I didn't think the cameras were rolling...
まさかカメラが回ってたとは…。
I was just confused.
I carefully wrapped my palm around the small object...
...I couldn't help but wonder...
...what it was he'd given me.

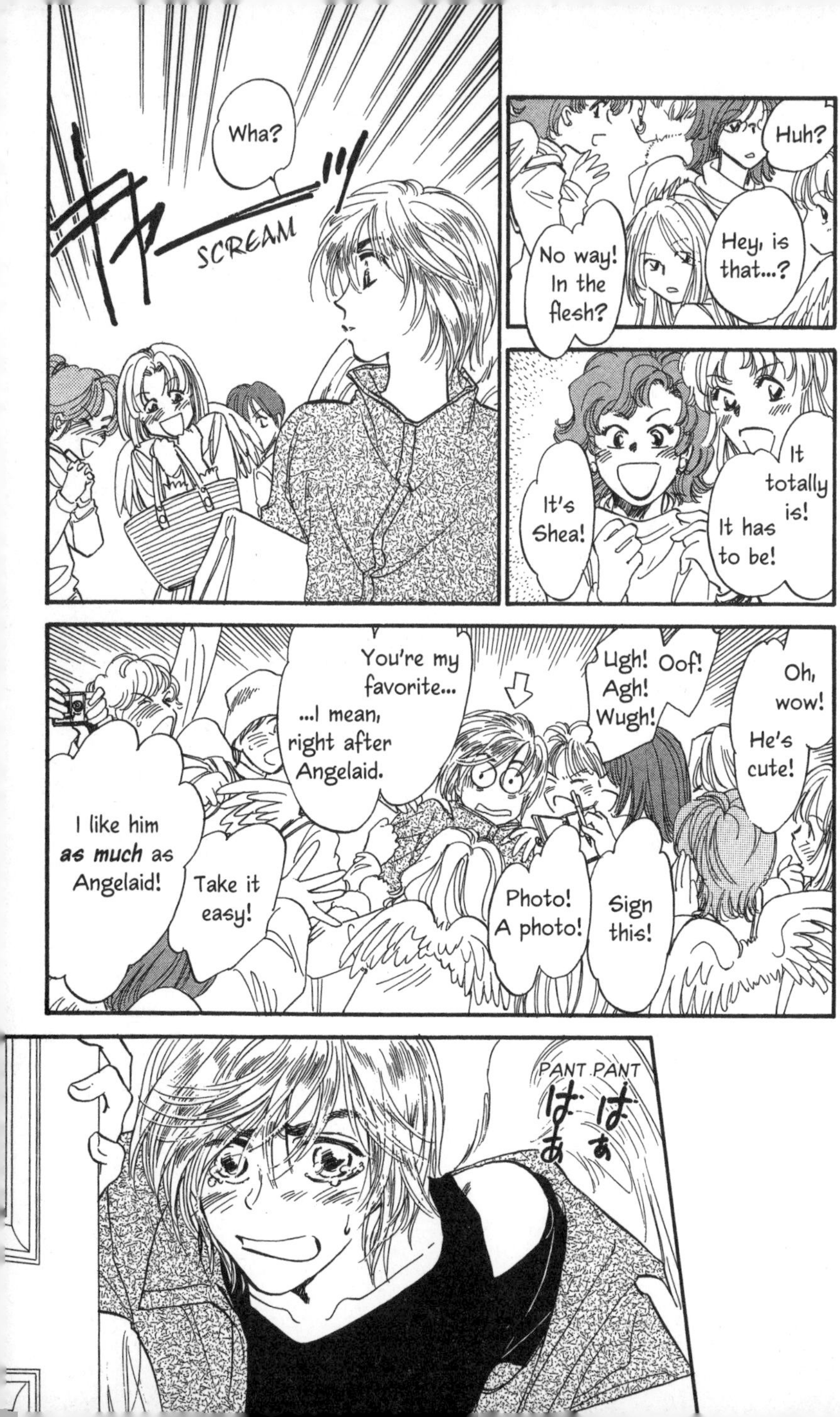
Huh?
Hey, is that...?
No way! In the flesh?
It totally is!
It has to be!
It's Shea!
Wha?
SCREAM
Oh, wow!
He's cute!
Ugh! Oof!
Agh! Wugh!
Sign this!
Photo! A photo!
You're my favorite...
...I mean, right after Angelaid.
Take it easy!
I like him **as much** as Angelaid!
PANT PANT

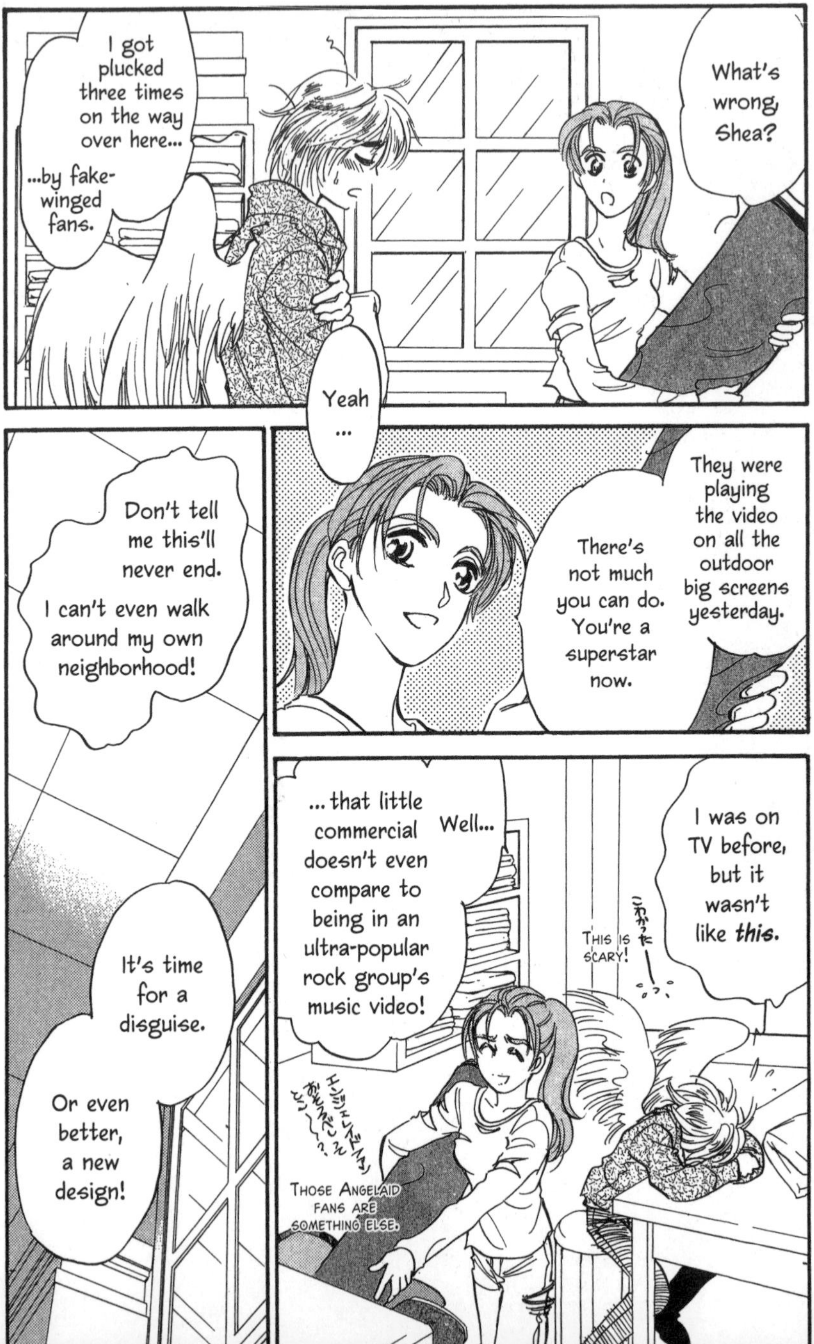
What's wrong, Shea?
I got plucked three times on the way over here...
...by fake-winged fans.
Yeah ...
They were playing the video on all the outdoor big screens yesterday.
There's not much you can do. You're a superstar now.
I was on TV before, but it wasn't like *this*.
Well...
... that little commercial doesn't even compare to being in an ultra-popular rock group's music video!
THIS IS SCARY!
THOSE ANGELAID FANS ARE SOMETHING ELSE.
Don't tell me this'll never end.
I can't even walk around my own neighborhood!
It's time for a disguise.
Or even better, a new design!

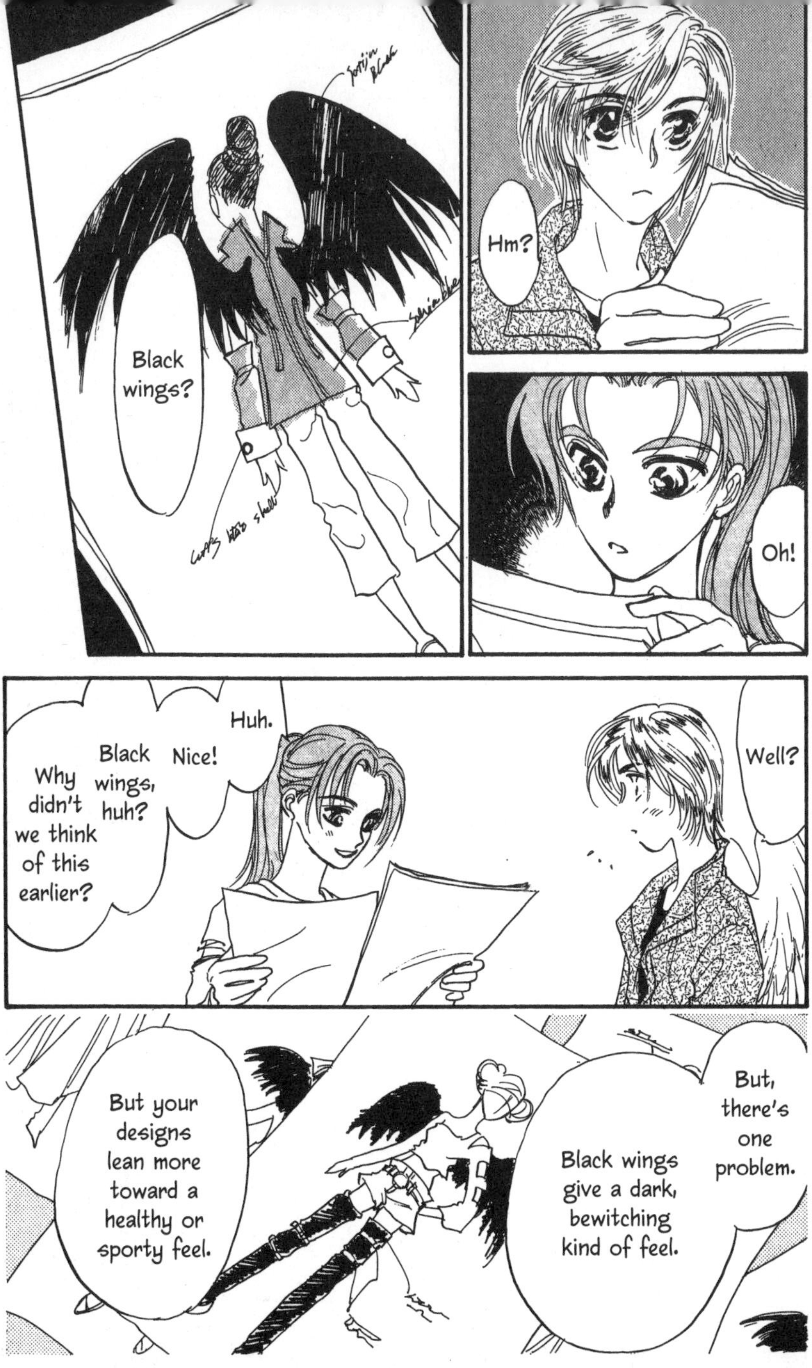
Hm?
Oh!
Black wings?
Well?
Huh.
Nice!
Black wings, huh?
Why didn't we think of this earlier?
But, there's one problem.
Black wings give a dark, bewitching kind of feel.
But your designs lean more toward a healthy or sporty feel.

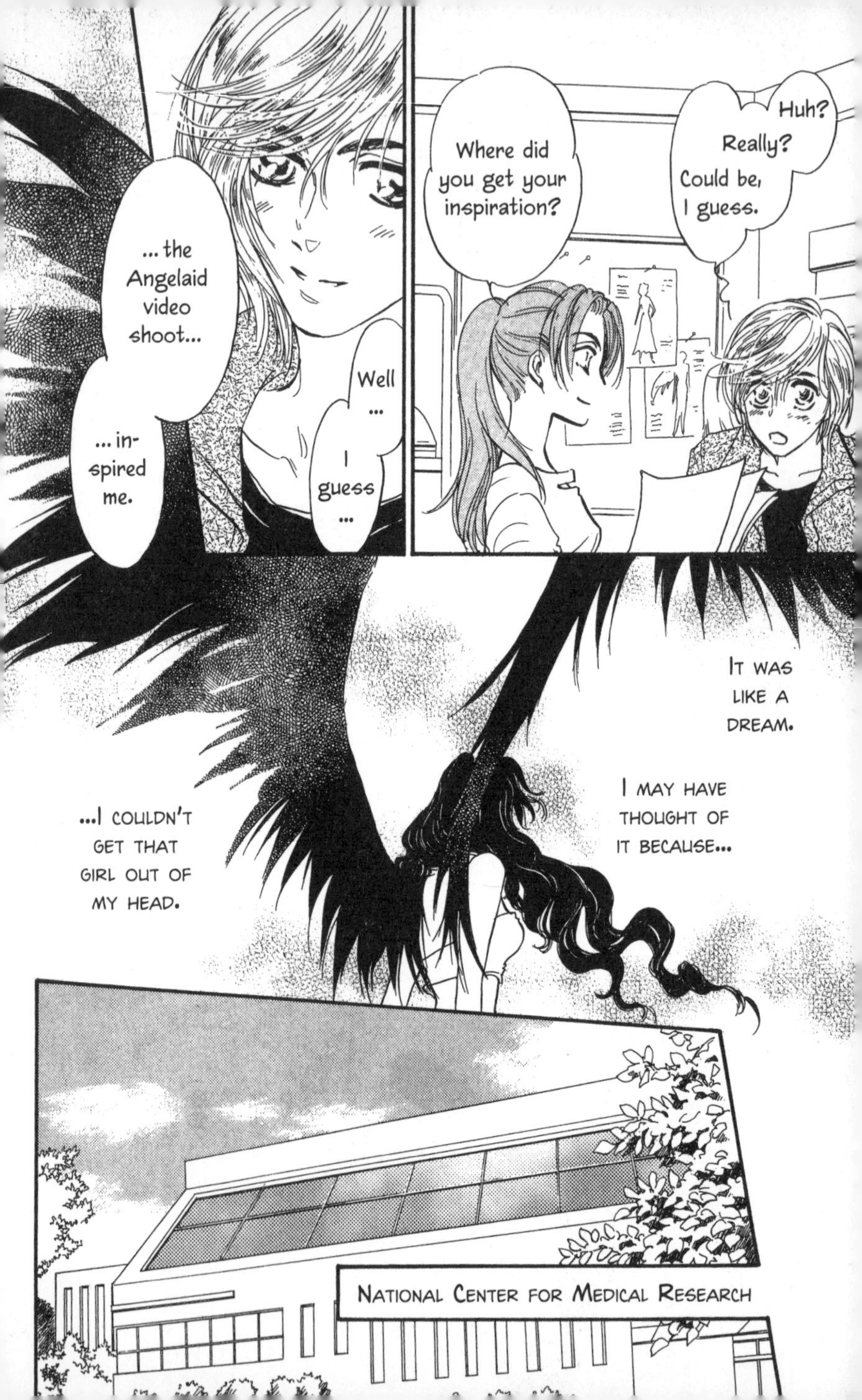
Huh? Really? Could be, I guess.
Where did you get your inspiration?
Well ... I guess ...
... the Angelaid video shoot...
... in-spired me.
It was like a dream.
I may have thought of it because...
...I couldn't get that girl out of my head.
National Center for Medical Research

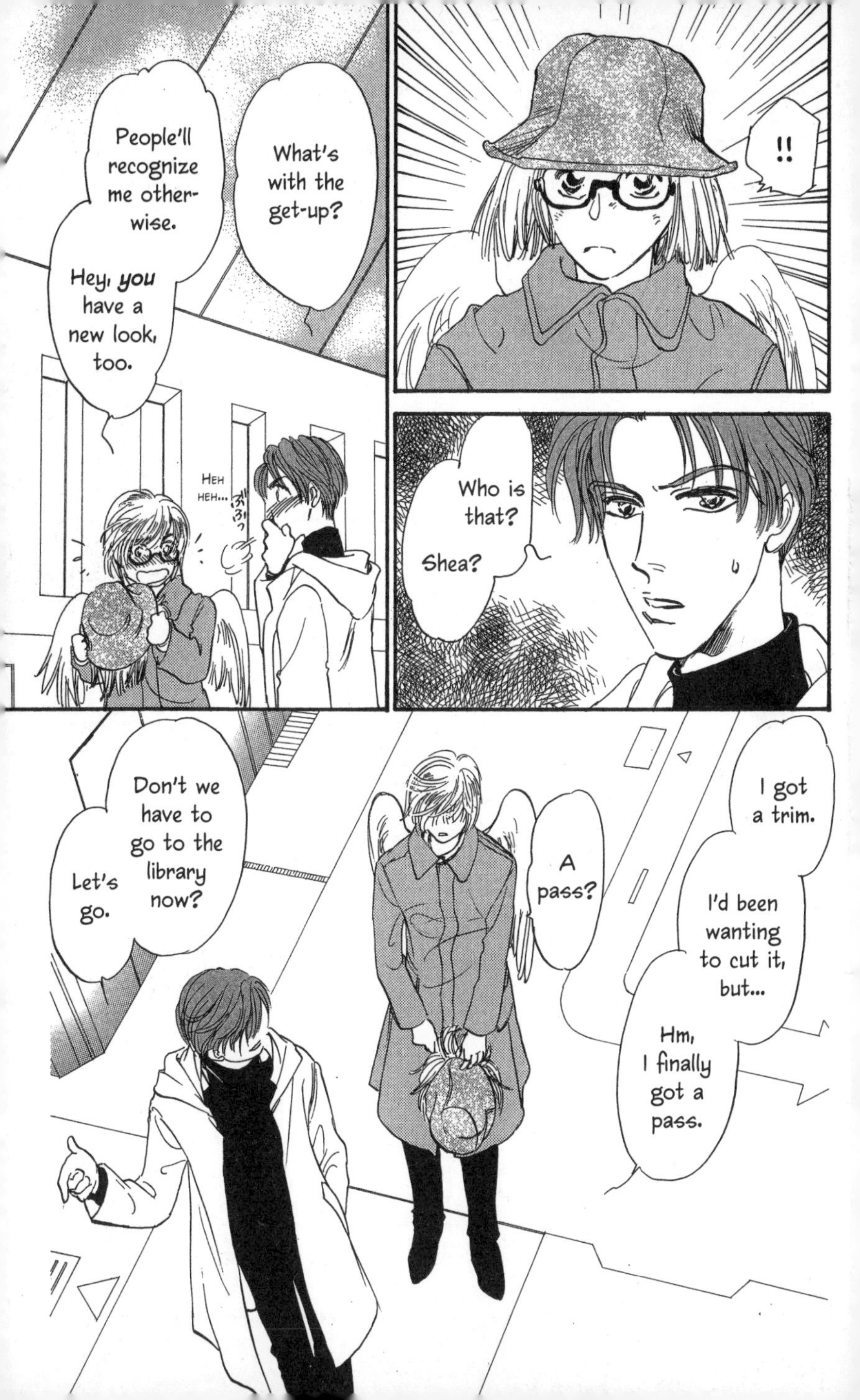
!!
Who is that?
Shea?
What's with the get-up?
People'll recognize me otherwise.
Hey, *you* have a new look, too.
Heh heh...
I got a trim.
I'd been wanting to cut it, but...
Hm, I finally got a pass.
A pass?
Don't we have to go to the library now?
Let's go.

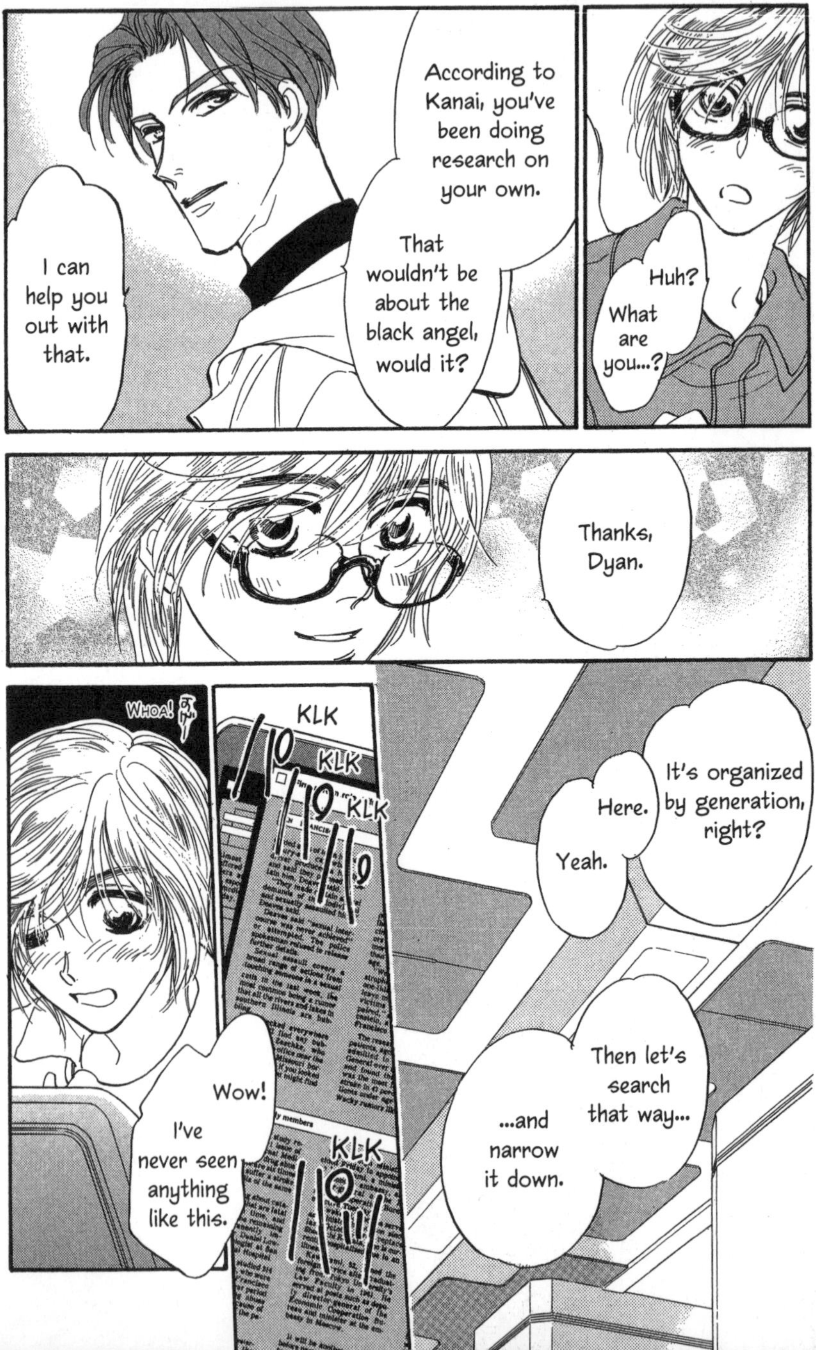
Huh? What are you...?
According to Kanai, you've been doing research on your own.
That wouldn't be about the black angel, would it?
I can help you out with that.
Thanks, Dyan.
It's organized by generation, right?
Here.
Yeah.
Then let's search that way...
...and narrow it down.
KLK
KLK
KLK
KLK
WHOA!
Wow!
I've never seen anything like this.

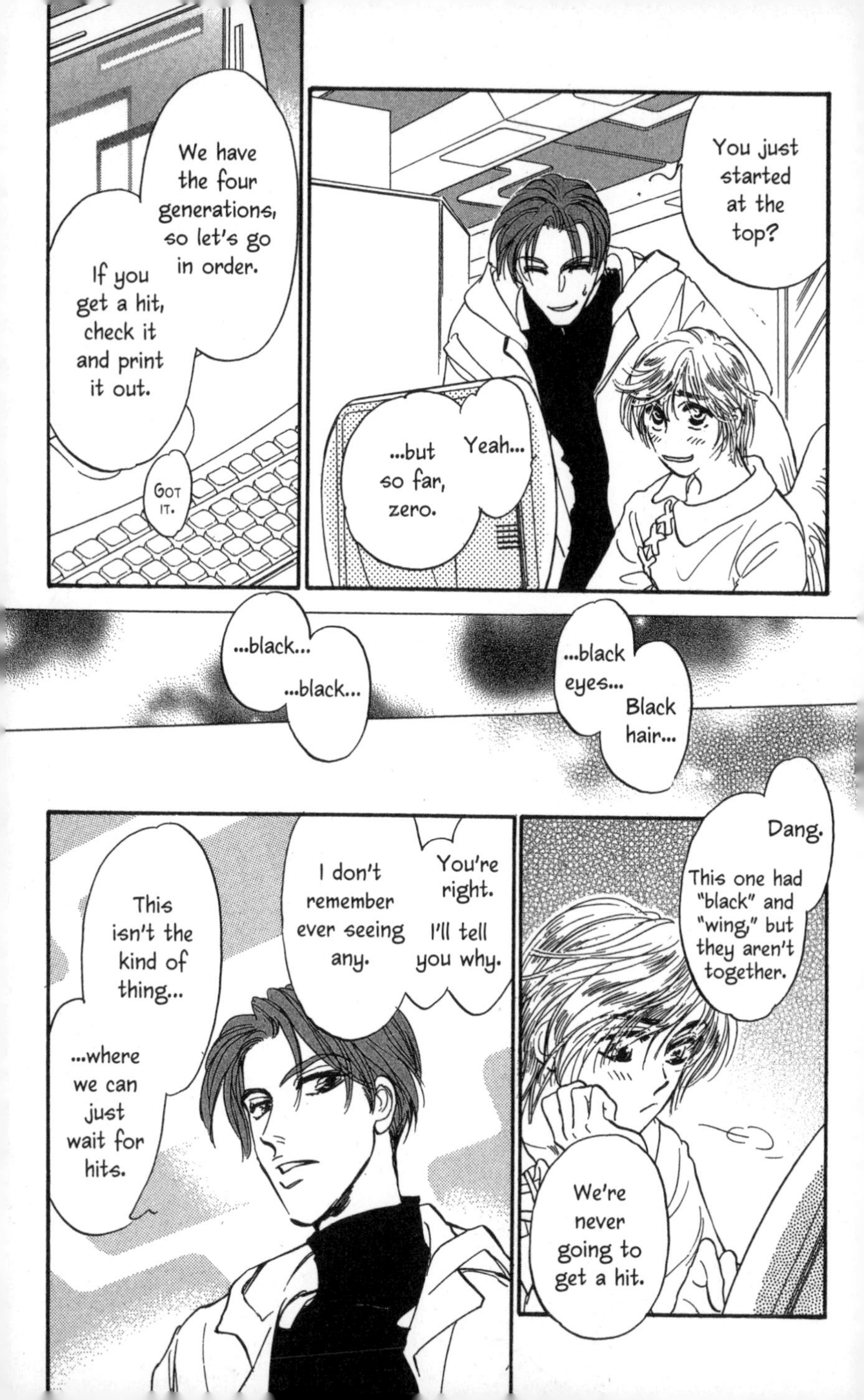

You just started at the top?
Yeah...
...but so far, zero.
We have the four generations, so let's go in order.
If you get a hit, check it and print it out.
Got it.
Black hair...
...black eyes...
...black...
...black...
Dang.
This one had "black" and "wing," but they aren't together.
We're never going to get a hit.
You're right.
I'll tell you why.
I don't remember ever seeing any.
This isn't the kind of thing...
...where we can just wait for hits.

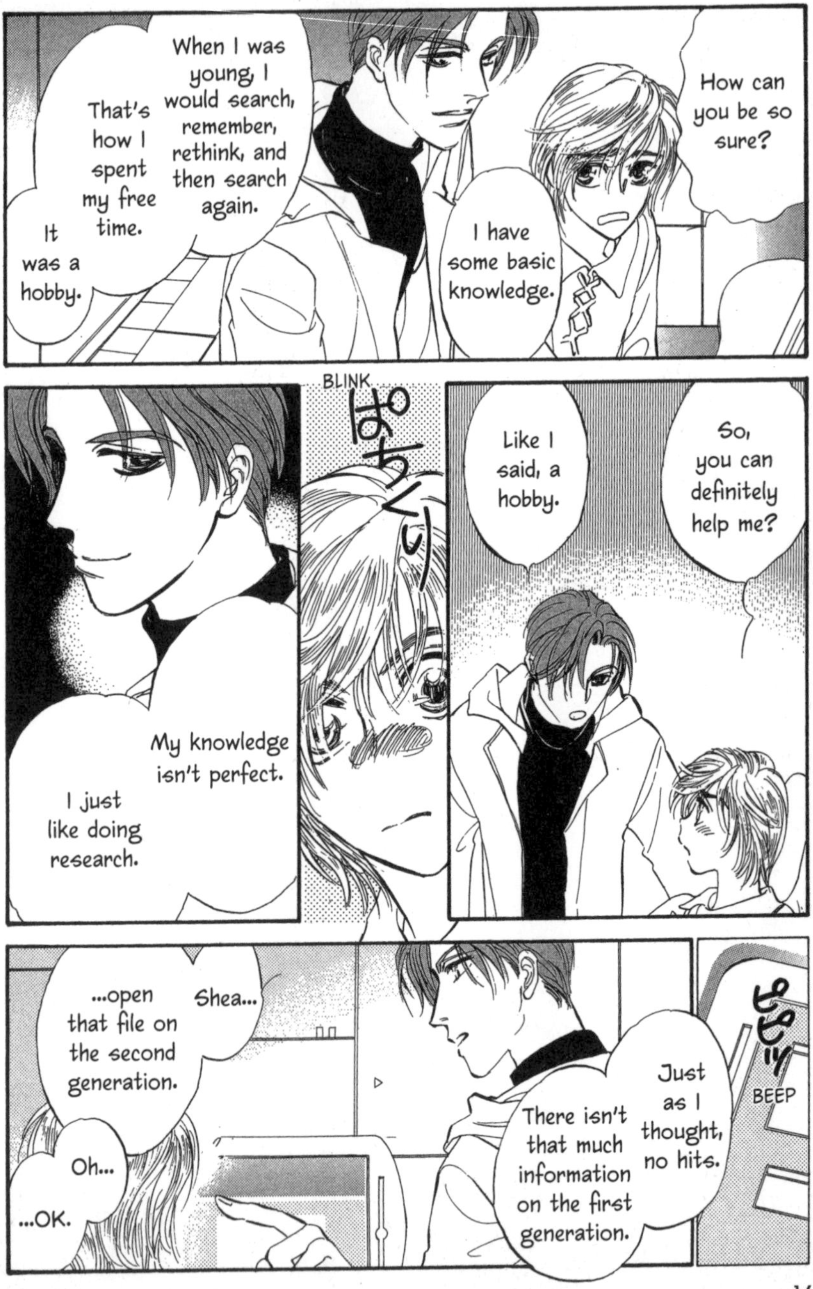
How can you be so sure?
I have some basic knowledge.
When I was young, I would search, remember, rethink, and then search again.
That's how I spent my free time.
It was a hobby.
So, you can definitely help me?
Like I said, a hobby.
BLINK
ぱちくり
My knowledge isn't perfect.
I just like doing research.
ピピッ
BEEP
Just as I thought, no hits.
There isn't that much information on the first generation.
Shea...
...open that file on the second generation.
Oh...
...OK.

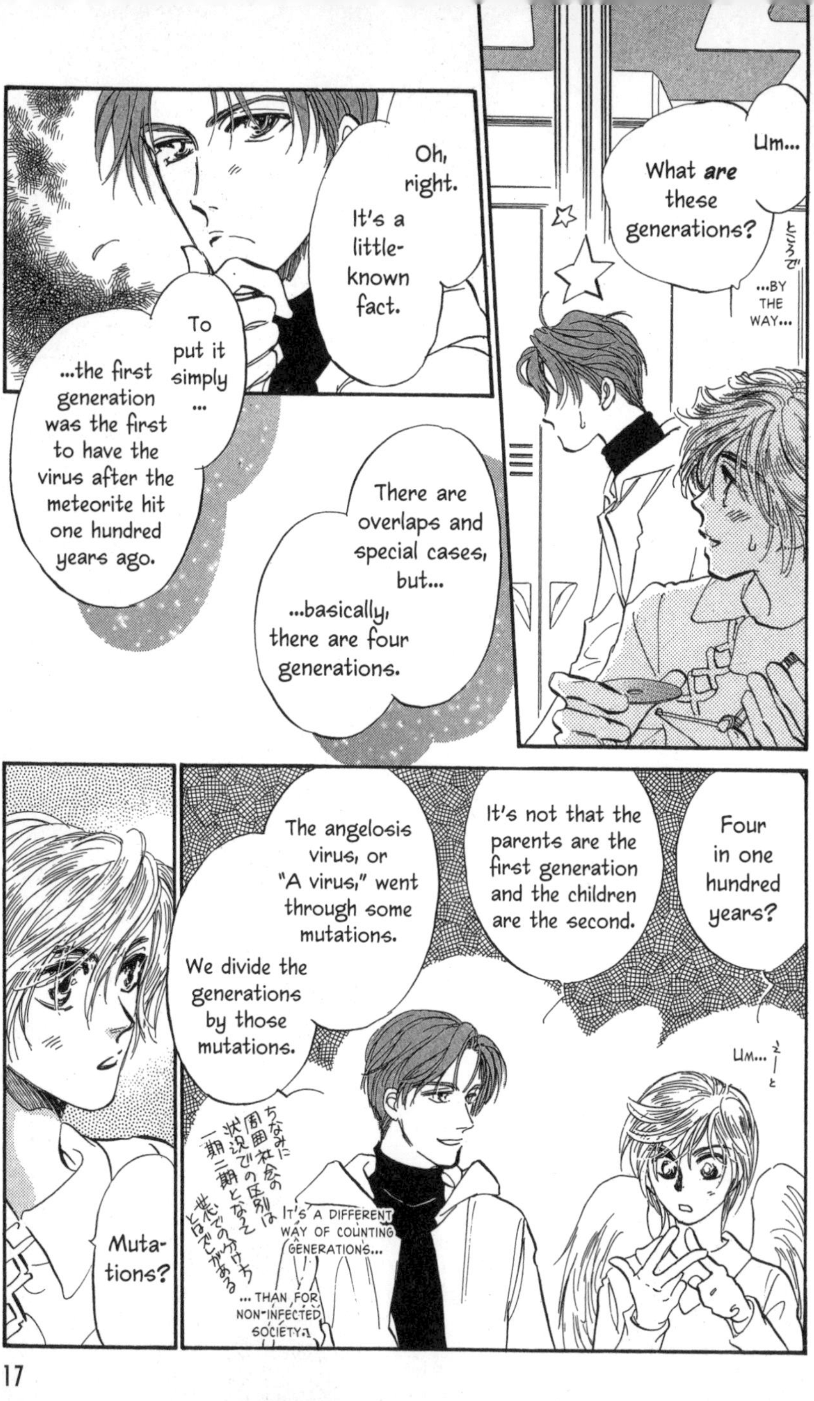
Um...
What **are** these generations?
ところで
...BY THE WAY...
Oh, right.
It's a little-known fact.
To put it simply...
...the first generation was the first to have the virus after the meteorite hit one hundred years ago.
There are overlaps and special cases, but...
...basically, there are four generations.
Four in one hundred years?
It's not that the parents are the first generation and the children are the second.
The angelosis virus, or "A virus," went through some mutations.
We divide the generations by those mutations.
Um...
えーと
ちなみに周囲社会の状況での区別は一期二期となってて世代での分け方とは違いがある
It's a different way of counting generations...
...than for non-infected society.
Muta-tions?

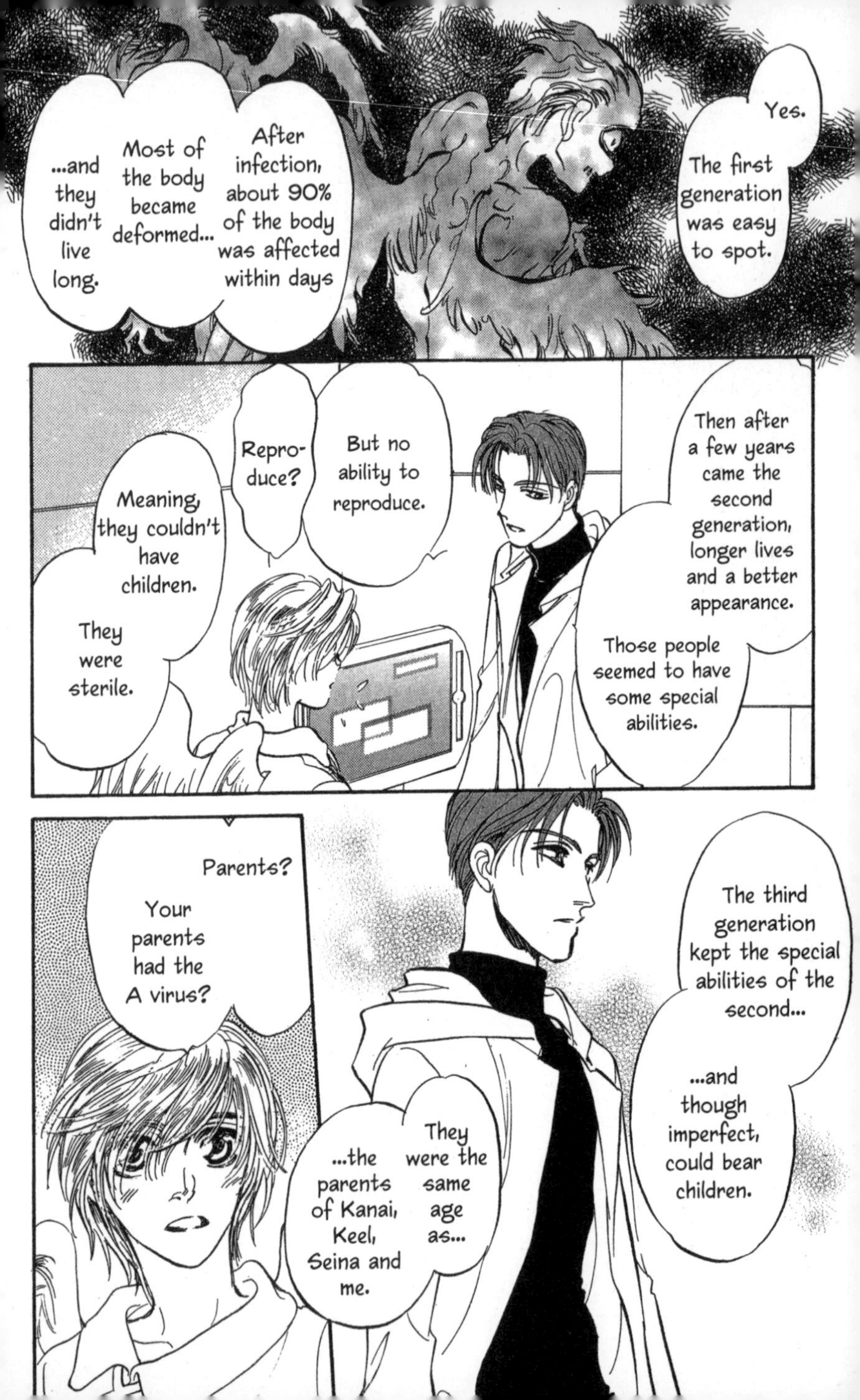

Yes.
The first generation was easy to spot.
After infection, about 90% of the body was affected within days
Most of the body became deformed...
...and they didn't live long.
Then after a few years came the second generation, longer lives and a better appearance.
Those people seemed to have some special abilities.
But no ability to reproduce.
Repro-duce?
Meaning, they couldn't have children.
They were sterile.
The third generation kept the special abilities of the second...
...and though imperfect, could bear children.
They were the same age as...
...the parents of Kanai, Keel, Seina and me.
Parents?
Your parents had the A virus?

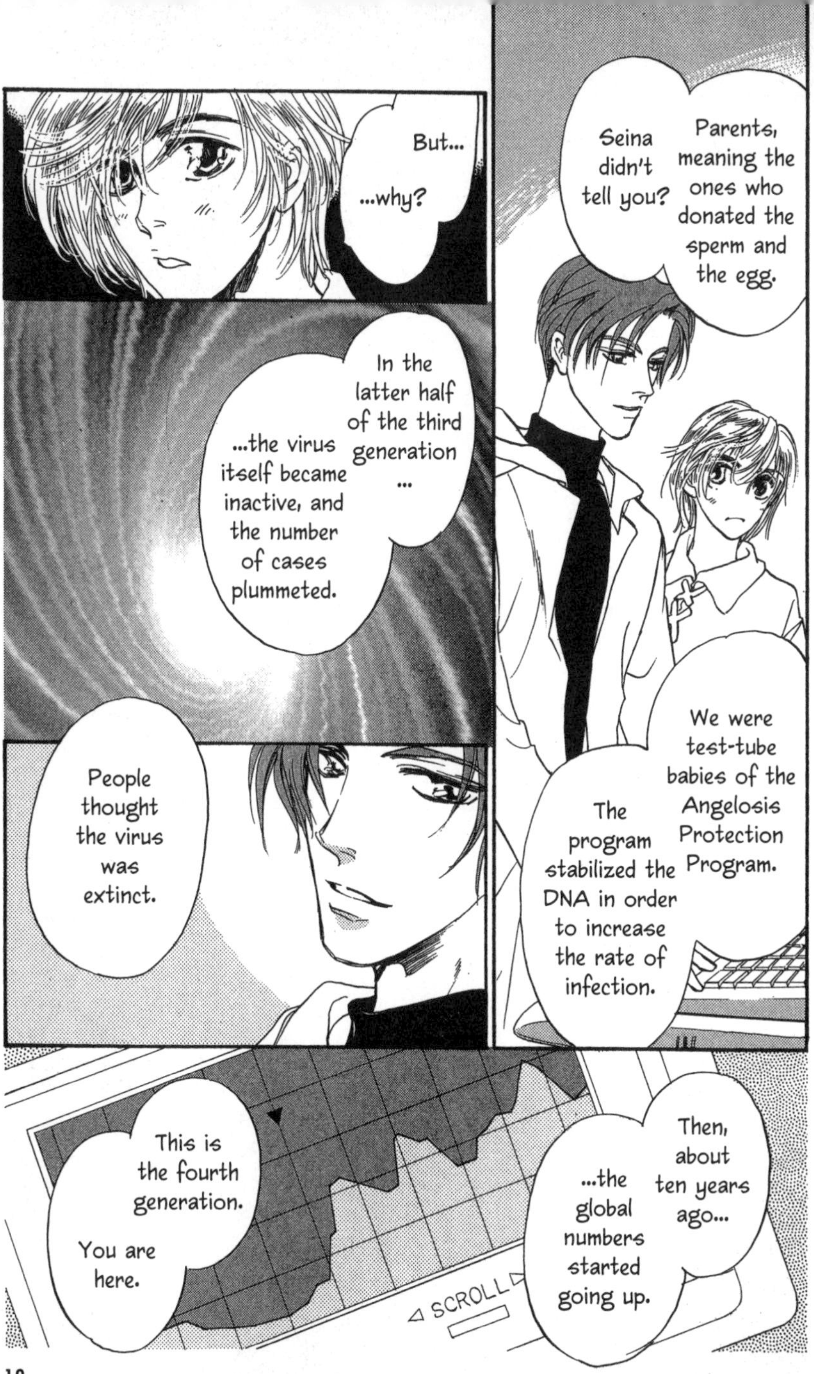
Parents, meaning the ones who donated the sperm and the egg.
Seina didn't tell you?
We were test-tube babies of the Angelosis Protection Program.
The program stabilized the DNA in order to increase the rate of infection.
But...
...why?
In the latter half of the third generation...
...the virus itself became inactive, and the number of cases plummeted.
People thought the virus was extinct.
Then, about ten years ago...
...the global numbers started going up.
SCROLL
This is the fourth generation.
You are here.

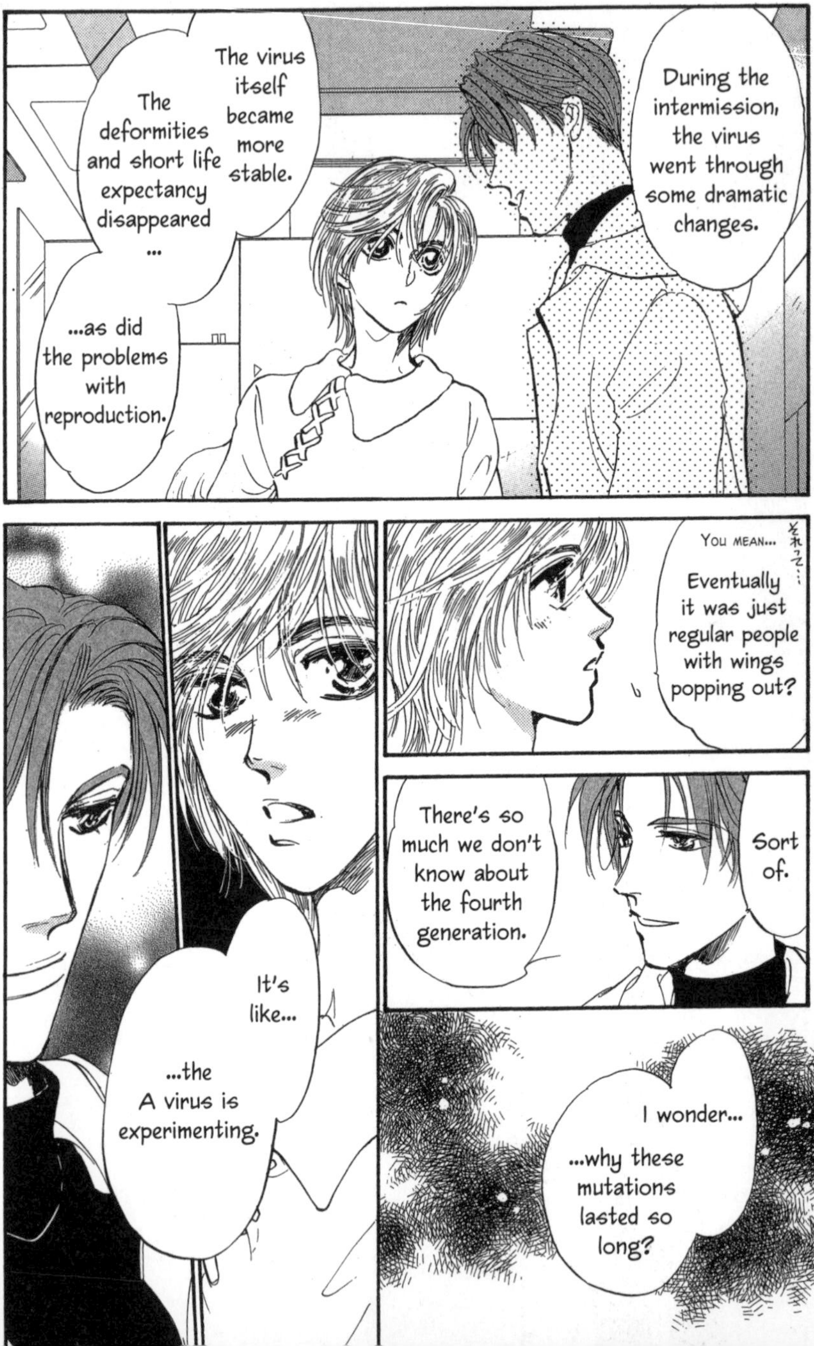
During the intermission, the virus went through some dramatic changes.
The virus itself became more stable.
The deformities and short life expectancy disappeared ...
...as did the problems with reproduction.
You mean...
Eventually it was just regular people with wings popping out?
Sort of.
There's so much we don't know about the fourth generation.
I wonder...
...why these mutations lasted so long?
It's like...
...the A virus is experimenting.

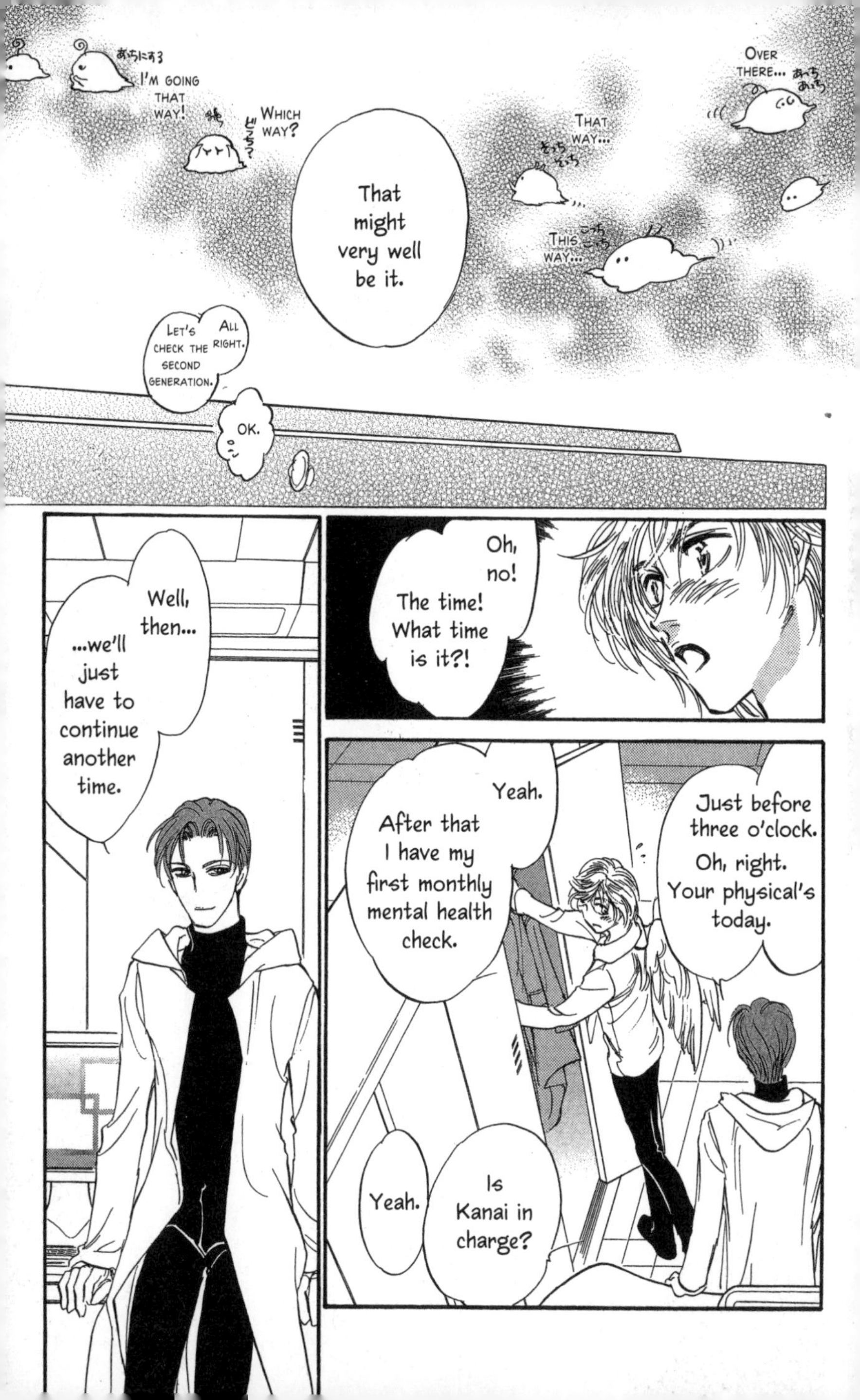

OVER THERE... あっちあっち
THAT WAY... そっちそっち
THIS WAY... こっちこっち
That might very well be it.
WHICH WAY? どっち?
あっちにする I'M GOING THAT WAY!
ALL RIGHT.
LET'S CHECK THE SECOND GENERATION.
OK.
Oh, no! The time! What time is it?!
Just before three o'clock. Oh, right. Your physical's today.
Yeah. After that I have my first monthly mental health check.
Is Kanai in charge?
Yeah.
Well, then... ...we'll just have to continue another time.

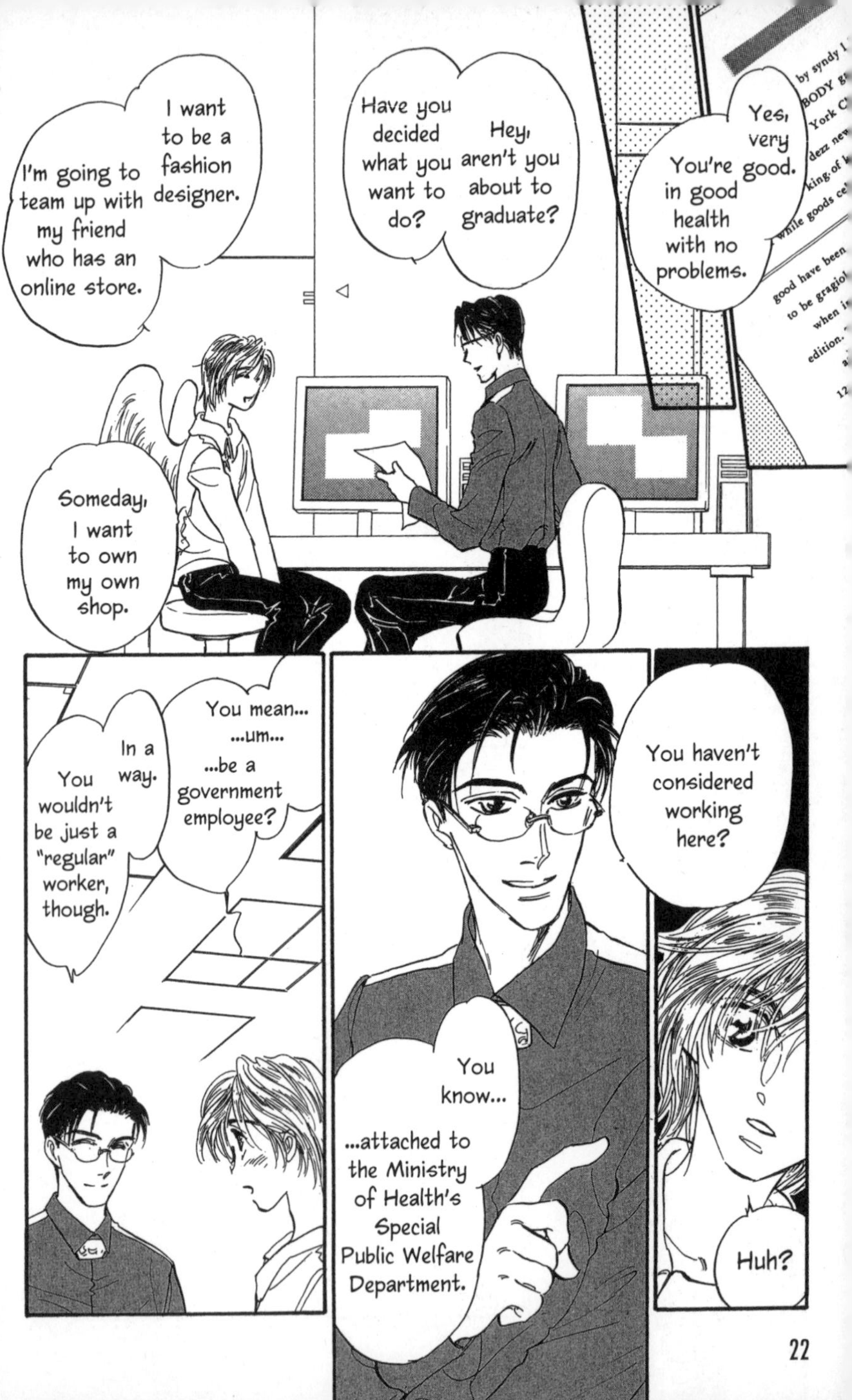
Yes, very good.
You're in good health with no problems.
Hey, aren't you about to graduate?
Have you decided what you want to do?
I want to be a fashion designer.
I'm going to team up with my friend who has an online store.
Someday, I want to own my own shop.
You haven't considered working here?
Huh?
You know...
...attached to the Ministry of Health's Special Public Welfare Department.
You mean... ...um... ...be a government employee?
In a way.
You wouldn't be just a "regular" worker, though.

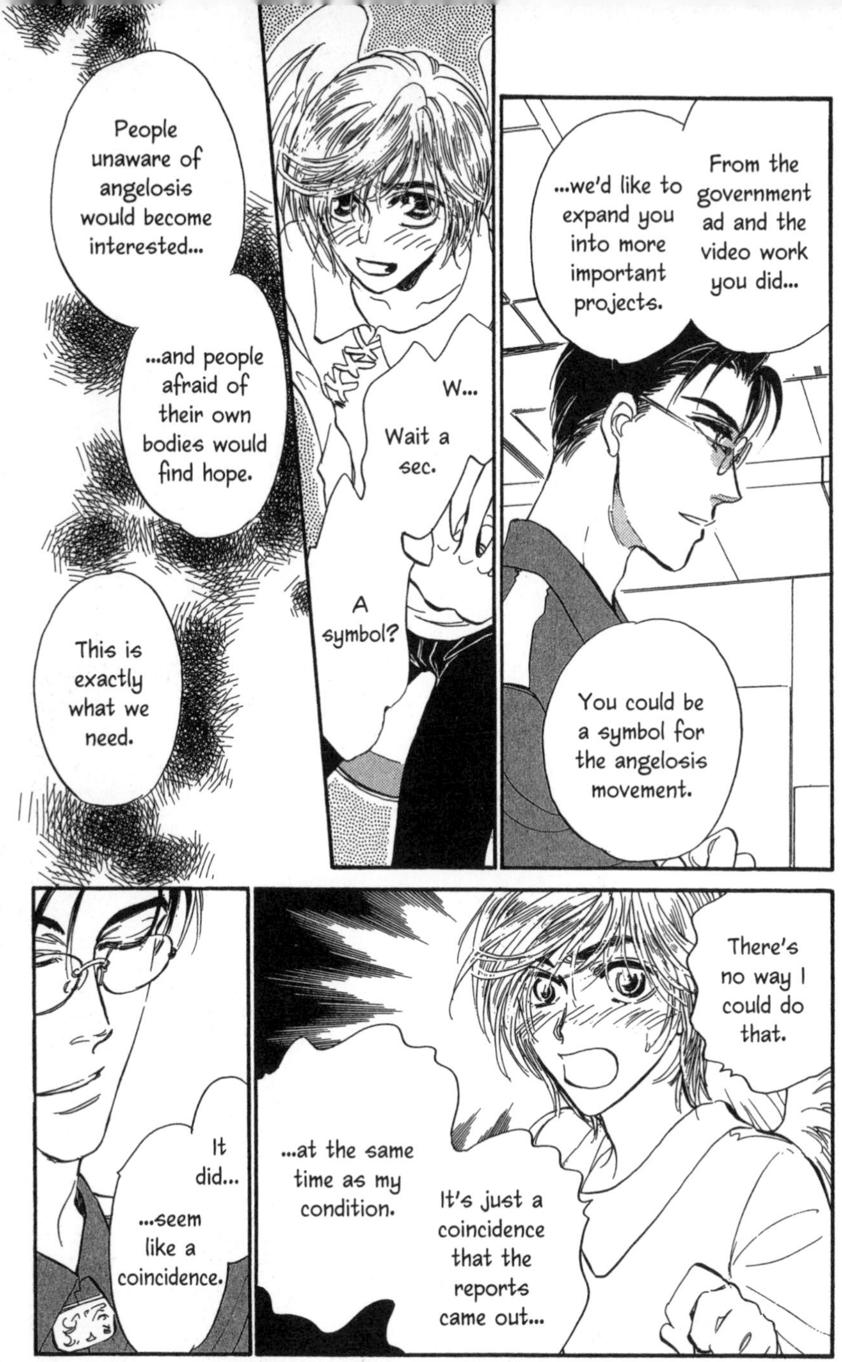
From the government ad and the video work you did...
...we'd like to expand you into more important projects.
You could be a symbol for the angelosis movement.
W... Wait a sec.
A symbol?
People unaware of angelosis would become interested...
...and people afraid of their own bodies would find hope.
This is exactly what we need.
There's no way I could do that.
It's just a coincidence that the reports came out...
...at the same time as my condition.
It did...
...seem like a coincidence.

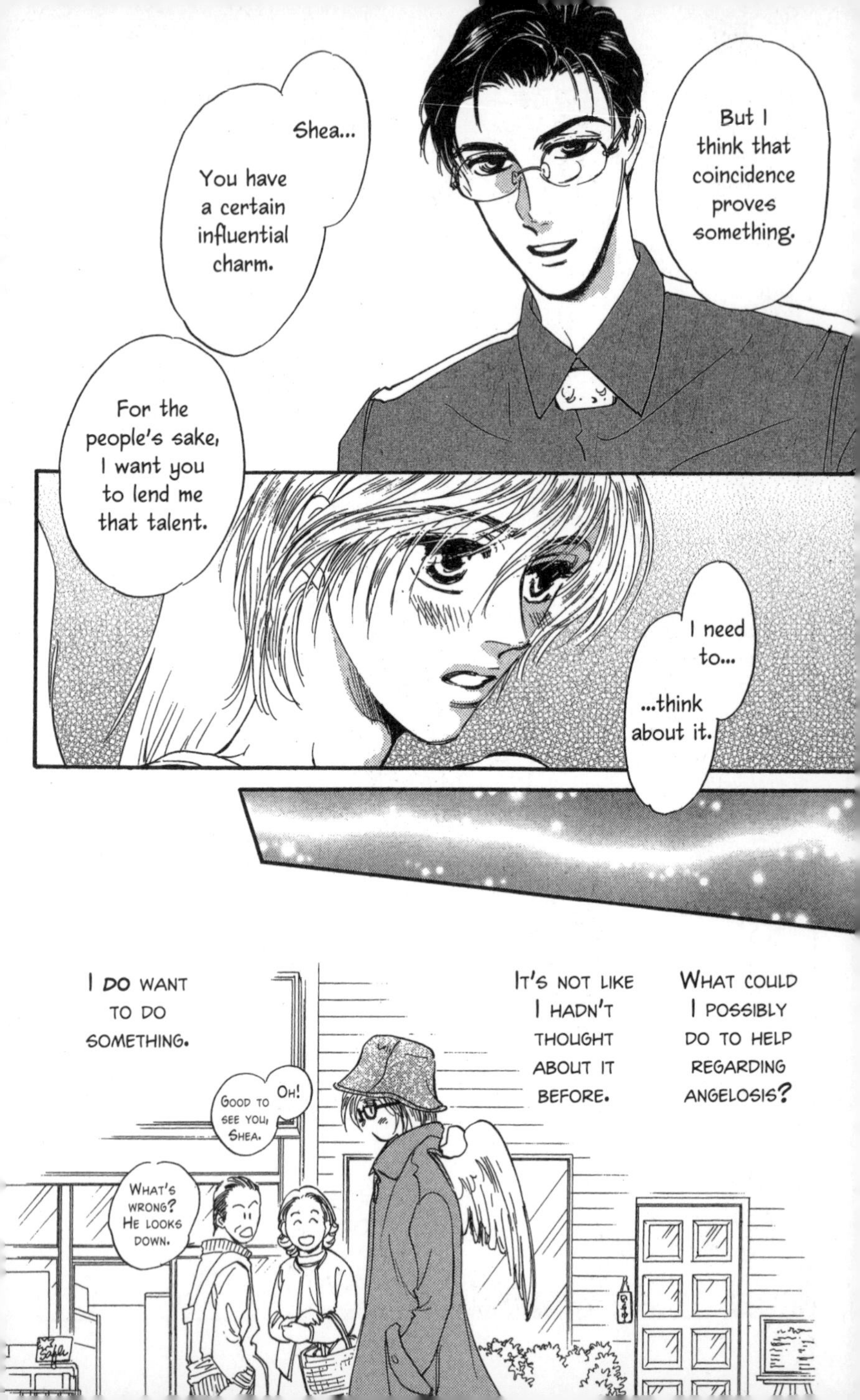
But I think that coincidence proves something.
Shea... You have a certain influential charm.
For the people's sake, I want you to lend me that talent.
I need to... ...think about it.
WHAT COULD I POSSIBLY DO TO HELP REGARDING ANGELOSIS?
IT'S NOT LIKE I HADN'T THOUGHT ABOUT IT BEFORE.
I ***DO*** WANT TO DO SOMETHING.
OH!
GOOD TO SEE YOU, SHEA.
WHAT'S WRONG? HE LOOKS DOWN.

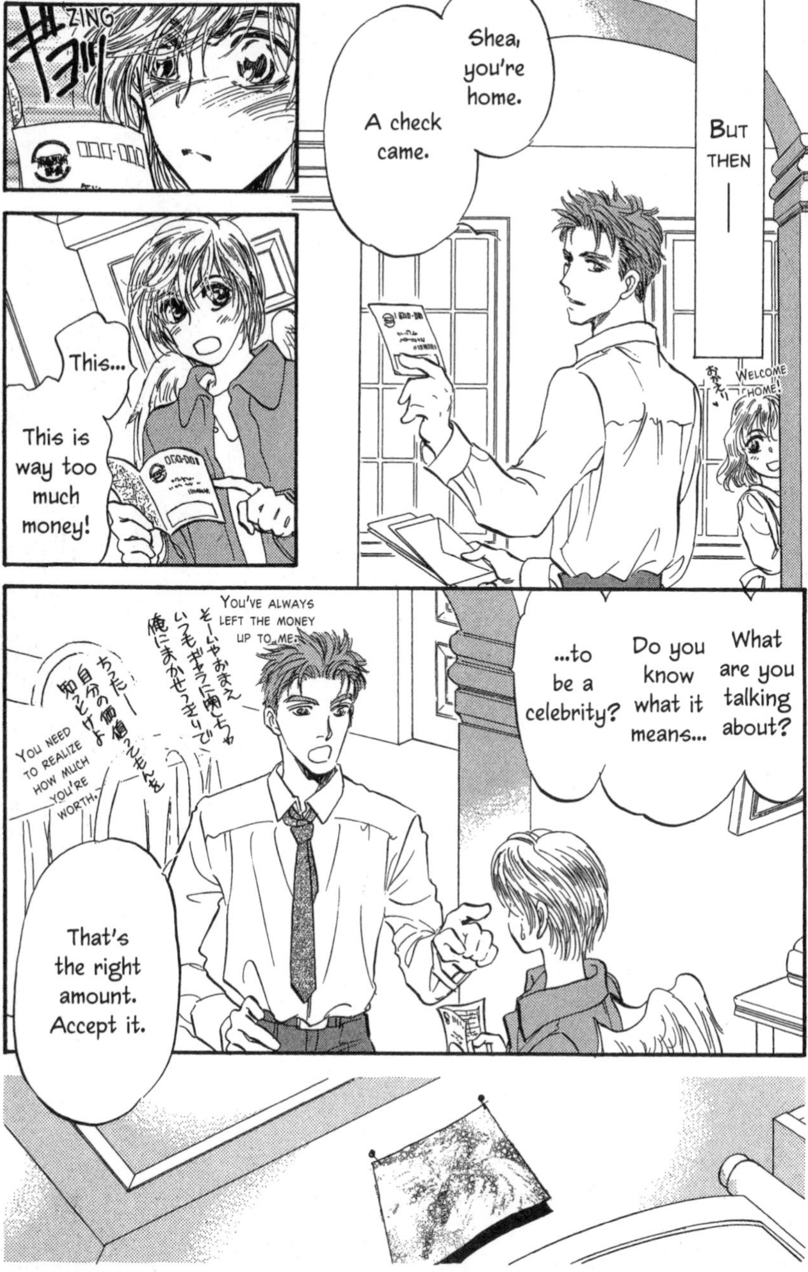
BUT THEN —
Shea, you're home.
A check came.
おかえり♥
WELCOME HOME!
ギョッ
ZING
This...
This is way too much money!
What are you talking about?
Do you know what it means...
...to be a celebrity?
そーいやおまえ いつもギャラに関しちゃ 俺にまかせっきりで
YOU'VE ALWAYS LEFT THE MONEY UP TO ME.
ちったー 自分の価値ってもんを 知っとけよ
YOU NEED TO REALIZE HOW MUCH YOU'RE WORTH.
That's the right amount. Accept it.

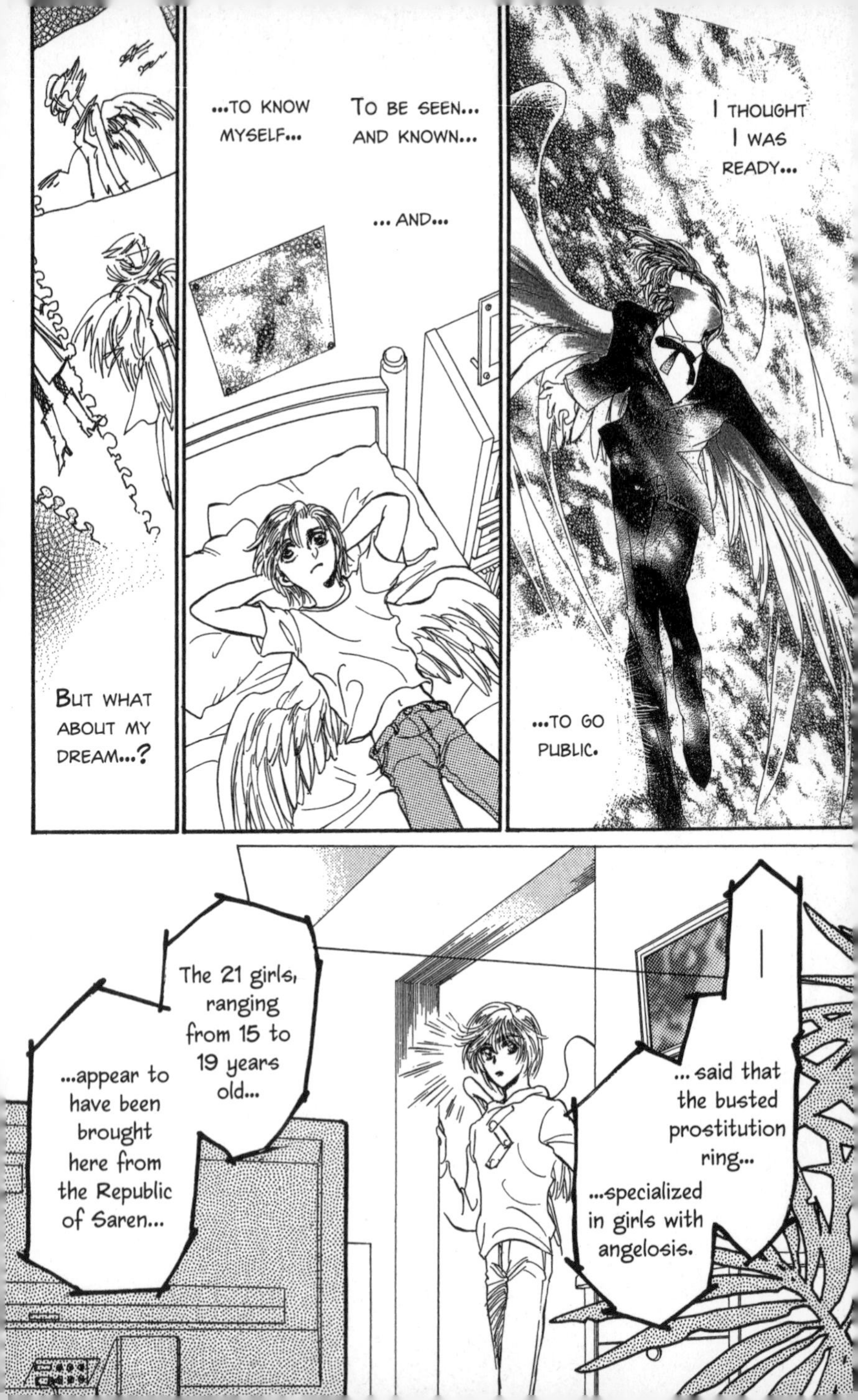
I THOUGHT I WAS READY...
...TO GO PUBLIC.
TO BE SEEN... AND KNOWN...
...TO KNOW MYSELF...
... AND...
BUT WHAT ABOUT MY DREAM...?
... said that the busted prostitution ring...
...specialized in girls with angelosis.
The 21 girls, ranging from 15 to 19 years old...
...appear to have been brought here from the Republic of Saren...

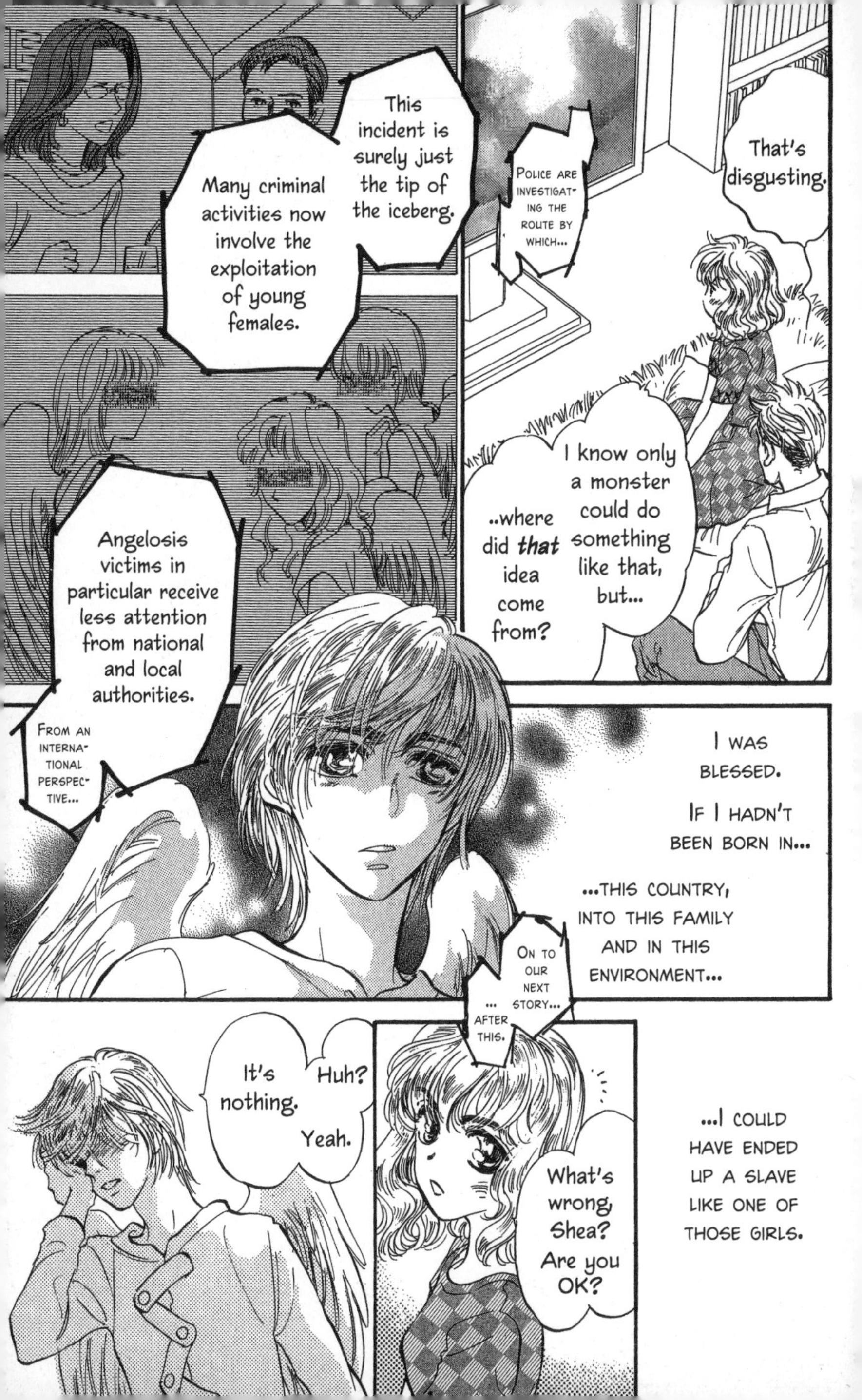
Police are investigating the route by which...
That's disgusting.
I know only a monster could do something like that, but...
..where did *that* idea come from?
This incident is surely just the tip of the iceberg.
Many criminal activities now involve the exploitation of young females.
Angelosis victims in particular receive less attention from national and local authorities.
From an international perspective...
I was blessed.
If I hadn't been born in...
...this country, into this family and in this environment...
On to our next story...
... after this.
...I could have ended up a slave like one of those girls.
What's wrong, Shea? Are you OK?
Huh?
It's nothing.
Yeah.

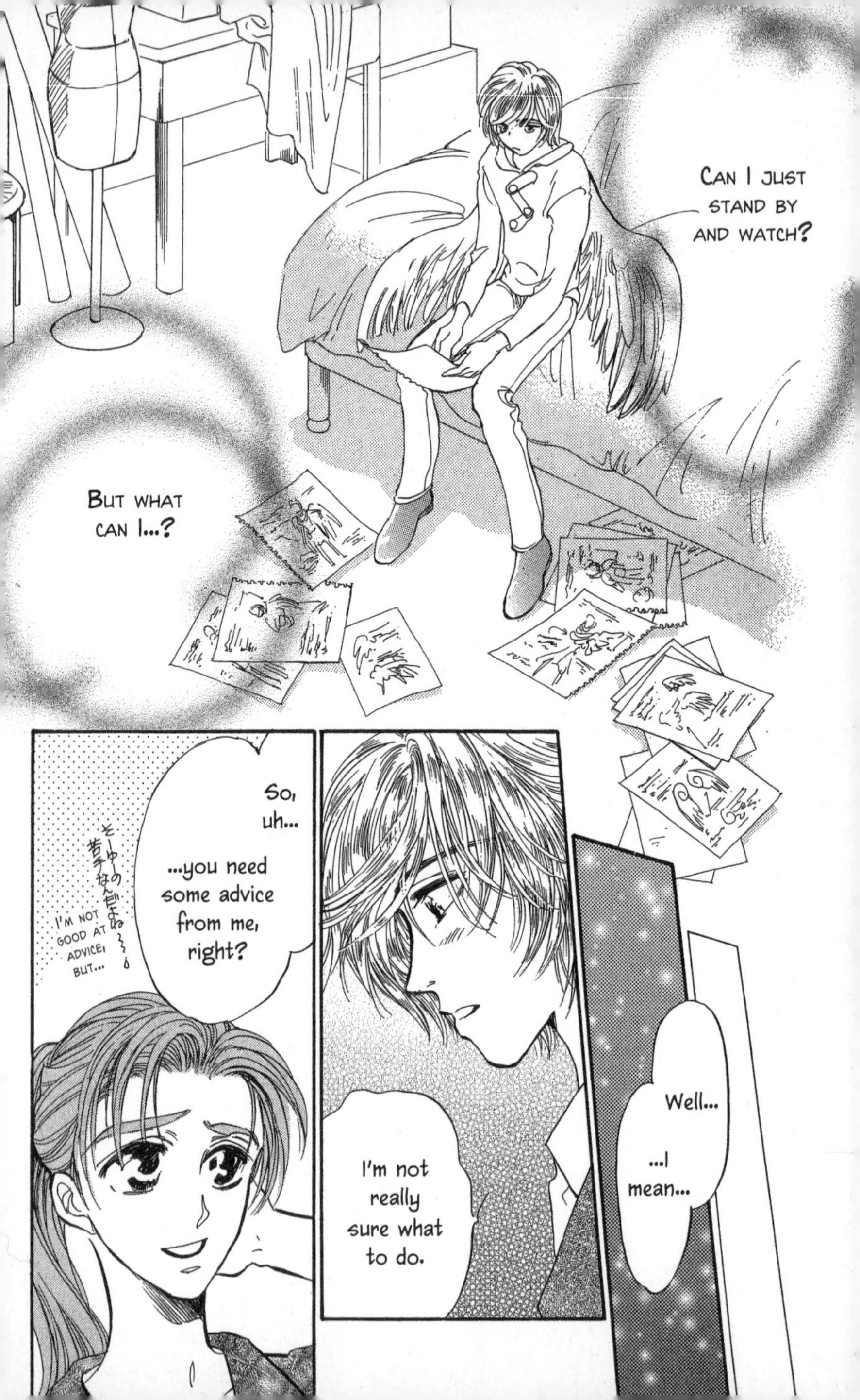

Can I just stand by and watch?
But what can I...?
Well...
...I mean...
I'm not really sure what to do.
So, uh...
...you need some advice from me, right?
そーゆーの苦手なんだよね～～
I'm not good at advice, but...

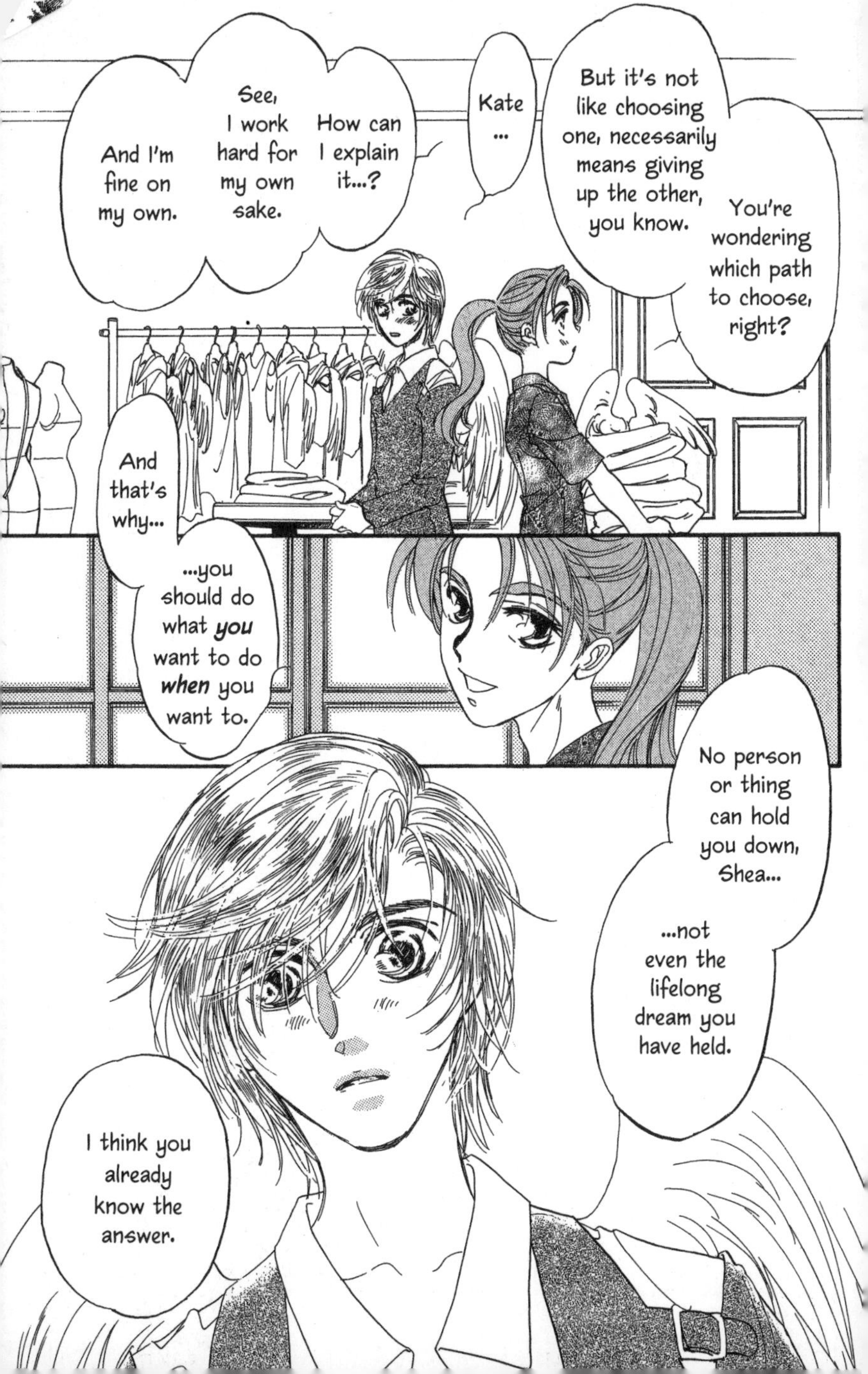
You're wondering which path to choose, right?
But it's not like choosing one, necessarily means giving up the other, you know.
Kate...
How can I explain it...?
See, I work hard for my own sake.
And I'm fine on my own.
And that's why...
...you should do what *you* want to do *when* you want to.
No person or thing can hold you down, Shea...
...not even the lifelong dream you have held.
I think you already know the answer.

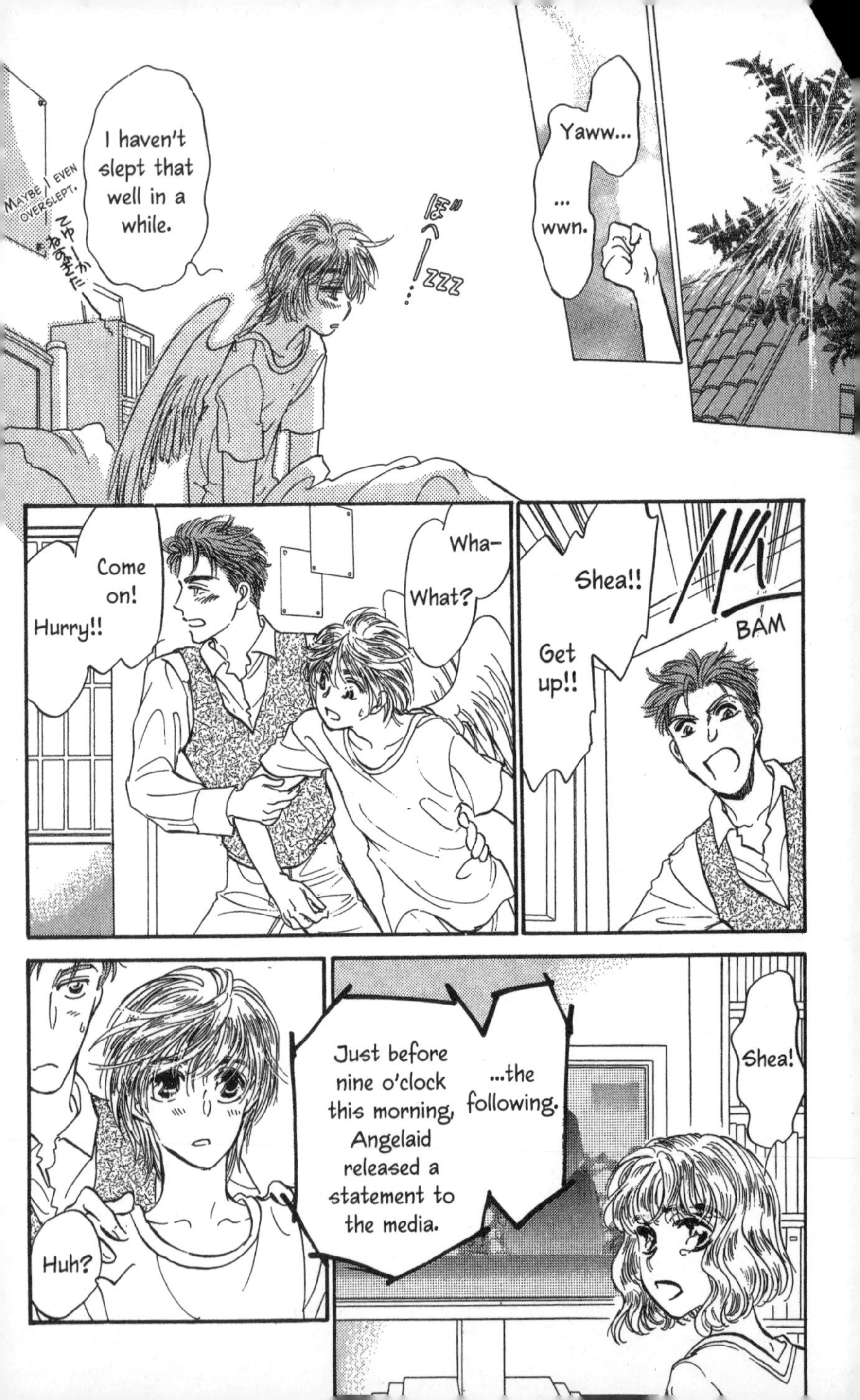
Yaww...
...wwn.
I haven't slept that well in a while.
Maybe I even overslept.
Shea!!
Get up!!
BAM
Wha-
What?
Come on!
Hurry!!
Shea!
Just before nine o'clock this morning, Angelaid released a statement to the media.
...the following.
Huh?

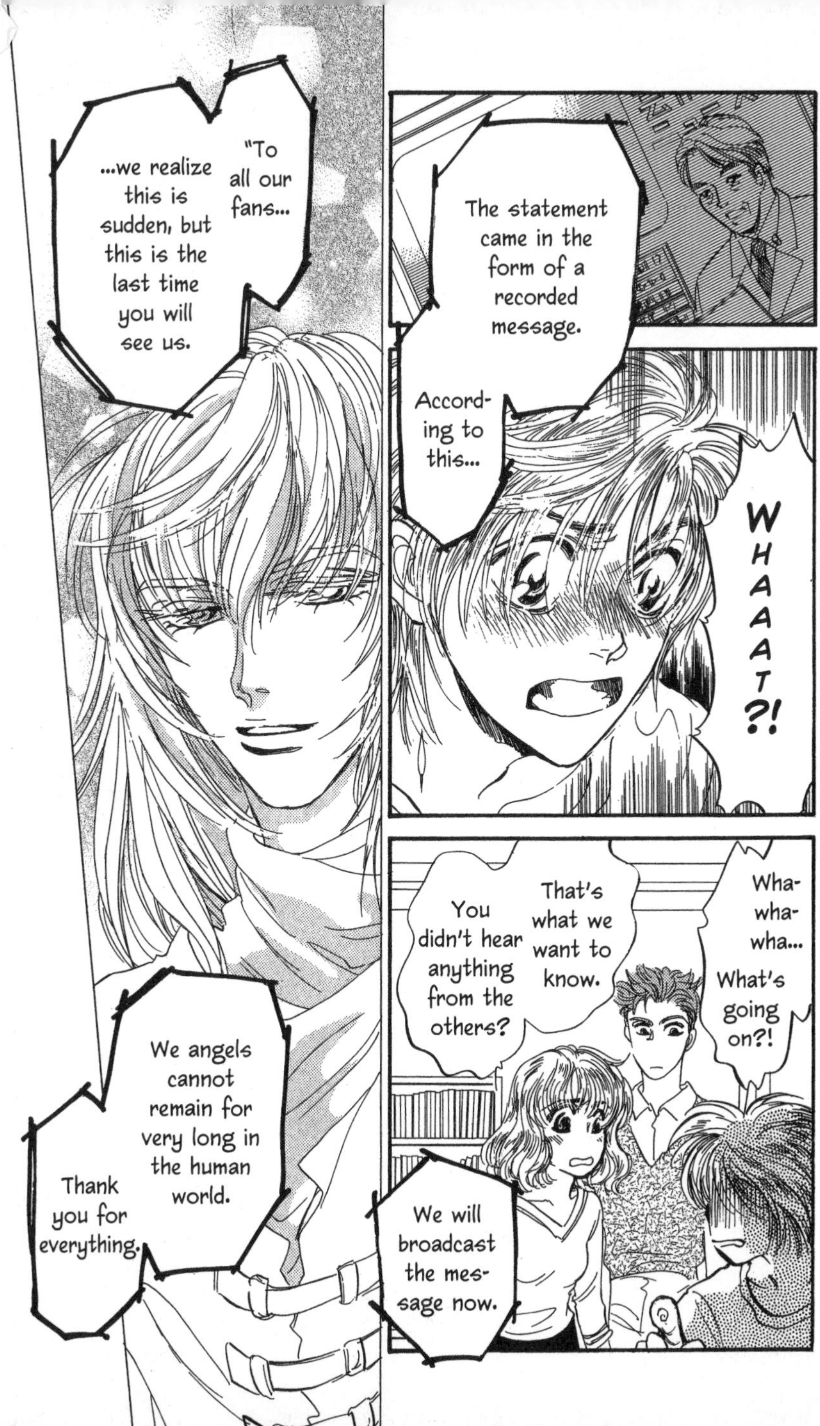
The statement came in the form of a recorded message.
According to this...
WHAAAAT?!
Wha-wha-wha...
What's going on?!
That's what we want to know.
You didn't hear anything from the others?
We will broadcast the message now.
"To all our fans...
...we realize this is sudden, but this is the last time you will see us.
We angels cannot remain for very long in the human world.
Thank you for everything.

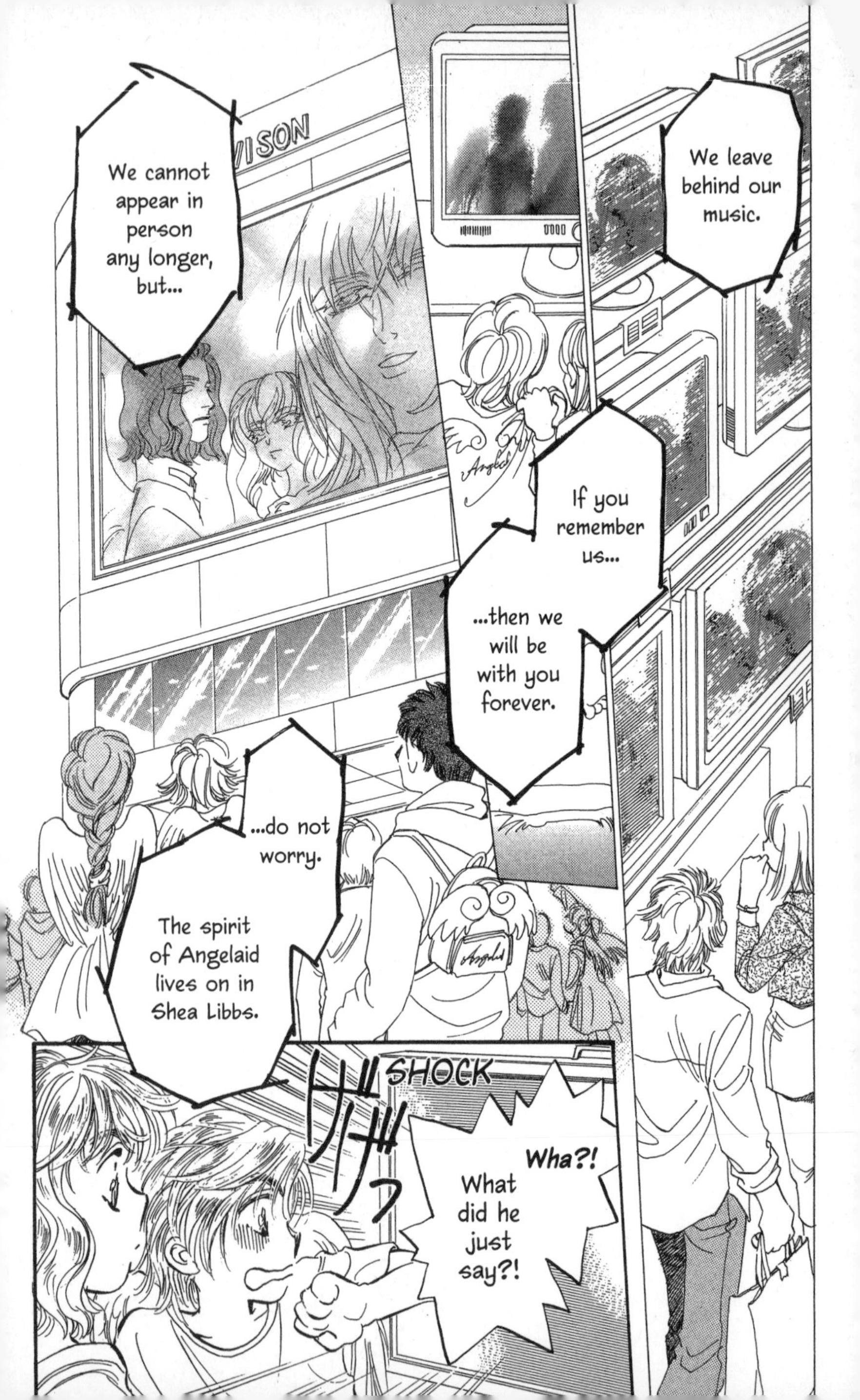

We leave behind our music.
If you remember us...
...then we will be with you forever.
VISON
We cannot appear in person any longer, but...
...do not worry.
The spirit of Angelaid lives on in Shea Libbs.
SHOCK
Wha?!
What did he just say?!

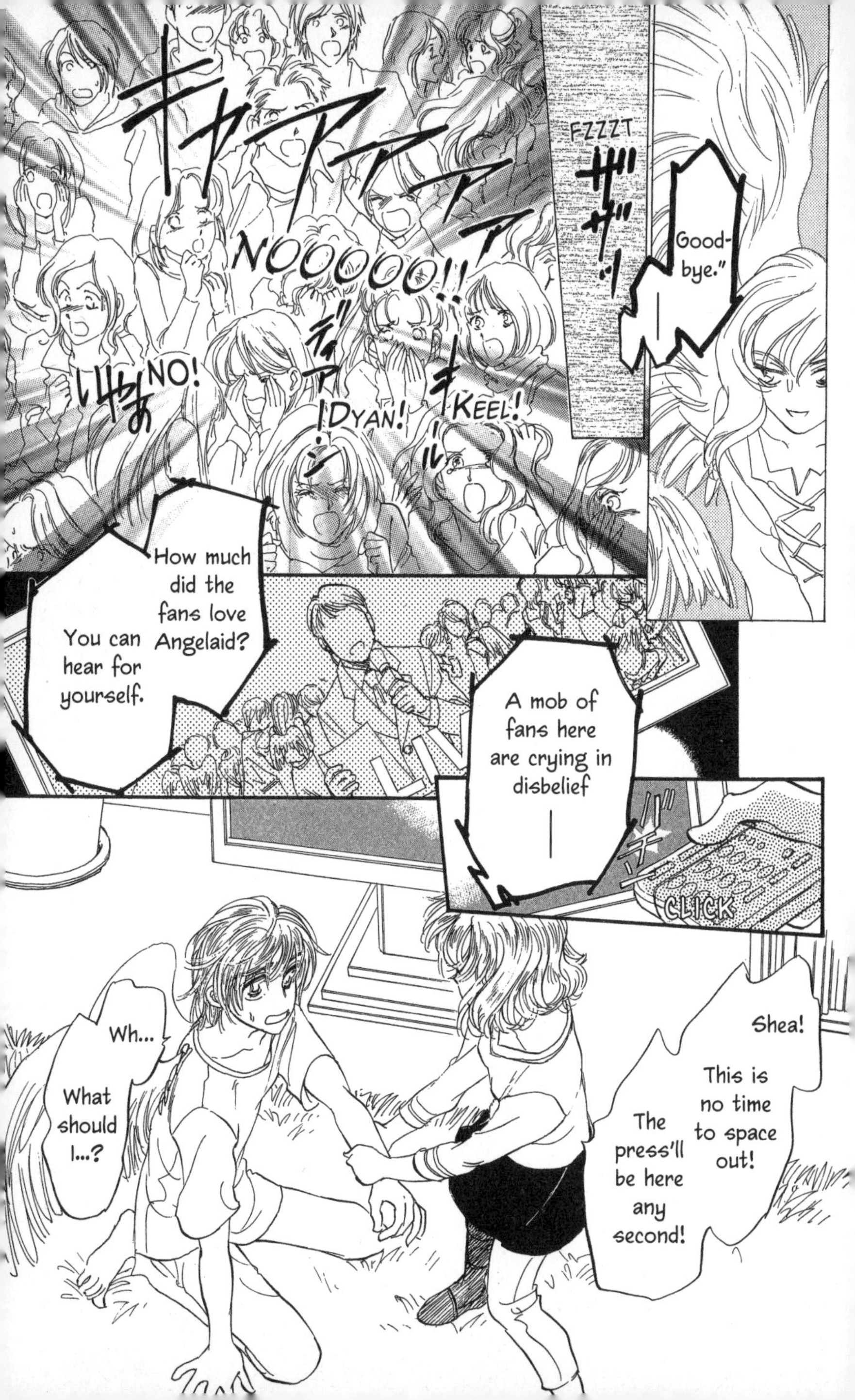
FZZZT
Good-bye."
NOOOOOO!!
NO!
DYAN!
KEEL!
A mob of fans here are crying in disbelief
How much did the fans love Angelaid? You can hear for yourself.
CLICK
Shea! This is no time to space out!
The press'll be here any second!
Wh...
What should I...?

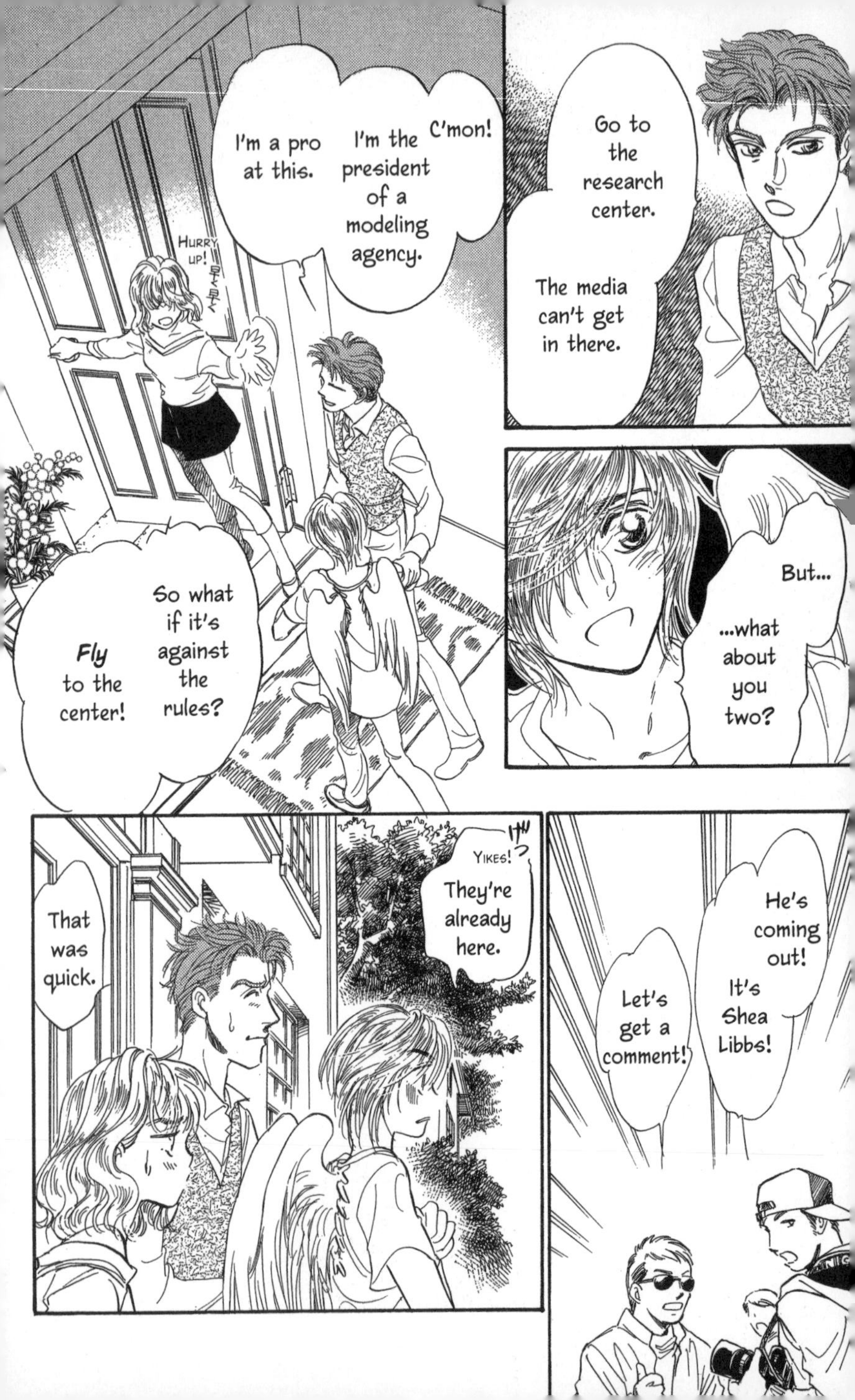
Go to the research center.
The media can't get in there.
But...
...what about you two?
C'mon!
I'm the president of a modeling agency.
I'm a pro at this.
Hurry up!
So what if it's against the rules?
Fly to the center!
He's coming out!
It's Shea Libbs!
Let's get a comment!
Yikes!
They're already here.
That was quick.

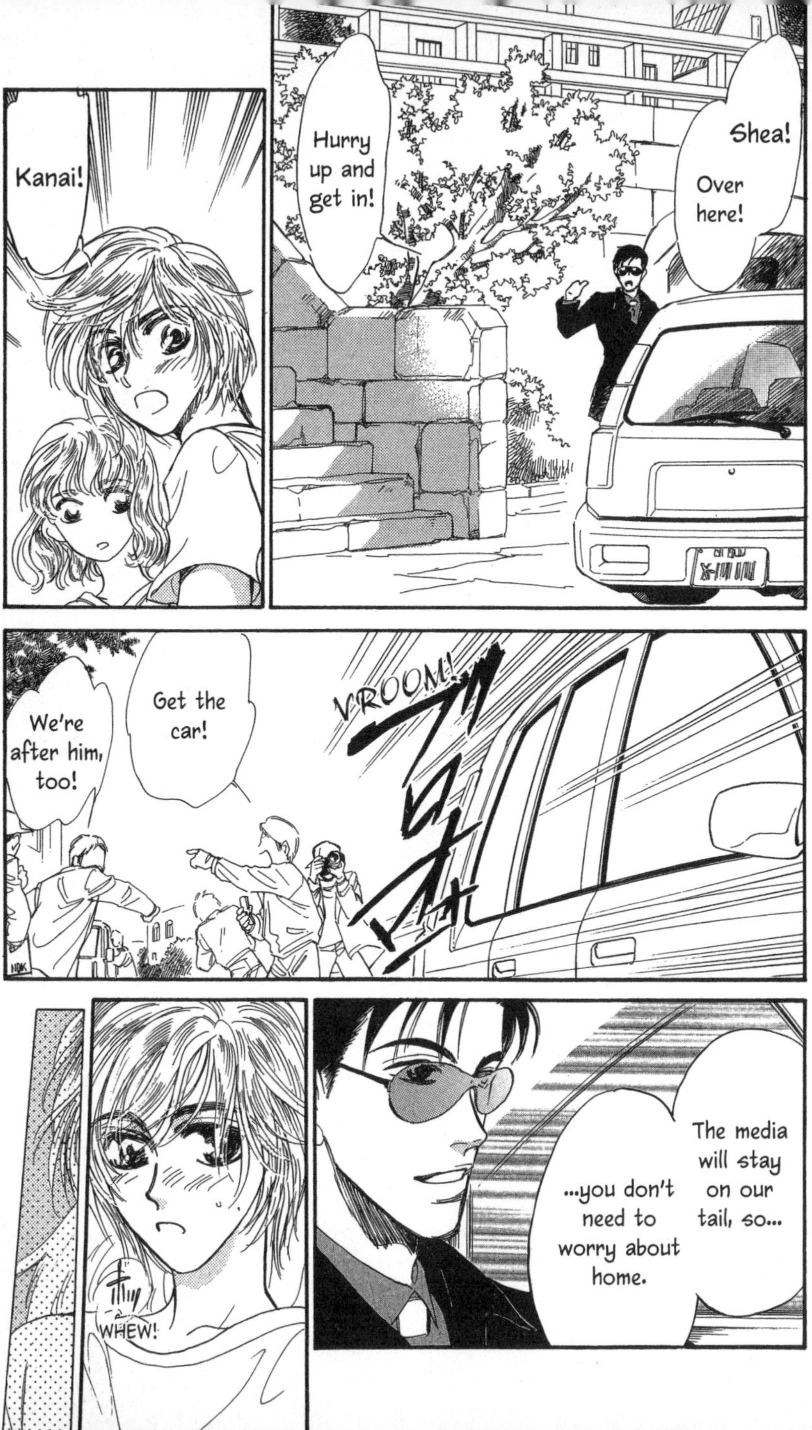
Shea!
Over here!
Hurry up and get in!
Kanai!
VROOM!
Get the car!
We're after him, too!
The media will stay on our tail, so...
...you don't need to worry about home.
WHEW!

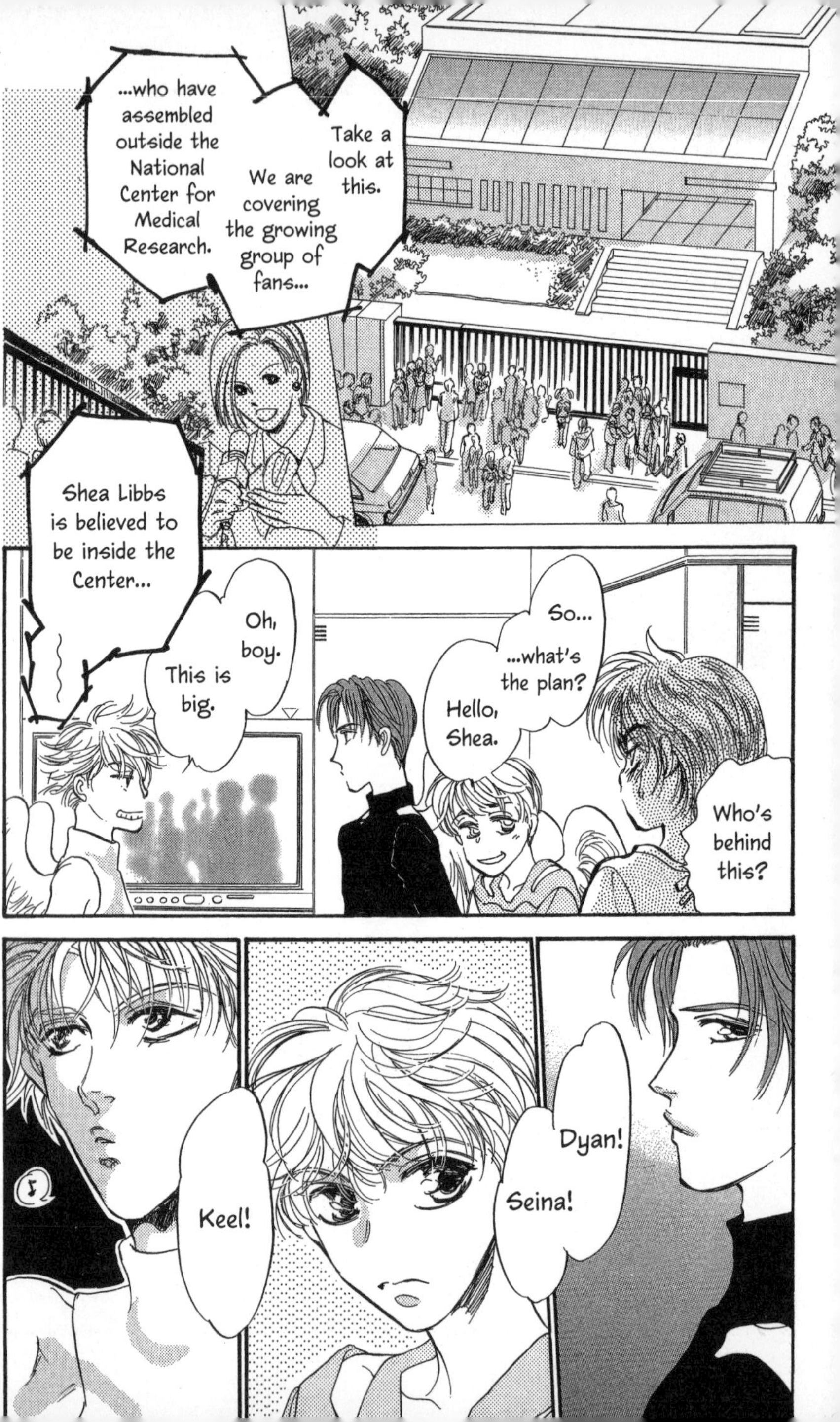
Take a look at this.
We are covering the growing group of fans...
...who have assembled outside the National Center for Medical Research.
Shea Libbs is believed to be inside the Center...
Who's behind this?
So... ...what's the plan?
Hello, Shea.
Oh, boy. This is big.
Dyan!
Seina!
Keel!

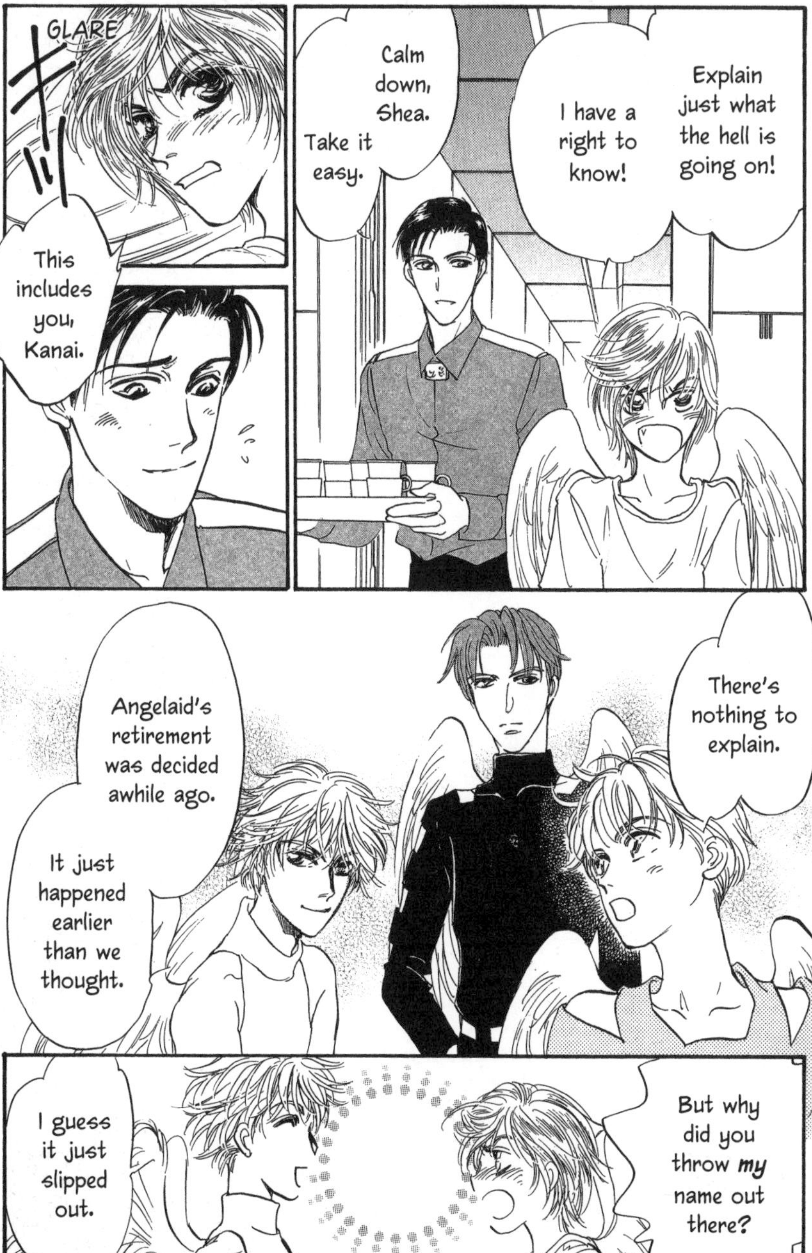
Explain just what the hell is going on!
I have a right to know!
Calm down, Shea.
Take it easy.
GLARE
This includes you, Kanai.
There's nothing to explain.
Angelaid's retirement was decided awhile ago.
It just happened earlier than we thought.
But why did you throw *my* name out there?
I guess it just slipped out.

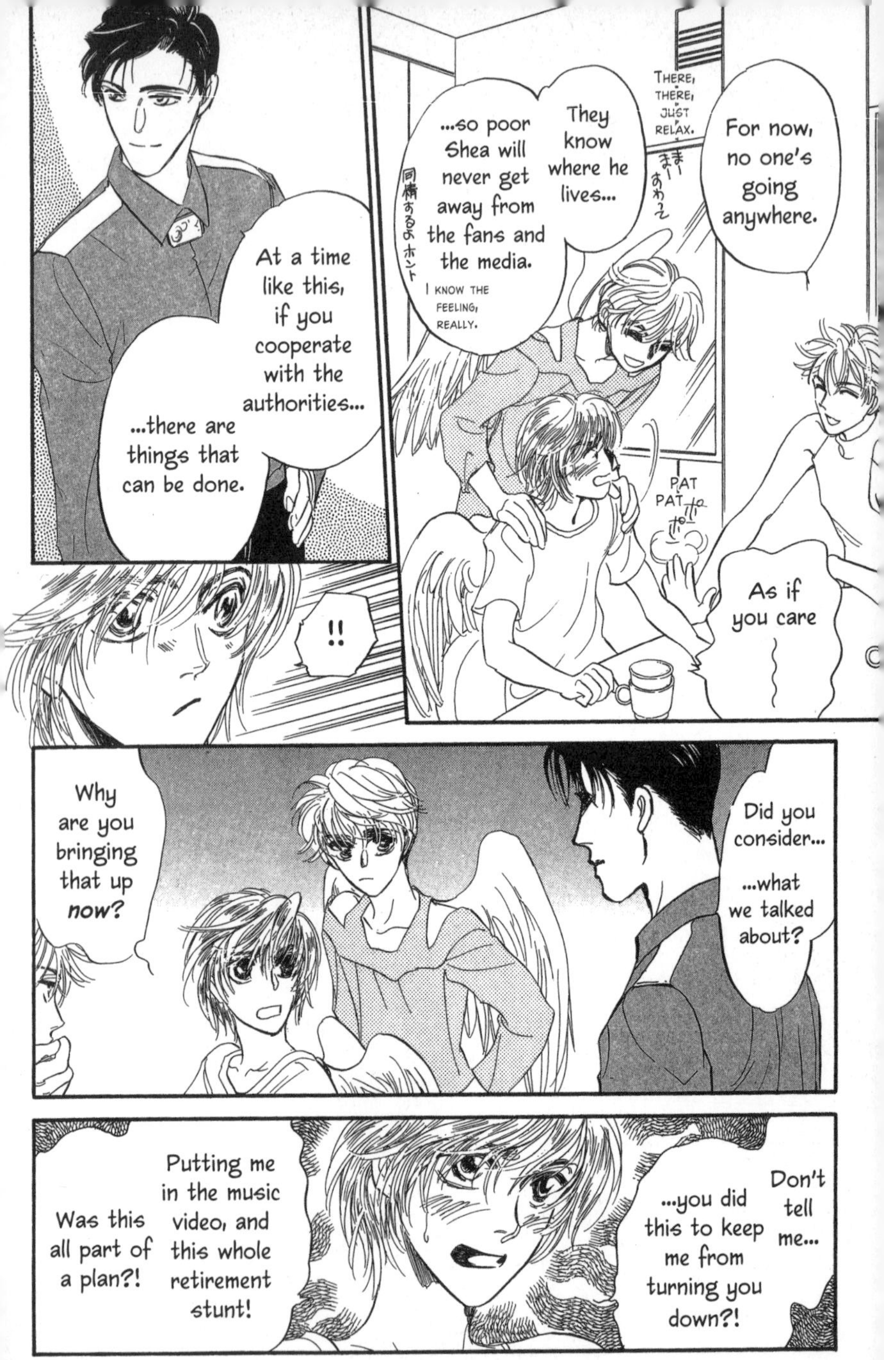
For now, no one's going anywhere.
THERE, THERE, JUST RELAX.
They know where he lives...
...so poor Shea will never get away from the fans and the media.
同情するよホント
I KNOW THE FEELING, REALLY.
PAT PAT
As if you care
At a time like this, if you cooperate with the authorities...
...there are things that can be done.
!!
Did you consider...
...what we talked about?
Why are you bringing that up *now*?
Don't tell me...
...you did this to keep me from turning you down?!
Putting me in the music video, and this whole retirement stunt!
Was this all part of a plan?!

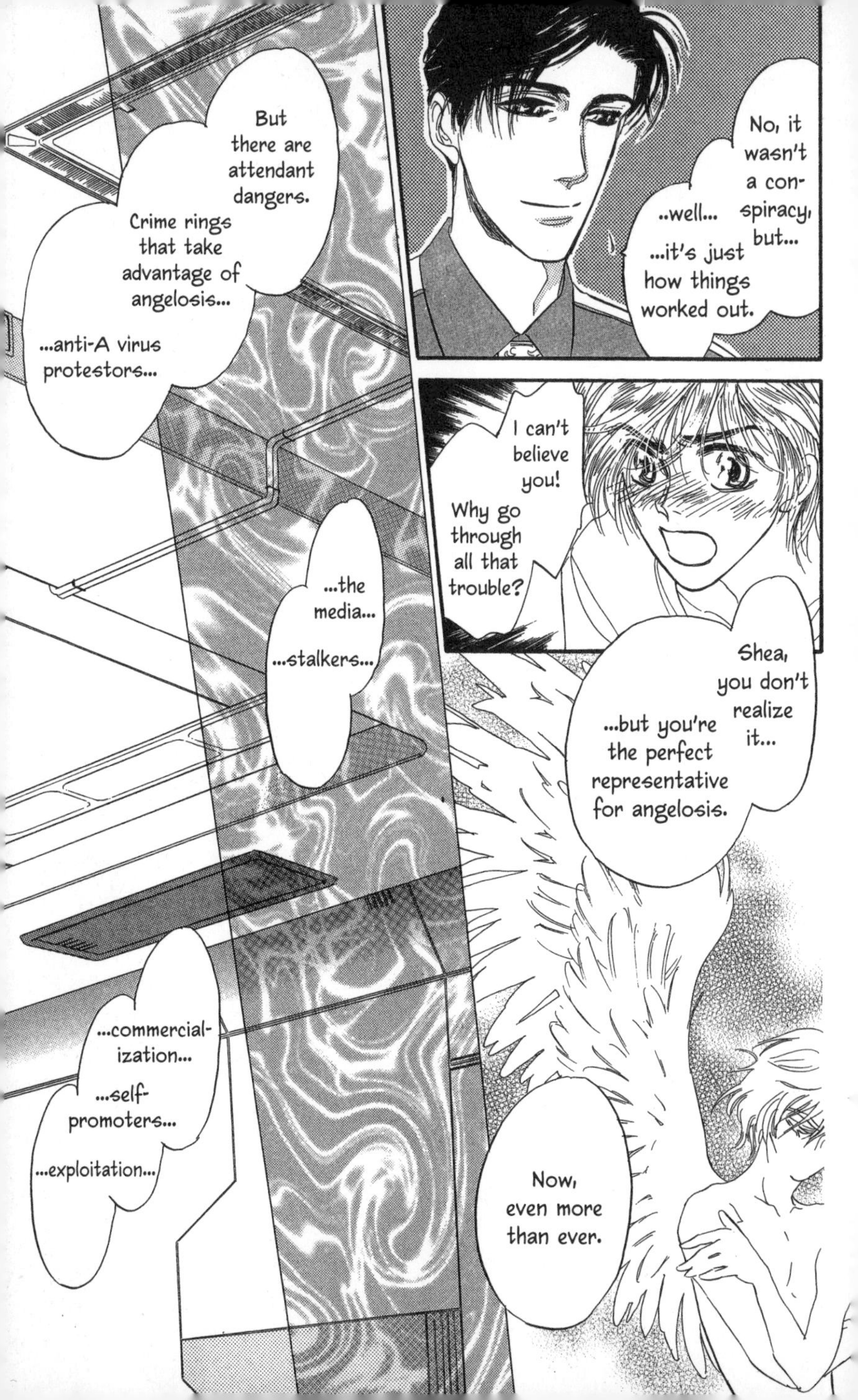
No, it wasn't a con-spiracy, but...
..well...
...it's just how things worked out.
I can't believe you!
Why go through all that trouble?
Shea, you don't realize it...
...but you're the perfect representative for angelosis.
Now, even more than ever.
But there are attendant dangers.
Crime rings that take advantage of angelosis...
...anti-A virus protestors...
...the media...
...stalkers...
...commercial-ization...
...self-promoters...
...exploitation...

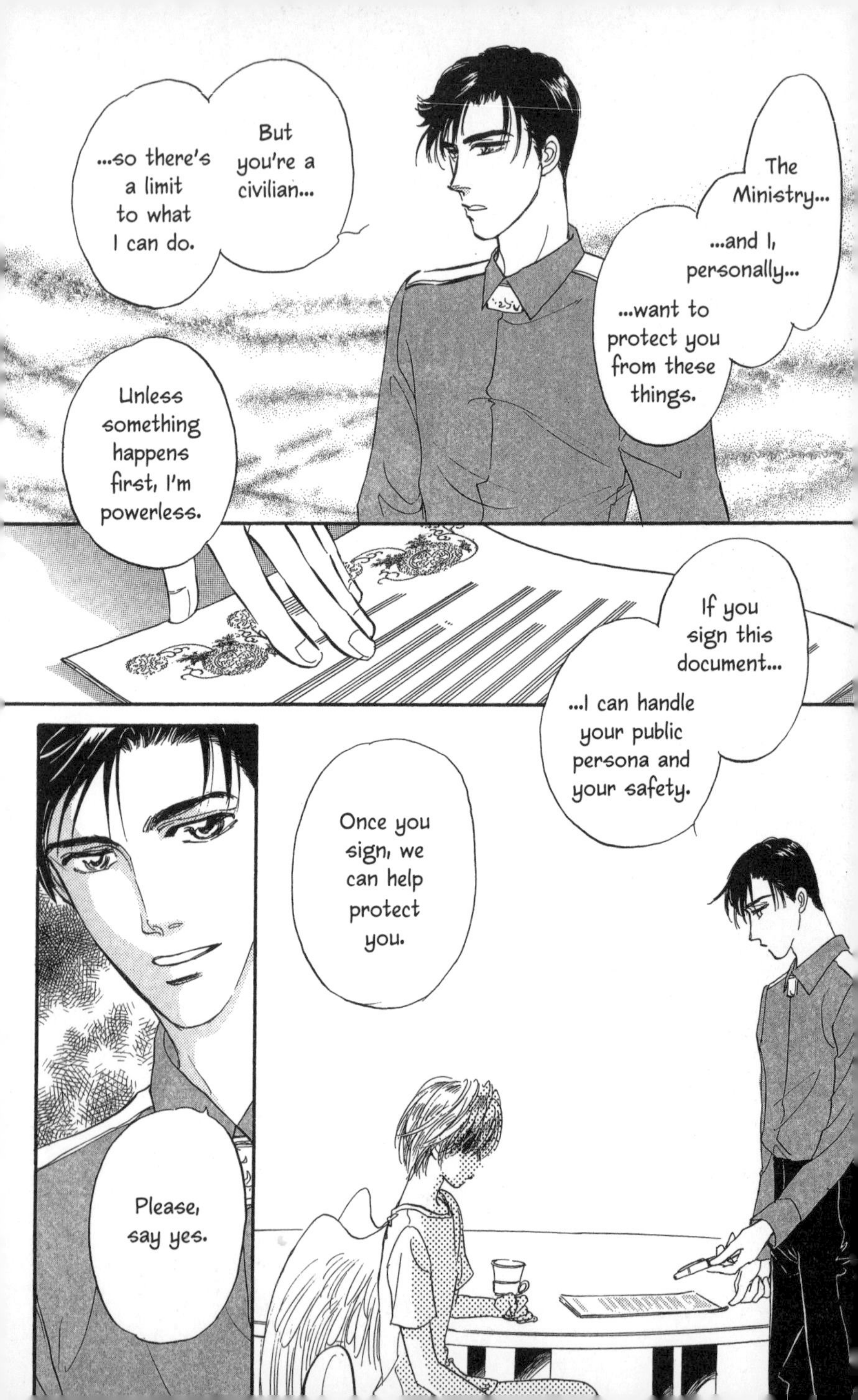
The Ministry...
...and I, personally...
...want to protect you from these things.
But you're a civilian...
...so there's a limit to what I can do.
Unless something happens first, I'm powerless.
If you sign this document...
...I can handle your public persona and your safety.
Once you sign, we can help protect you.
Please, say yes.

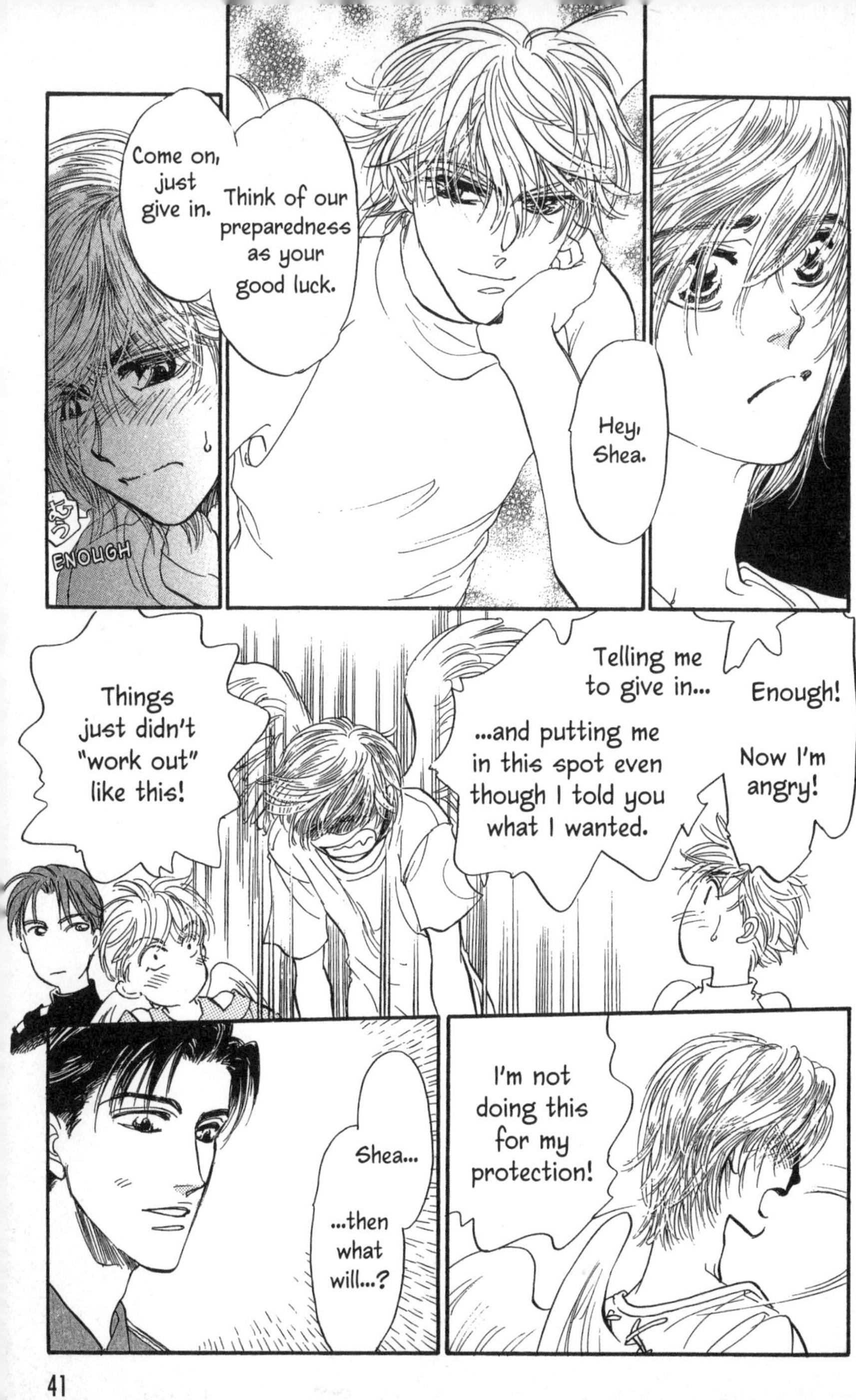
Hey, Shea.
Come on, just give in.
Think of our preparedness as your good luck.
ENOUGH
Enough!
Now I'm angry!
Telling me to give in...
...and putting me in this spot even though I told you what I wanted.
Things just didn't "work out" like this!
I'm not doing this for my protection!
Shea...
...then what will...?

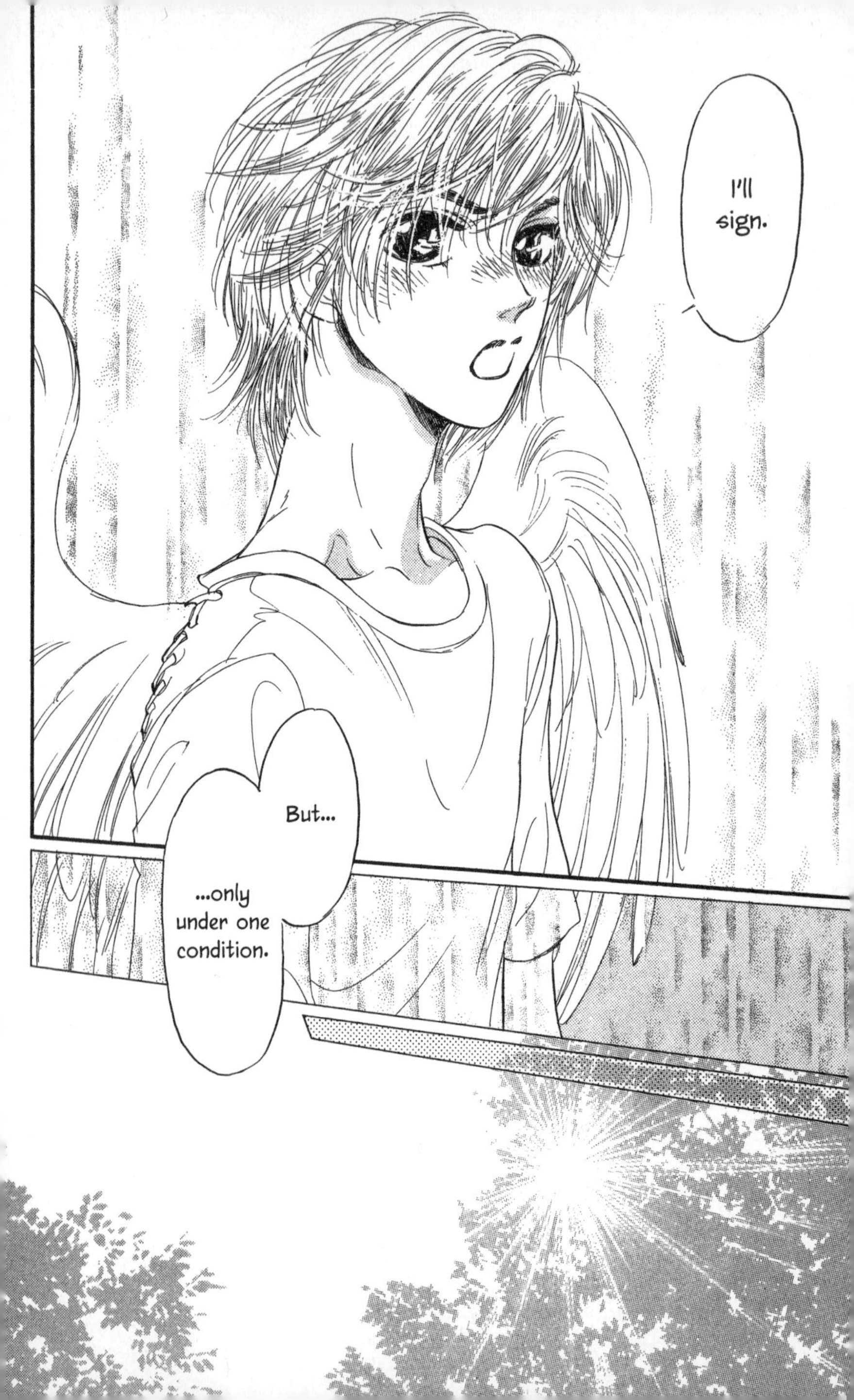
I'll sign.
But...
...only under one condition.

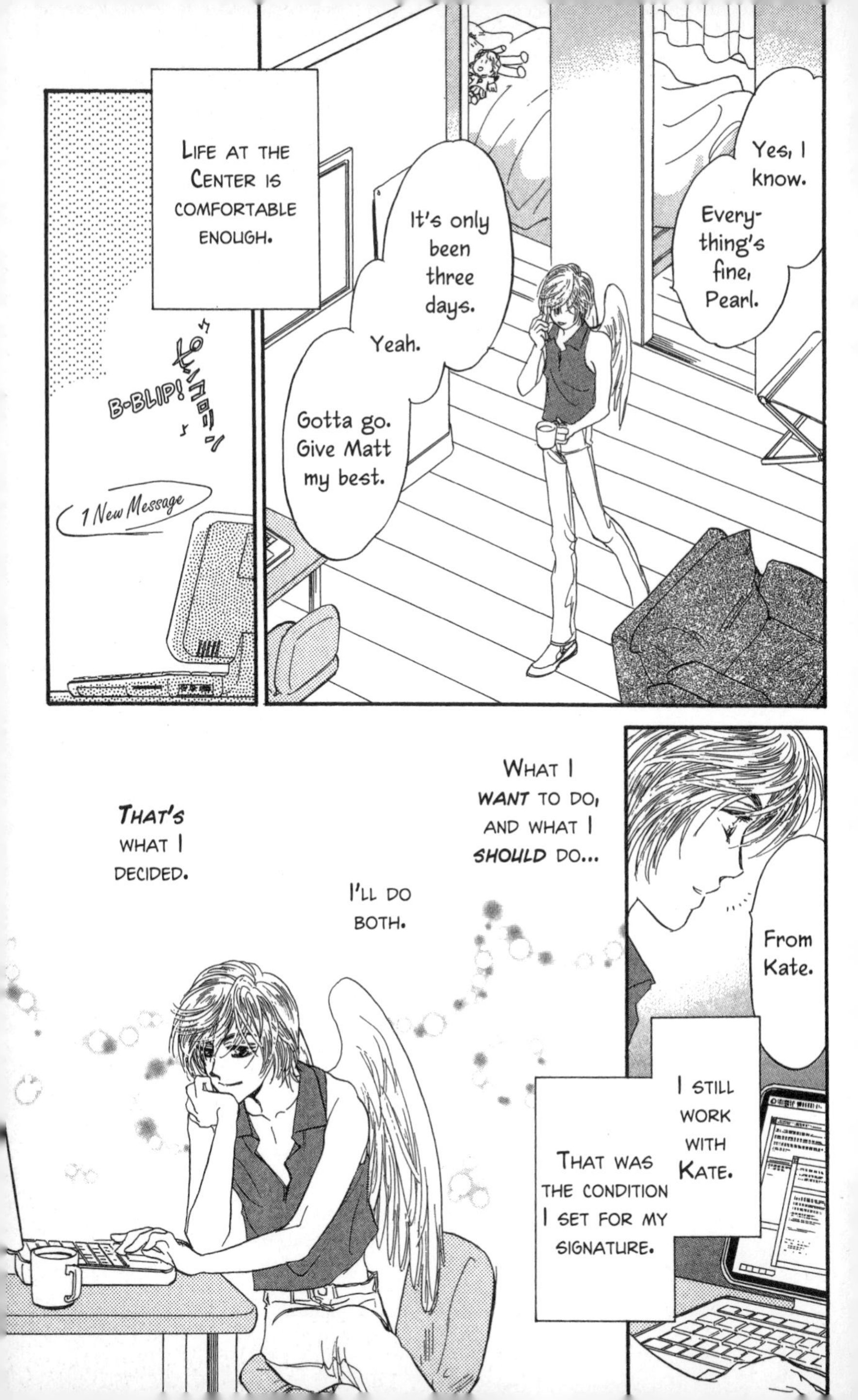
Yes, I know.
Every-thing's fine, Pearl.
It's only been three days.
Yeah.
Gotta go. Give Matt my best.
LIFE AT THE CENTER IS COMFORTABLE ENOUGH.
B-BLIP!
1 New Message
From Kate.
I STILL WORK WITH KATE.
THAT WAS THE CONDITION I SET FOR MY SIGNATURE.
WHAT I *WANT* TO DO, AND WHAT I *SHOULD* DO...
I'LL DO BOTH.
THAT'S WHAT I DECIDED.

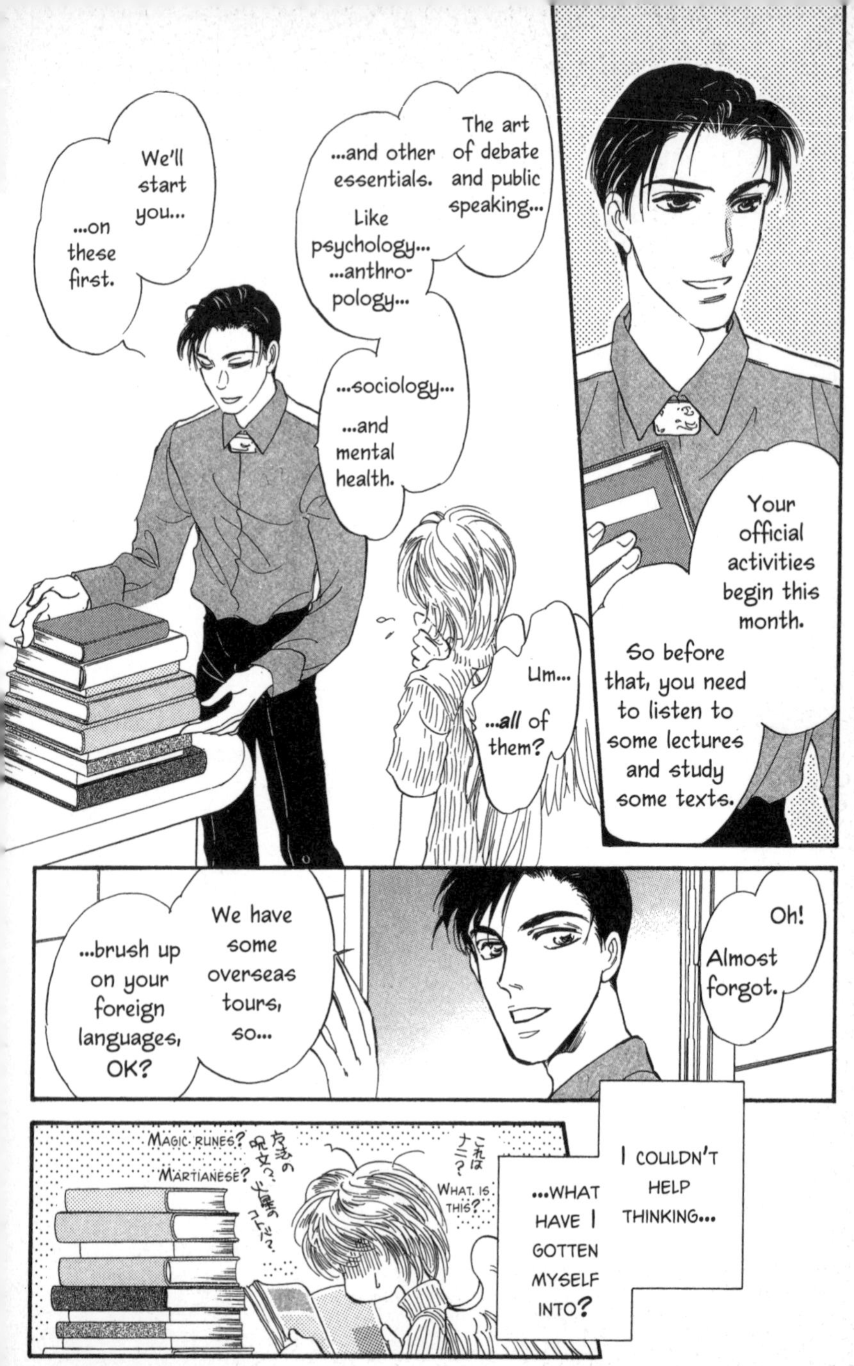
Your official activities begin this month.
So before that, you need to listen to some lectures and study some texts.
The art of debate and public speaking...
...and other essentials.
Like psychology... ...anthro-pology...
...sociology...
...and mental health.
We'll start you...
...on these first.
Um... ...all of them?
Oh! Almost forgot.
We have some overseas tours, so...
...brush up on your foreign languages, OK?
I couldn't help thinking...
...what have I gotten myself into?
これはナニ？
What. is this?
Magic runes?
Martianese?

Chapter 6 The End

Chapter 7

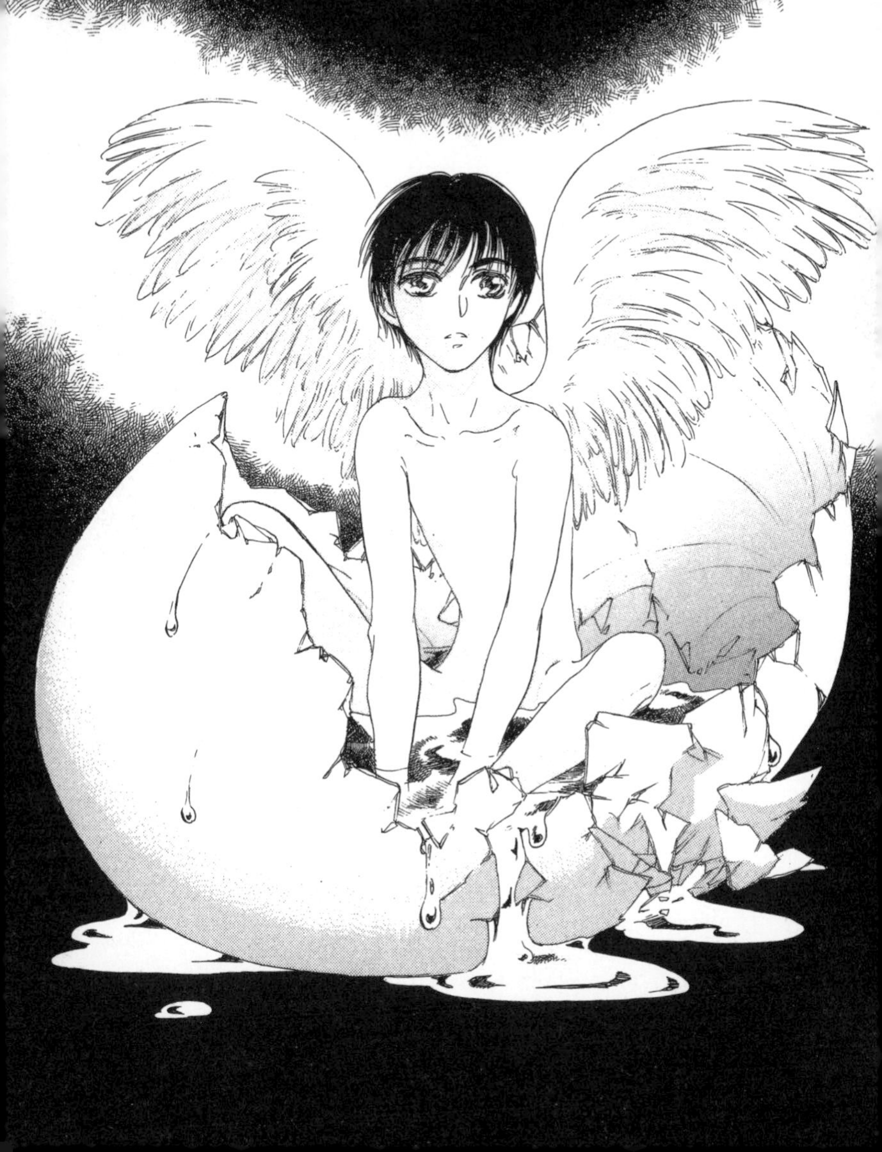

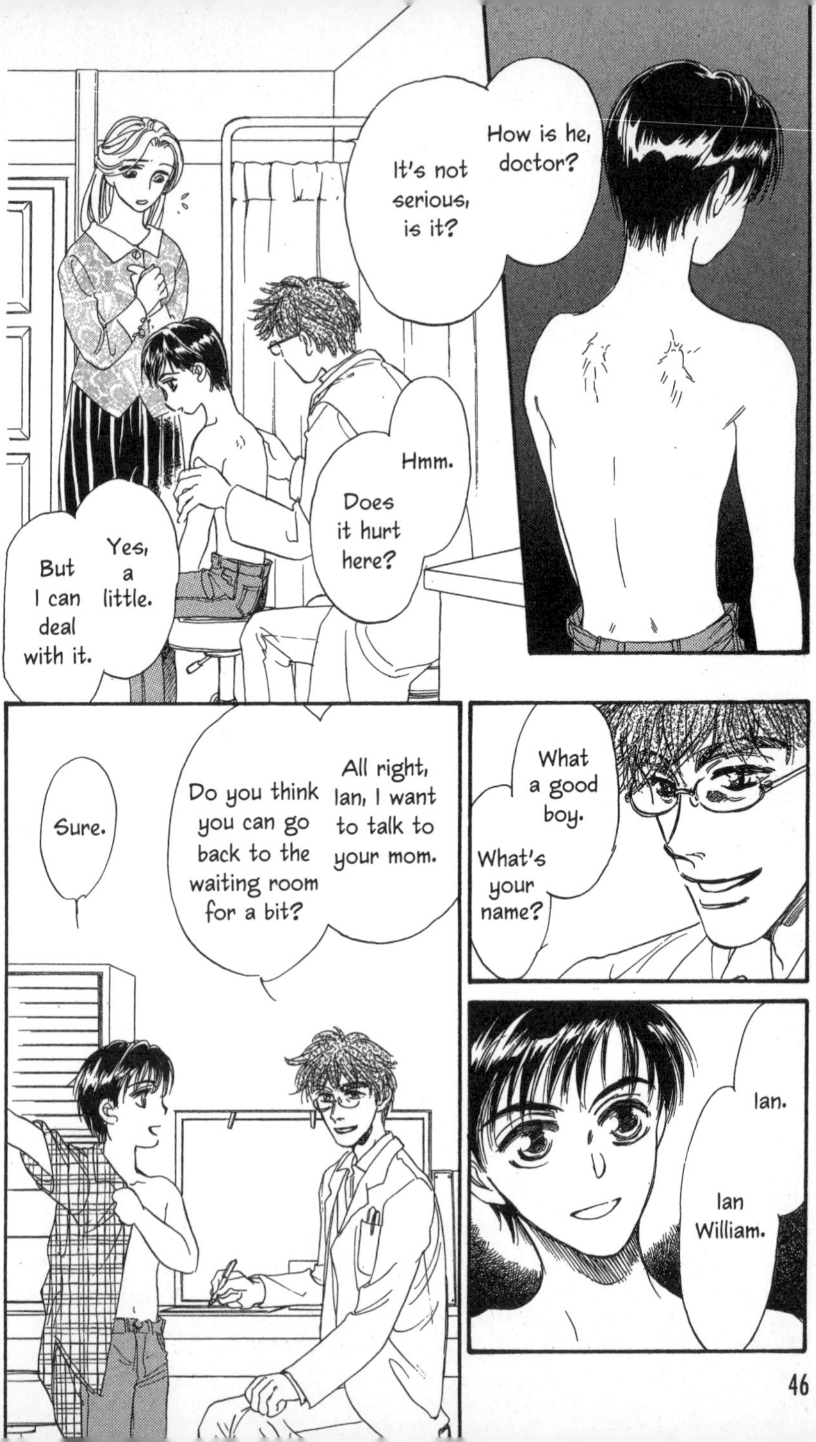
How is he, doctor?
It's not serious, is it?
Hmm.
Does it hurt here?
Yes, a little.
But I can deal with it.
What a good boy.
What's your name?
Ian.
Ian William.
All right, Ian, I want to talk to your mom.
Do you think you can go back to the waiting room for a bit?
Sure.

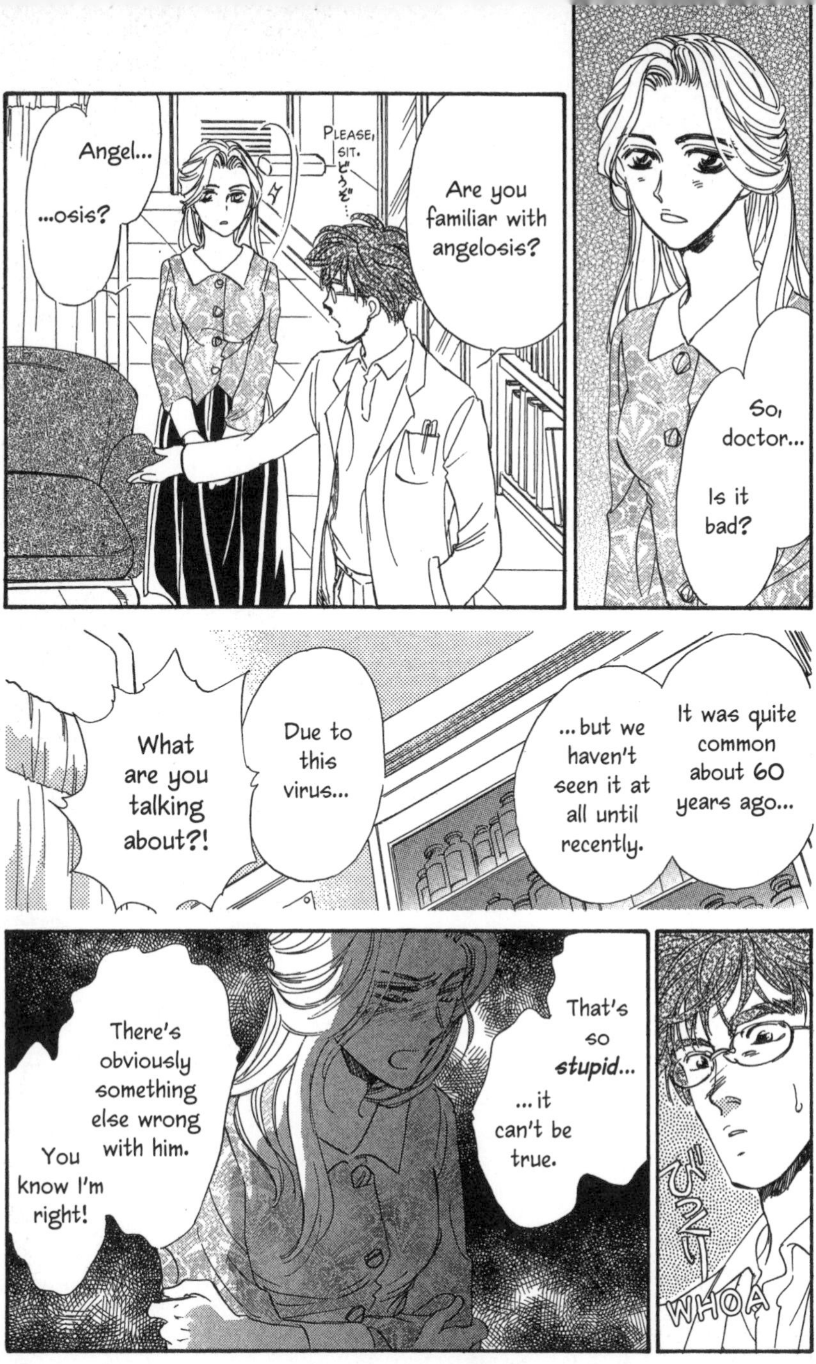
So, doctor...
Is it bad?
Are you familiar with angelosis?
Please, sit.
どうぞ...
Angel...
...osis?
It was quite common about 60 years ago...
...but we haven't seen it at all until recently.
Due to this virus...
What are you talking about?!
びくっ
WHOA
That's so *stupid*...
...it can't be true.
There's obviously something else wrong with him.
You know I'm right!

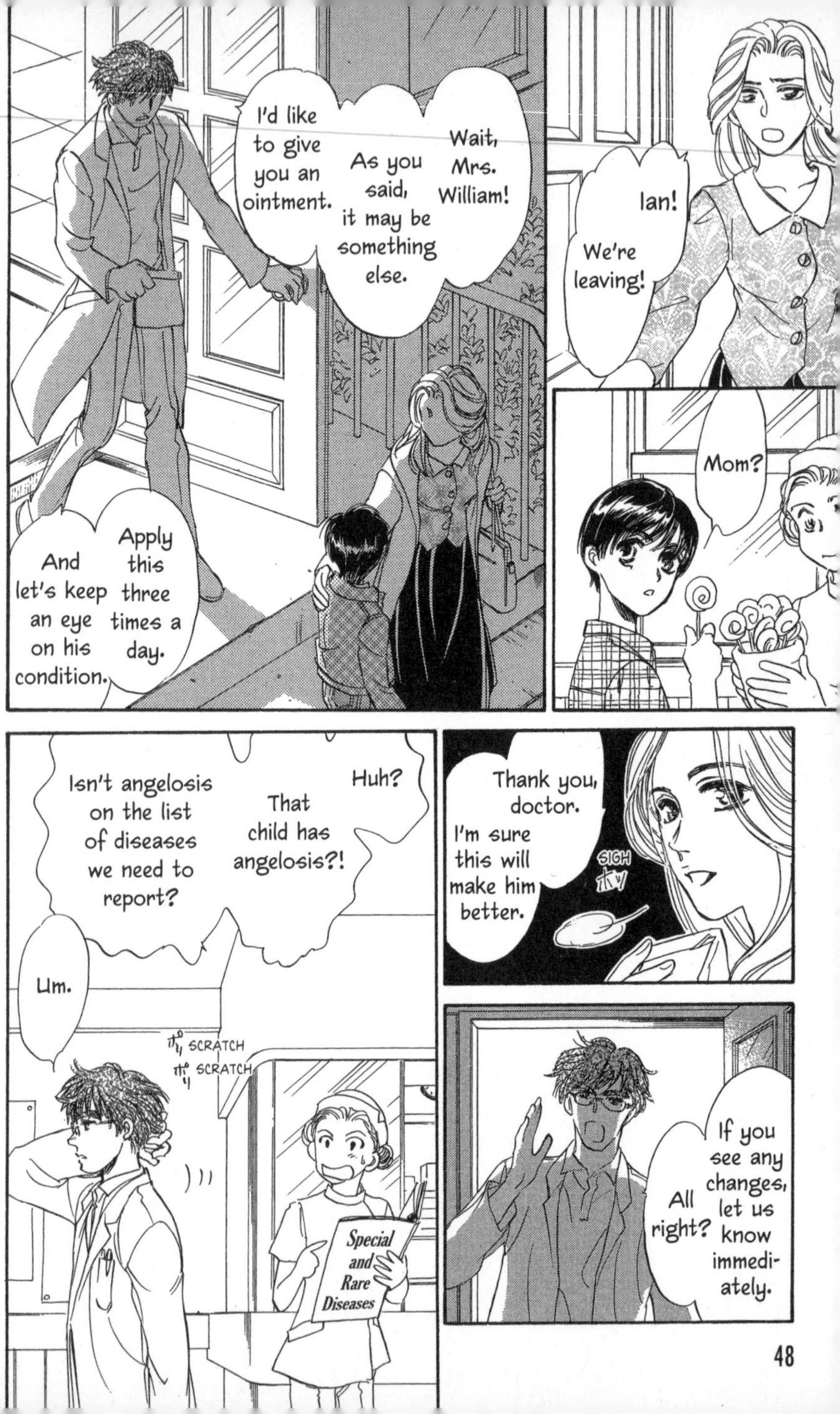
Ian!
We're leaving!
Mom?
Wait, Mrs. William!
As you said, it may be something else.
I'd like to give you an ointment.
Apply this three times a day.
And let's keep an eye on his condition.
Thank you, doctor.
I'm sure this will make him better.
SIGH
If you see any changes, let us know immediately.
All right?
Huh?
That child has angelosis?!
Isn't angelosis on the list of diseases we need to report?
Um.
SCRATCH
SCRATCH
Special and Rare Diseases

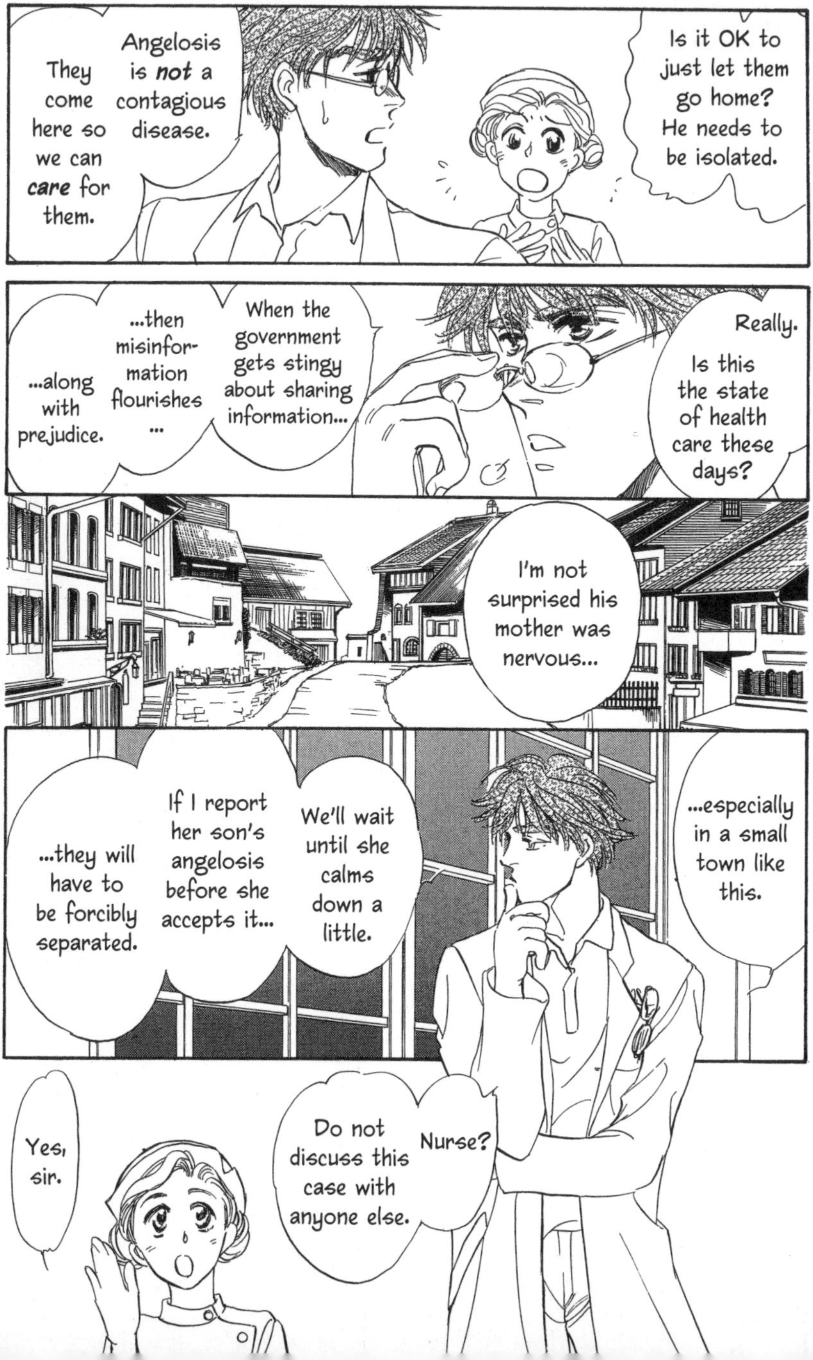
Is it OK to just let them go home? He needs to be isolated.
Angelosis is **not** a contagious disease.
They come here so we can **care** for them.
Really.
Is this the state of health care these days?
When the government gets stingy about sharing information...
...then misinformation flourishes...
...along with prejudice.
I'm not surprised his mother was nervous...
...especially in a small town like this.
We'll wait until she calms down a little.
If I report her son's angelosis before she accepts it...
...they will have to be forcibly separated.
Nurse?
Do not discuss this case with anyone else.
Yes, sir.

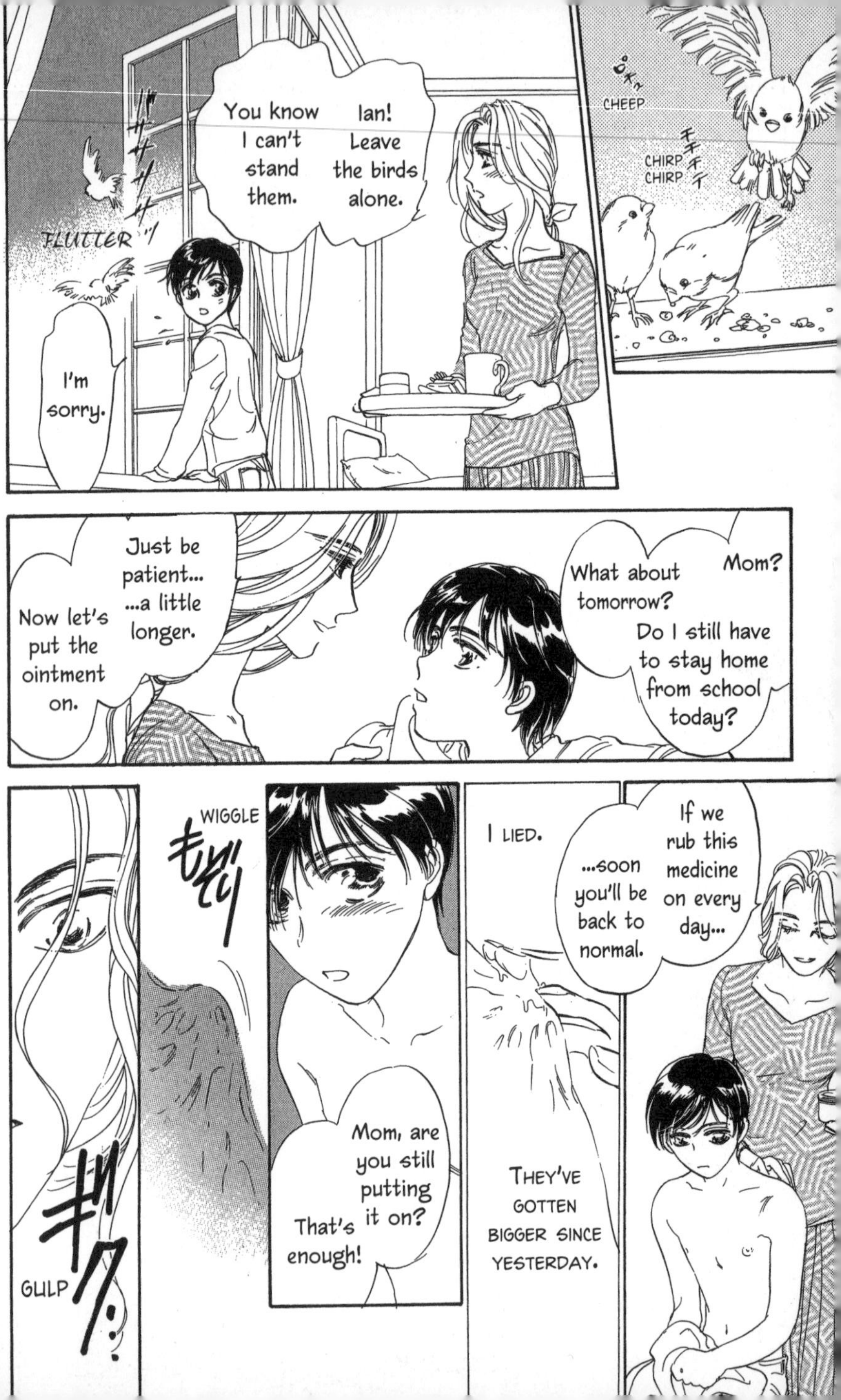
CHEEP
CHIRP CHIRP
Ian! Leave the birds alone.
You know I can't stand them.
FLUTTER
I'm sorry.
Mom?
What about tomorrow?
Do I still have to stay home from school today?
Just be patient... ...a little longer.
Now let's put the ointment on.
If we rub this medicine on every day...
...soon you'll be back to normal.
I LIED.
THEY'VE GOTTEN BIGGER SINCE YESTERDAY.
WIGGLE
Mom, are you still putting it on?
That's enough!
GULP

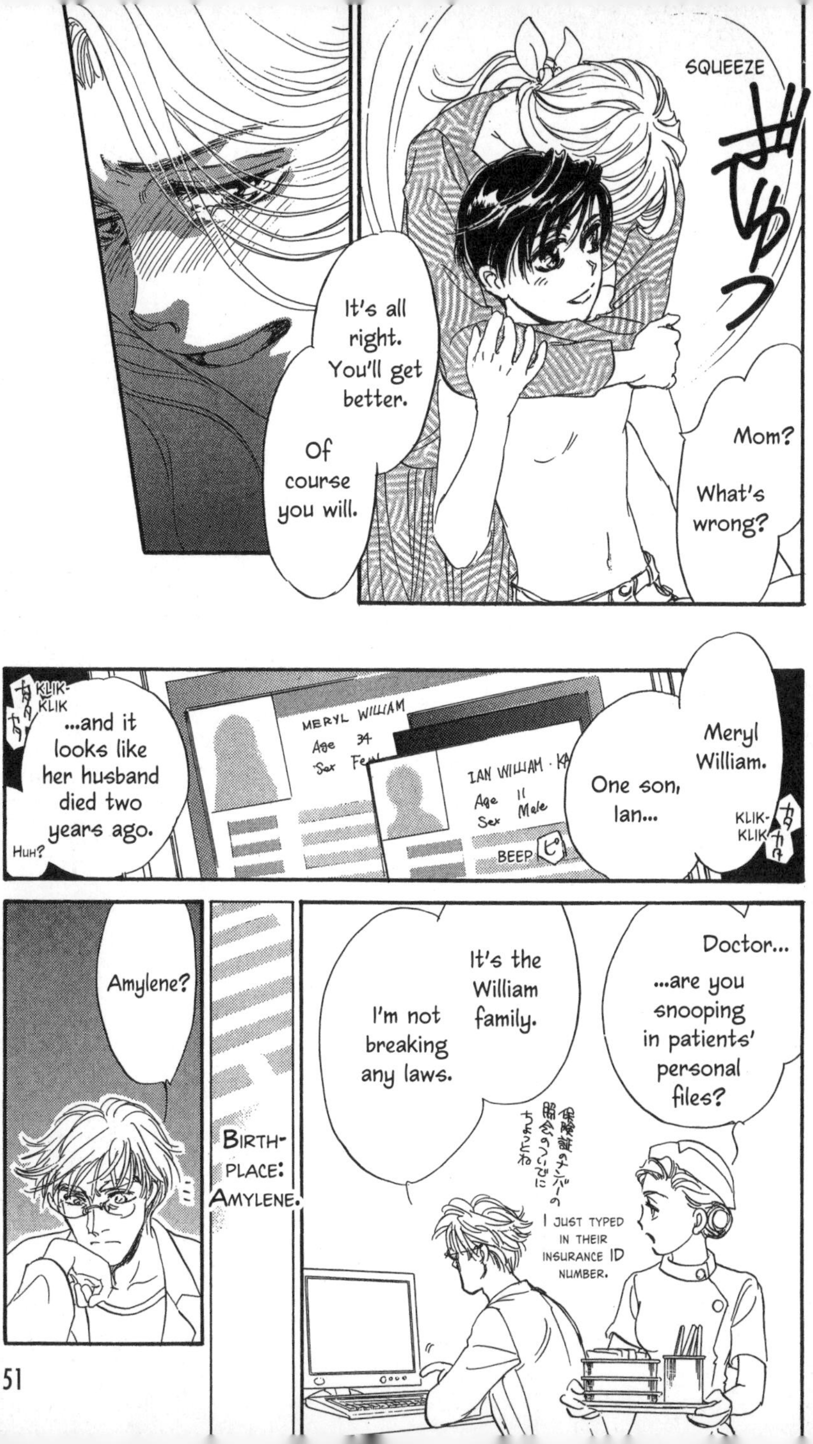
SQUEEZE
ぎゅっ
Mom?
What's wrong?
It's all right. You'll get better.
Of course you will.
Meryl William.
One son, Ian...
KLIK-KLIK
MERYL WILLIAM
Age 34
IAN WILLIAM
Age 11
Sex Male
BEEP
...and it looks like her husband died two years ago.
KLIK-KLIK
Huh?
Doctor...
...are you snooping in patients' personal files?
It's the William family.
I'm not breaking any laws.
保険証ナンバーの照会のついでにちょっとね
I just typed in their insurance ID number.
Birth-place: Amylene.
Amylene?

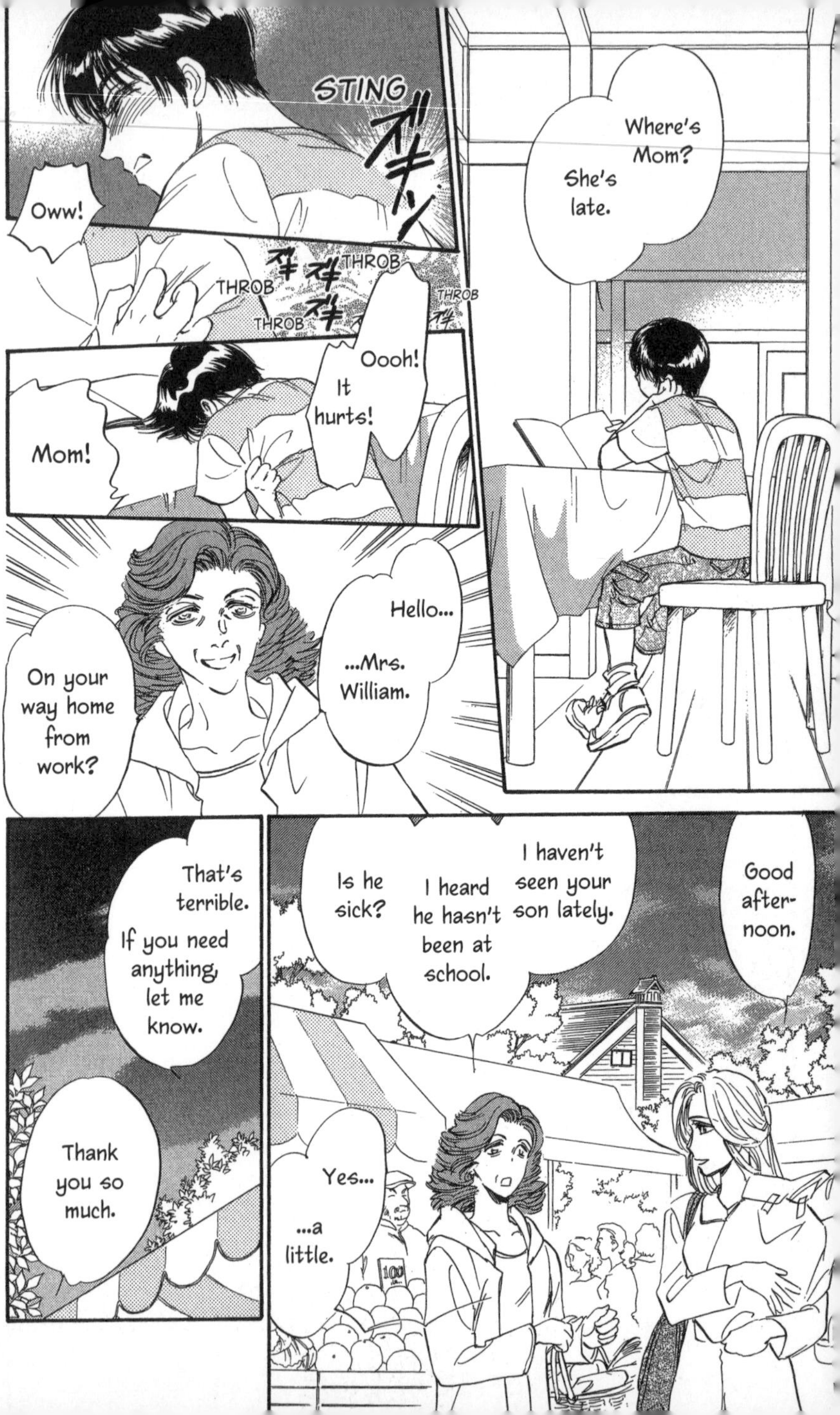
Where's Mom?
She's late.
STING
Oww!
THROB THROB THROB THROB
Mom!
Oooh!
It hurts!
Hello...
...Mrs. William.
On your way home from work?
Good afternoon.
I haven't seen your son lately.
I heard he hasn't been at school.
Is he sick?
Yes...
...a little.
That's terrible.
If you need anything, let me know.
Thank you so much.

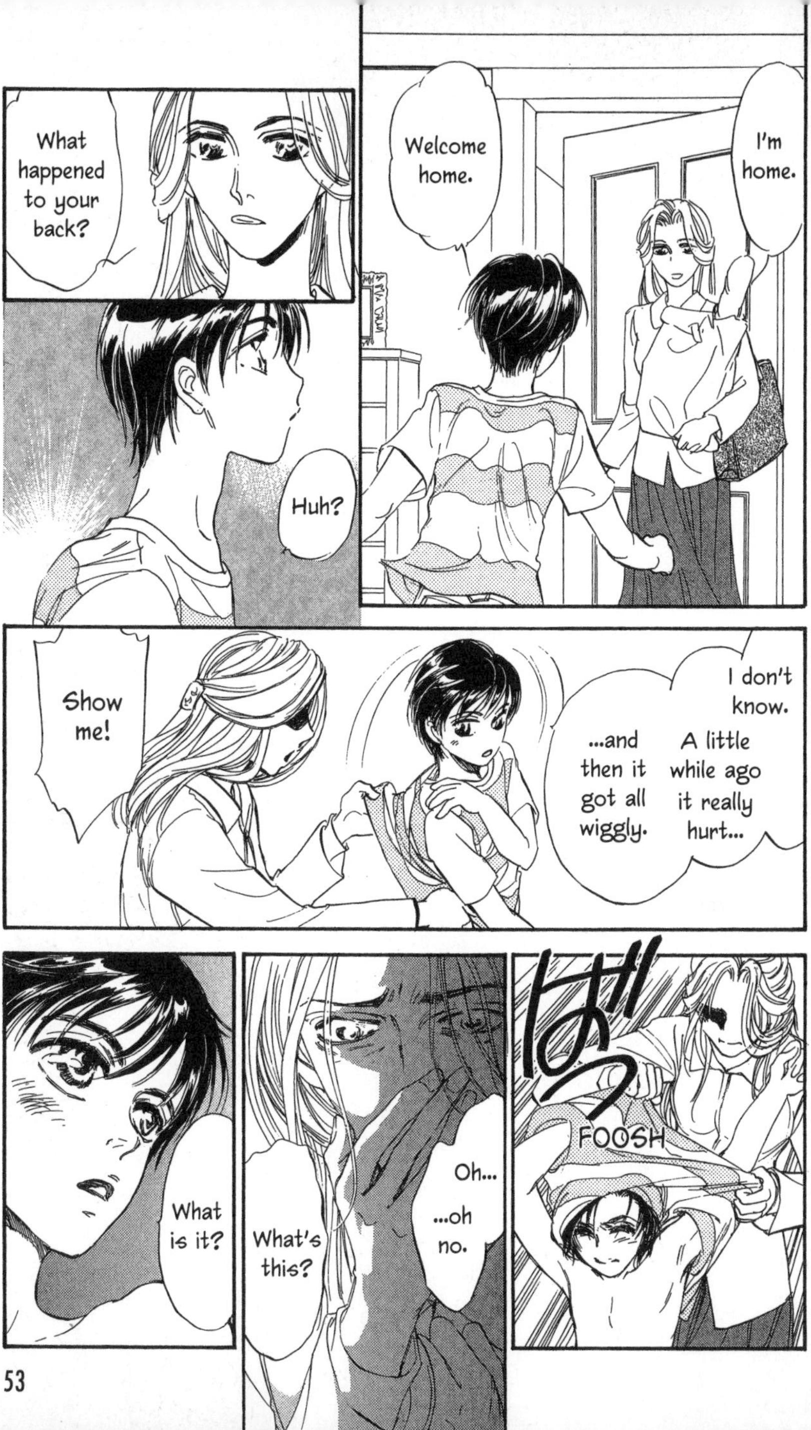
I'm home.
Welcome home.
What happened to your back?
Huh?
I don't know.
A little while ago it really hurt...
...and then it got all wiggly.
Show me!
ぱっ
FOOSH
Oh...
...oh no.
What's this?
What is it?

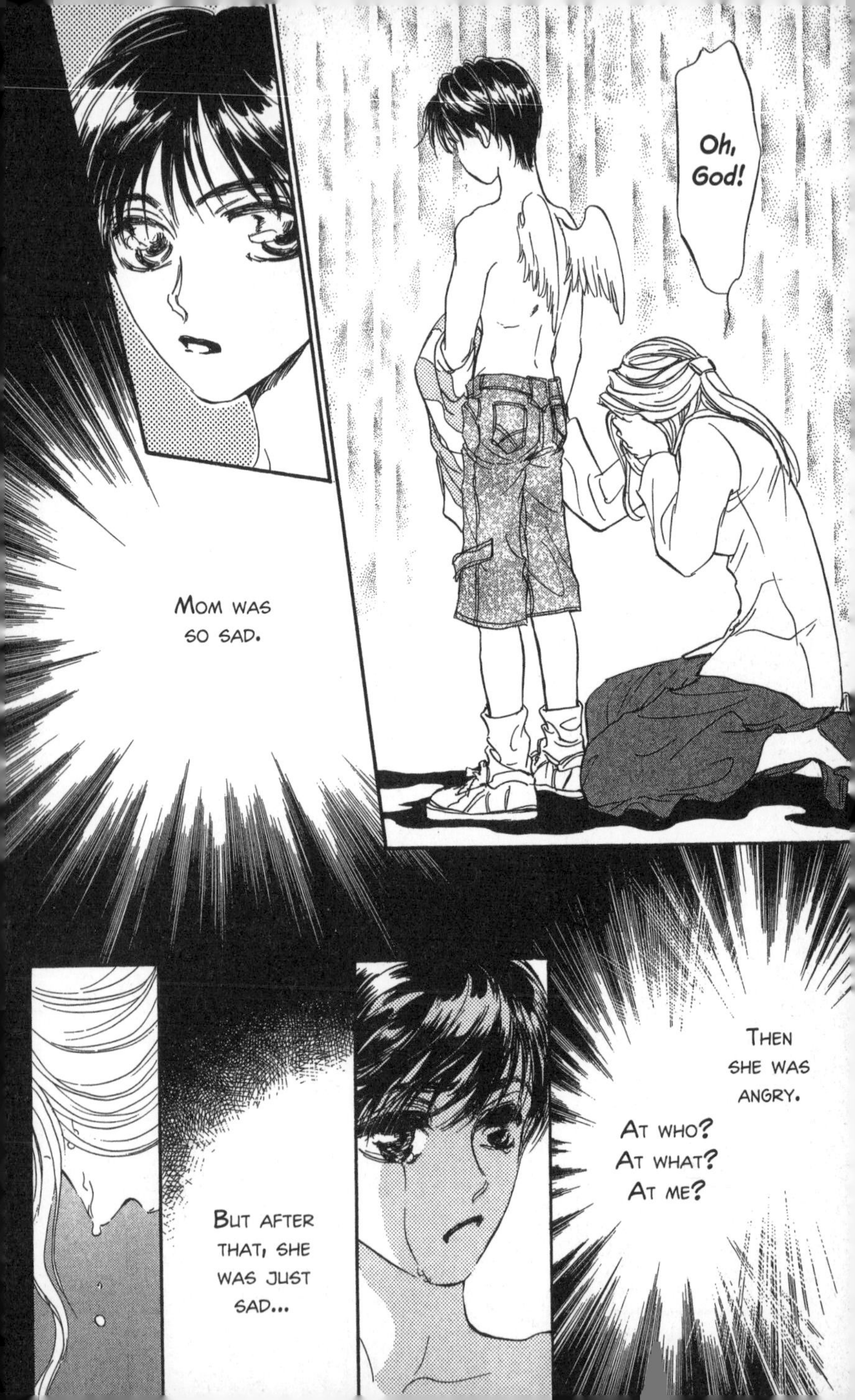
Oh, God!
Mom was so sad.
Then she was angry.
At who? At what? At me?
But after that, she was just sad...

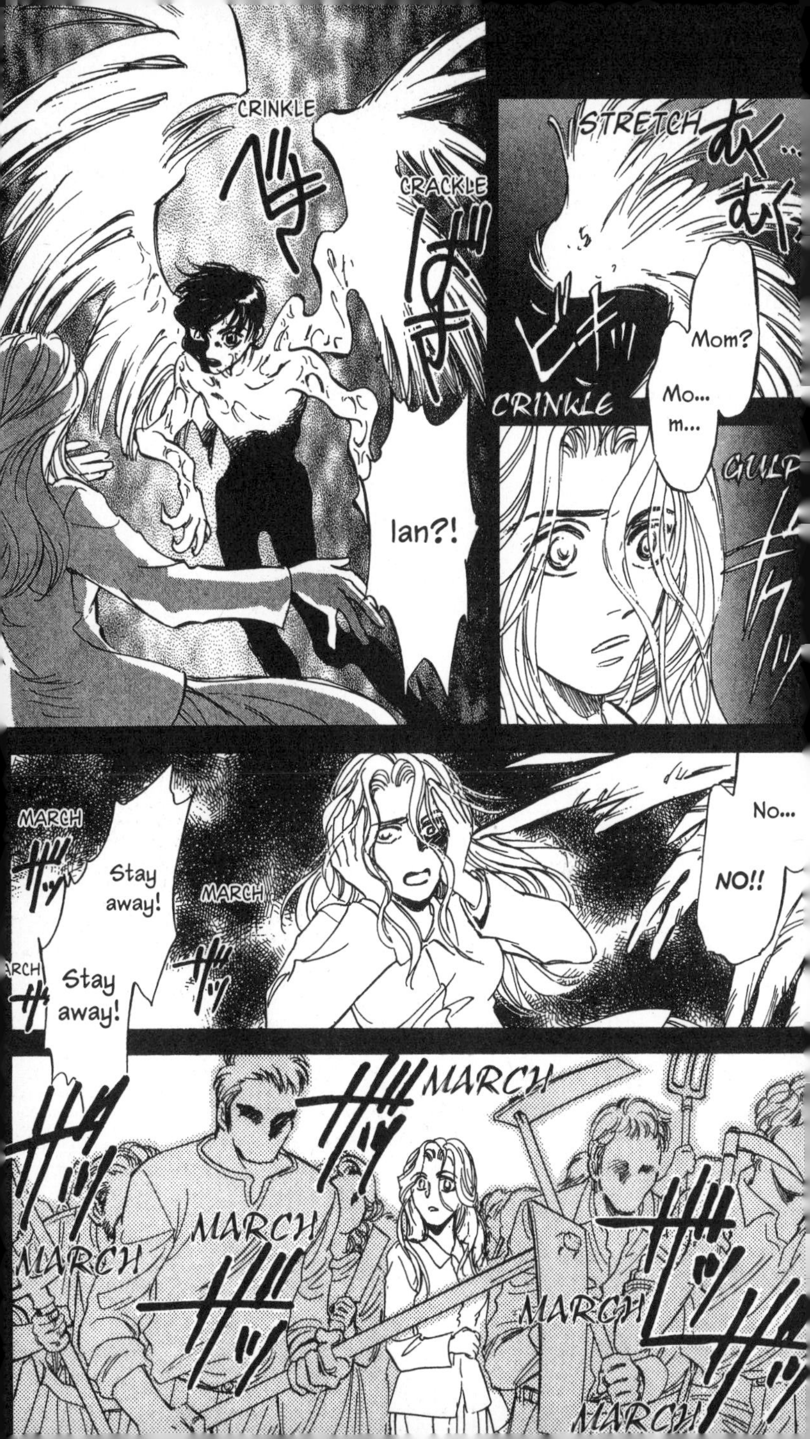
STRETCH
CRINKLE
Mom?
Mo... m...
GULP
CRACKLE
CRINKLE
Ian?!
No...
NO!!
MARCH
Stay away!
MARCH
Stay away!
MARCH
MARCH
MARCH
MARCH
MARCH
MARCH

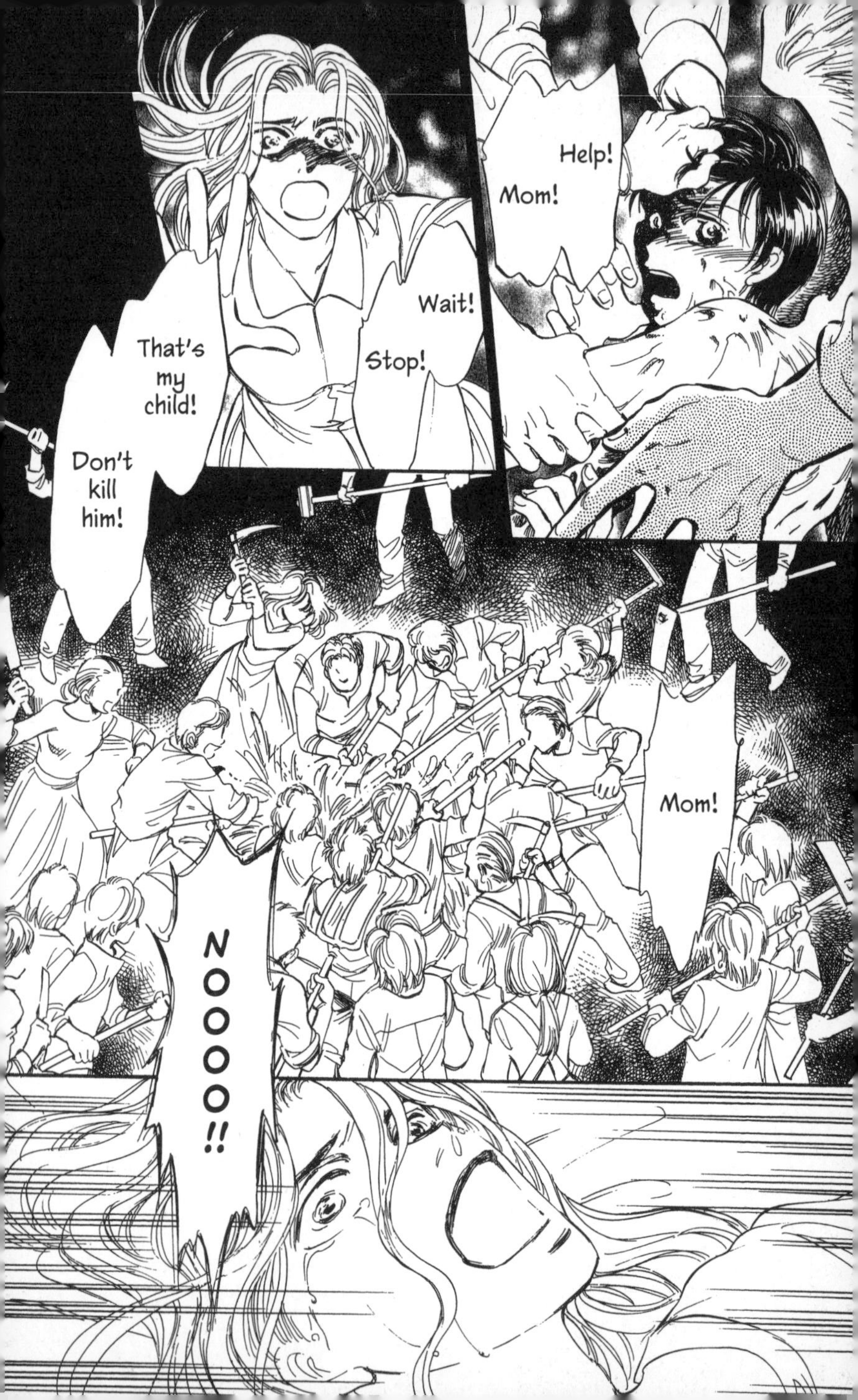
Help! Mom!
Wait! Stop!
That's my child! Don't kill him!
Mom!
NOOOOO!!

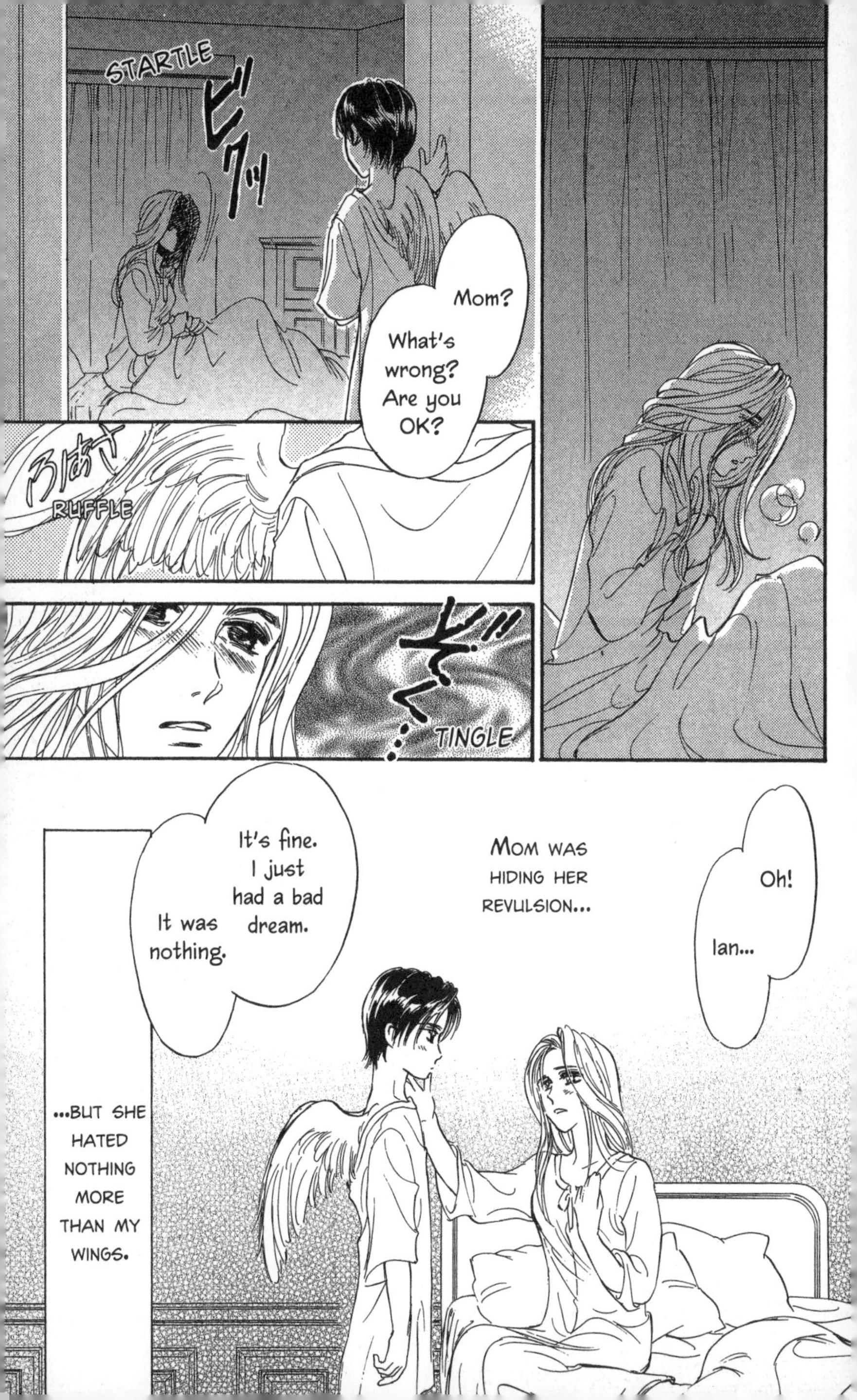
STARTLE
ビクッ
Mom?
What's wrong? Are you OK?
RUFFLE
TINGLE
Oh!
Ian...
MOM WAS HIDING HER REVULSION...
It's fine. I just had a bad dream.
It was nothing.
...BUT SHE HATED NOTHING MORE THAN MY WINGS.

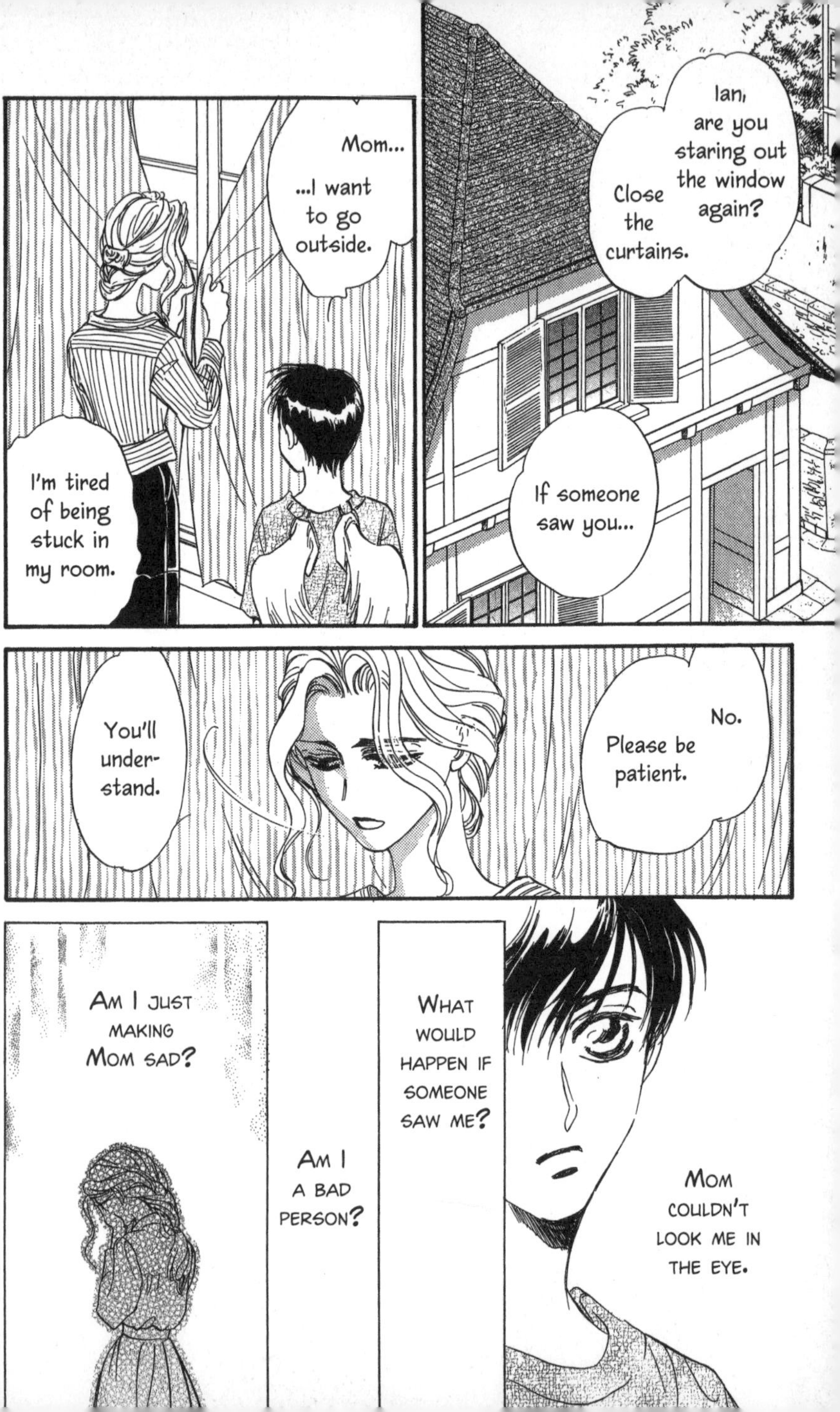
Ian, are you staring out the window again?
Close the curtains.
If someone saw you...
Mom...
...I want to go outside.
I'm tired of being stuck in my room.
No.
Please be patient.
You'll understand.
Mom couldn't look me in the eye.
What would happen if someone saw me?
Am I a bad person?
Am I just making Mom sad?

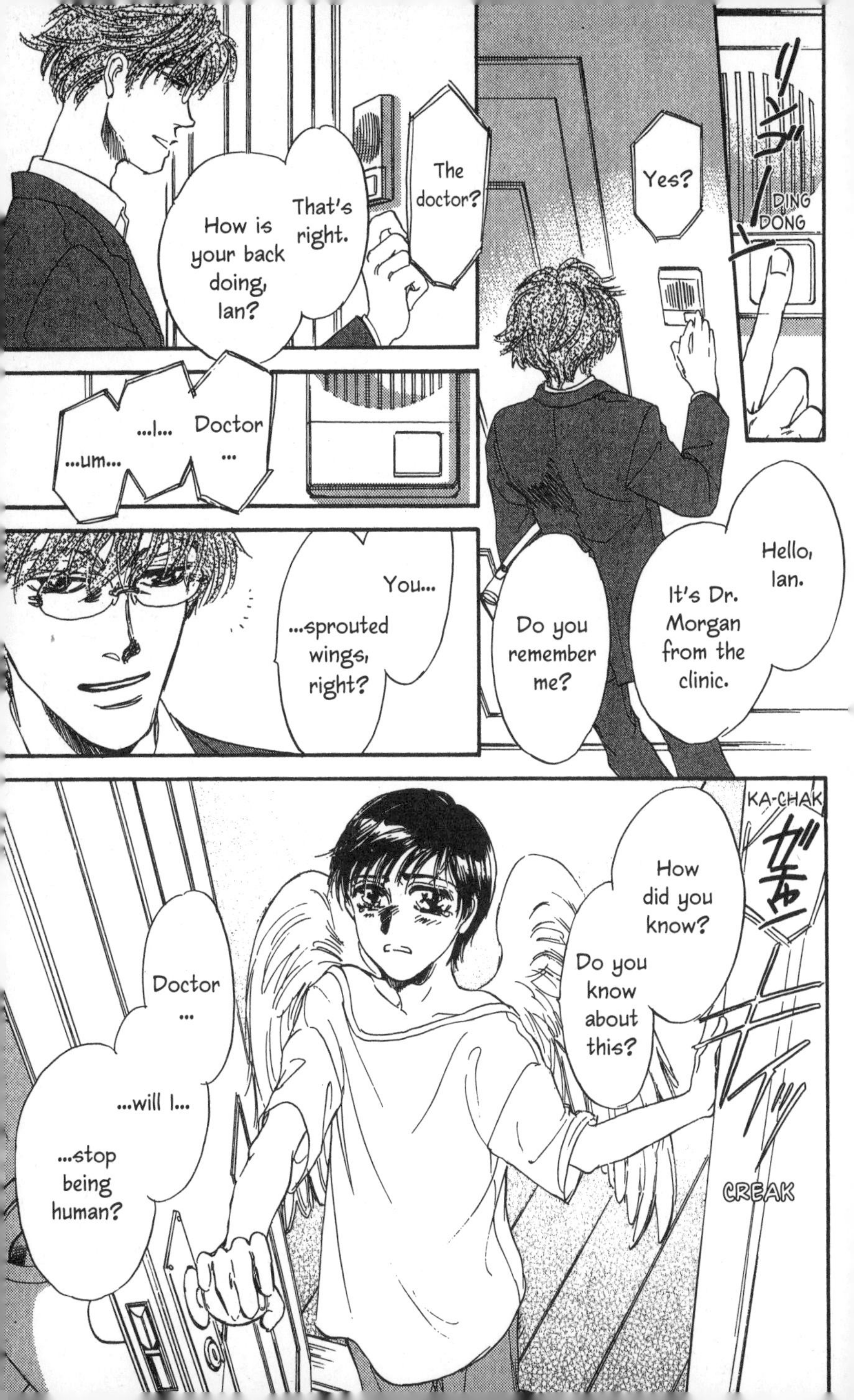
DING DONG
Yes?
Hello, Ian. It's Dr. Morgan from the clinic.
Do you remember me?
The doctor?
That's right.
How is your back doing, Ian?
Doctor ...
...I...
...um...
You...
...sprouted wings, right?
KA-CHAK
CREAK
How did you know?
Do you know about this?
Doctor ...
...will I...
...stop being human?

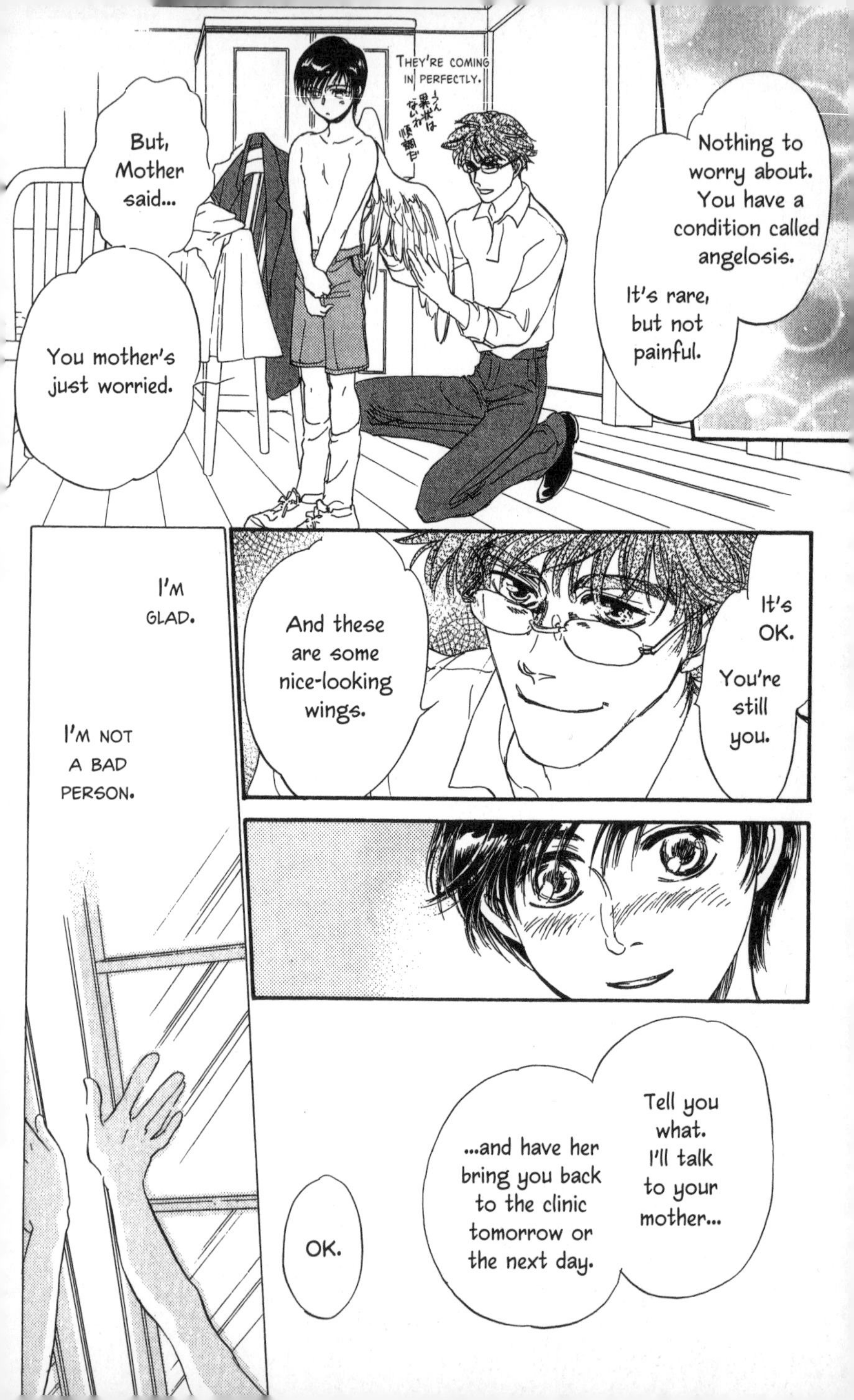
Nothing to worry about. You have a condition called angelosis.
It's rare, but not painful.
THEY'RE COMING IN PERFECTLY.
But, Mother said...
You mother's just worried.
It's OK.
You're still you.
And these are some nice-looking wings.
Tell you what. I'll talk to your mother...
...and have her bring you back to the clinic tomorrow or the next day.
OK.
I'M GLAD.
I'M NOT A BAD PERSON.

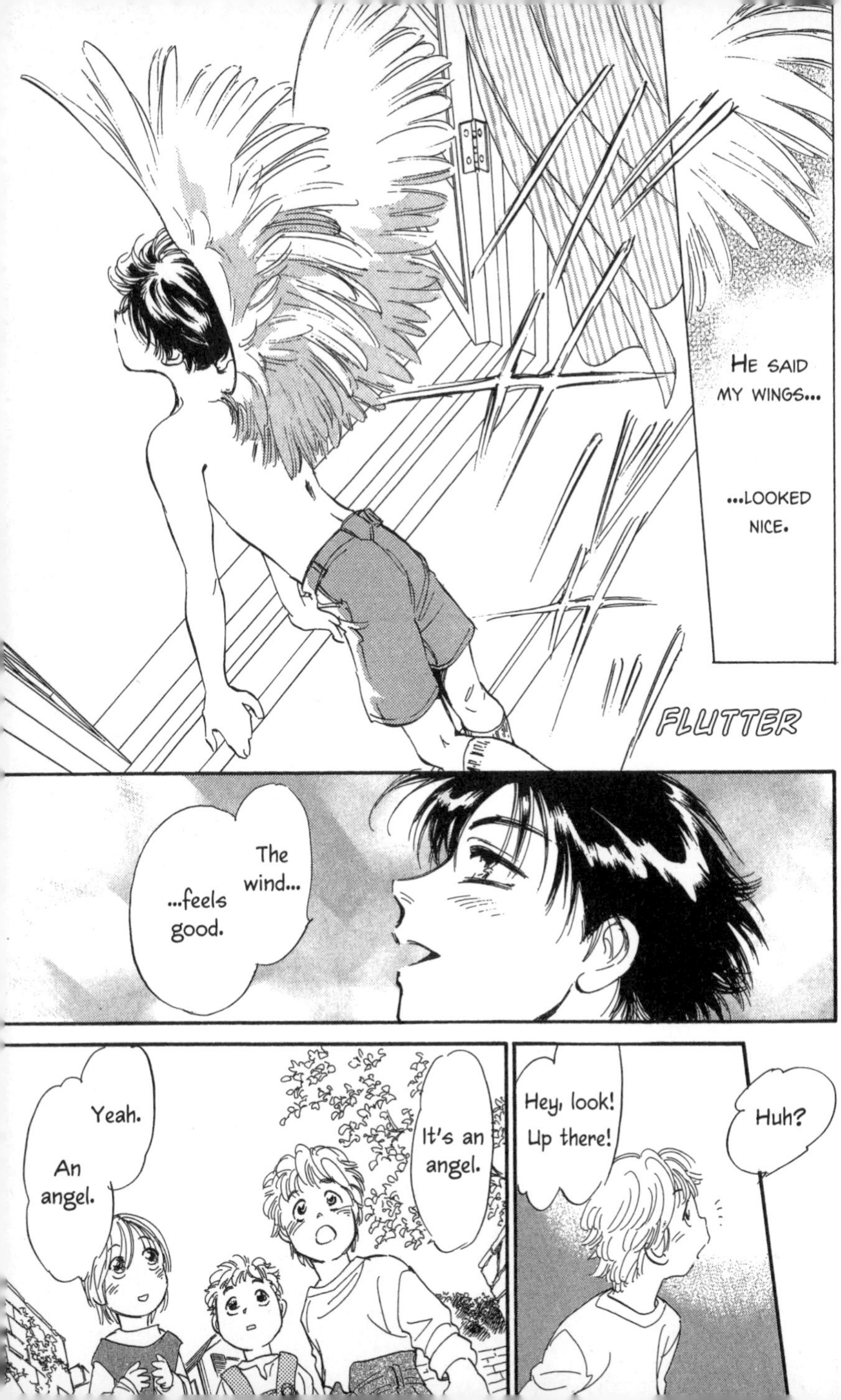
He said my wings...
...looked nice.
FLUTTER
The wind...
...feels good.
Huh?
Hey, look! Up there!
It's an angel.
Yeah.
An angel.

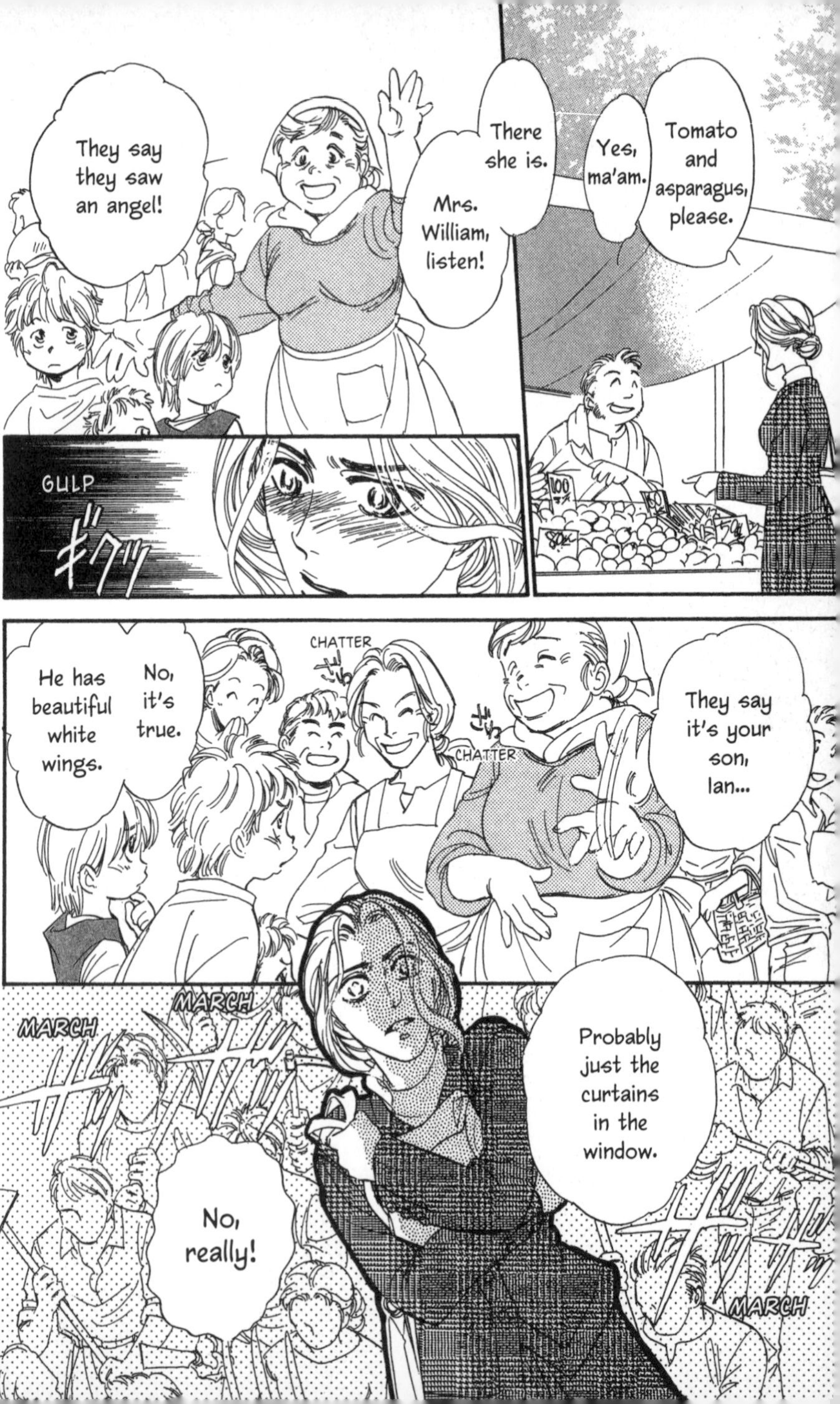
Tomato and asparagus, please.
Yes, ma'am.
There she is.
Mrs. William, listen!
They say they saw an angel!
GULP
ギクッ
They say it's your son, Ian...
CHATTER
CHATTER
No, it's true.
He has beautiful white wings.
Probably just the curtains in the window.
MARCH
No, really!
MARCH
MARCH

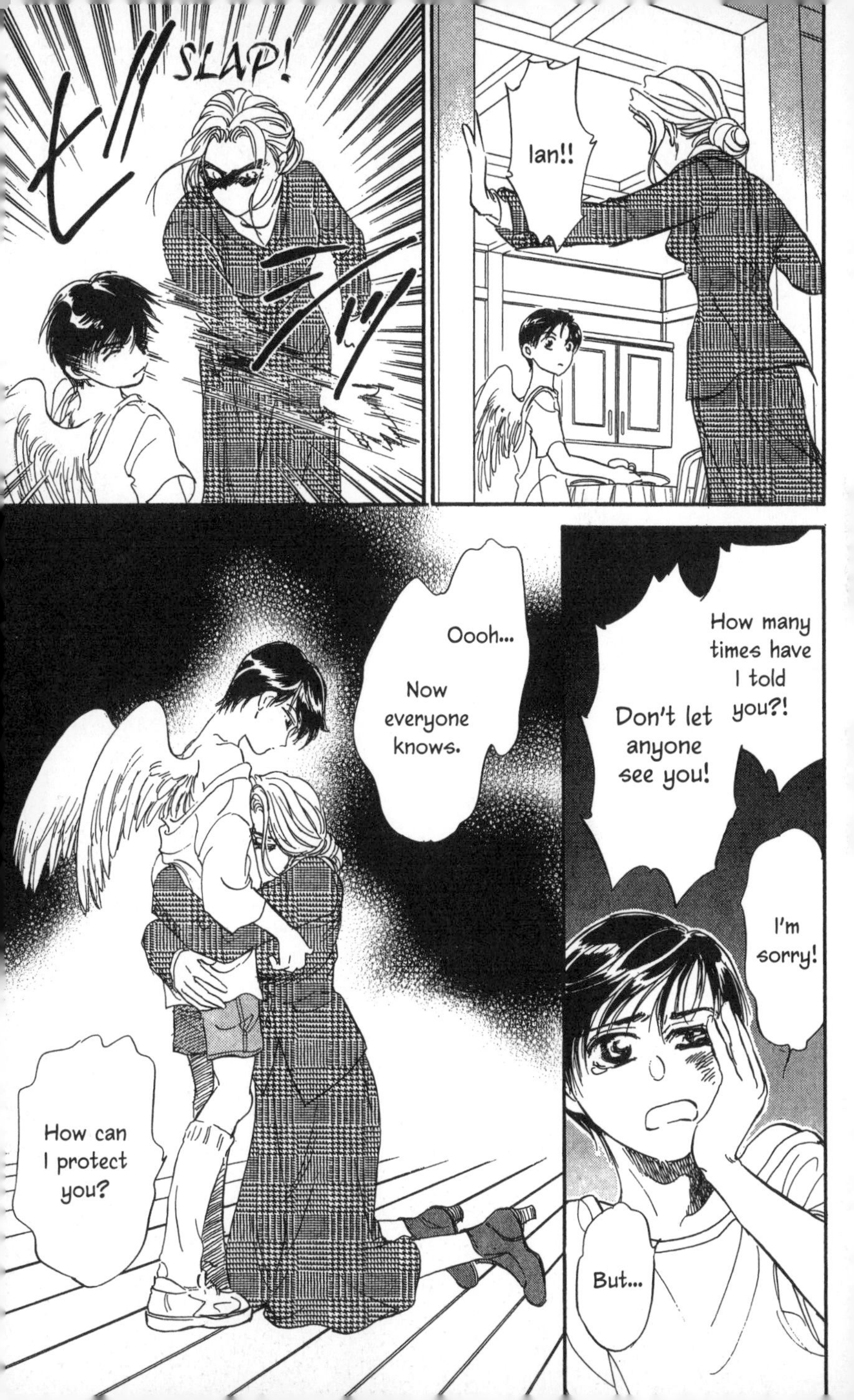
Ian!!
SLAP!
How many times have I told you?!
Don't let anyone see you!
I'm sorry!
But...
Oooh...
Now everyone knows.
How can I protect you?

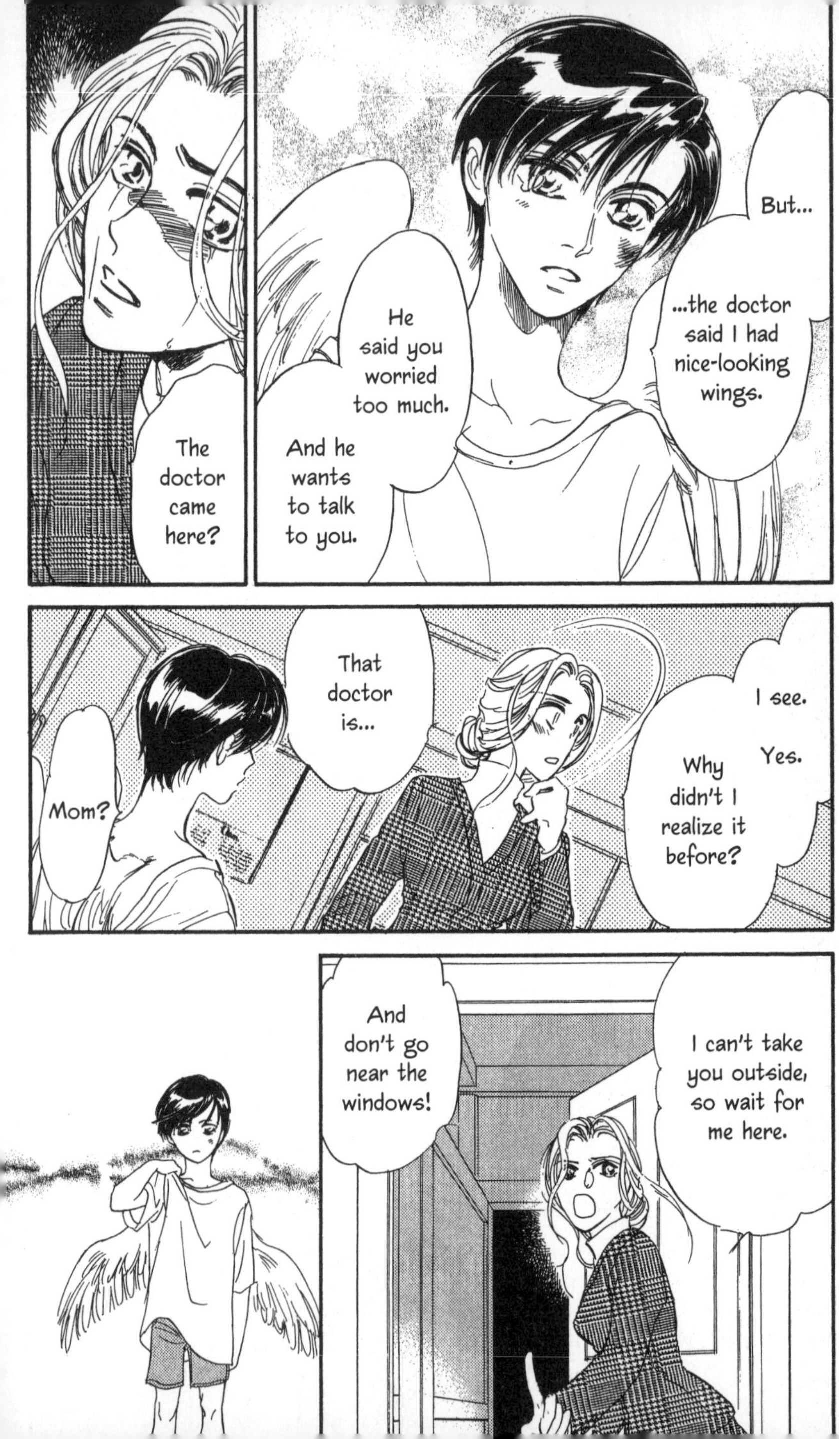
But...
...the doctor said I had nice-looking wings.
He said you worried too much.
And he wants to talk to you.
The doctor came here?
I see.
Yes.
Why didn't I realize it before?
That doctor is...
Mom?
I can't take you outside, so wait for me here.
And don't go near the windows!

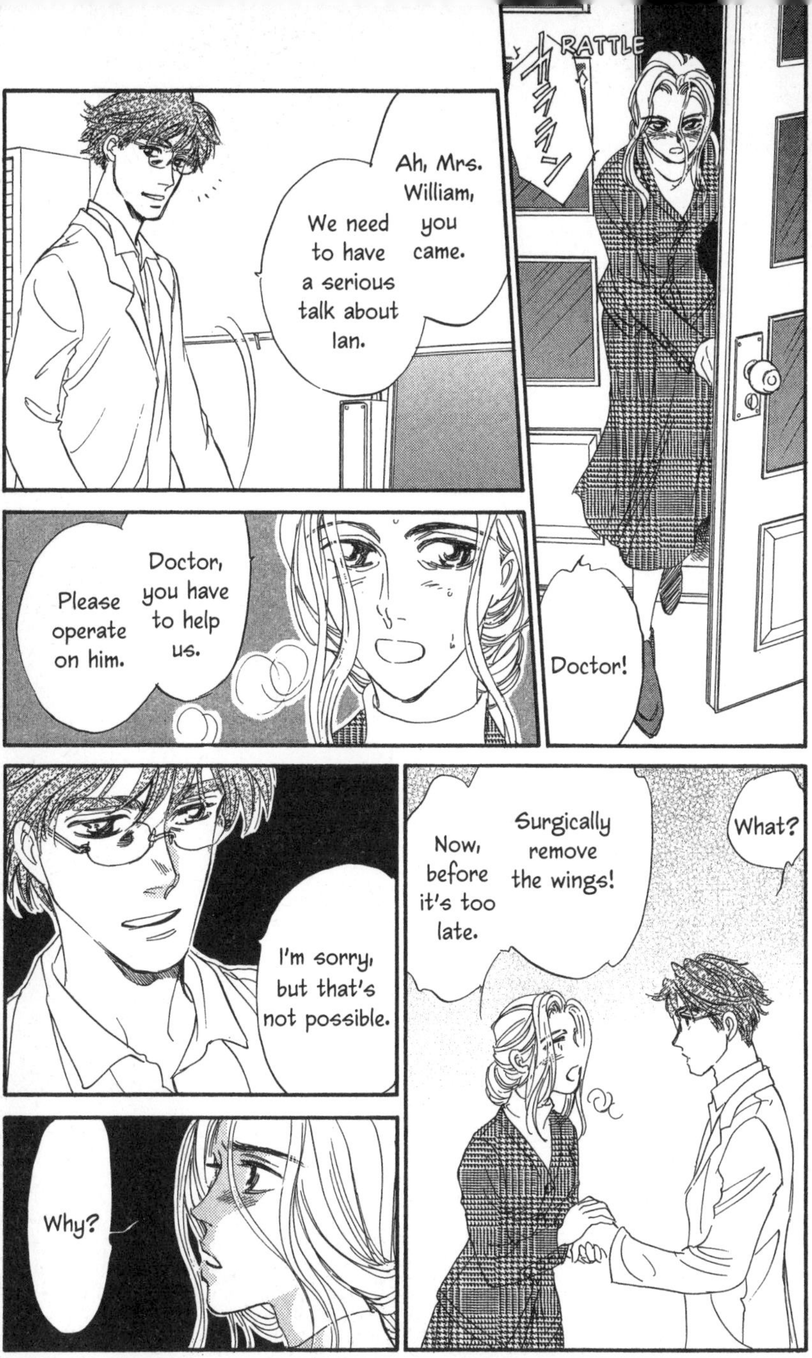

RATTLE
Doctor!
Ah, Mrs. William, you came.
We need to have a serious talk about Ian.
Doctor, you have to help us.
Please operate on him.
What?
Surgically remove the wings!
Now, before it's too late.
I'm sorry, but that's not possible.
Why?

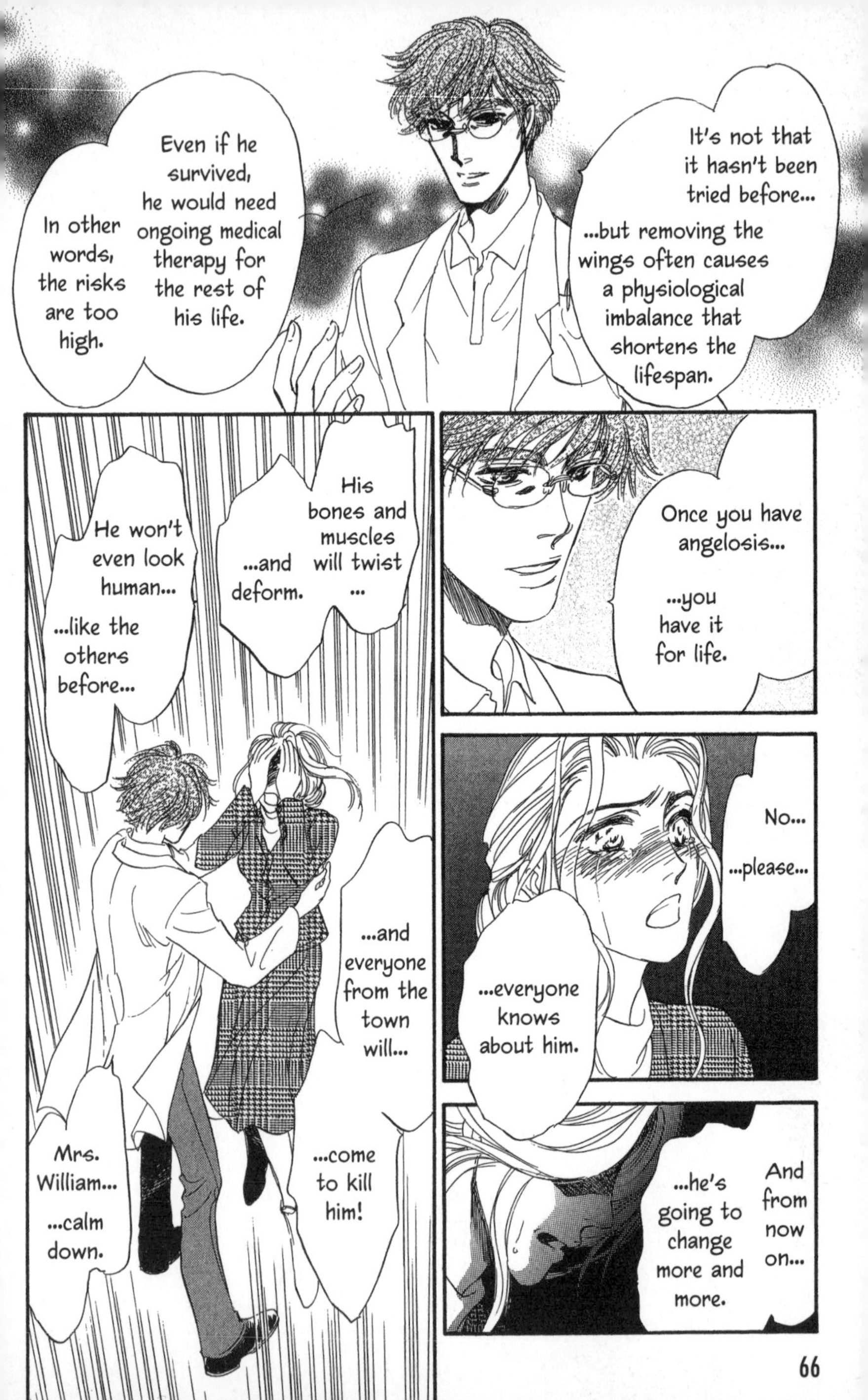

It's not that it hasn't been tried before...
...but removing the wings often causes a physiological imbalance that shortens the lifespan.
Even if he survived, he would need ongoing medical therapy for the rest of his life.
In other words, the risks are too high.
Once you have angelosis...
...you have it for life.
No...
...please...
...everyone knows about him.
And from now on...
...he's going to change more and more.
His bones and muscles will twist ...
...and deform.
He won't even look human...
...like the others before...
...and everyone from the town will...
...come to kill him!
Mrs. William...
...calm down.

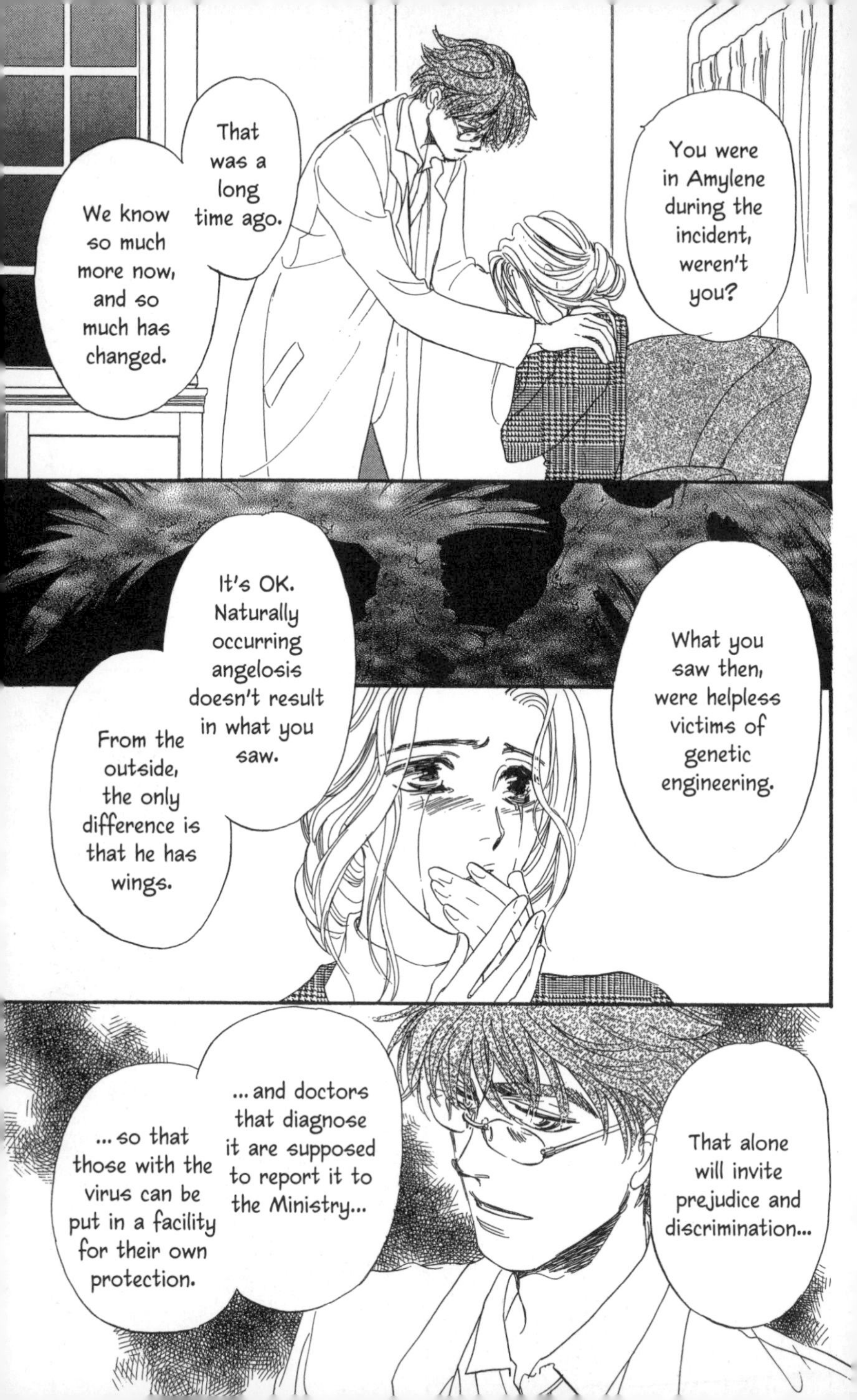
You were in Amylene during the incident, weren't you?
That was a long time ago.
We know so much more now, and so much has changed.
What you saw then, were helpless victims of genetic engineering.
It's OK. Naturally occurring angelosis doesn't result in what you saw.
From the outside, the only difference is that he has wings.
That alone will invite prejudice and discrimination...
...and doctors that diagnose it are supposed to report it to the Ministry...
...so that those with the virus can be put in a facility for their own protection.

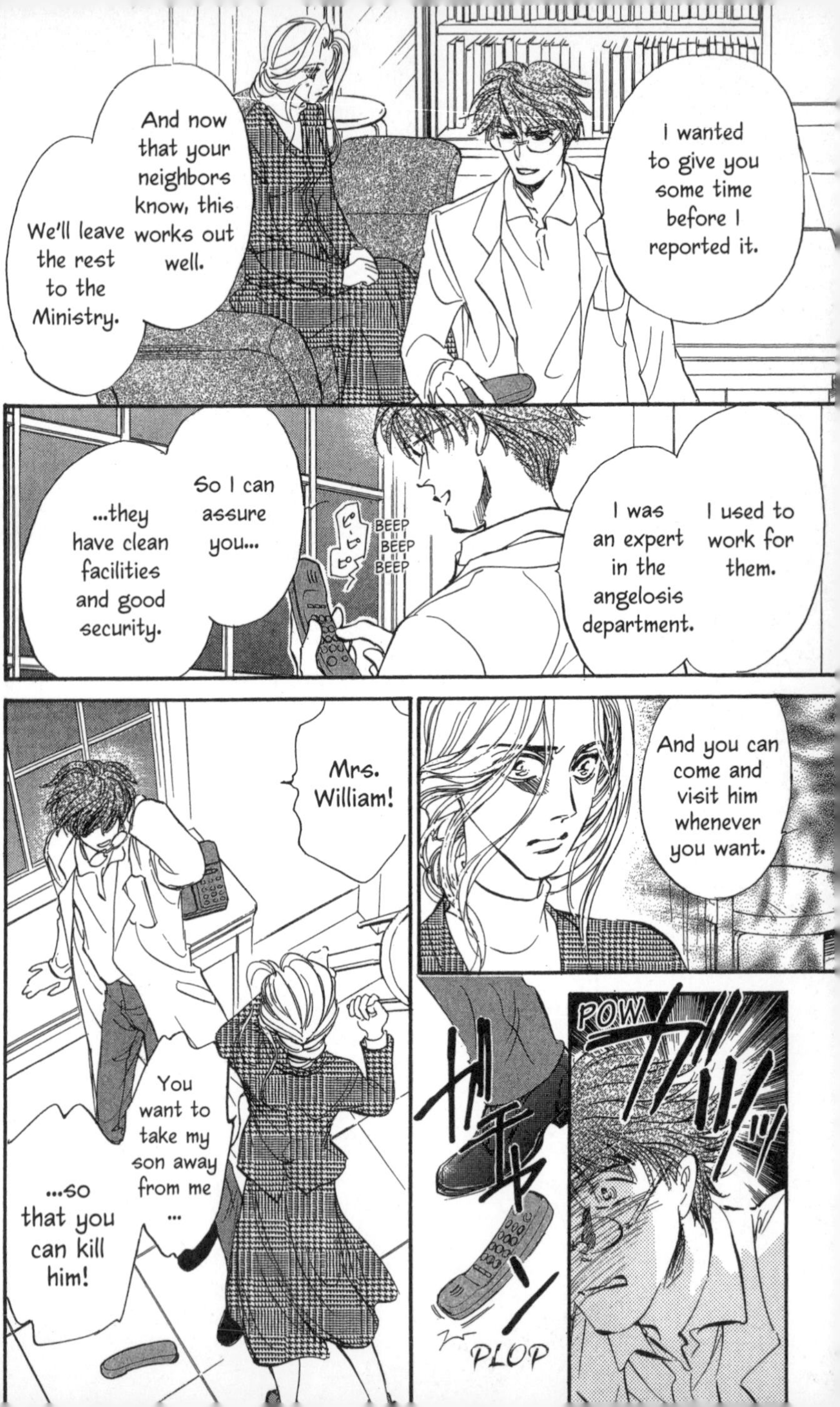
I wanted to give you some time before I reported it.
And now that your neighbors know, this works out well.
We'll leave the rest to the Ministry.
I used to work for them.
I was an expert in the angelosis department.
BEEP BEEP BEEP
So I can assure you...
...they have clean facilities and good security.
And you can come and visit him whenever you want.
POW
PLOP
Mrs. William!
You want to take my son away from me ...
...so that you can kill him!

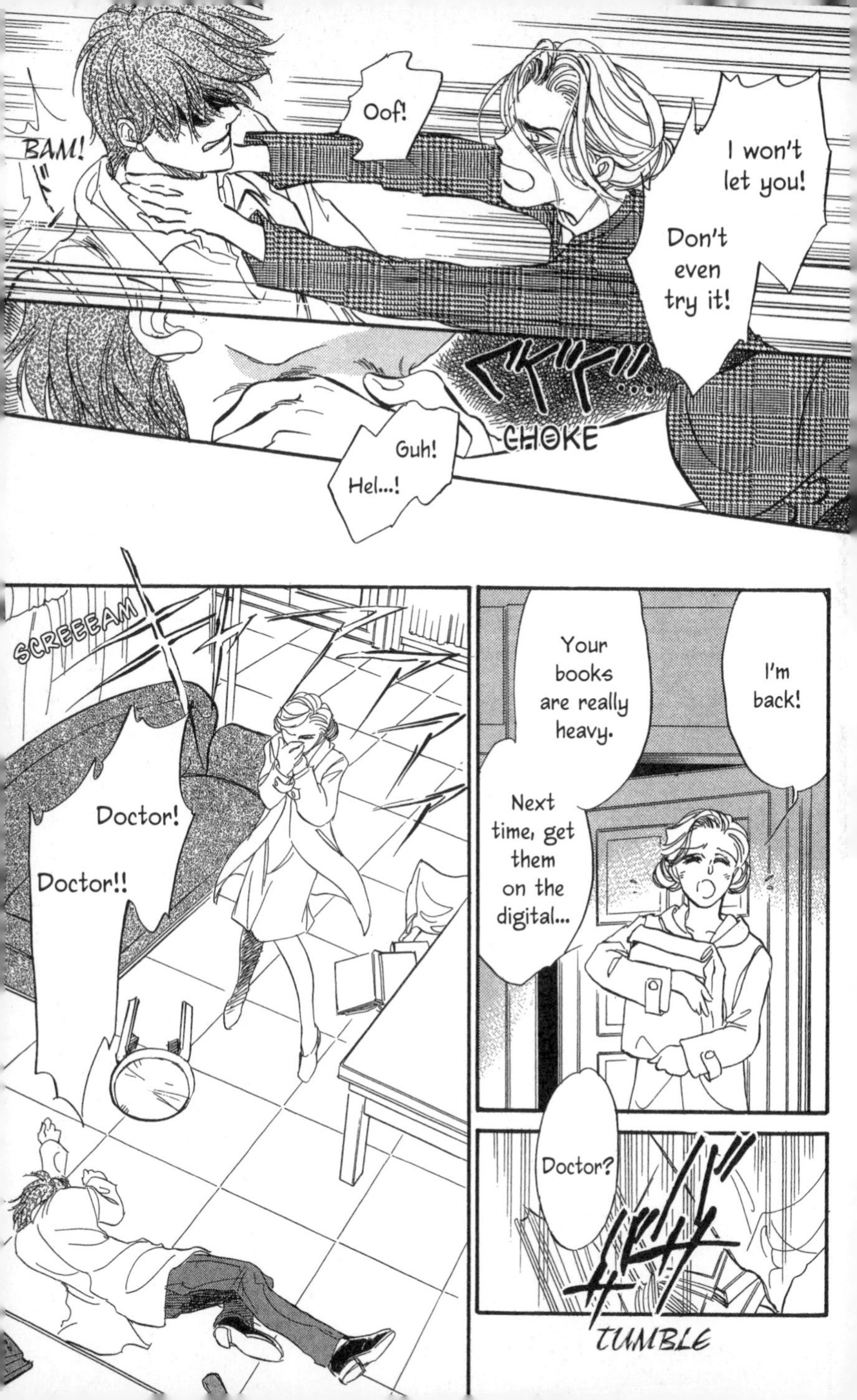
I won't let you!
Don't even try it!
Oof!
BAM!
CHOKE
Guh!
Hel...!
I'm back!
Your books are really heavy.
Next time, get them on the digital...
Doctor?
TUMBLE
SCREEEAM
Doctor!
Doctor!!

Mom?

HUFF

HUFF

HUFF

SLAM

...ONLY ME...

I HAVE TO PROTECT HIM...

What is it?

What happened?

YANK

Come, Ian!

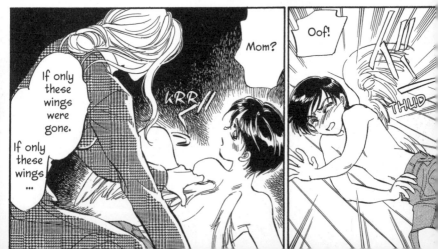

If only these wings were gone.

If only these wings...

kRR//

Mom?

Oof!

THUD

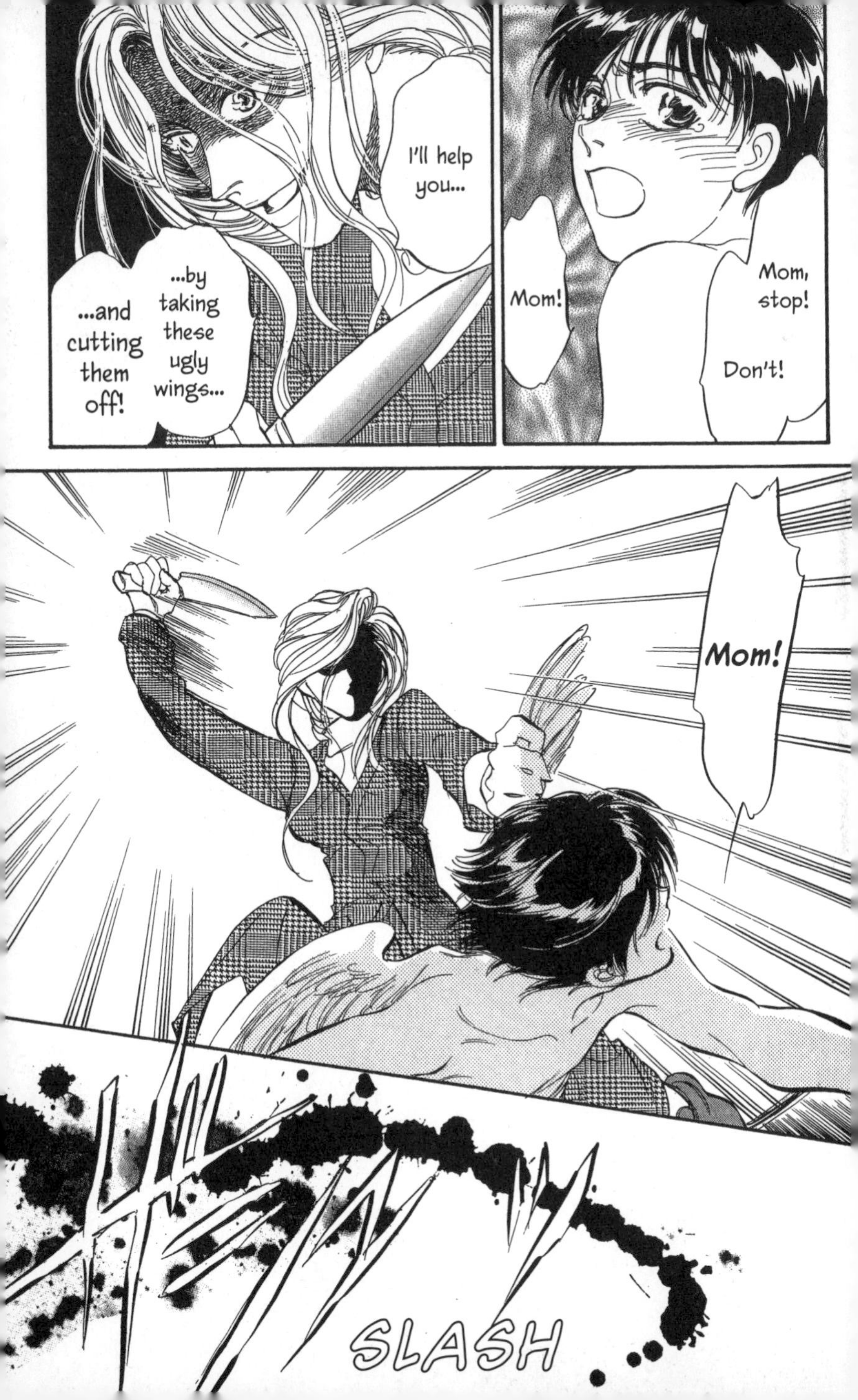
Mom, stop!
Don't!
Mom!
I'll help you...
...by taking these ugly wings...
...and cutting them off!
Mom!
SLASH

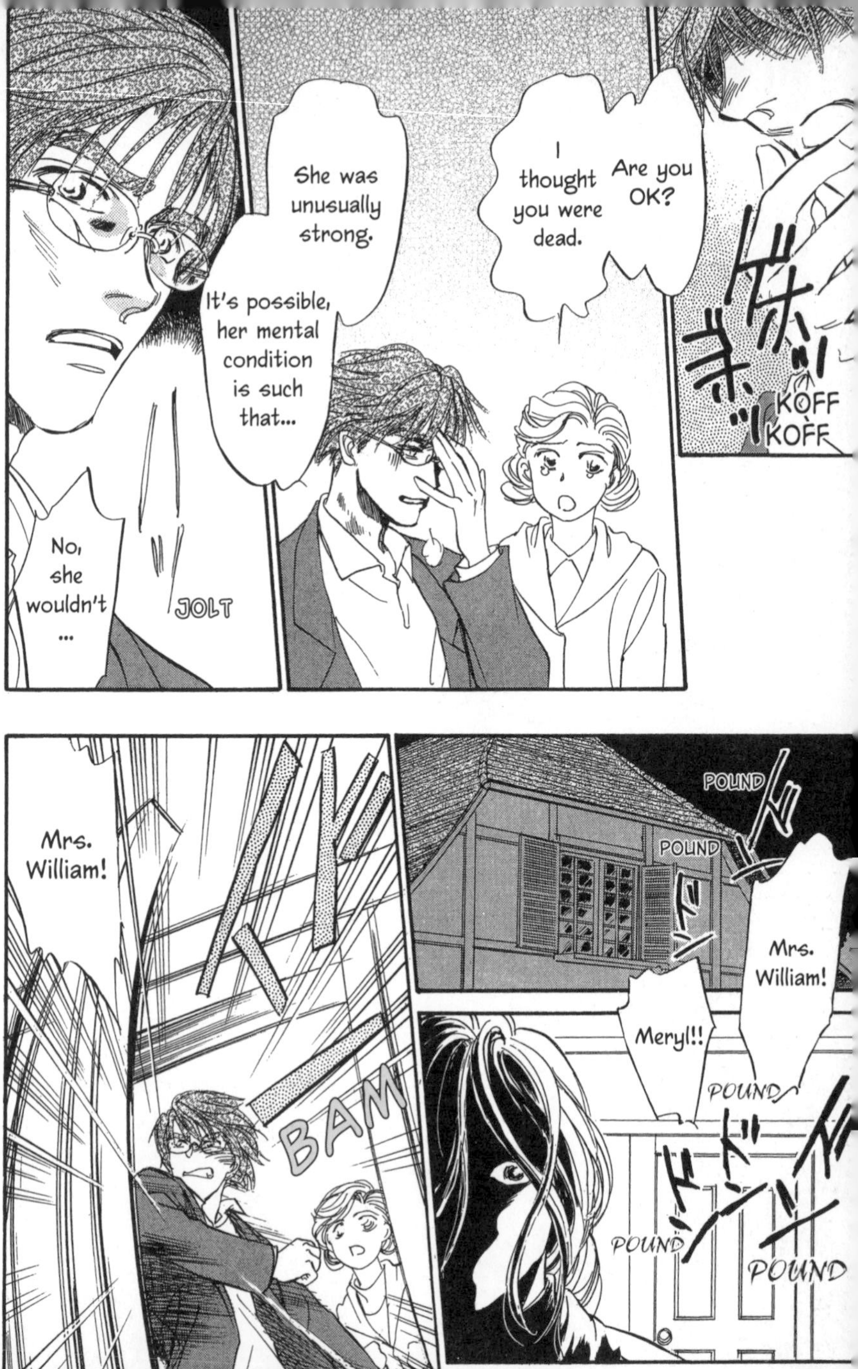
KOFF
KOFF
Are you OK?
I thought you were dead.
She was unusually strong.
It's possible, her mental condition is such that...
JOLT
No, she wouldn't ...
POUND
POUND
Mrs. William!
Meryl!!
POUND
POUND
POUND
BAM
Mrs. William!

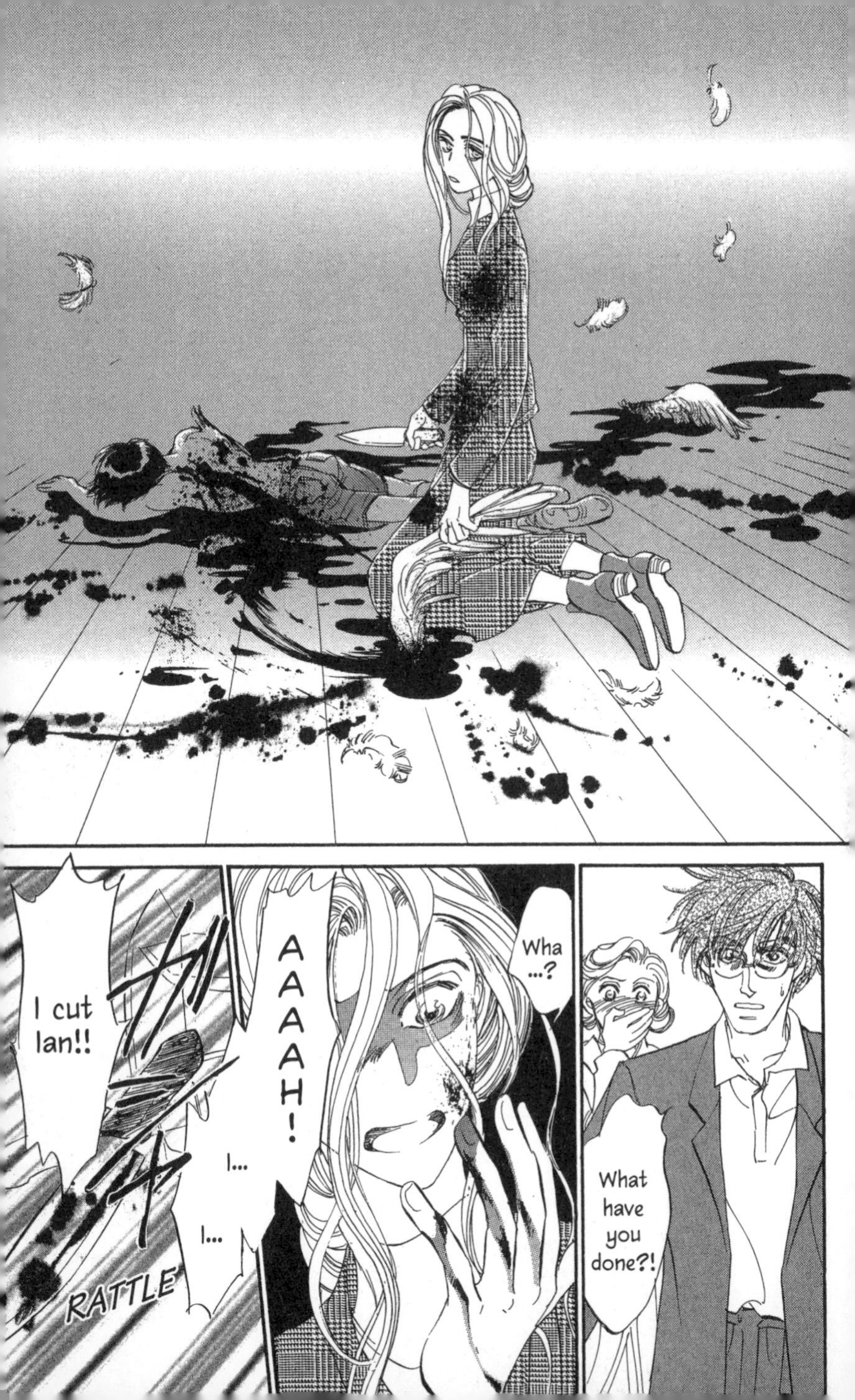
What have you done?!
Wha...?
AAAAAH!
I... I...
I cut Ian!!
RATTLE

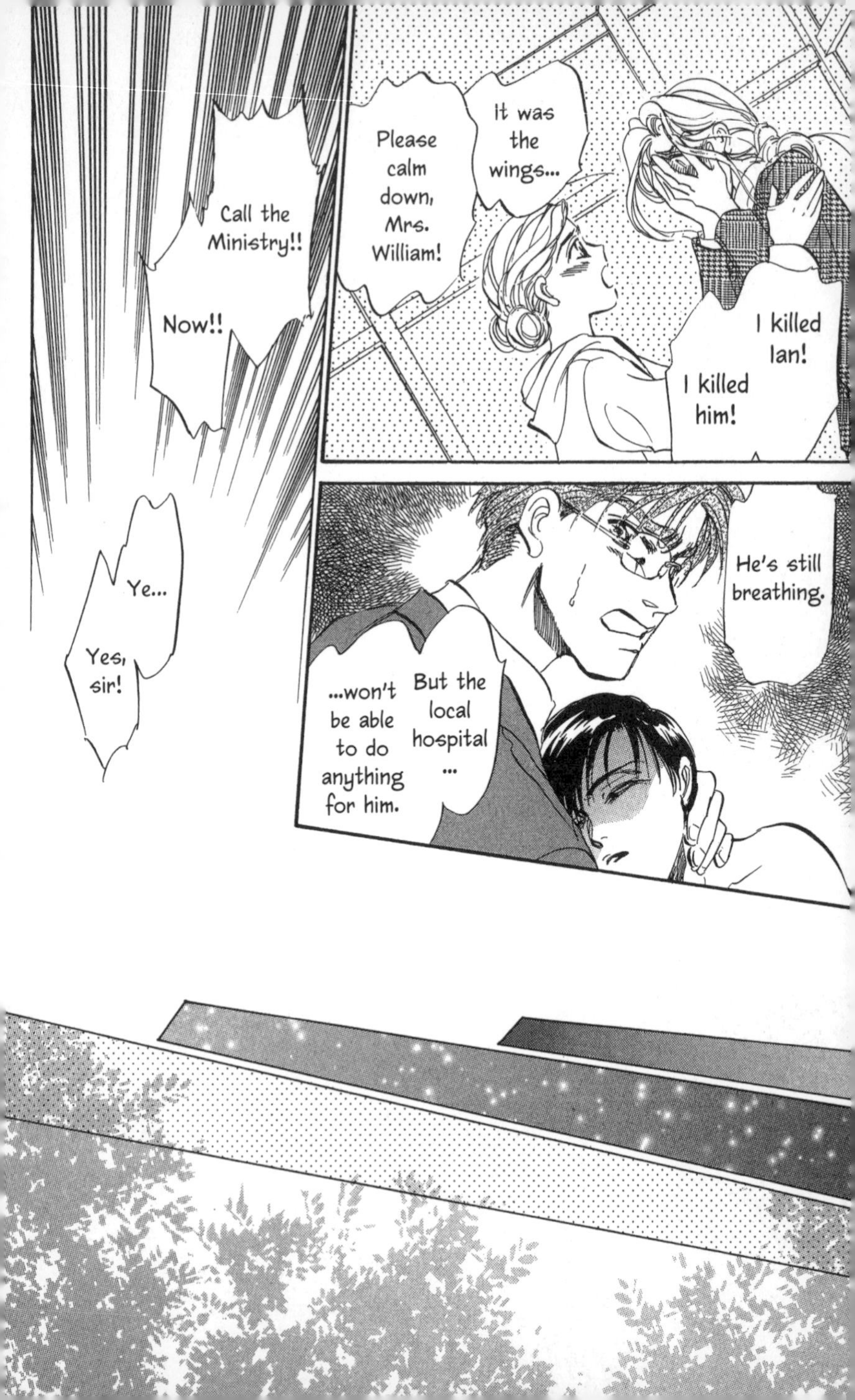
It was the wings...
Please calm down, Mrs. William!
I killed Ian!
I killed him!
He's still breathing.
But the local hospital...
...won't be able to do anything for him.
Call the Ministry!!
Now!!
Ye...
Yes, sir!

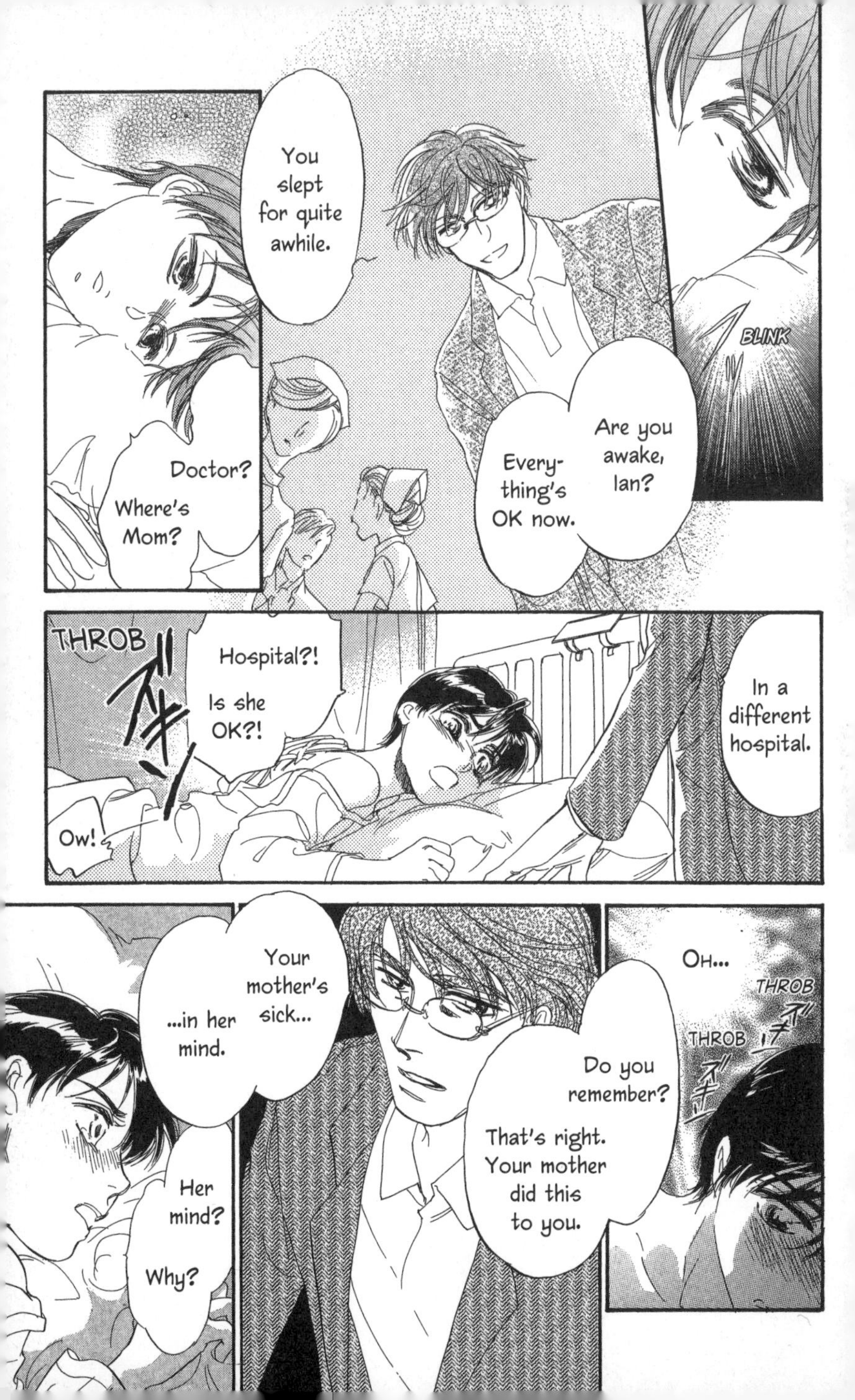
BLINK
Are you awake, Ian?
Every-thing's OK now.
You slept for quite awhile.
Doctor?
Where's Mom?
THROB
Ow!
Hospital?!
Is she OK?!
In a different hospital.
Oh...
THROB
THROB
Do you remember?
That's right. Your mother did this to you.
Your mother's sick...
...in her mind.
Her mind?
Why?

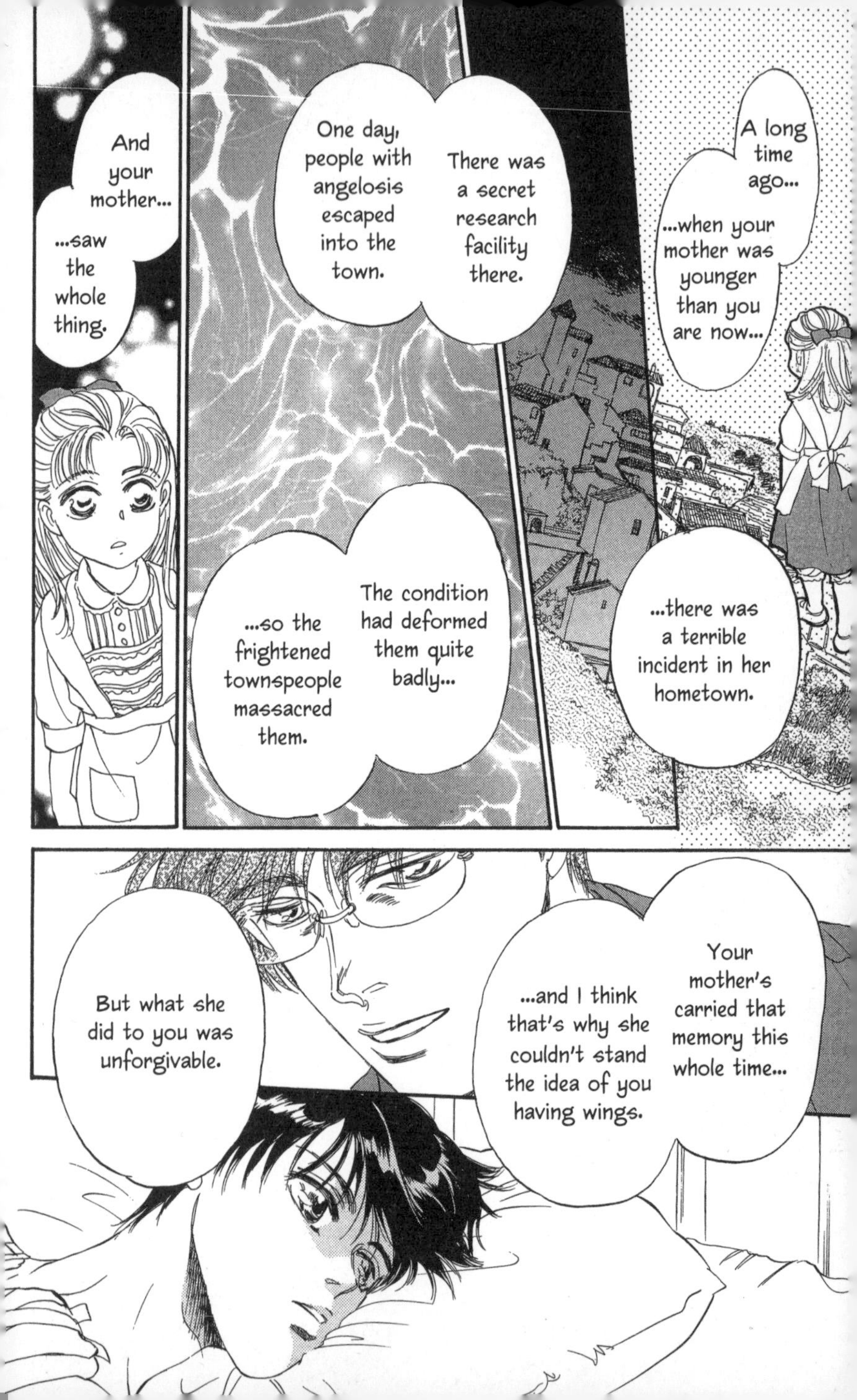
A long time ago...
...when your mother was younger than you are now...
...there was a terrible incident in her hometown.
There was a secret research facility there.
One day, people with angelosis escaped into the town.
The condition had deformed them quite badly...
...so the frightened townspeople massacred them.
And your mother...
...saw the whole thing.
Your mother's carried that memory this whole time...
...and I think that's why she couldn't stand the idea of you having wings.
But what she did to you was unforgivable.

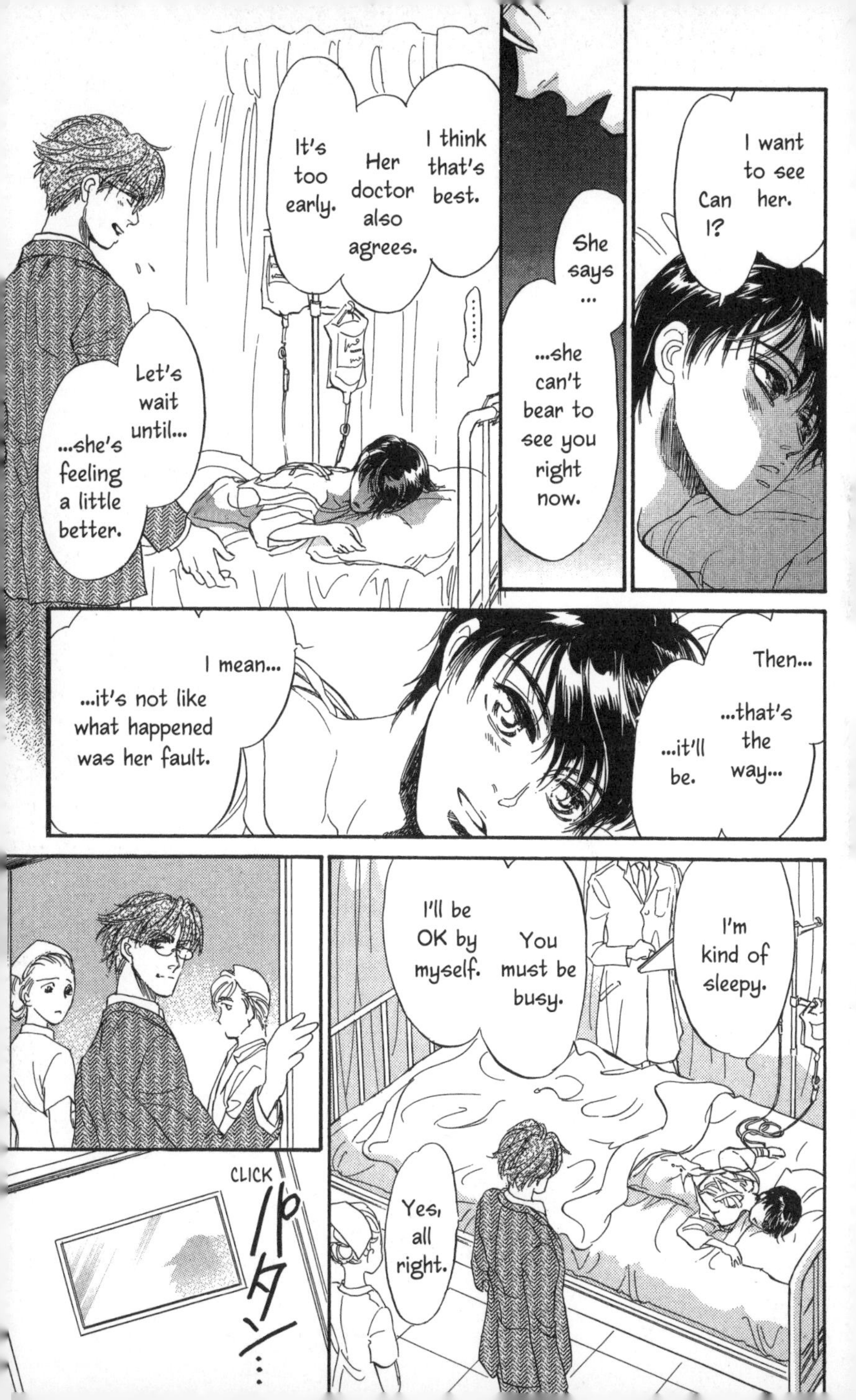
I want to see her.
Can I?
She says...
...she can't bear to see you right now.
I think that's best.
Her doctor also agrees.
It's too early.
......
Let's wait until...
...she's feeling a little better.
Then...
...that's the way...
...it'll be.
I mean...
...it's not like what happened was her fault.
I'm kind of sleepy.
You must be busy.
I'll be OK by myself.
Yes, all right.
CLICK

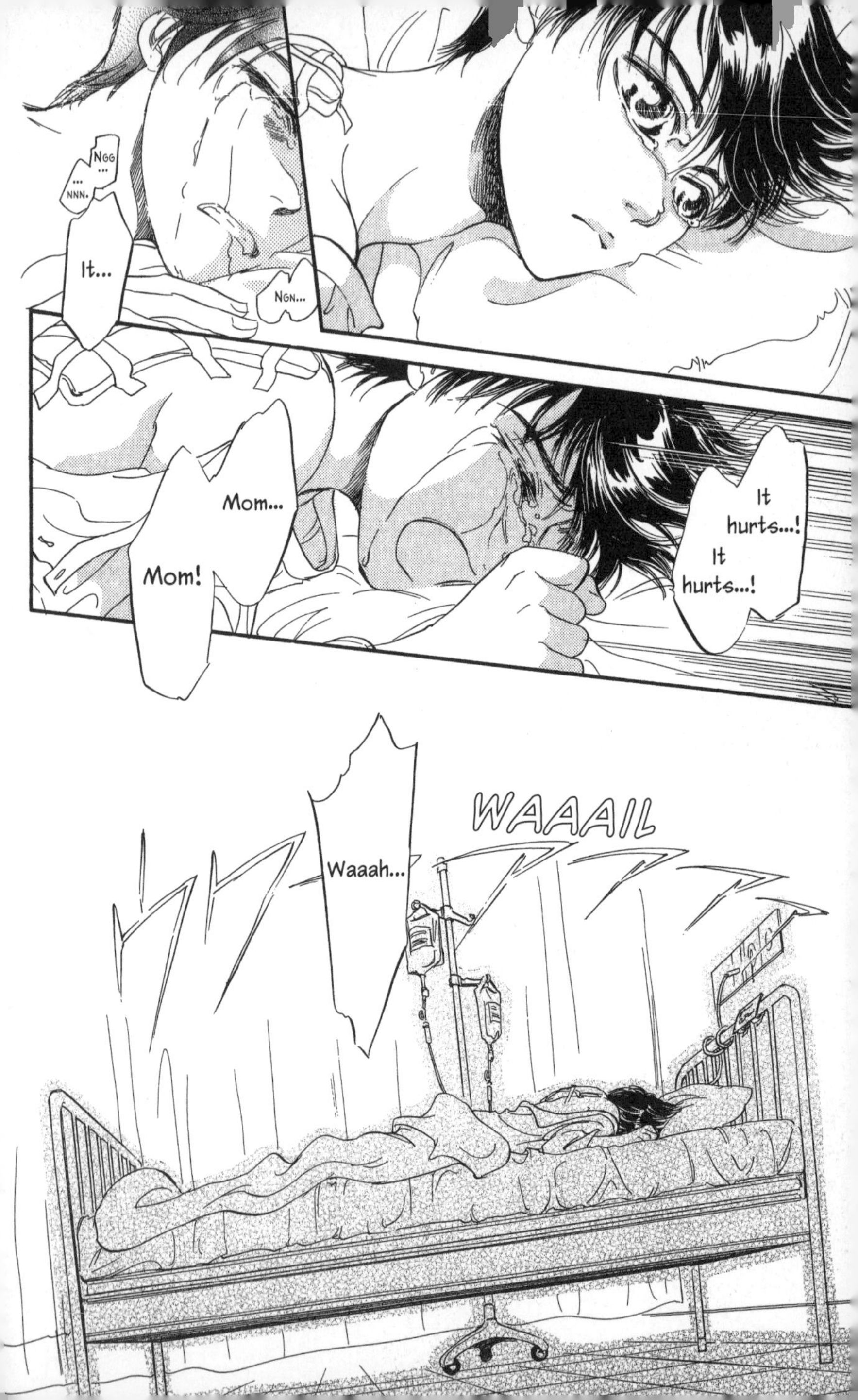

Ngn...
Ngg...
...nnn.
It...
It hurts...!
It hurts...!
Mom...
Mom!
WAAAIL
Waaah...

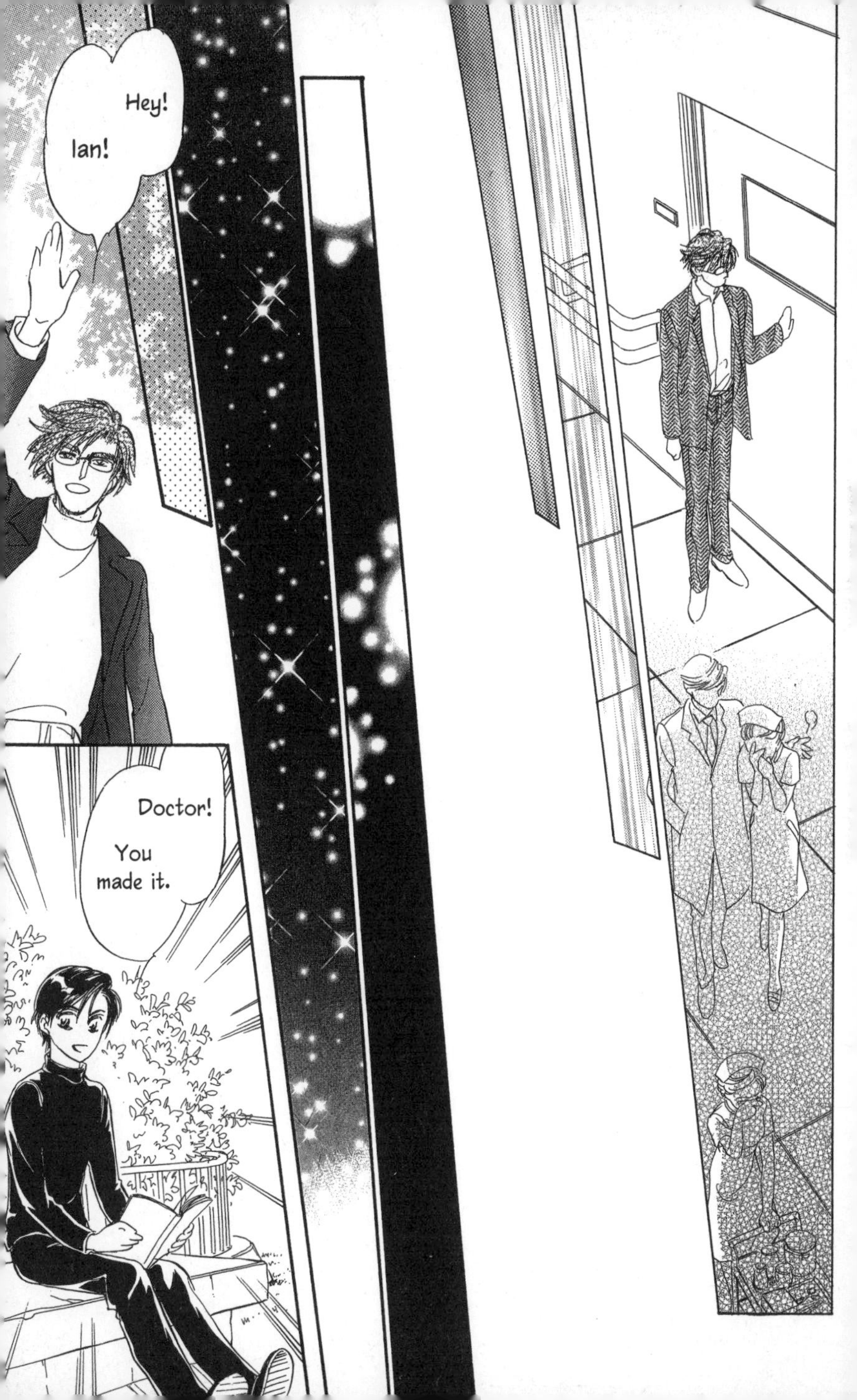
Hey! Ian!
Doctor! You made it.

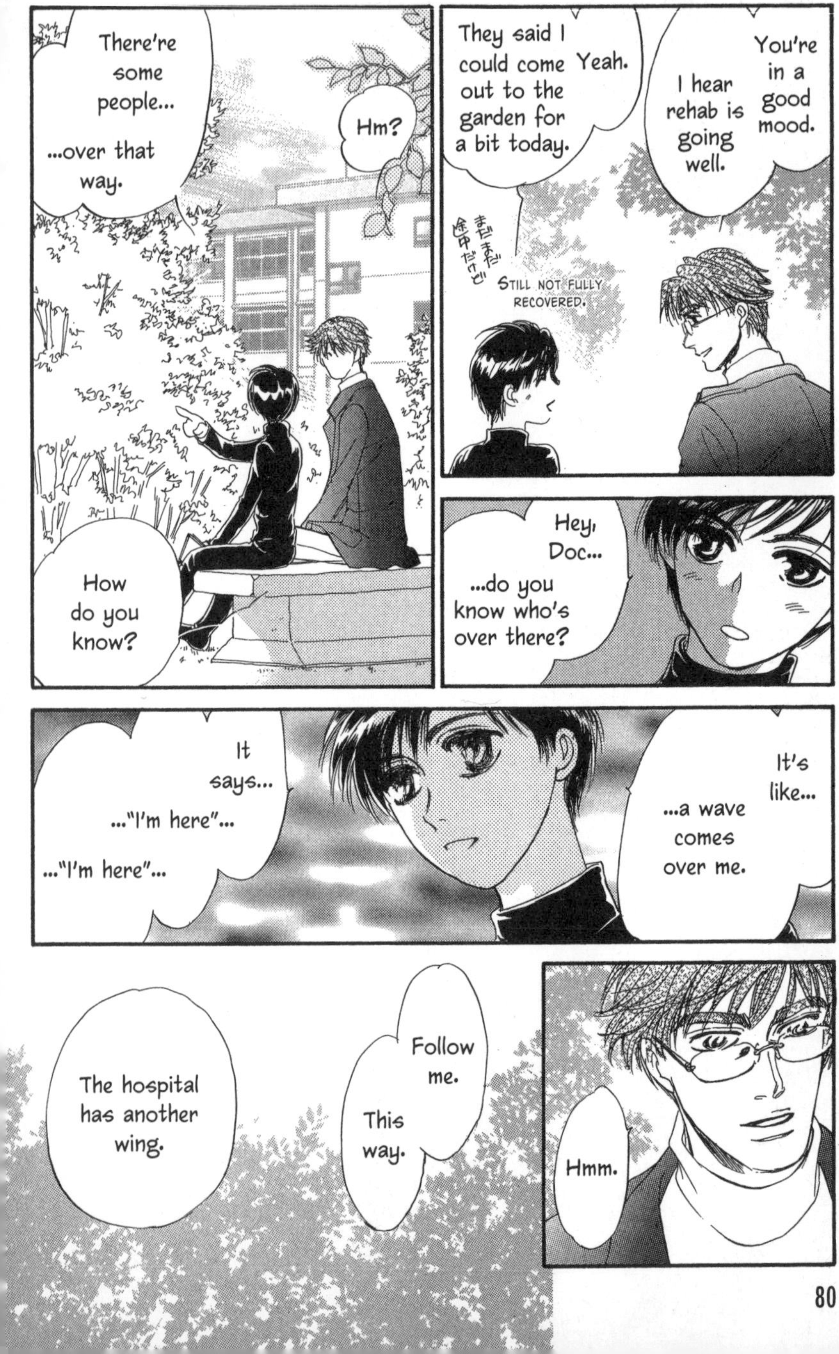
You're in a good mood.
I hear rehab is going well.
Yeah.
They said I could come out to the garden for a bit today.
まだまだ途中だけど
STILL NOT FULLY RECOVERED.
Hey, Doc... ...do you know who's over there?
Hm?
There're some people... ...over that way.
How do you know?
It's like... ...a wave comes over me.
It says... ..."I'm here"... ..."I'm here"...
Hmm.
Follow me. This way.
The hospital has another wing.

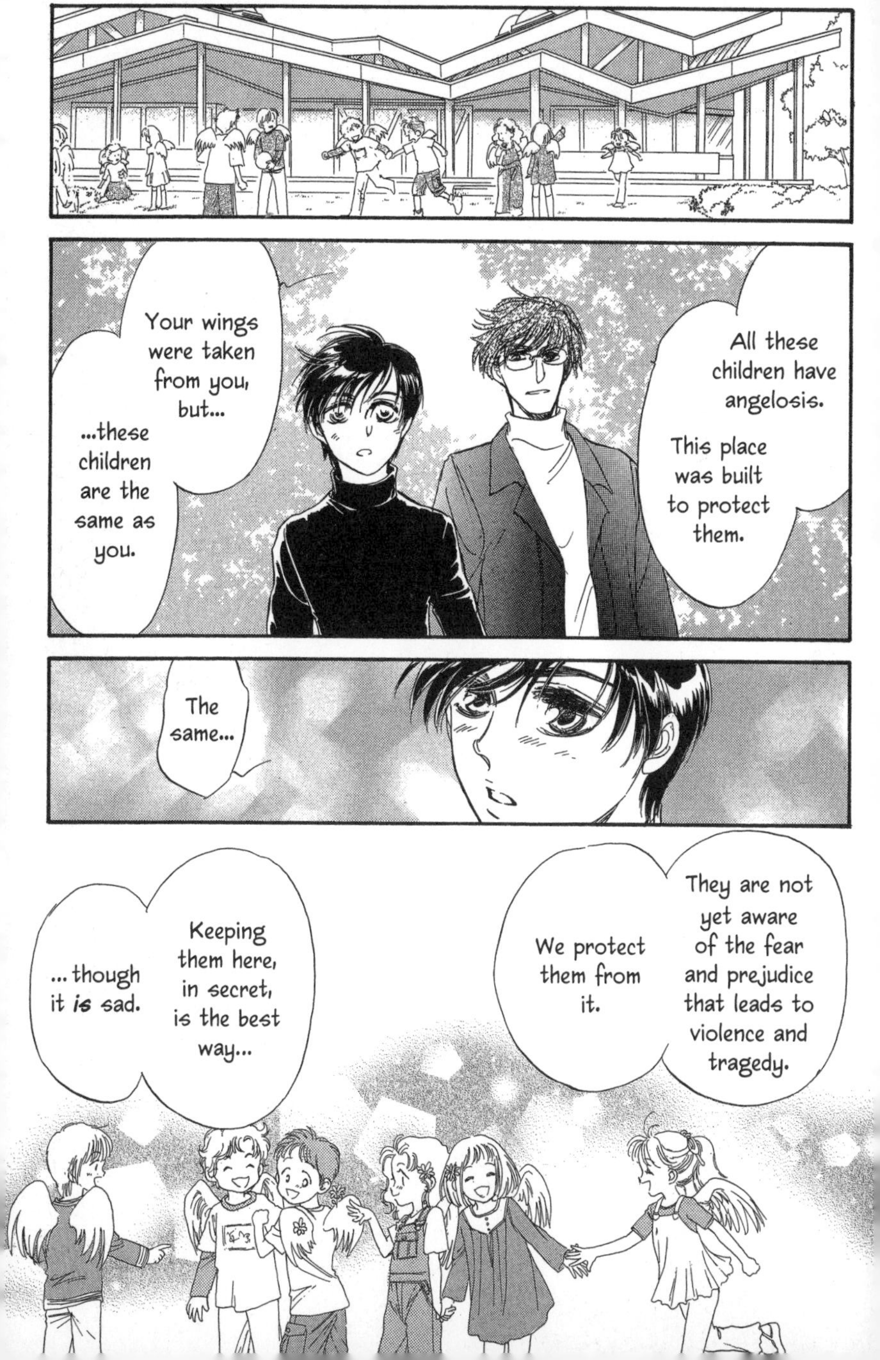
All these children have angelosis.
This place was built to protect them.
Your wings were taken from you, but...
...these children are the same as you.
The same...
They are not yet aware of the fear and prejudice that leads to violence and tragedy.
We protect them from it.
Keeping them here, in secret, is the best way...
... though it *is* sad.

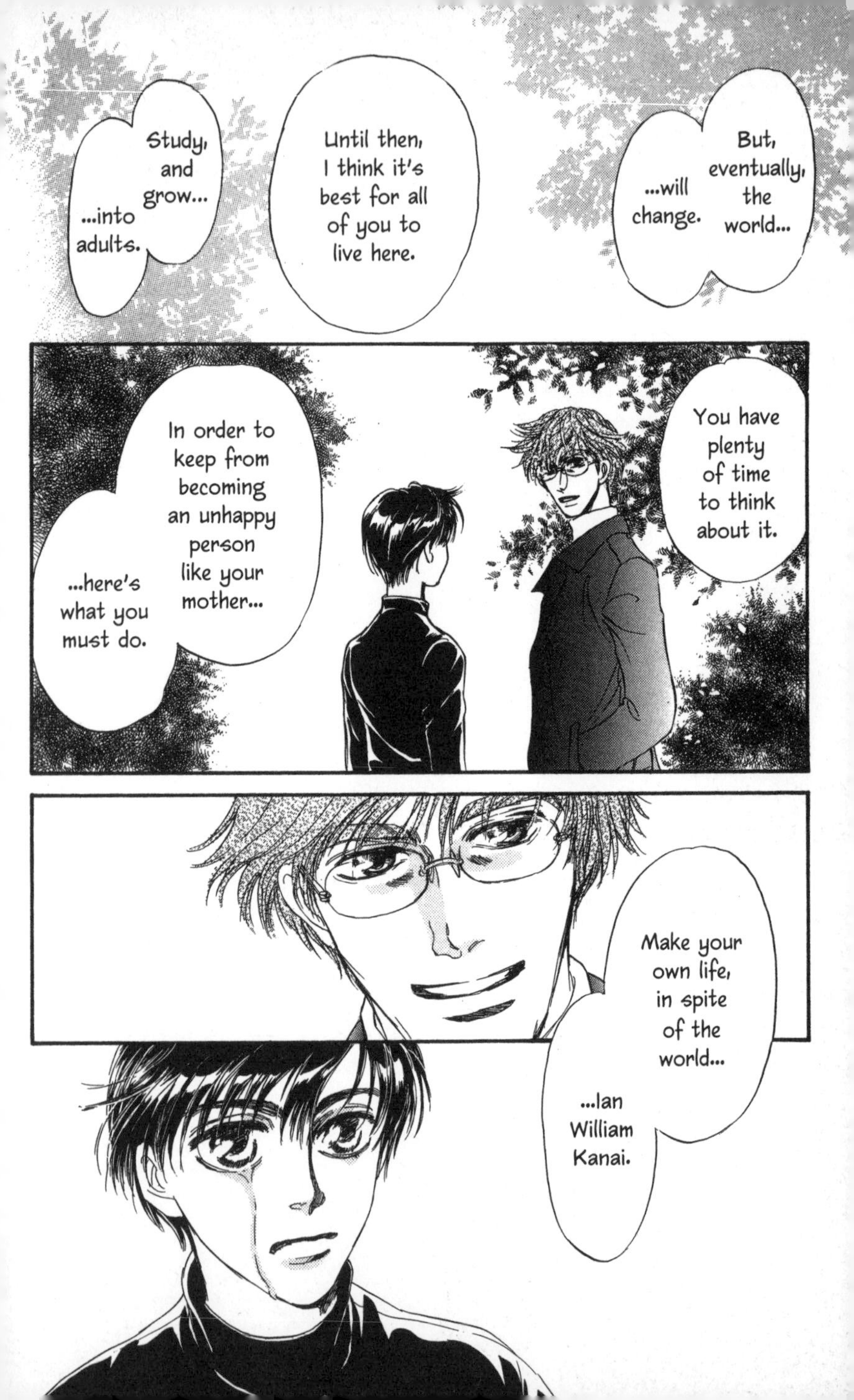
But, eventually, the world...
...will change.
Until then, I think it's best for all of you to live here.
Study, and grow...
...into adults.
You have plenty of time to think about it.
In order to keep from becoming an unhappy person like your mother...
...here's what you must do.
Make your own life, in spite of the world...
...Ian William Kanai.

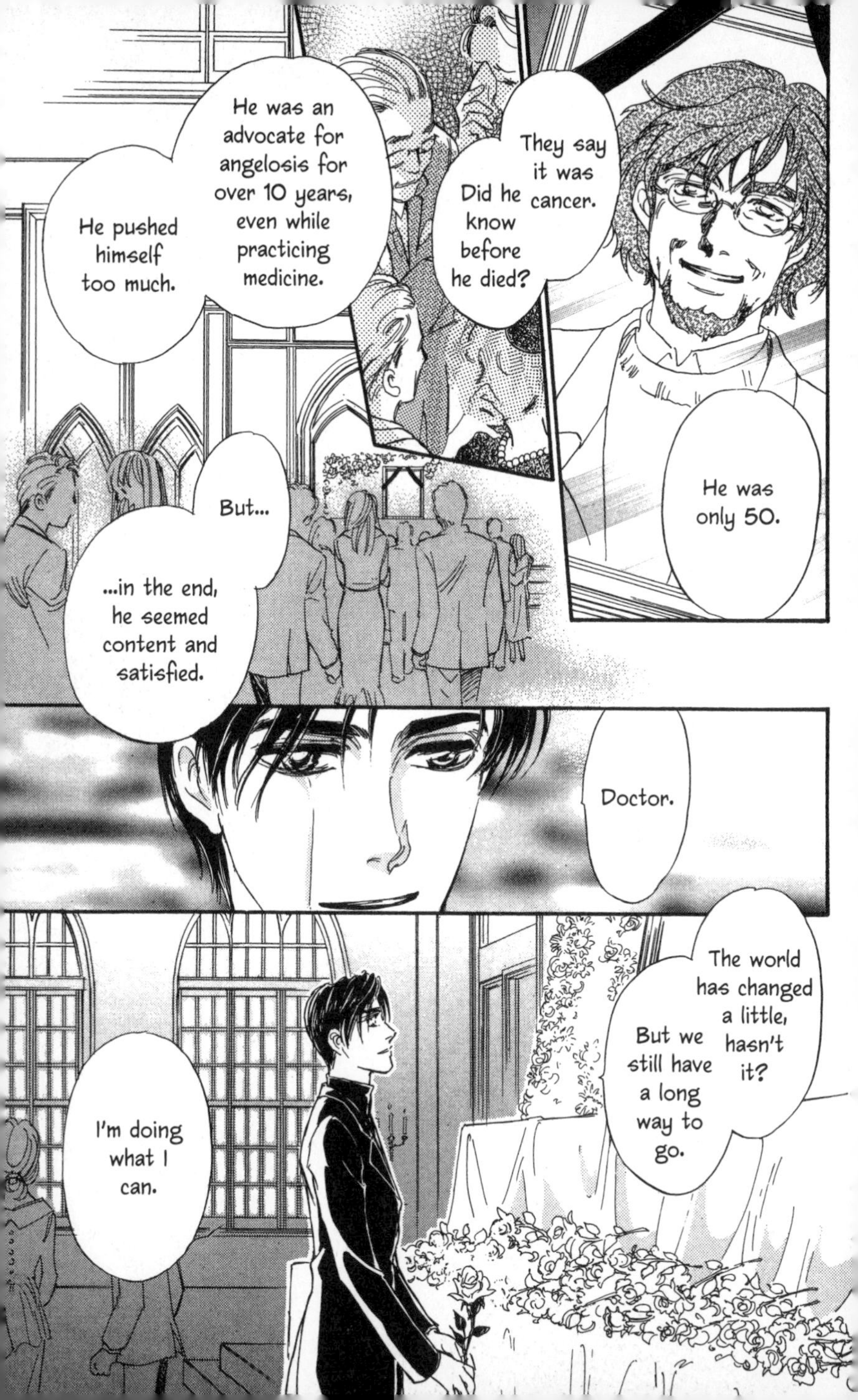
He was only 50.
They say it was cancer.
Did he know before he died?
He was an advocate for angelosis for over 10 years, even while practicing medicine.
He pushed himself too much.
But...
...in the end, he seemed content and satisfied.
Doctor.
The world has changed a little, hasn't it?
But we still have a long way to go.
I'm doing what I can.

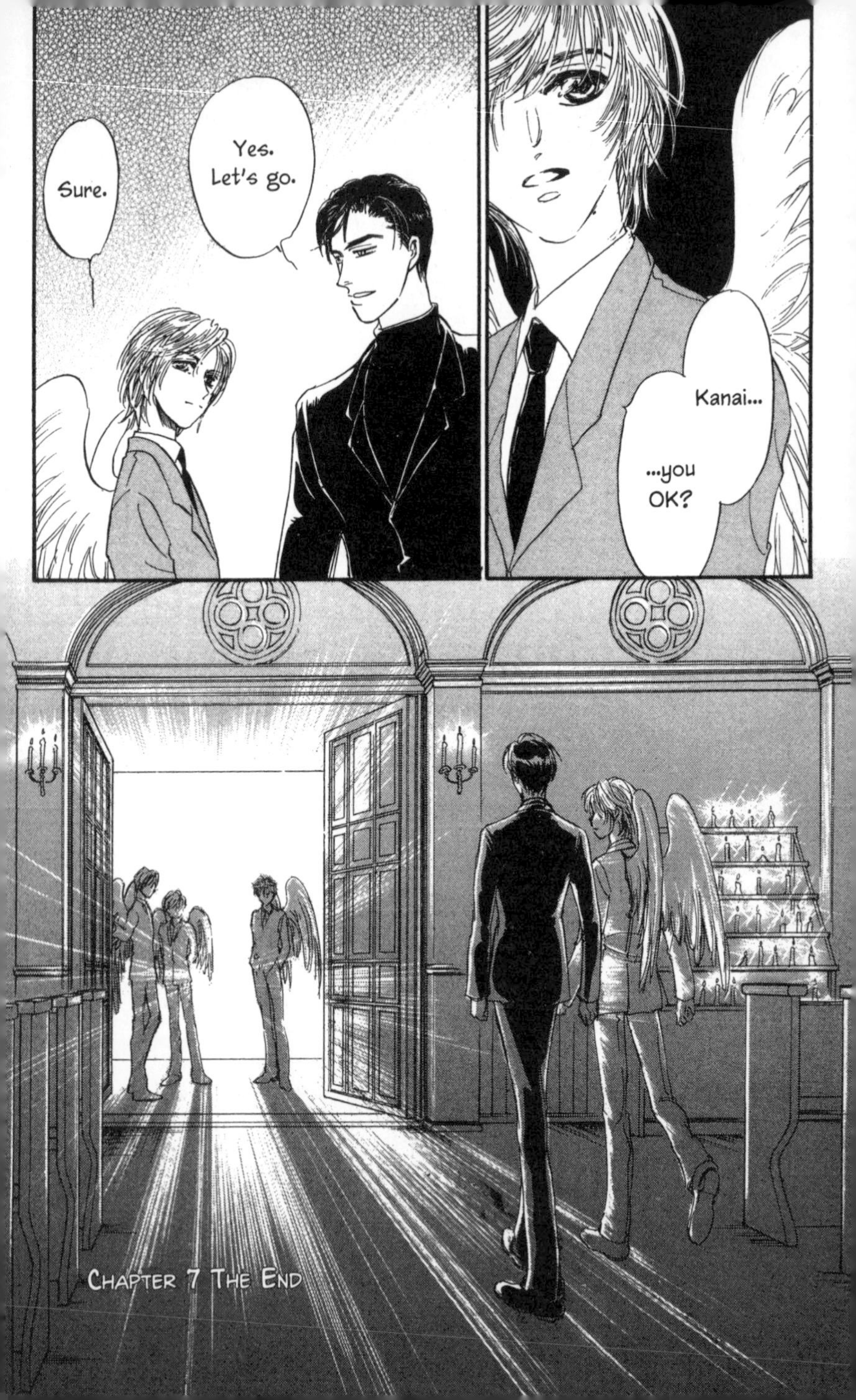
Kanai...
...you OK?
Yes. Let's go.
Sure.
Chapter 7 The End

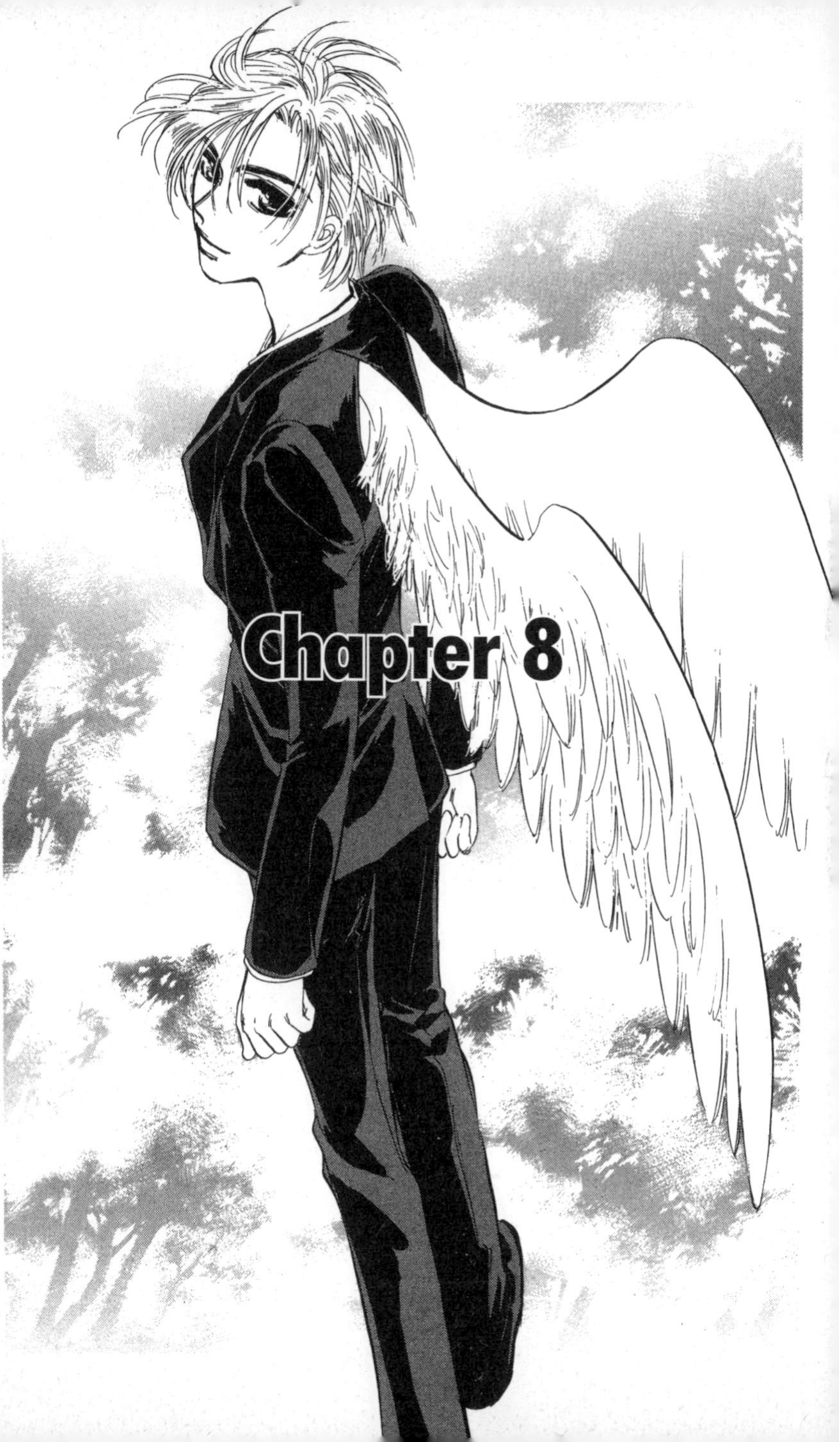
Chapter 8

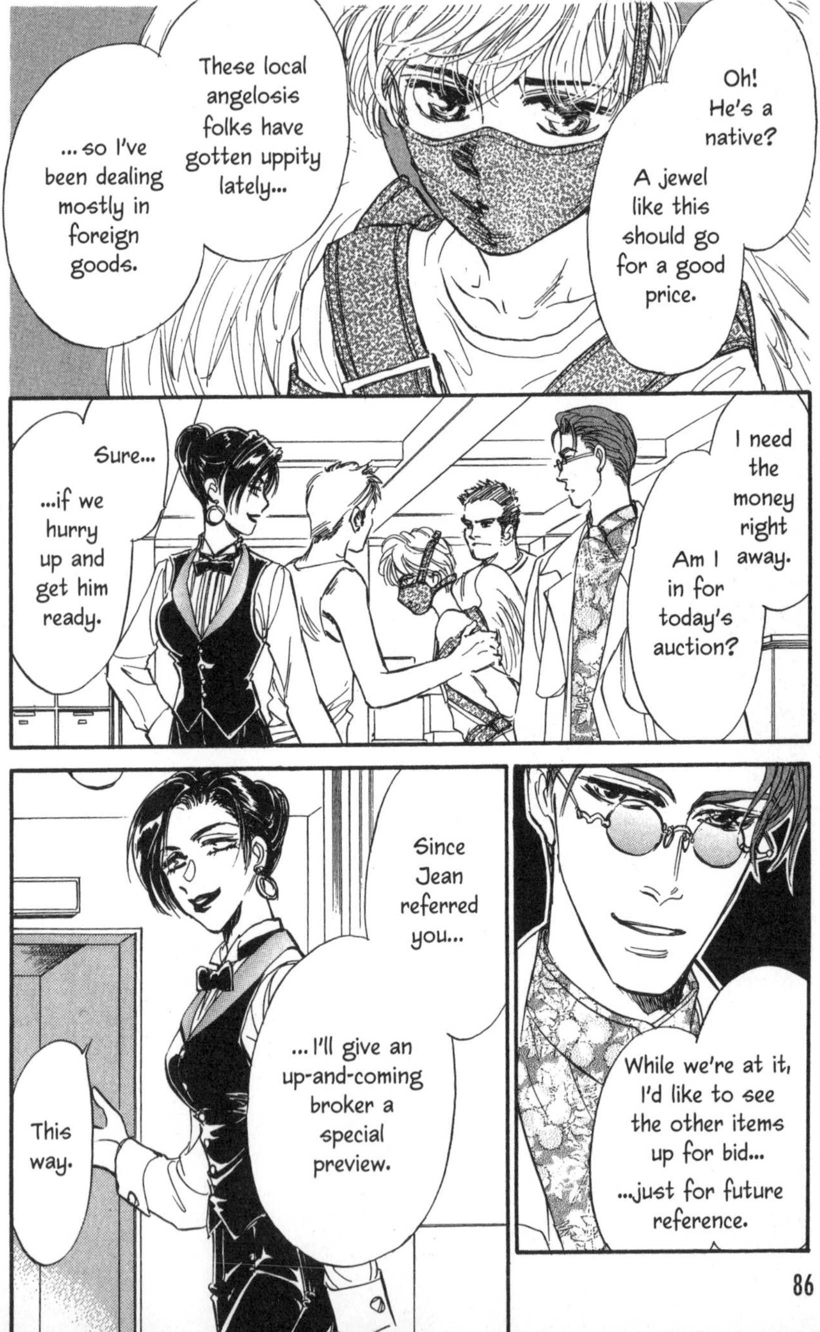
Oh! He's a native?
A jewel like this should go for a good price.
These local angelosis folks have gotten uppity lately...
... so I've been dealing mostly in foreign goods.
I need the money right away.
Am I in for today's auction?
Sure...
...if we hurry up and get him ready.
While we're at it, I'd like to see the other items up for bid...
...just for future reference.
Since Jean referred you...
... I'll give an up-and-coming broker a special preview.
This way.

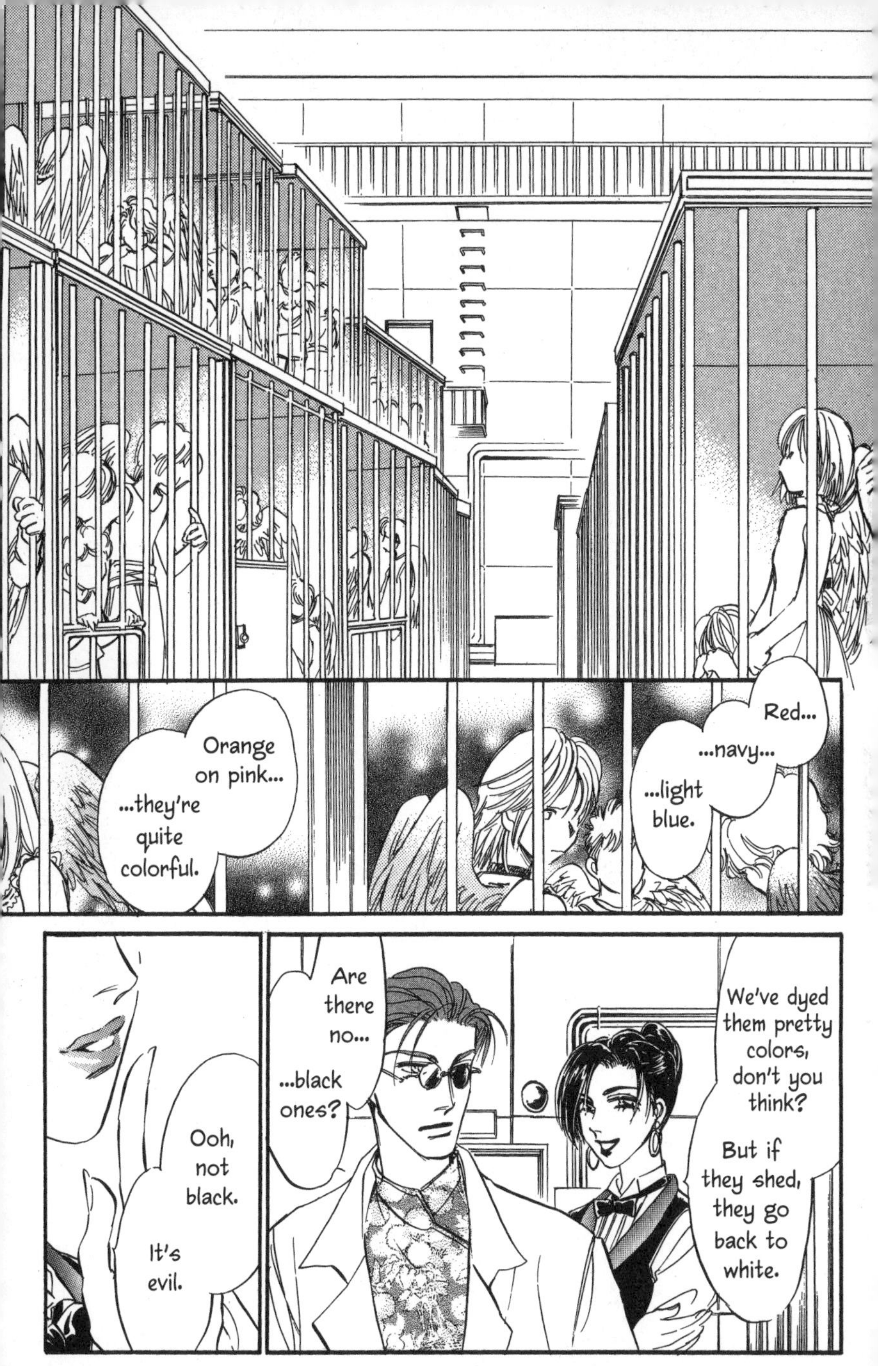
Red... ...navy... ...light blue.
Orange on pink... ...they're quite colorful.
We've dyed them pretty colors, don't you think?
But if they shed, they go back to white.
Are there no... ...black ones?
Ooh, not black.
It's evil.

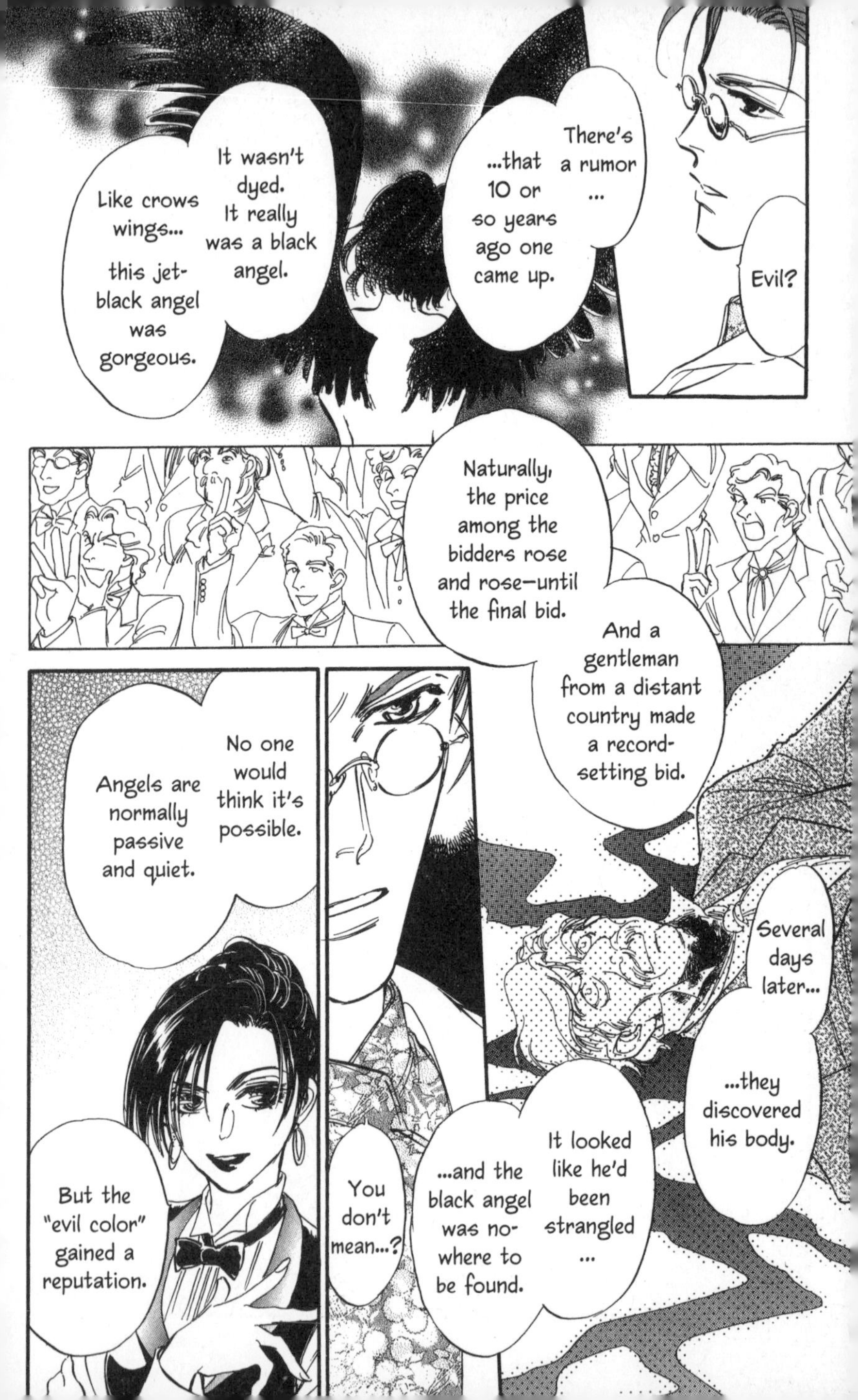
Evil?
There's a rumor ...
...that 10 or so years ago one came up.
It wasn't dyed. It really was a black angel.
Like crows wings... this jet-black angel was gorgeous.
Naturally, the price among the bidders rose and rose—until the final bid.
And a gentleman from a distant country made a record-setting bid.
Several days later...
...they discovered his body.
It looked like he'd been strangled ...
...and the black angel was no-where to be found.
You don't mean...?
No one would think it's possible.
Angels are normally passive and quiet.
But the "evil color" gained a reputation.

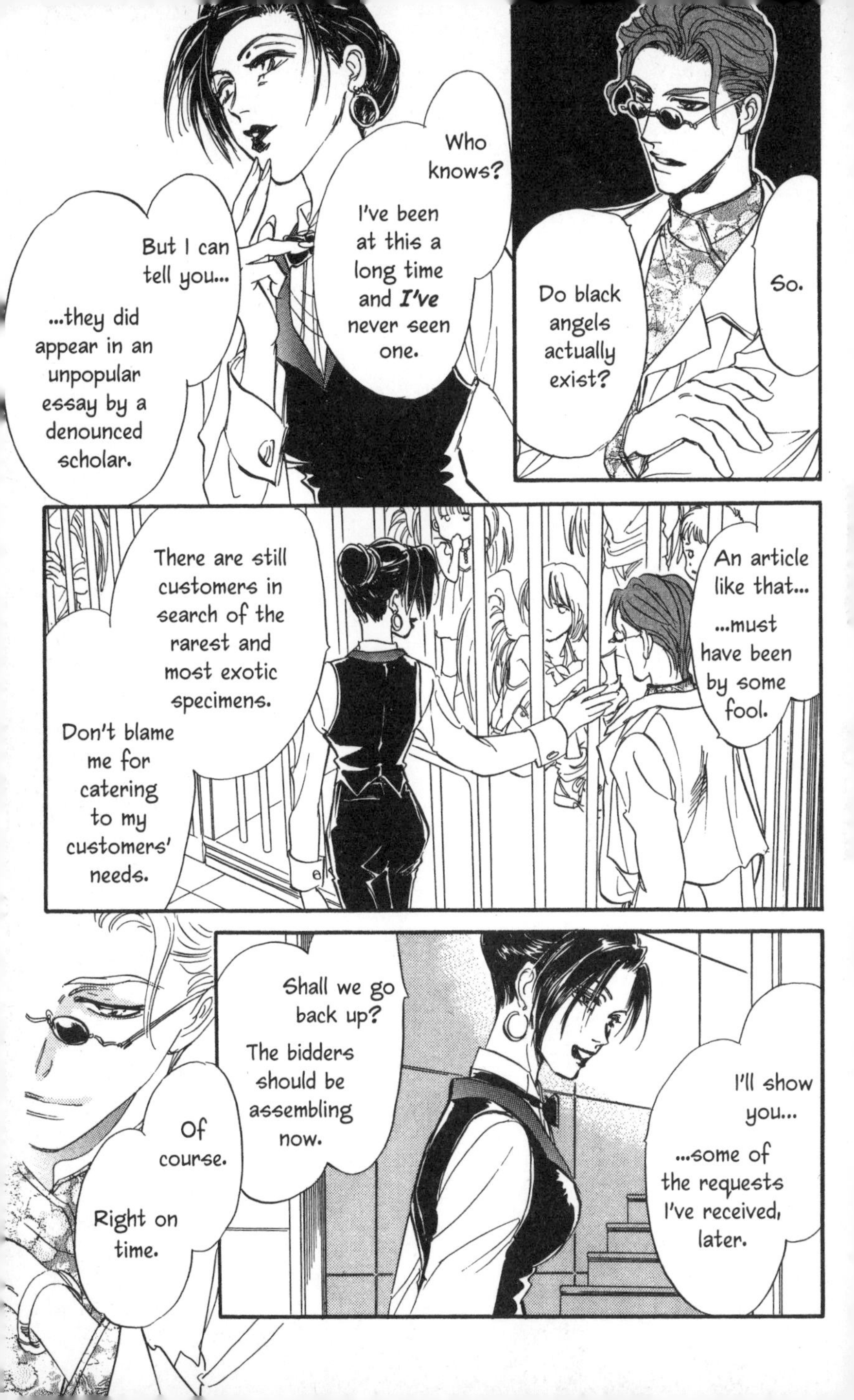
So.
Do black angels actually exist?
Who knows?
I've been at this a long time and *I've* never seen one.
But I can tell you...
...they did appear in an unpopular essay by a denounced scholar.
An article like that...
...must have been by some fool.
There are still customers in search of the rarest and most exotic specimens.
Don't blame me for catering to my customers' needs.
I'll show you...
...some of the requests I've received, later.
Shall we go back up?
The bidders should be assembling now.
Of course.
Right on time.

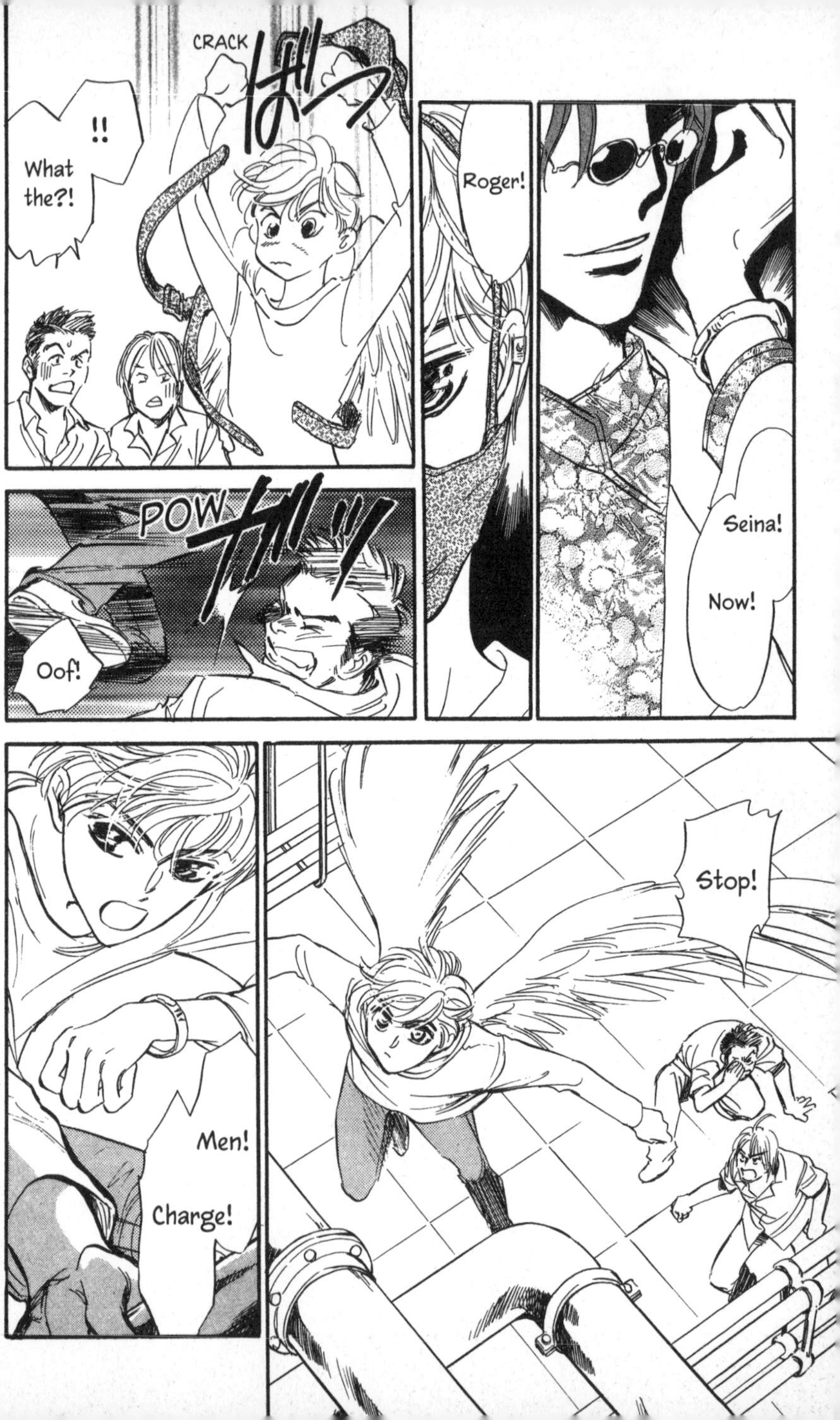

Seina! Now!
Roger!
CRACK
!!
What the?!
POW
Oof!
Stop!
Men! Charge!

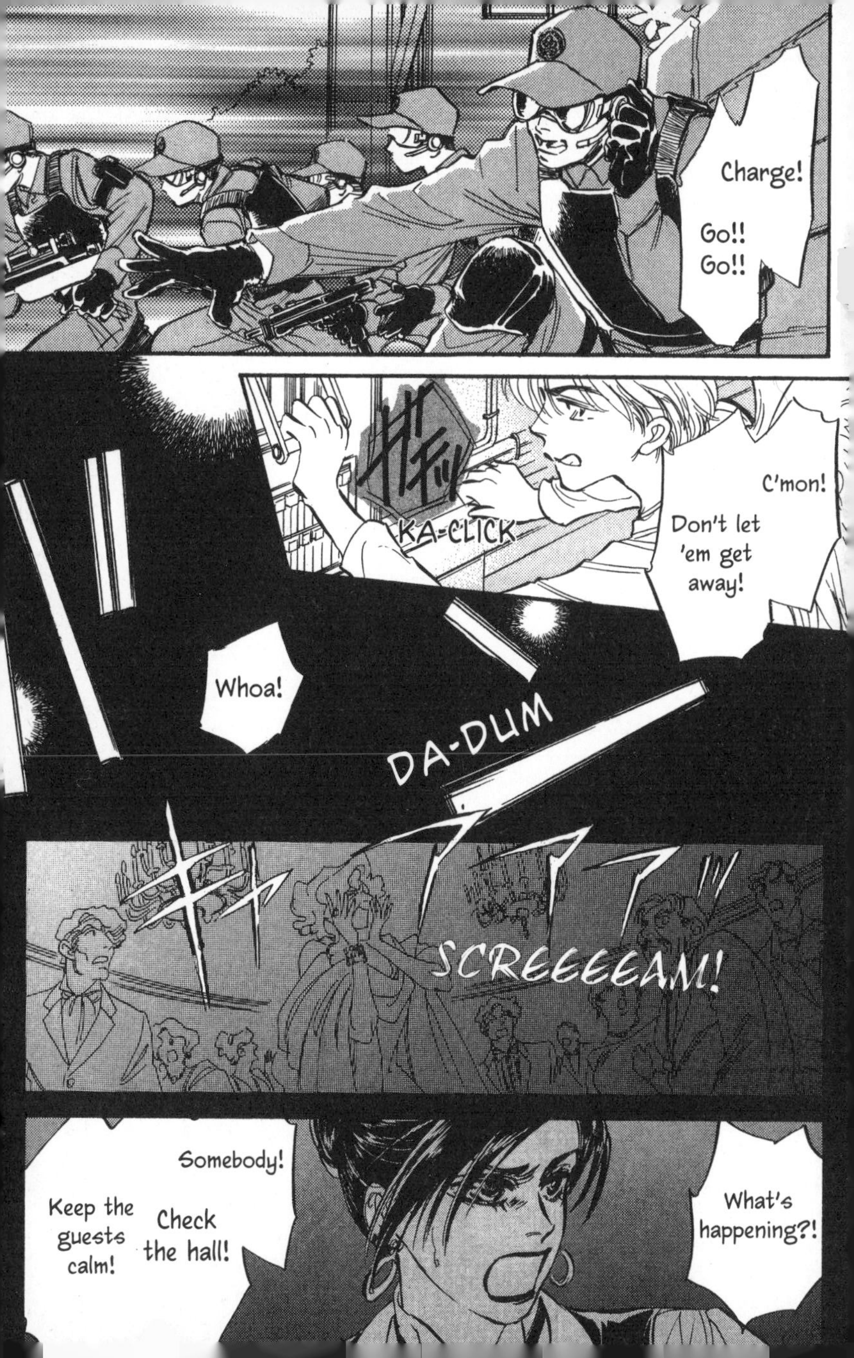
Charge!
Go!! Go!!
C'mon! Don't let 'em get away!
KA-CLICK
Whoa!
DA-DUM
SCREEEEEAM!
What's happening?!
Somebody!
Check the hall!
Keep the guests calm!

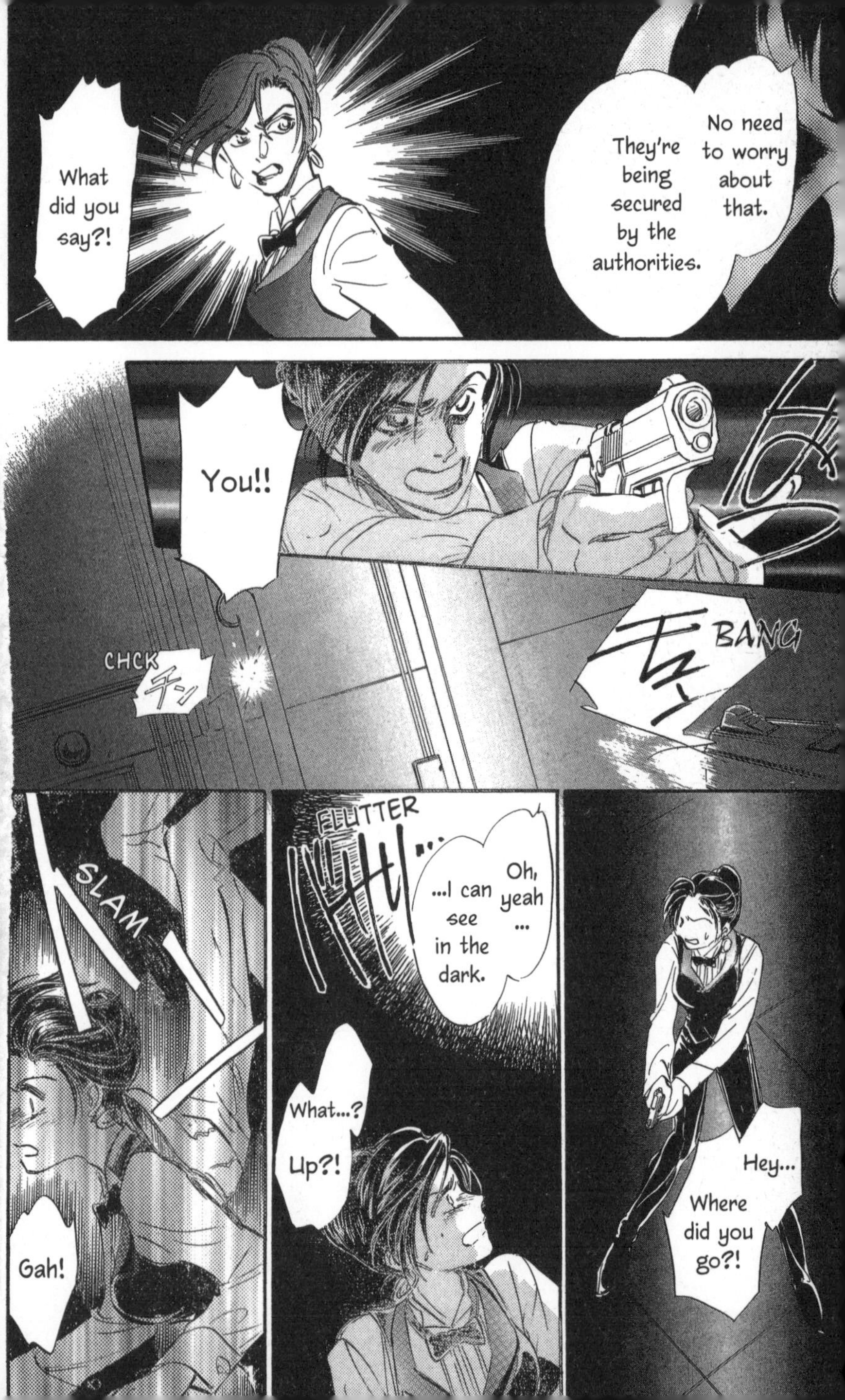
No need to worry about that.
They're being secured by the authorities.
What did you say?!
You!!
BANG
CHCK
Hey...
Where did you go?!
FLUTTER
Oh, yeah ...
...I can see in the dark.
What...?
Up?!
SLAM
Gah!

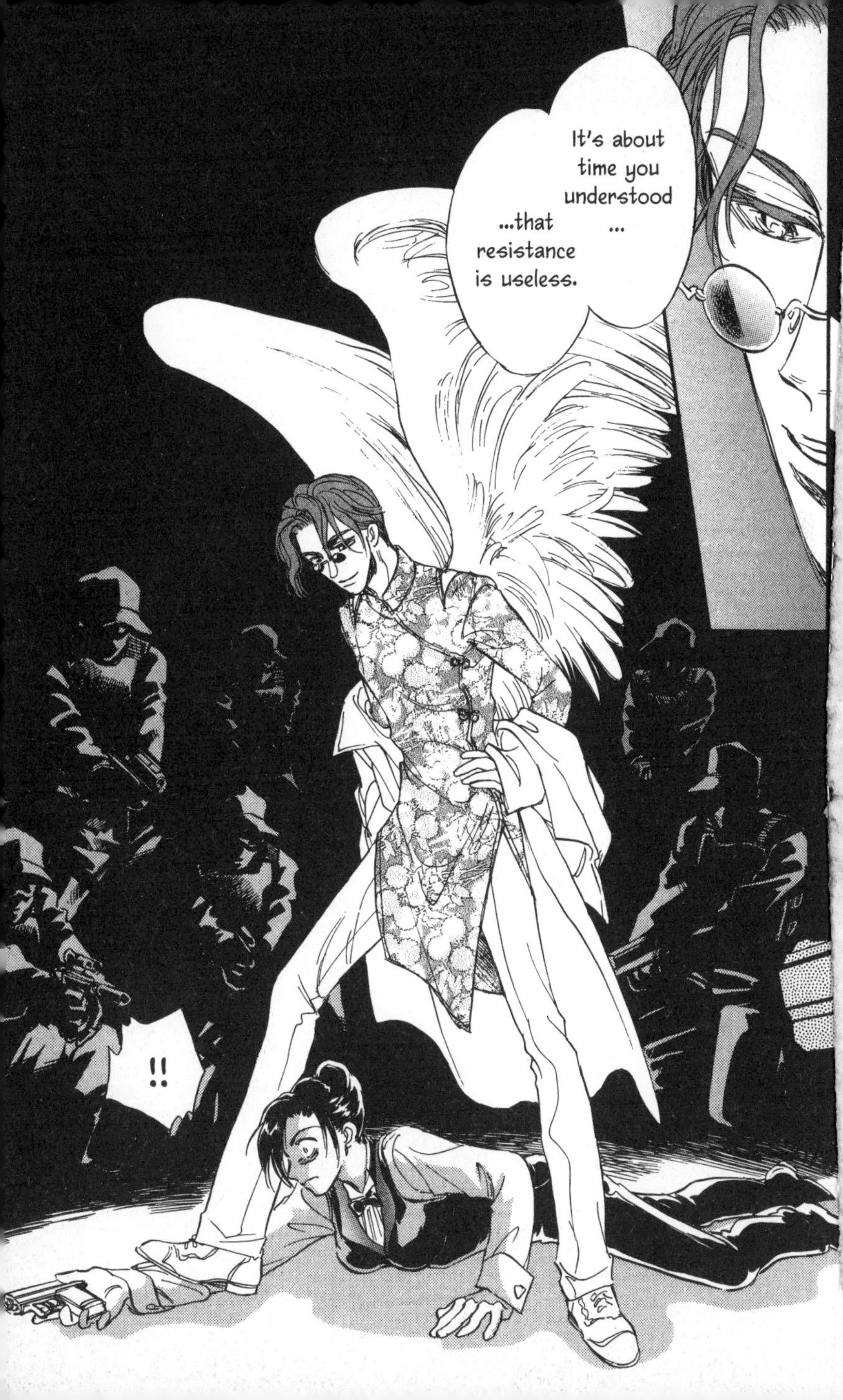
It's about time you understood ... ...that resistance is useless.
!!

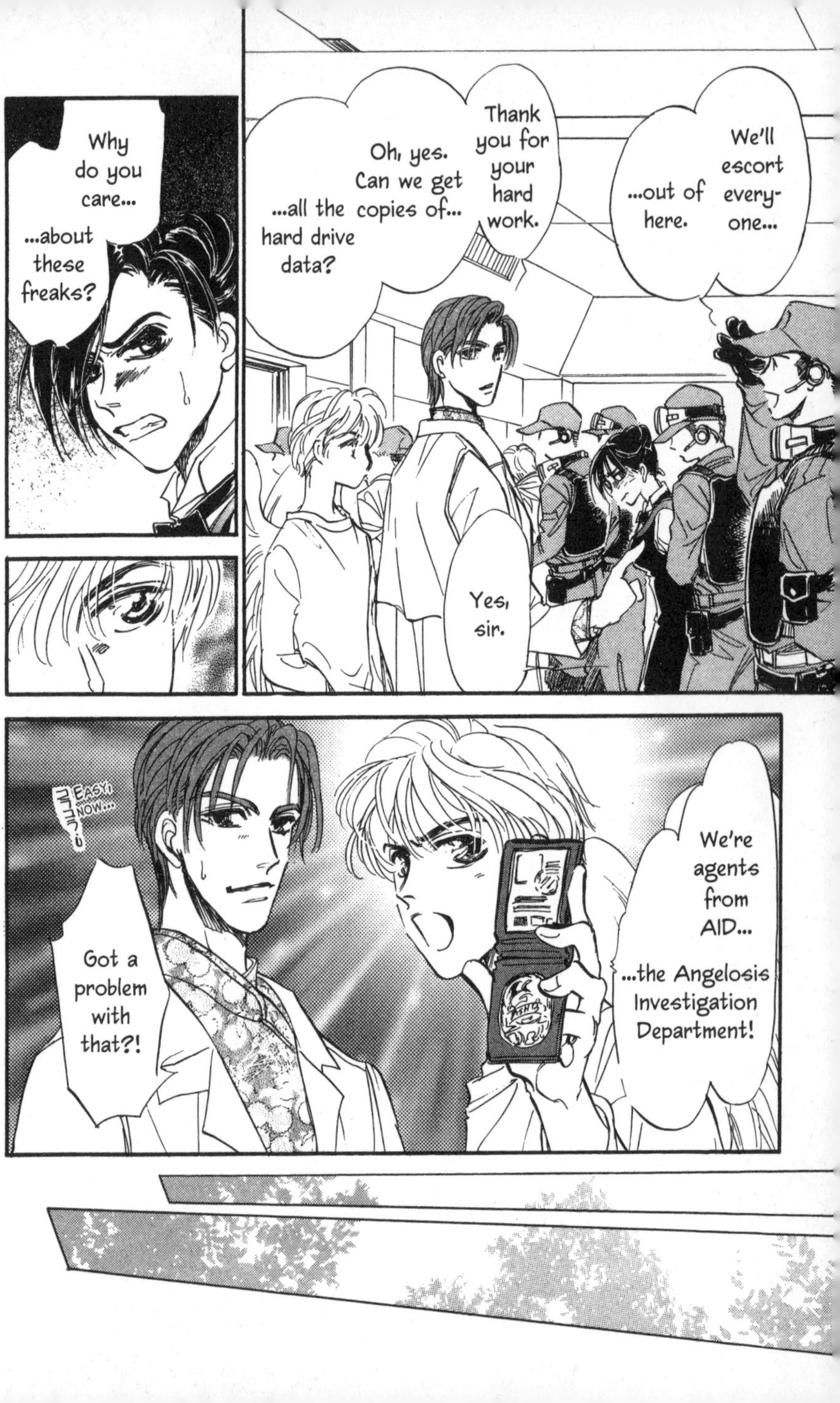
We'll escort every-one...
...out of here.
Thank you for your hard work.
Oh, yes. Can we get ...all the copies of... hard drive data?
Yes, sir.
Why do you care...
...about these freaks?
We're agents from AID...
...the Angelosis Investigation Department!
EASY, NOW...
Got a problem with that?!

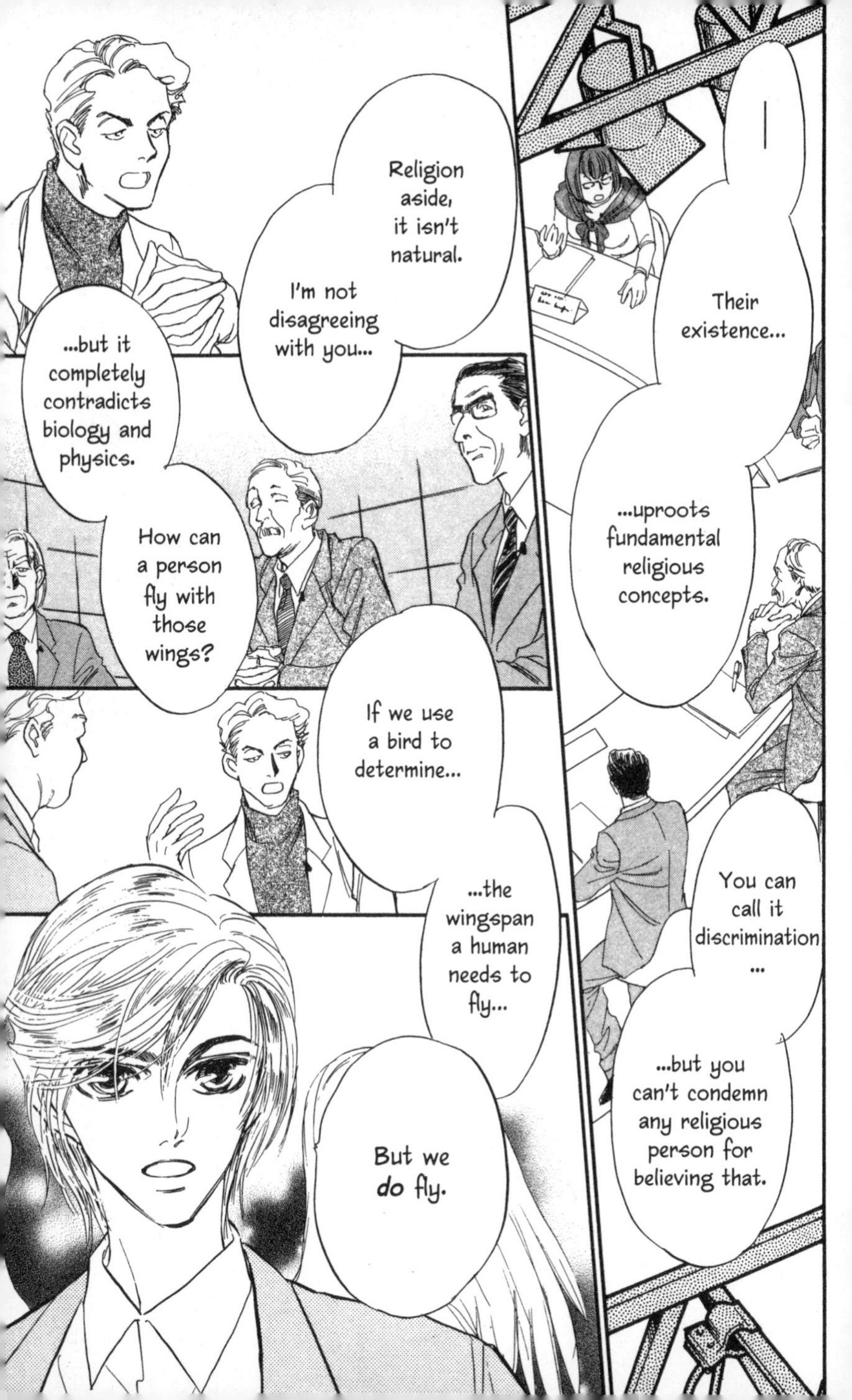

—
Their existence...
...uproots fundamental religious concepts.
You can call it discrimination...
...but you can't condemn any religious person for believing that.
Religion aside, it isn't natural.
I'm not disagreeing with you...
...but it completely contradicts biology and physics.
How can a person fly with those wings?
If we use a bird to determine...
...the wingspan a human needs to fly...
But we *do* fly.

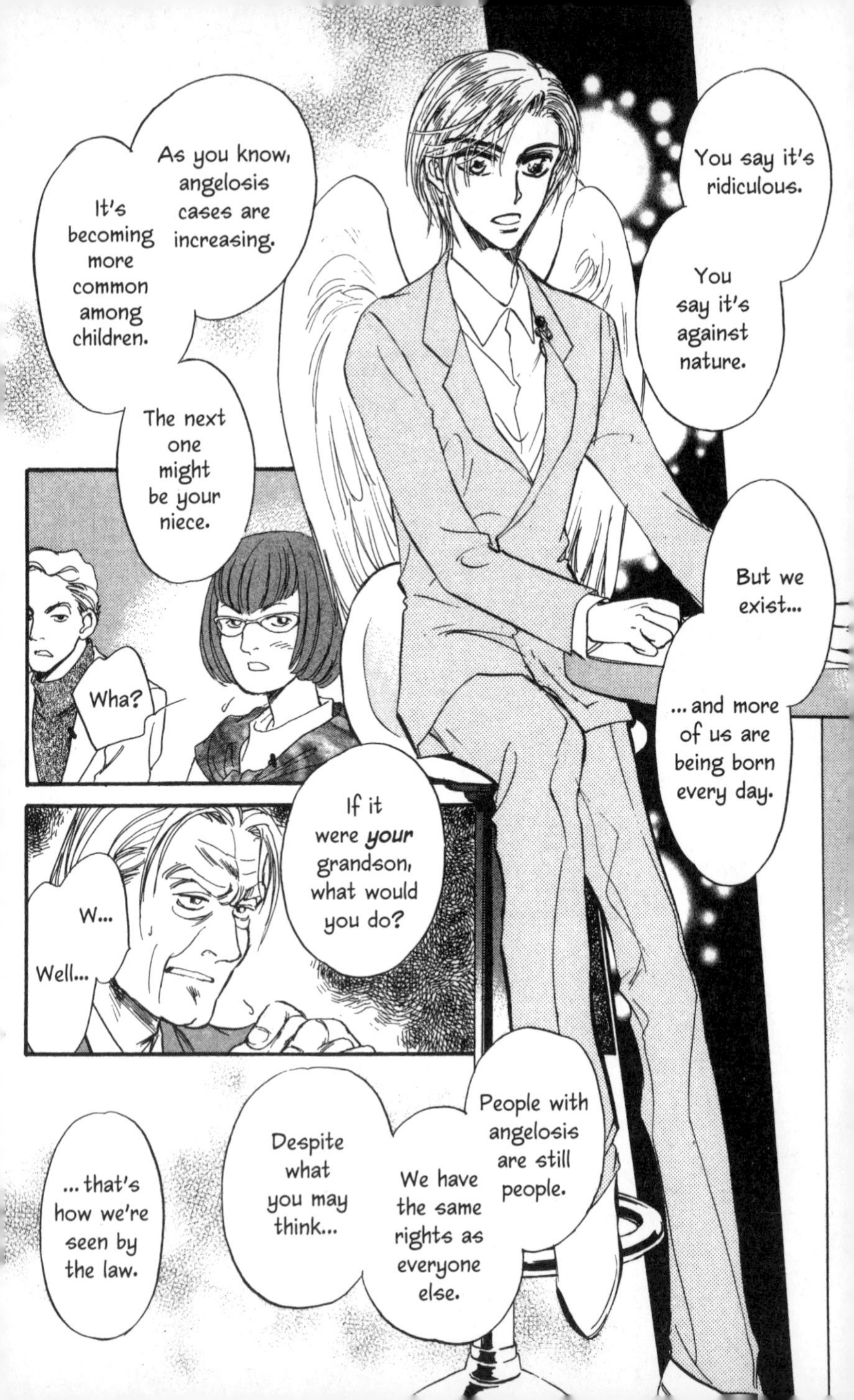
You say it's ridiculous.
You say it's against nature.
As you know, angelosis cases are increasing.
It's becoming more common among children.
The next one might be your niece.
But we exist...
...and more of us are being born every day.
Wha?
If it were *your* grandson, what would you do?
W...
Well...
People with angelosis are still people.
We have the same rights as everyone else.
Despite what you may think...
...that's how we're seen by the law.

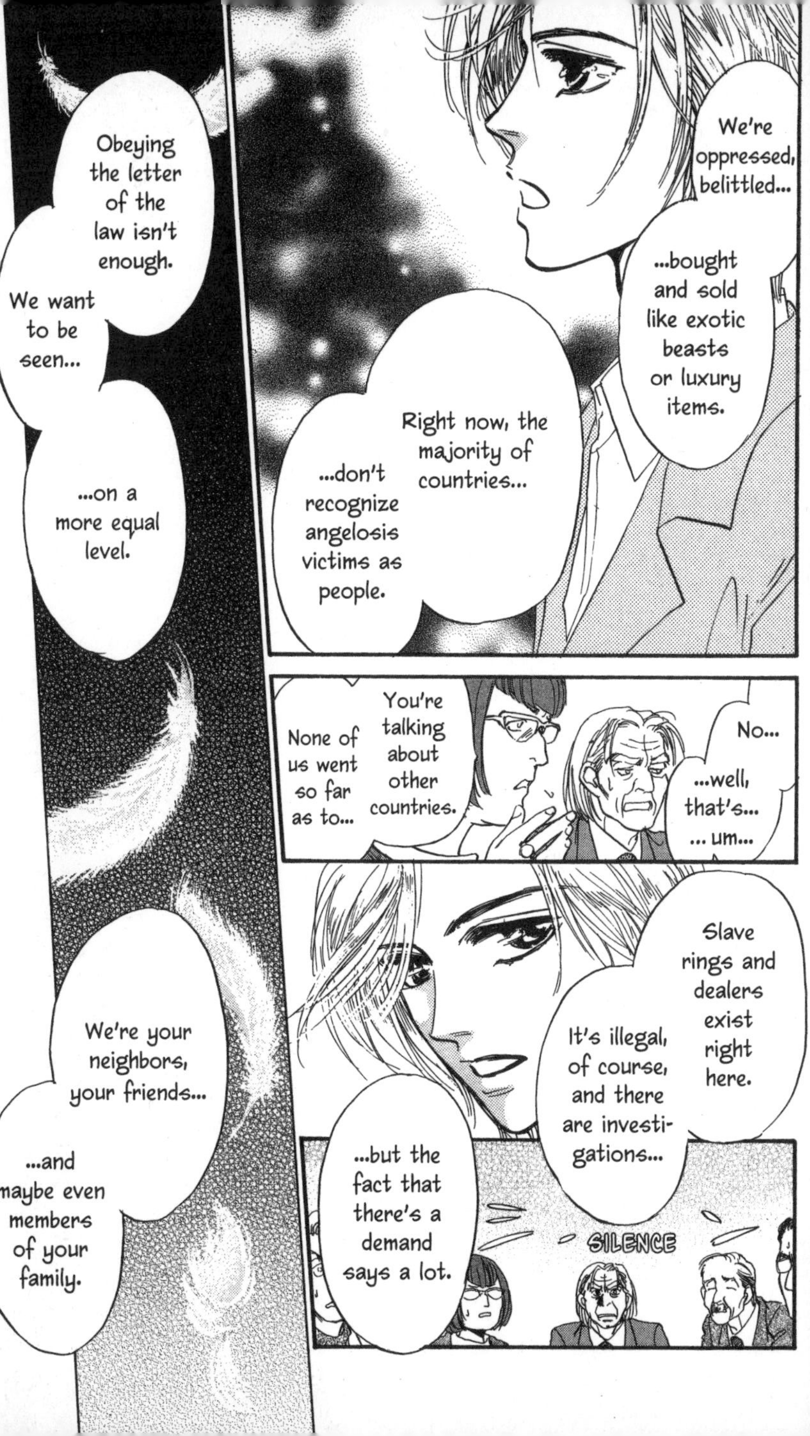
We're oppressed, belittled...
...bought and sold like exotic beasts or luxury items.
Right now, the majority of countries...
...don't recognize angelosis victims as people.
No...
...well, that's...
... um...
You're talking about other countries.
None of us went so far as to...
Slave rings and dealers exist right here.
It's illegal, of course, and there are investigations...
...but the fact that there's a demand says a lot.
SILENCE
Obeying the letter of the law isn't enough.
We want to be seen...
...on a more equal level.
We're your neighbors, your friends...
...and maybe even members of your family.

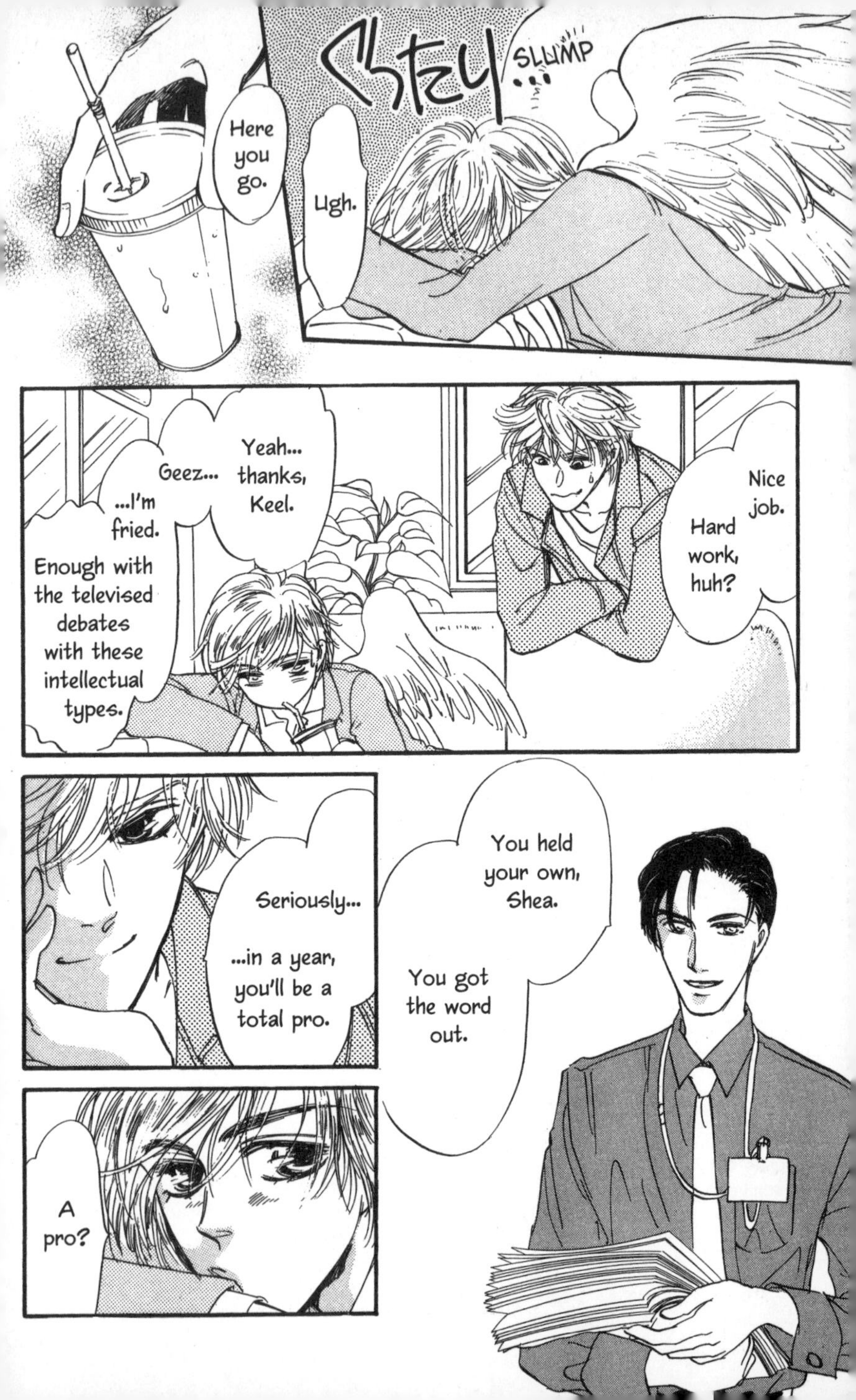
ぐったり
SLUMP
...
Ugh.
Here you go.
Nice job.
Hard work, huh?
Yeah... thanks, Keel.
Geez...
...I'm fried.
Enough with the televised debates with these intellectual types.
You held your own, Shea.
You got the word out.
Seriously...
...in a year, you'll be a total pro.
A pro?

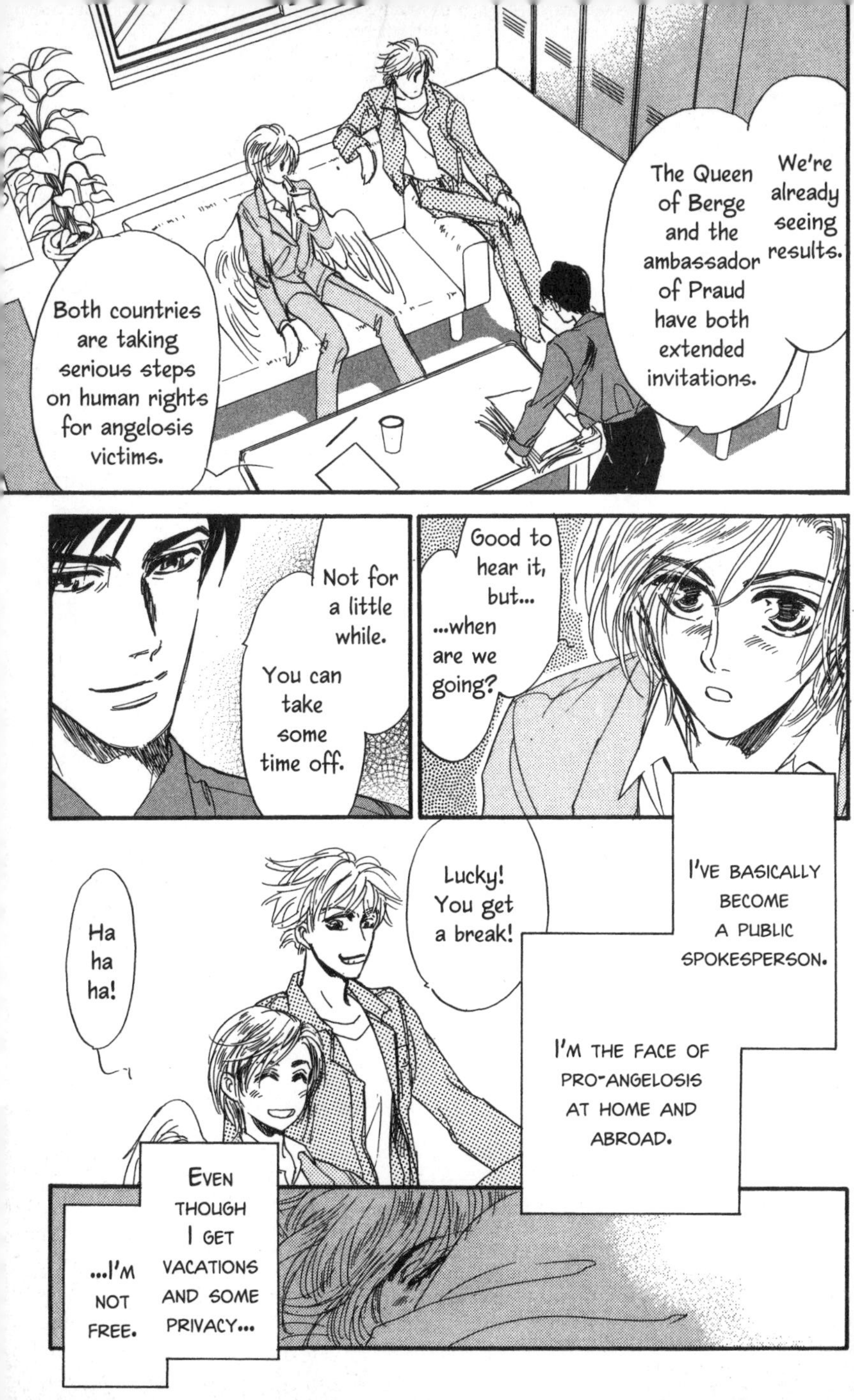
We're already seeing results.
The Queen of Berge and the ambassador of Praud have both extended invitations.
Both countries are taking serious steps on human rights for angelosis victims.
Good to hear it, but... ...when are we going?
Not for a little while.
You can take some time off.
I've basically become a public spokesperson.
I'm the face of pro-angelosis at home and abroad.
Lucky! You get a break!
Ha ha ha!
Even though I get vacations and some privacy...
...I'm not free.

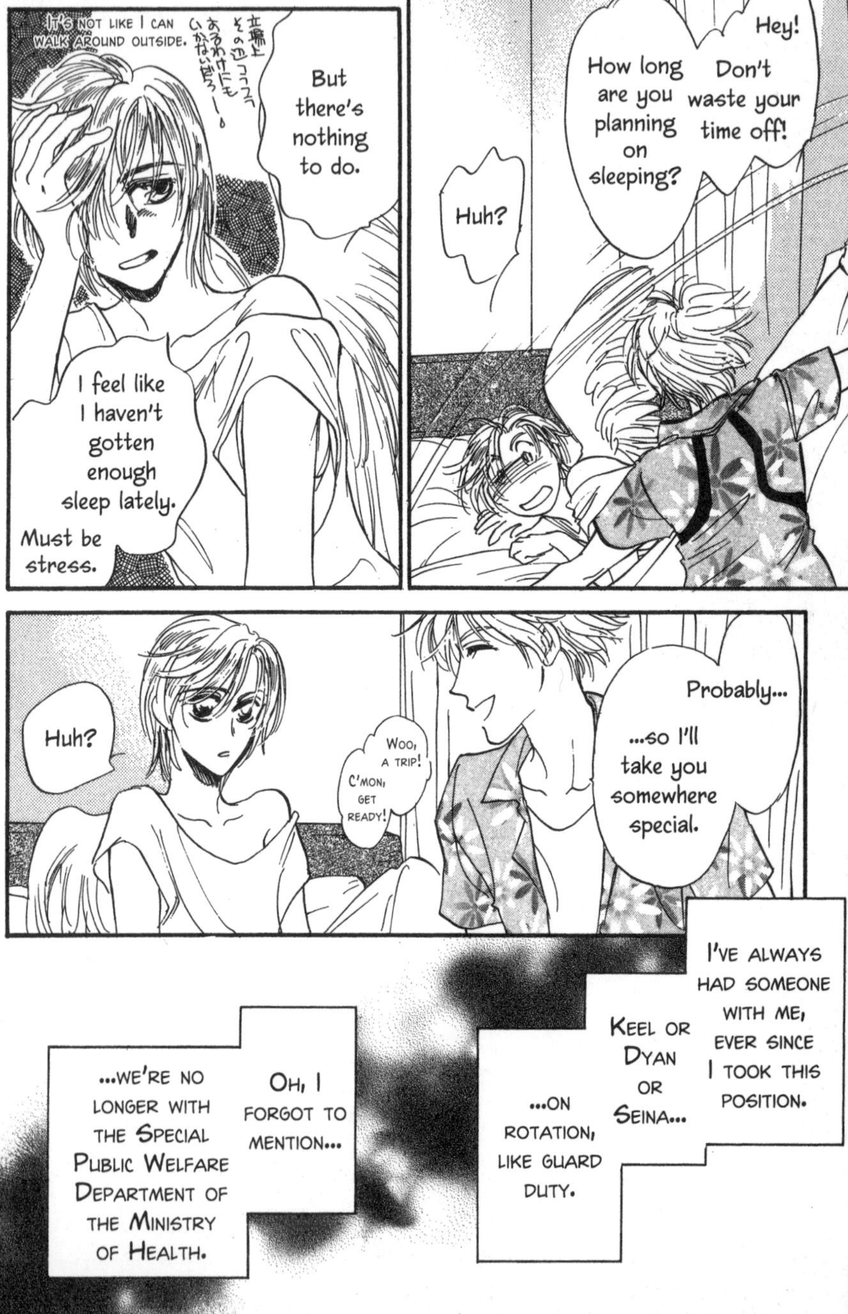
Hey! Don't waste your time off!
How long are you planning on sleeping?
Huh?
But there's nothing to do.
It's not like I can walk around outside.
I feel like I haven't gotten enough sleep lately.
Must be stress.
Probably...
...so I'll take you somewhere special.
Woo, a trip! C'mon, get ready!
Huh?
I've always had someone with me, ever since I took this position.
Keel or Dyan or Seina...
...on rotation, like guard duty.
Oh, I forgot to mention...
...we're no longer with the Special Public Welfare Department of the Ministry of Health.

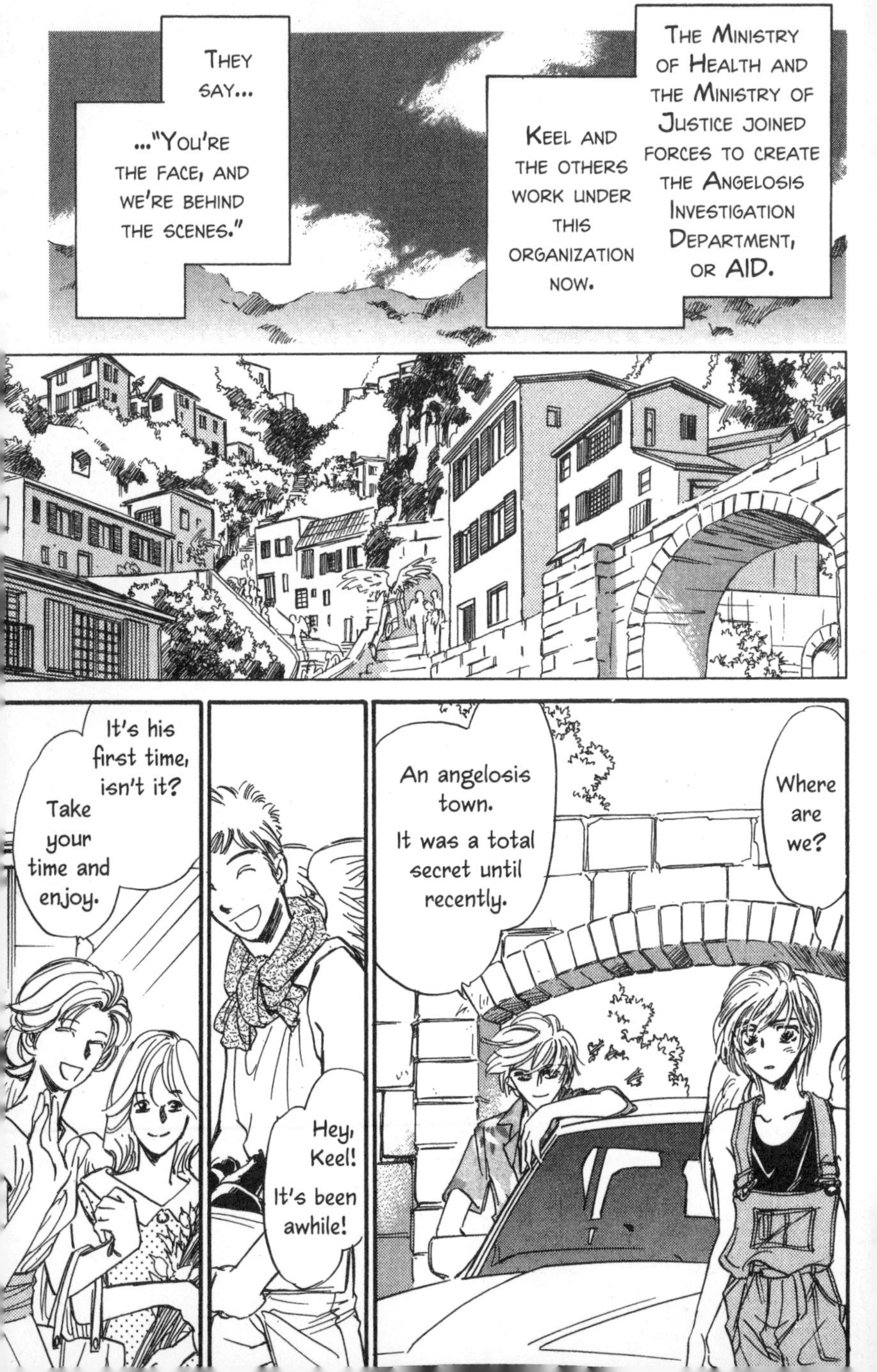
The Ministry of Health and the Ministry of Justice joined forces to create the Angelosis Investigation Department, or AID.
Keel and the others work under this organization now.
They say...
..."You're the face, and we're behind the scenes."
Where are we?
An angelosis town.
It was a total secret until recently.
Hey, Keel!
It's been awhile!
It's his first time, isn't it?
Take your time and enjoy.

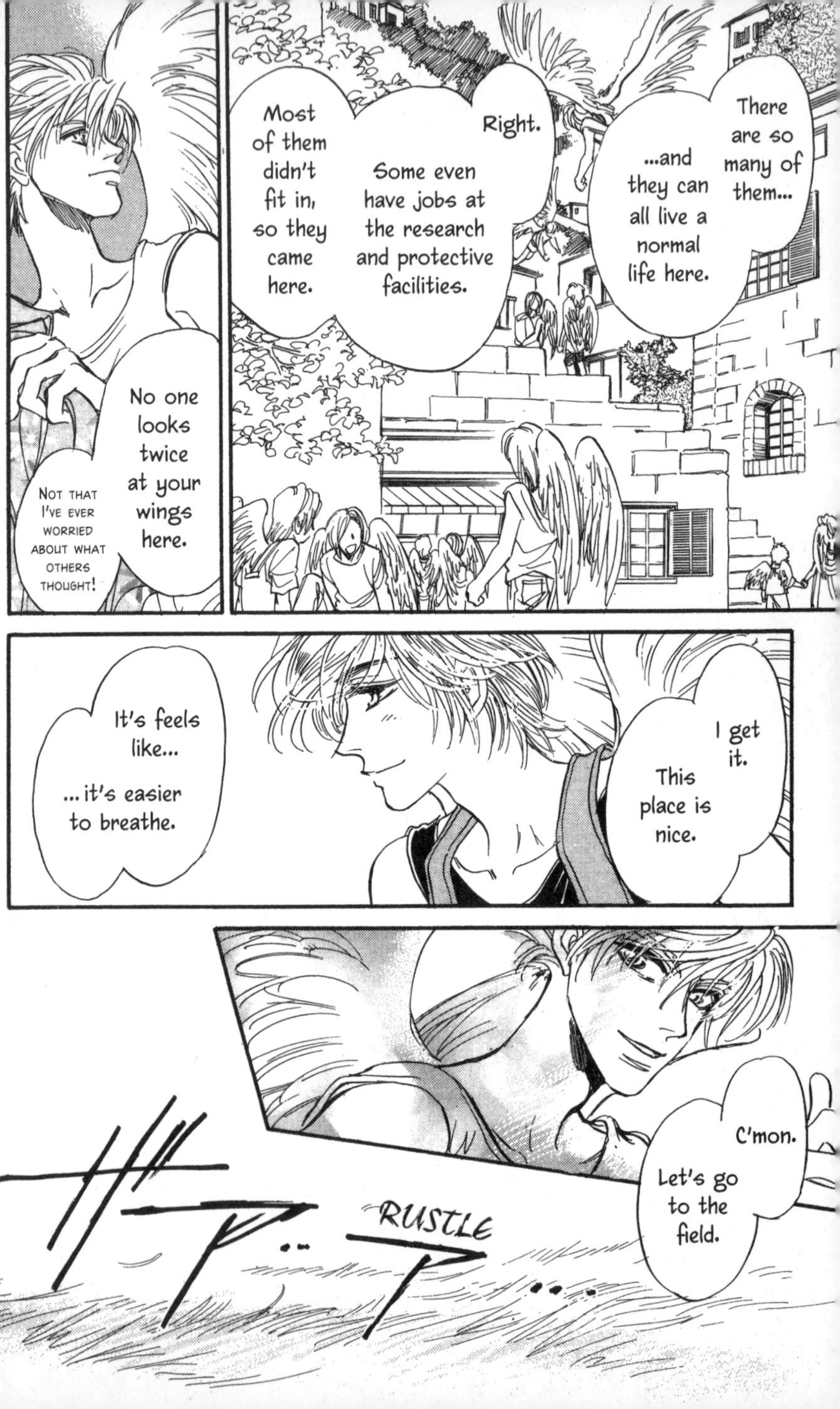
There are so many of them...
...and they can all live a normal life here.
Right.
Most of them didn't fit in, so they came here.
Some even have jobs at the research and protective facilities.
No one looks twice at your wings here.
Not that I've ever worried about what others thought!
I get it.
This place is nice.
It's feels like...
...it's easier to breathe.
C'mon.
Let's go to the field.
RUSTLE

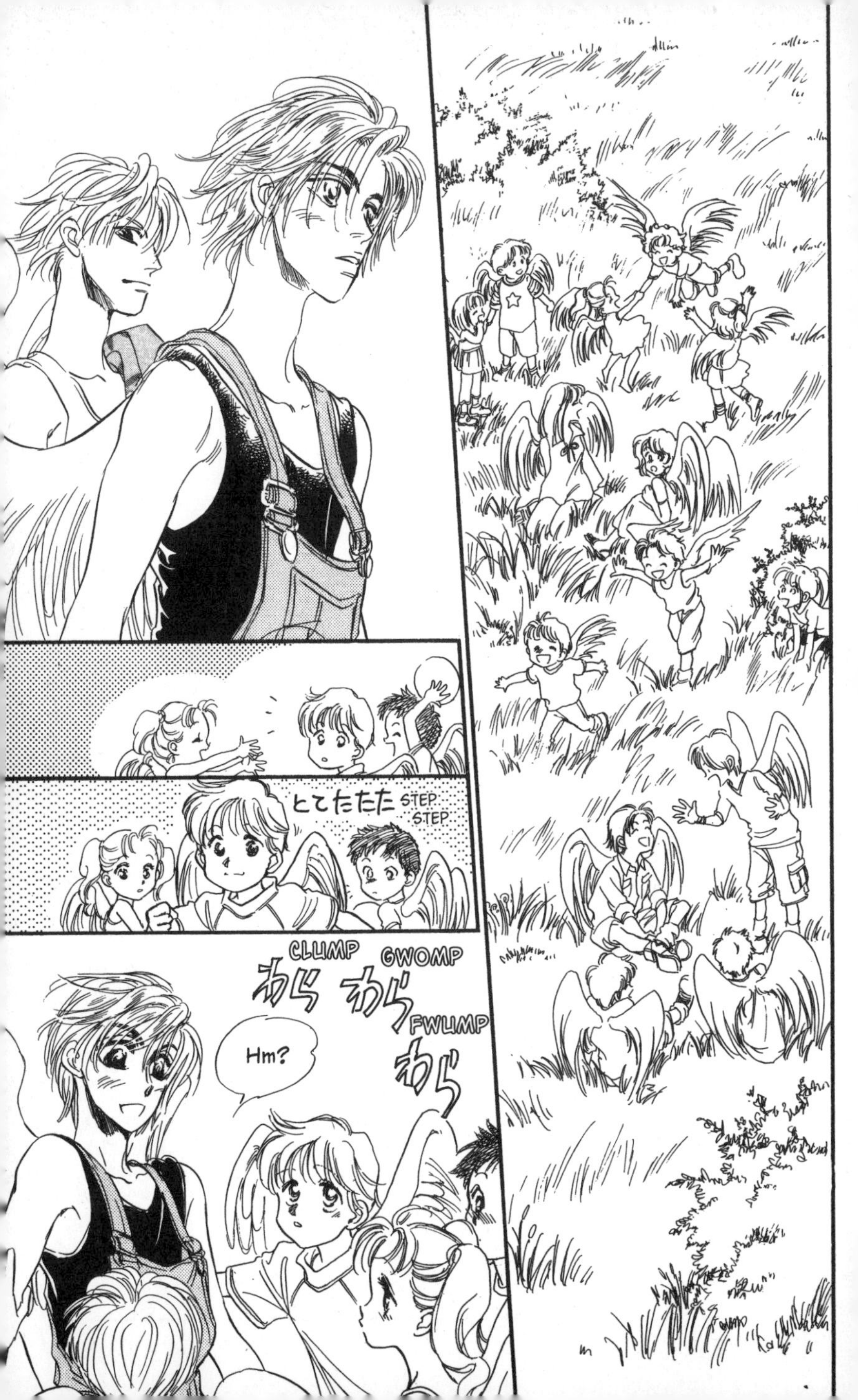
とてたたた
STEP STEP
わら わら わら
CLUMP GWOMP FWUMP
Hm?

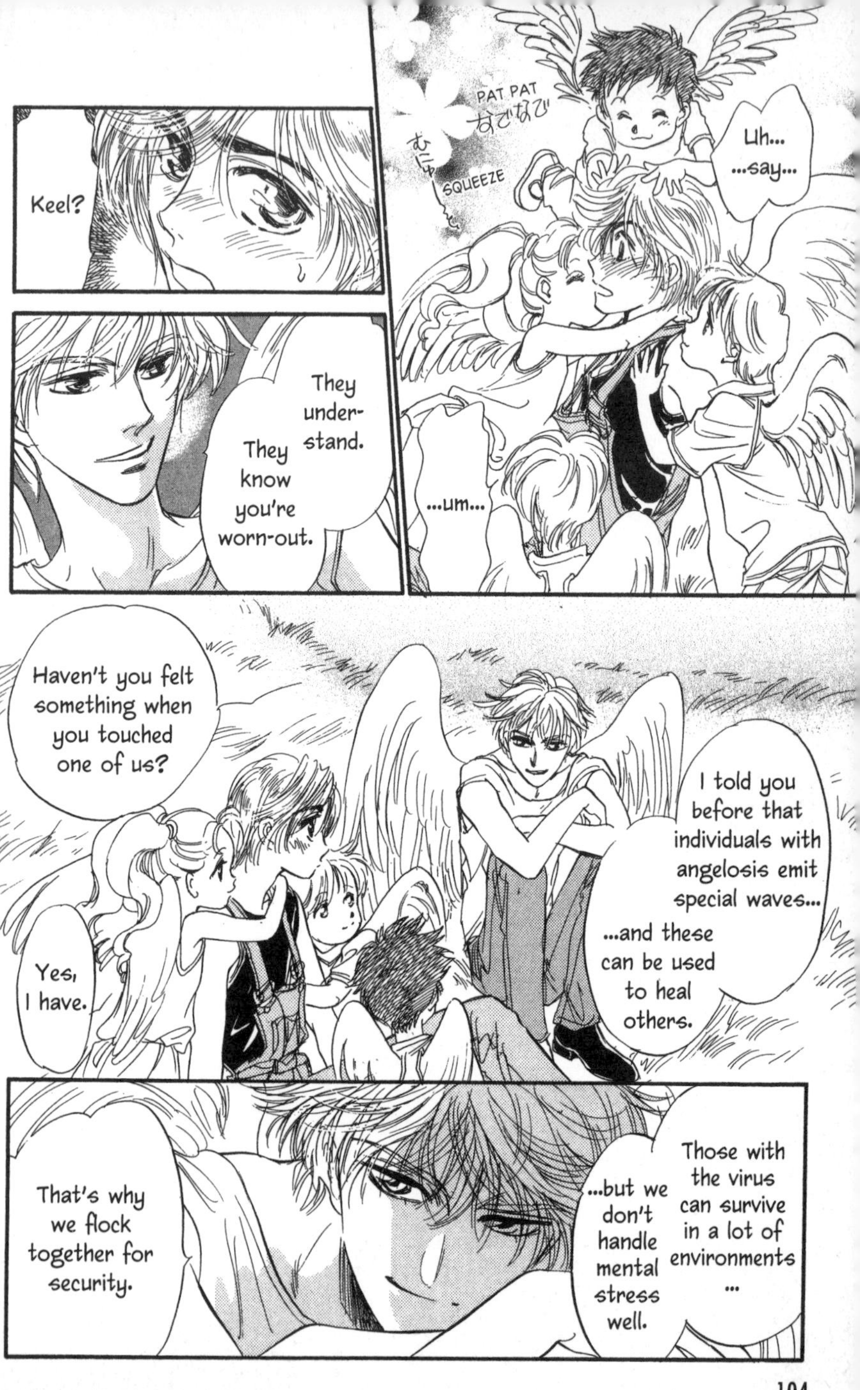
Uh...
...say...
PAT PAT
なでなで
むにゅ
SQUEEZE
...um...
Keel?
They understand.
They know you're worn-out.
Haven't you felt something when you touched one of us?
Yes, I have.
I told you before that individuals with angelosis emit special waves...
...and these can be used to heal others.
Those with the virus can survive in a lot of environments...
...but we don't handle mental stress well.
That's why we flock together for security.

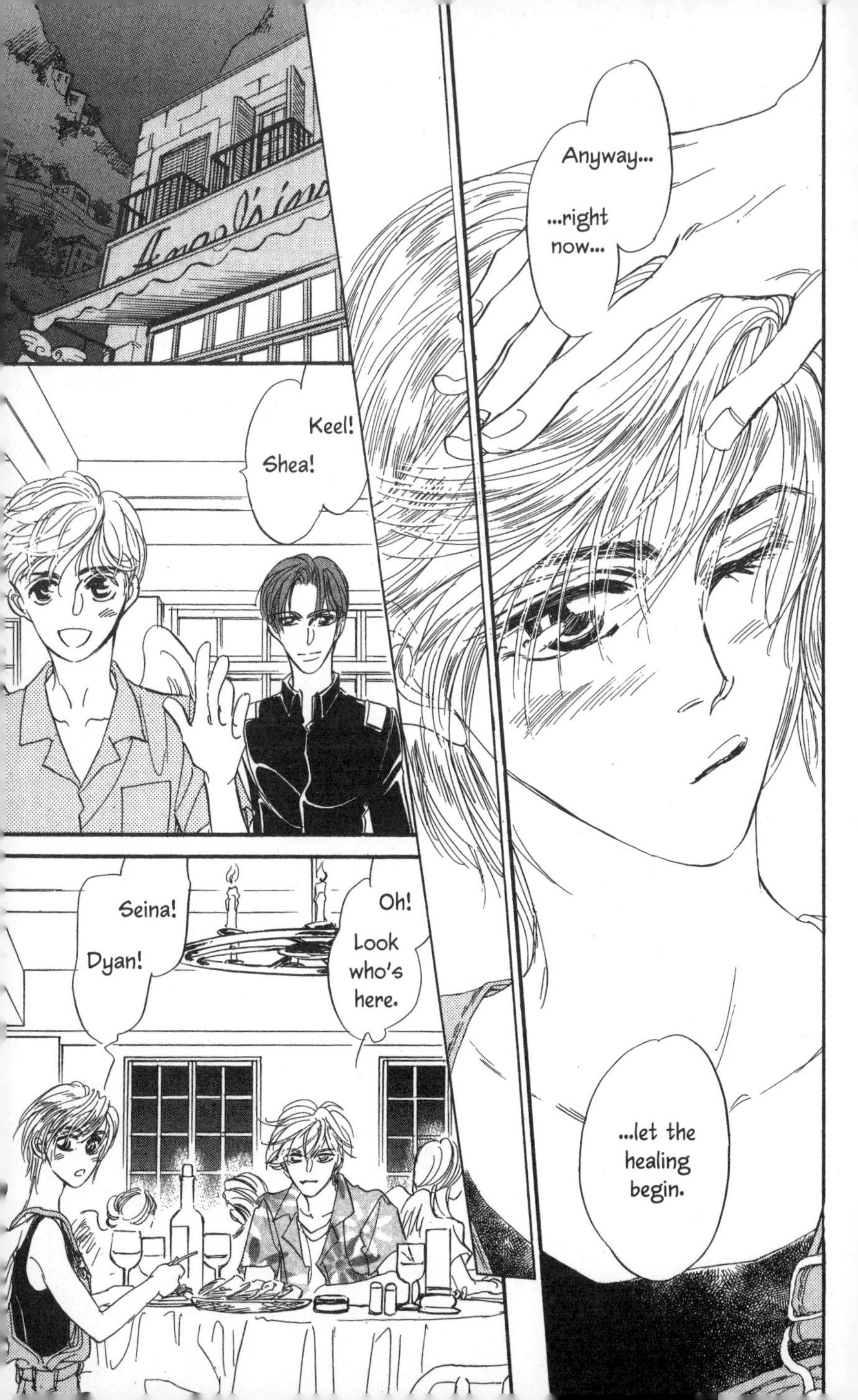
Anyway...
...right now...
...let the healing begin.
Keel!
Shea!
Oh!
Look who's here.
Seina!
Dyan!

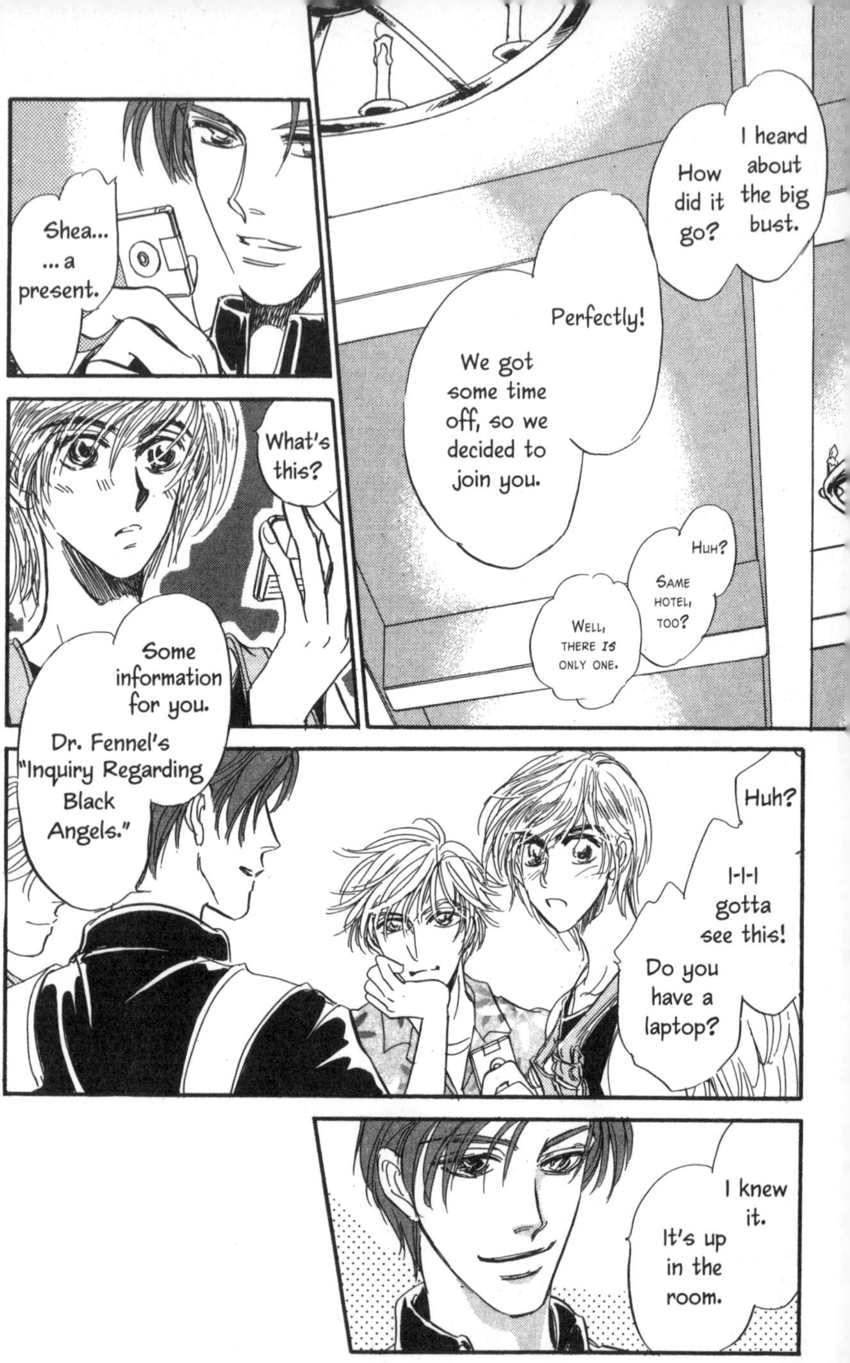
I heard about the big bust.
How did it go?
Perfectly!
We got some time off, so we decided to join you.
Huh?
Same hotel, too?
Well, there *is* only one.
Shea...
...a present.
What's this?
Some information for you.
Dr. Fennel's "Inquiry Regarding Black Angels."
Huh?
I-I-I gotta see this!
Do you have a laptop?
I knew it.
It's up in the room.

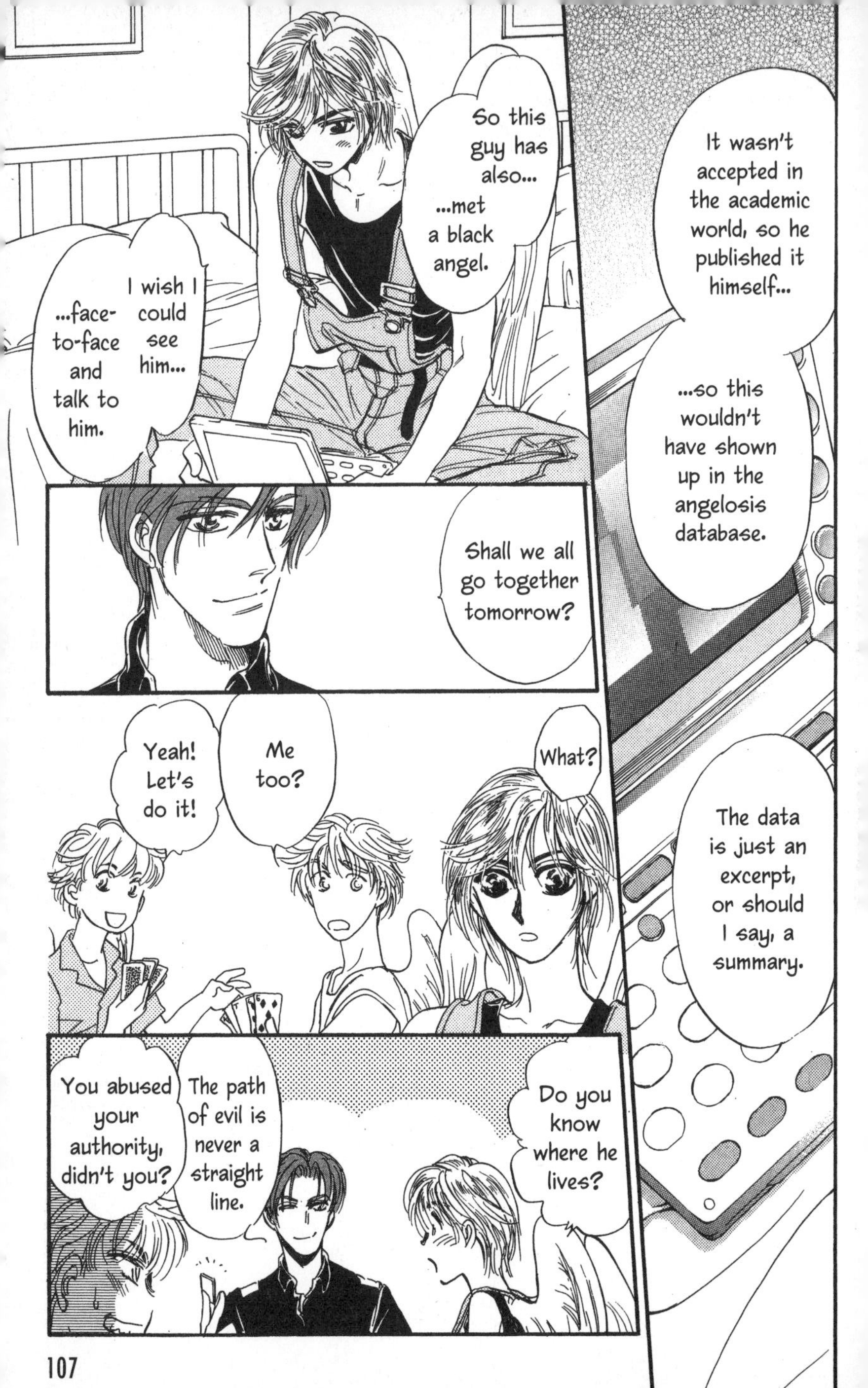
It wasn't accepted in the academic world, so he published it himself...
...so this wouldn't have shown up in the angelosis database.
The data is just an excerpt, or should I say, a summary.
So this guy has also...
...met a black angel.
I wish I could see him...
...face-to-face and talk to him.
Shall we all go together tomorrow?
What?
Me too?
Yeah! Let's do it!
Do you know where he lives?
The path of evil is never a straight line.
You abused your authority, didn't you?

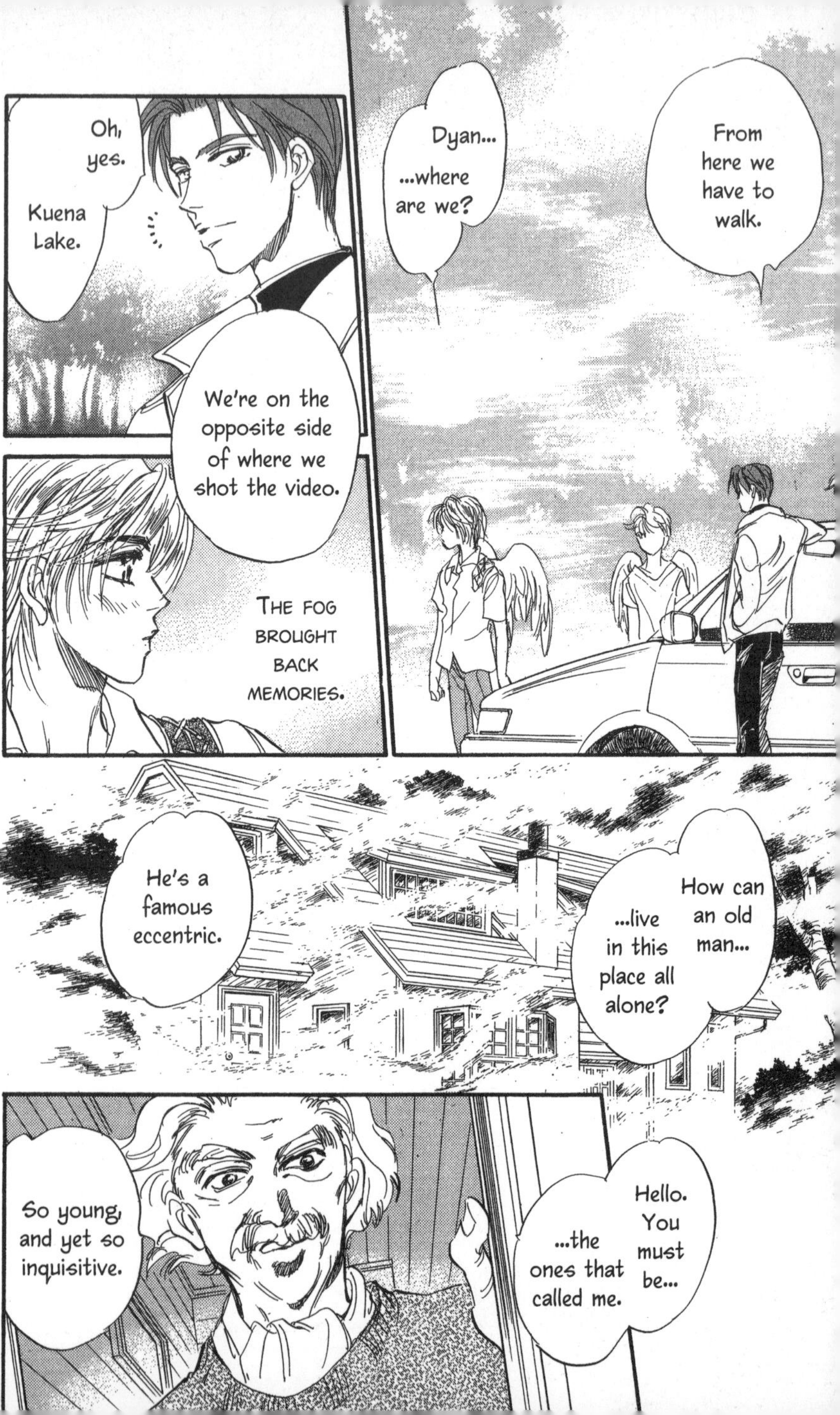
Dyan... ...where are we?
From here we have to walk.
Oh, yes.
Kuena Lake.
We're on the opposite side of where we shot the video.
THE FOG BROUGHT BACK MEMORIES.
How can an old man...
...live in this place all alone?
He's a famous eccentric.
Hello. You must be...
...the ones that called me.
So young, and yet so inquisitive.

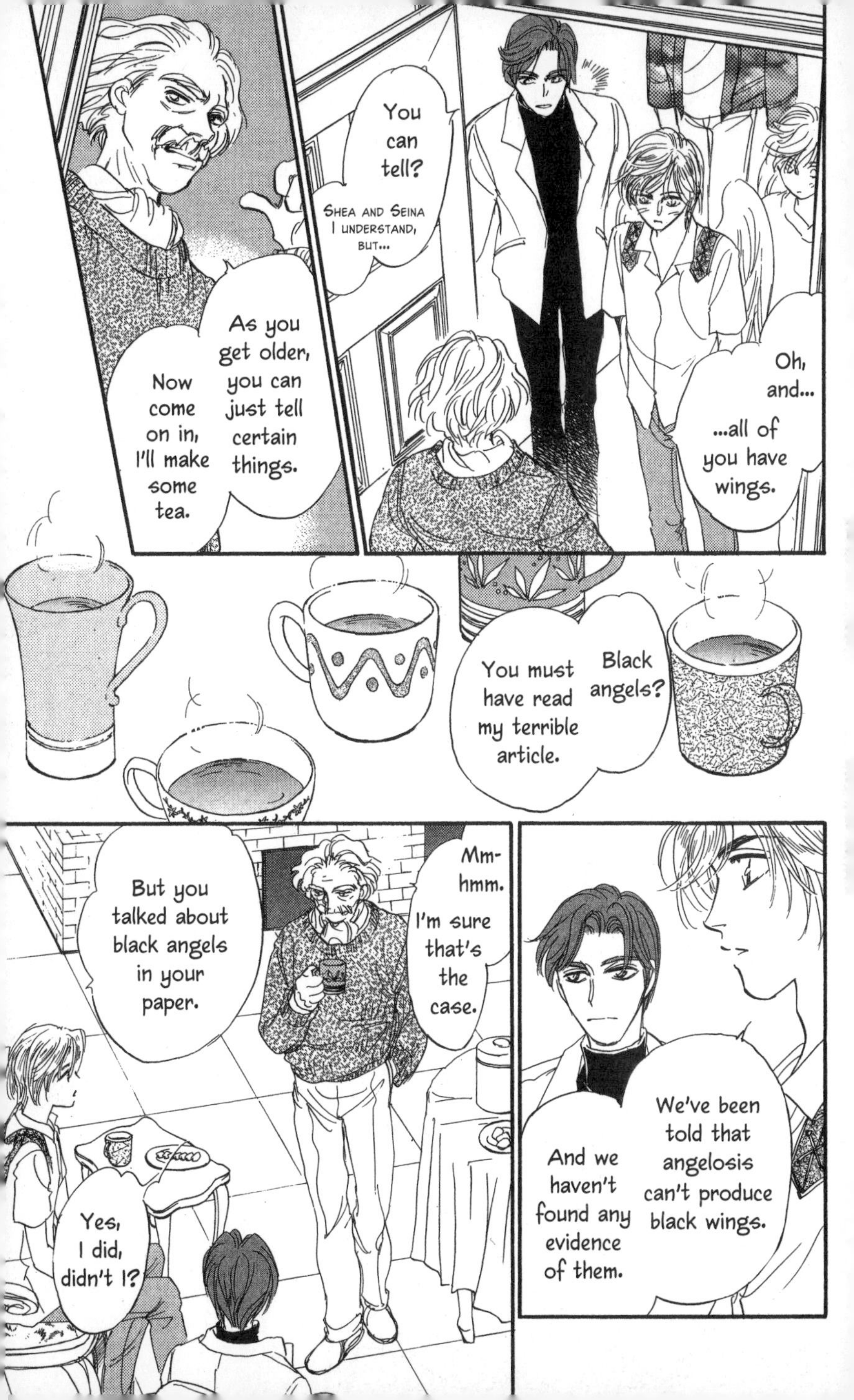
You can tell?
Shea and Seina I understand, but...
Oh, and...
...all of you have wings.
As you get older, you can just tell certain things.
Now come on in, I'll make some tea.
Black angels?
You must have read my terrible article.
We've been told that angelosis can't produce black wings.
And we haven't found any evidence of them.
Mm-hmm.
I'm sure that's the case.
But you talked about black angels in your paper.
Yes, I did, didn't I?

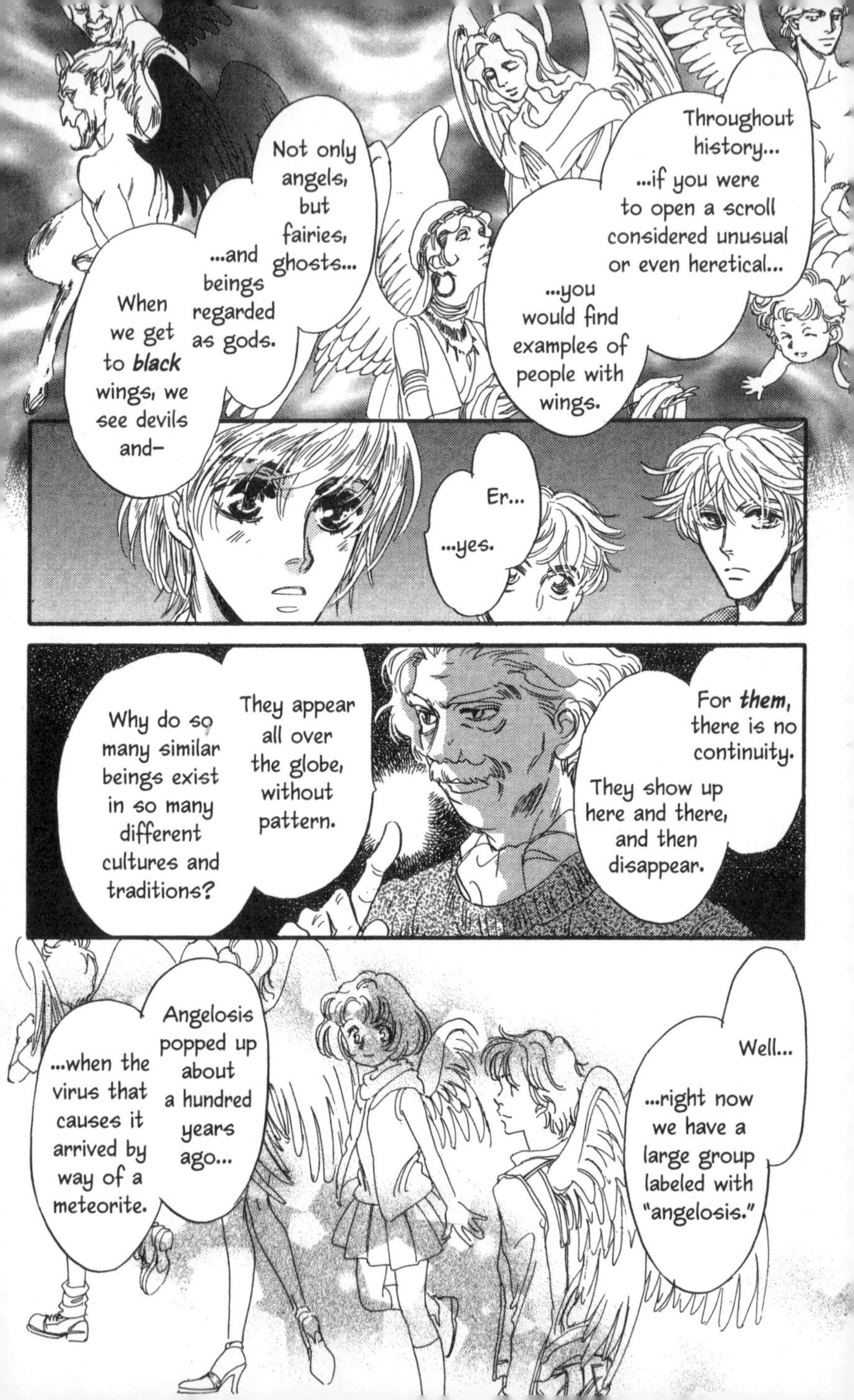
Throughout history...
...if you were to open a scroll considered unusual or even heretical...
...you would find examples of people with wings.
Not only angels, but fairies, ghosts...
...and beings regarded as gods.
When we get to ***black*** wings, we see devils and–
Er...
...yes.
For ***them***, there is no continuity.
They show up here and there, and then disappear.
They appear all over the globe, without pattern.
Why do so many similar beings exist in so many different cultures and traditions?
Well...
...right now we have a large group labeled with "angelosis."
Angelosis popped up about a hundred years ago...
...when the virus that causes it arrived by way of a meteorite.

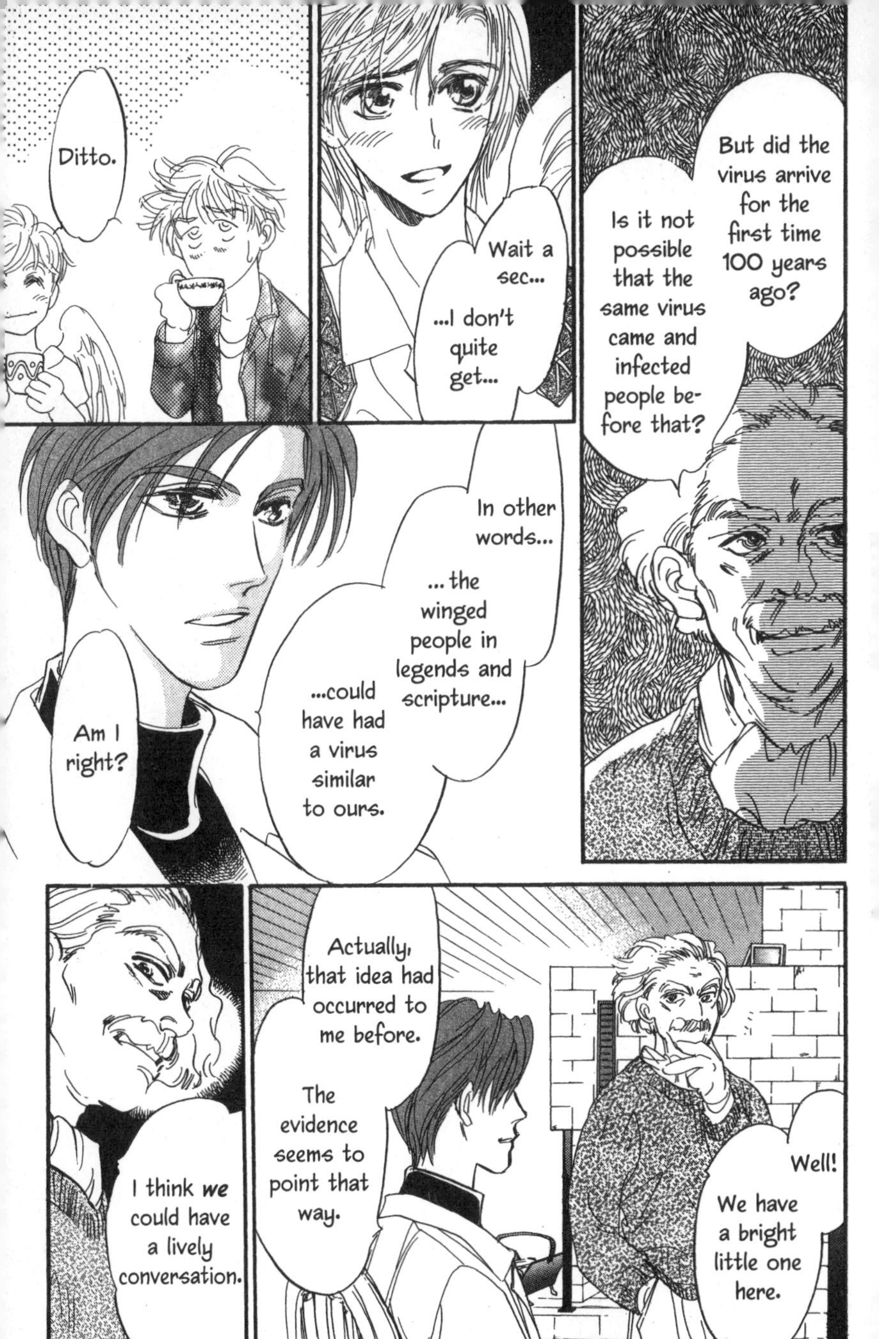

But did the virus arrive for the first time 100 years ago?
Is it not possible that the same virus came and infected people be-fore that?
Wait a sec...
...I don't quite get...
Ditto.
In other words...
... the winged people in legends and scripture...
...could have had a virus similar to ours.
Am I right?
Well!
We have a bright little one here.
Actually, that idea had occurred to me before.
The evidence seems to point that way.
I think *we* could have a lively conversation.

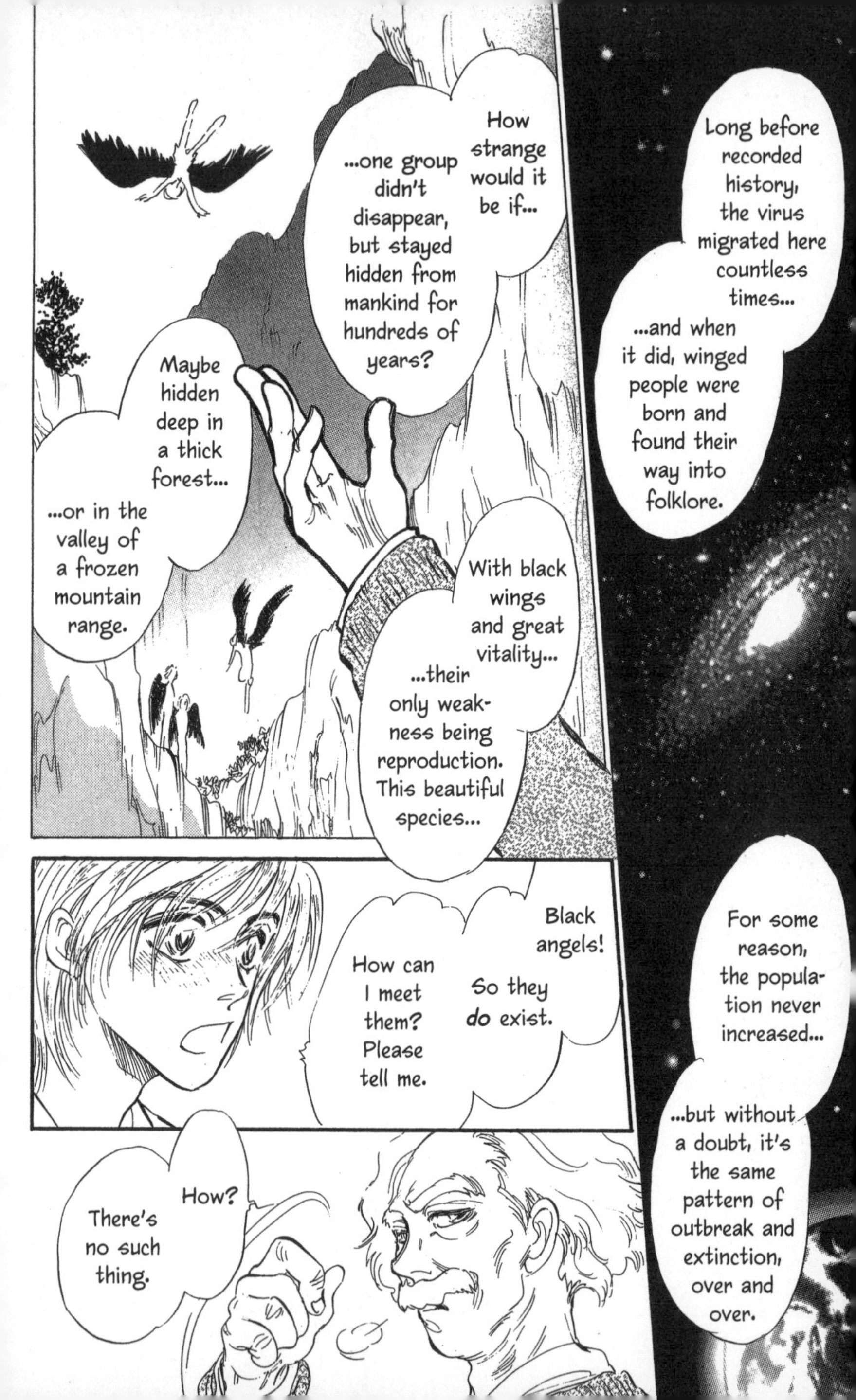
Long before recorded history, the virus migrated here countless times...
...and when it did, winged people were born and found their way into folklore.
For some reason, the population never increased...
...but without a doubt, it's the same pattern of outbreak and extinction, over and over.
How strange would it be if...
...one group didn't disappear, but stayed hidden from mankind for hundreds of years?
Maybe hidden deep in a thick forest...
...or in the valley of a frozen mountain range.
With black wings and great vitality...
...their only weakness being reproduction. This beautiful species...
Black angels!
So they *do* exist.
How can I meet them? Please tell me.
How?
There's no such thing.

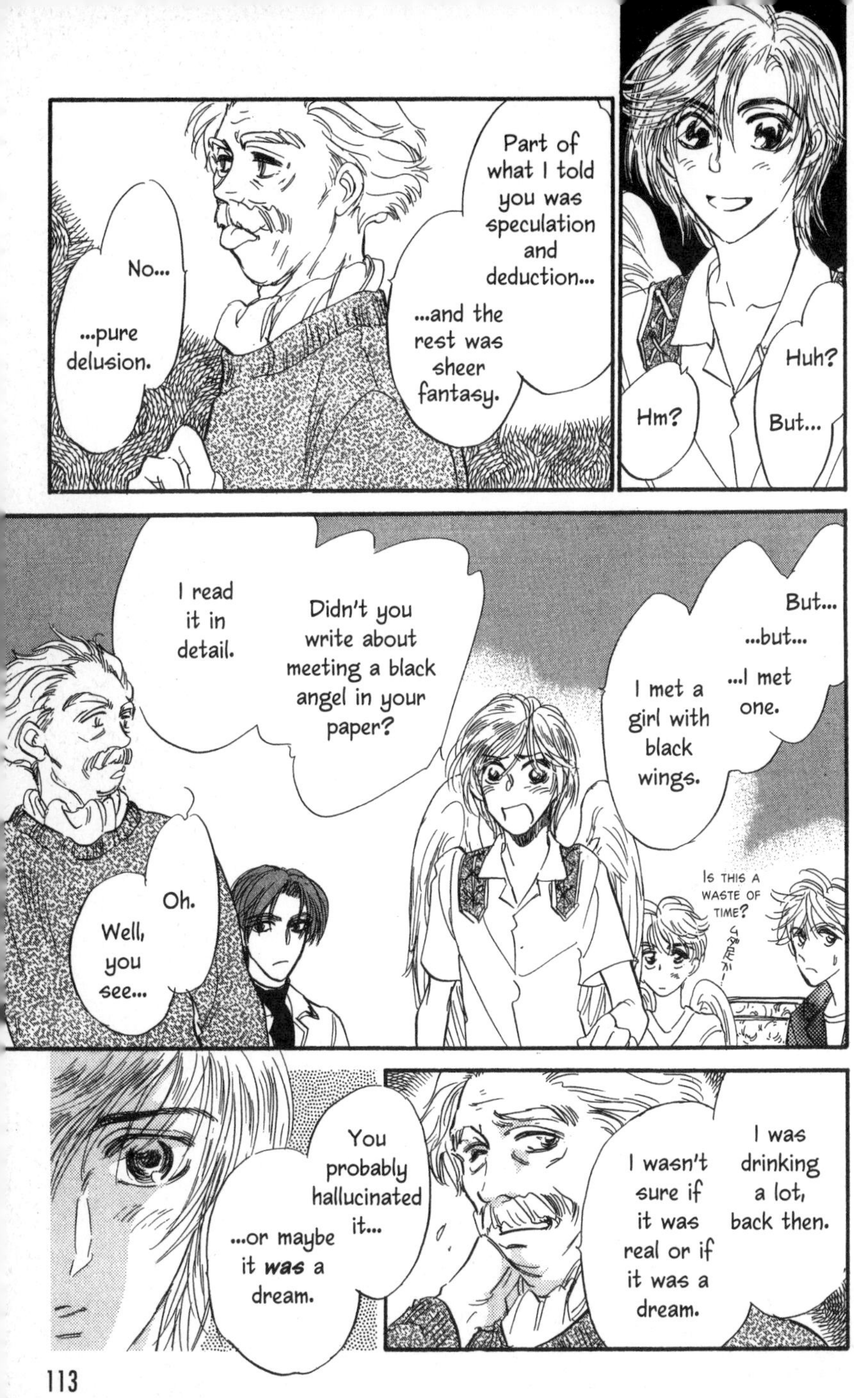
Huh? But...
Hm?
Part of what I told you was speculation and deduction...
...and the rest was sheer fantasy.
No...
...pure delusion.
But... ...but... ...I met one.
I met a girl with black wings.
Didn't you write about meeting a black angel in your paper?
I read it in detail.
Is this a waste of time?
Oh.
Well, you see...
I was drinking a lot, back then.
I wasn't sure if it was real or if it was a dream.
You probably hallucinated it...
...or maybe it *was* a dream.

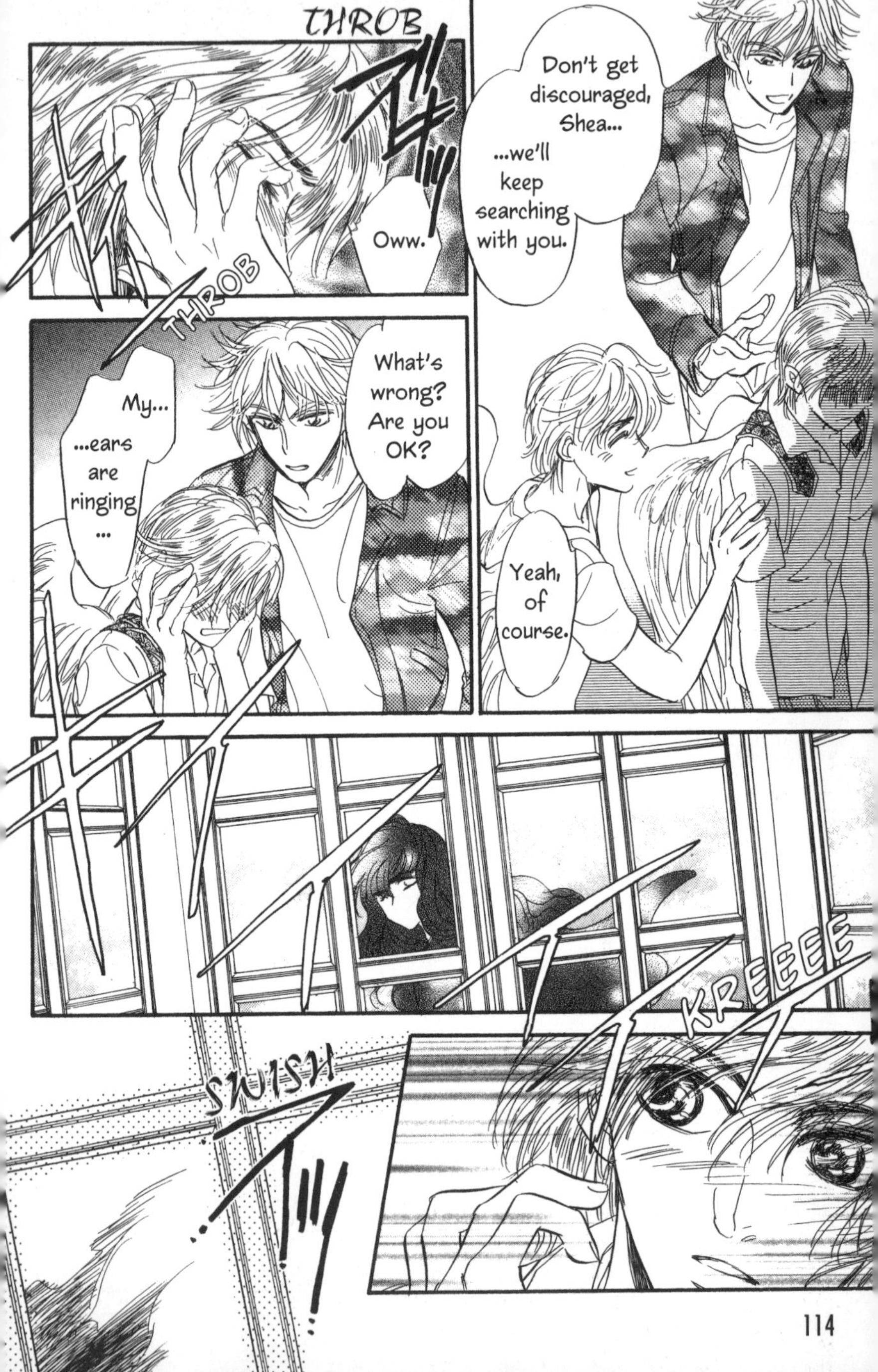
Don't get discouraged, Shea...
...we'll keep searching with you.
Yeah, of course.
THROB
Oww.
THROB
What's wrong? Are you OK?
My...
...ears are ringing...
KREEEE
SWISH
...

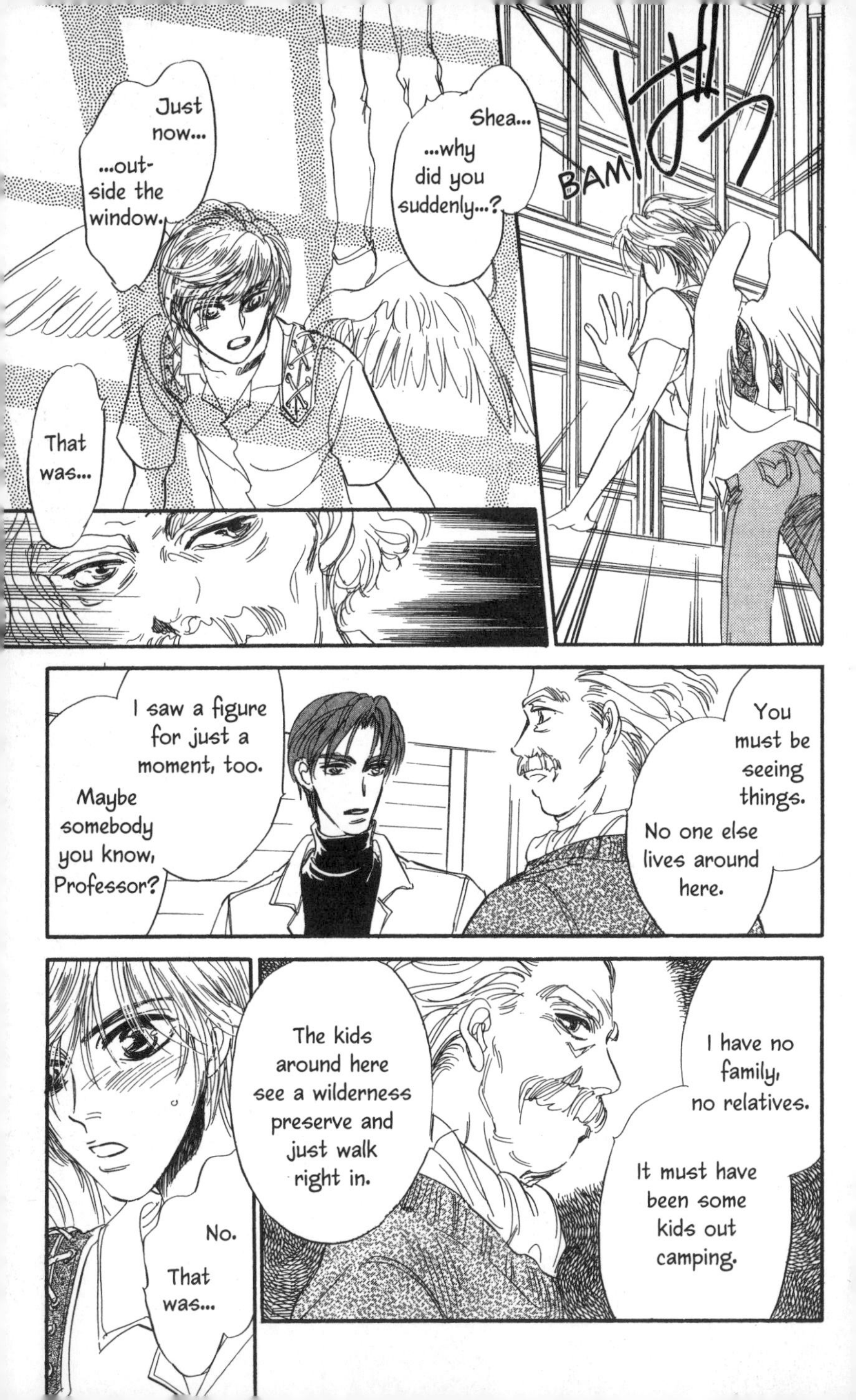
BAM
Shea...
...why did you suddenly...?
Just now...
...out-side the window.
That was...
You must be seeing things.
No one else lives around here.
I saw a figure for just a moment, too.
Maybe somebody you know, Professor?
I have no family, no relatives.
It must have been some kids out camping.
The kids around here see a wilderness preserve and just walk right in.
No.
That was...

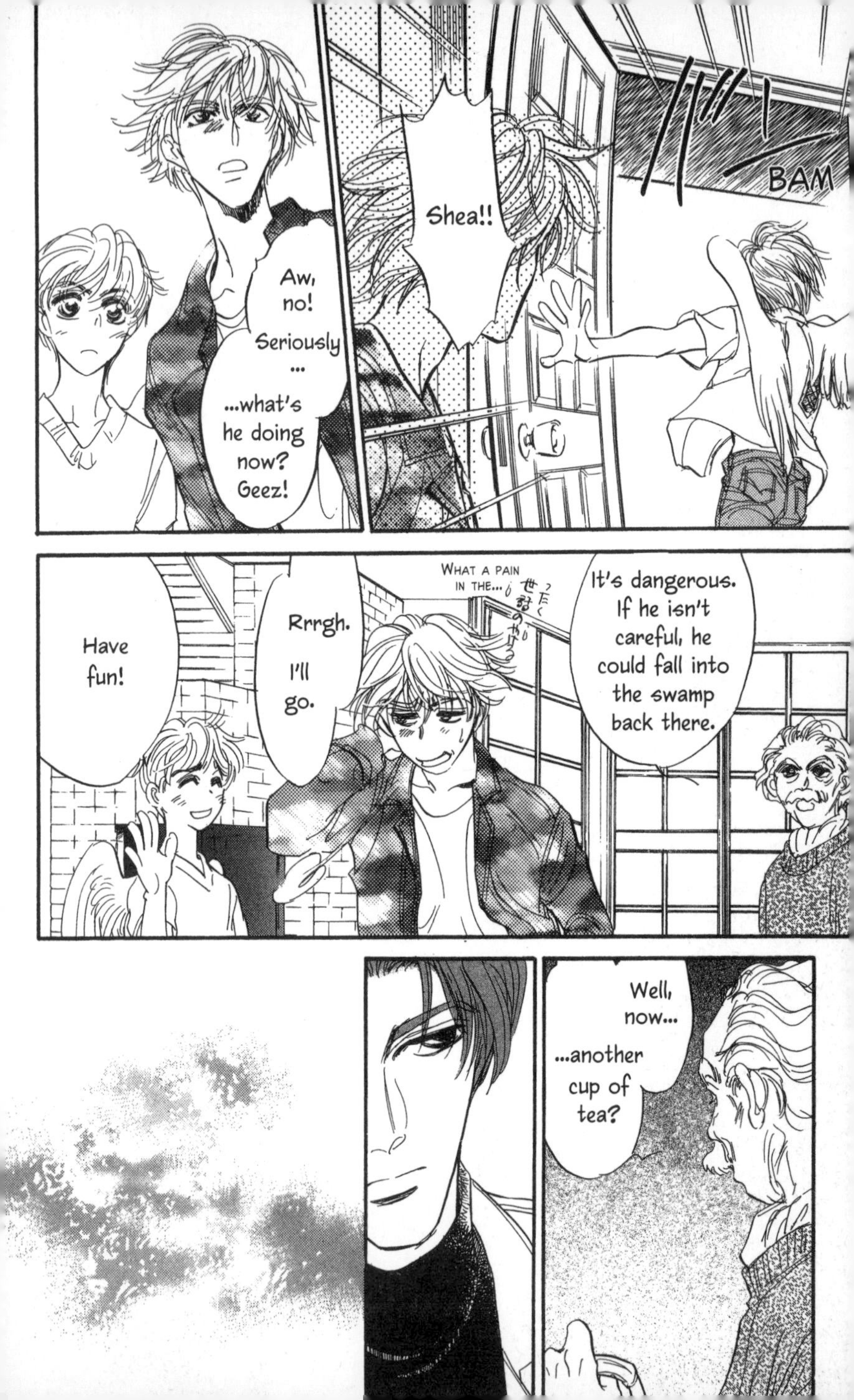
BAM
Shea!!
Aw, no!
Seriously...
...what's he doing now? Geez!
It's dangerous. If he isn't careful, he could fall into the swamp back there.
WHAT A PAIN IN THE...
Rrrgh.
I'll go.
Have fun!
Well, now...
...another cup of tea?

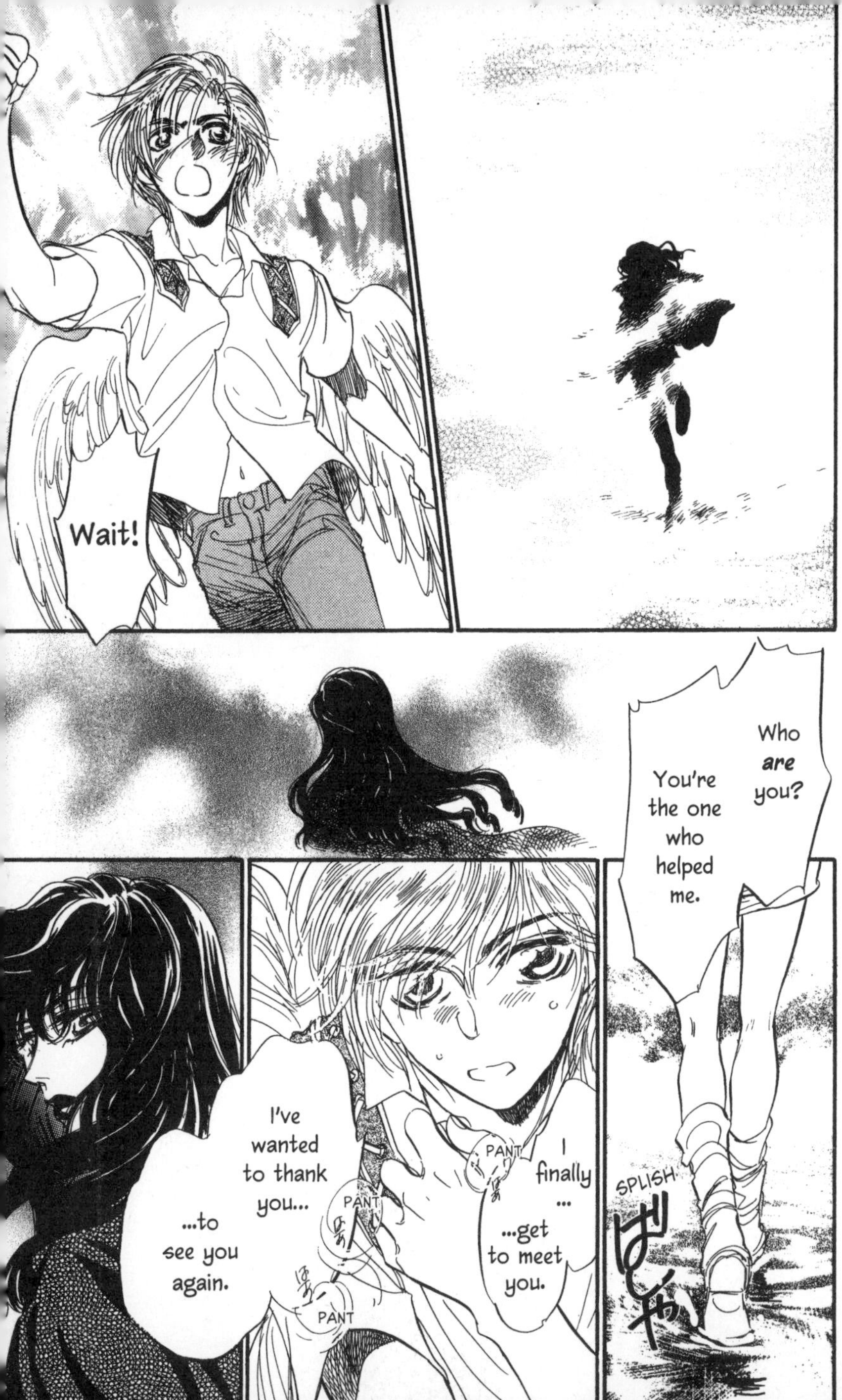
Wait!
Who **are** you?
You're the one who helped me.
SPLISH
ぱしゃ
PANT
I finally...
...get to meet you.
PANT
PANT
I've wanted to thank you...
...to see you again.

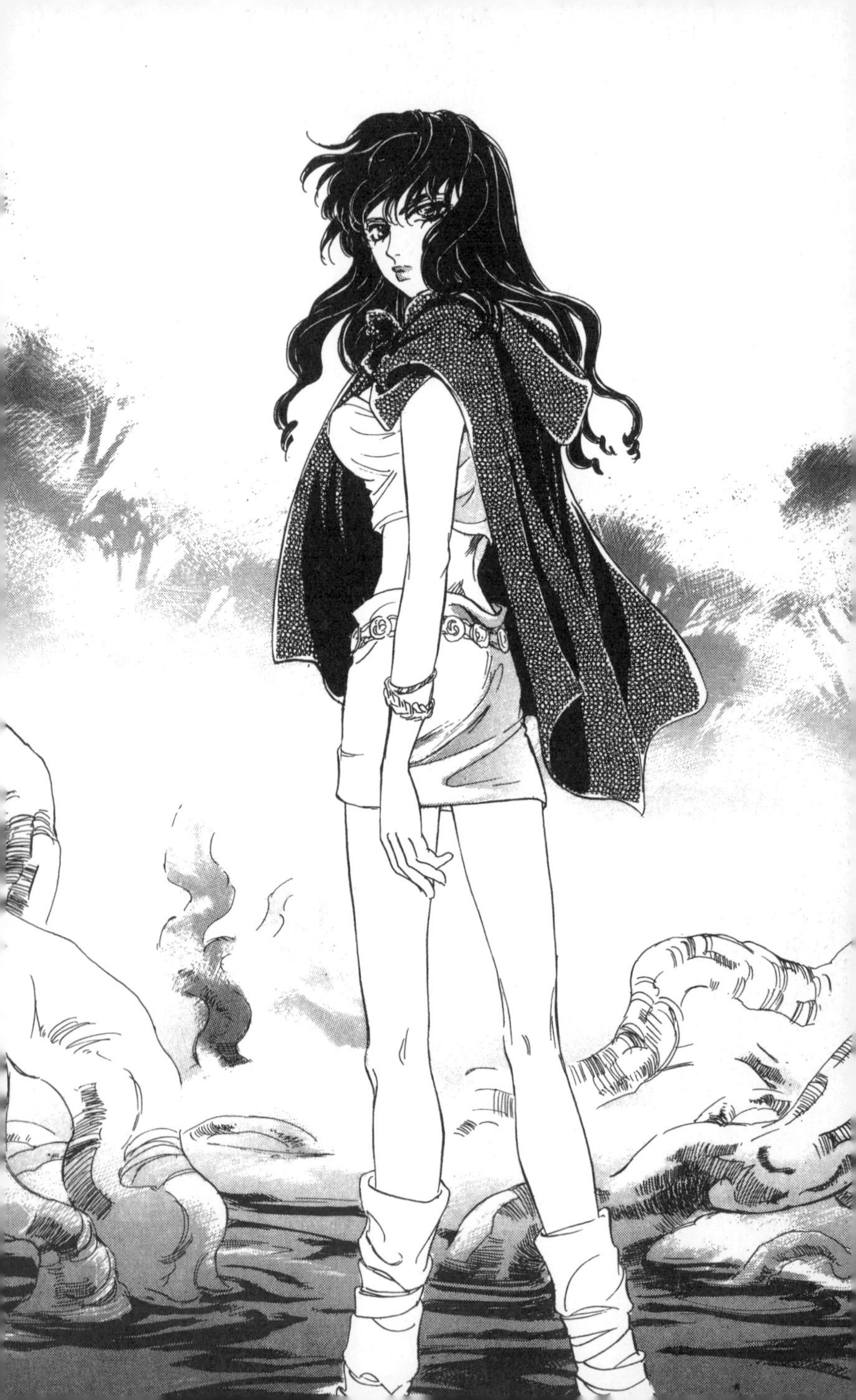

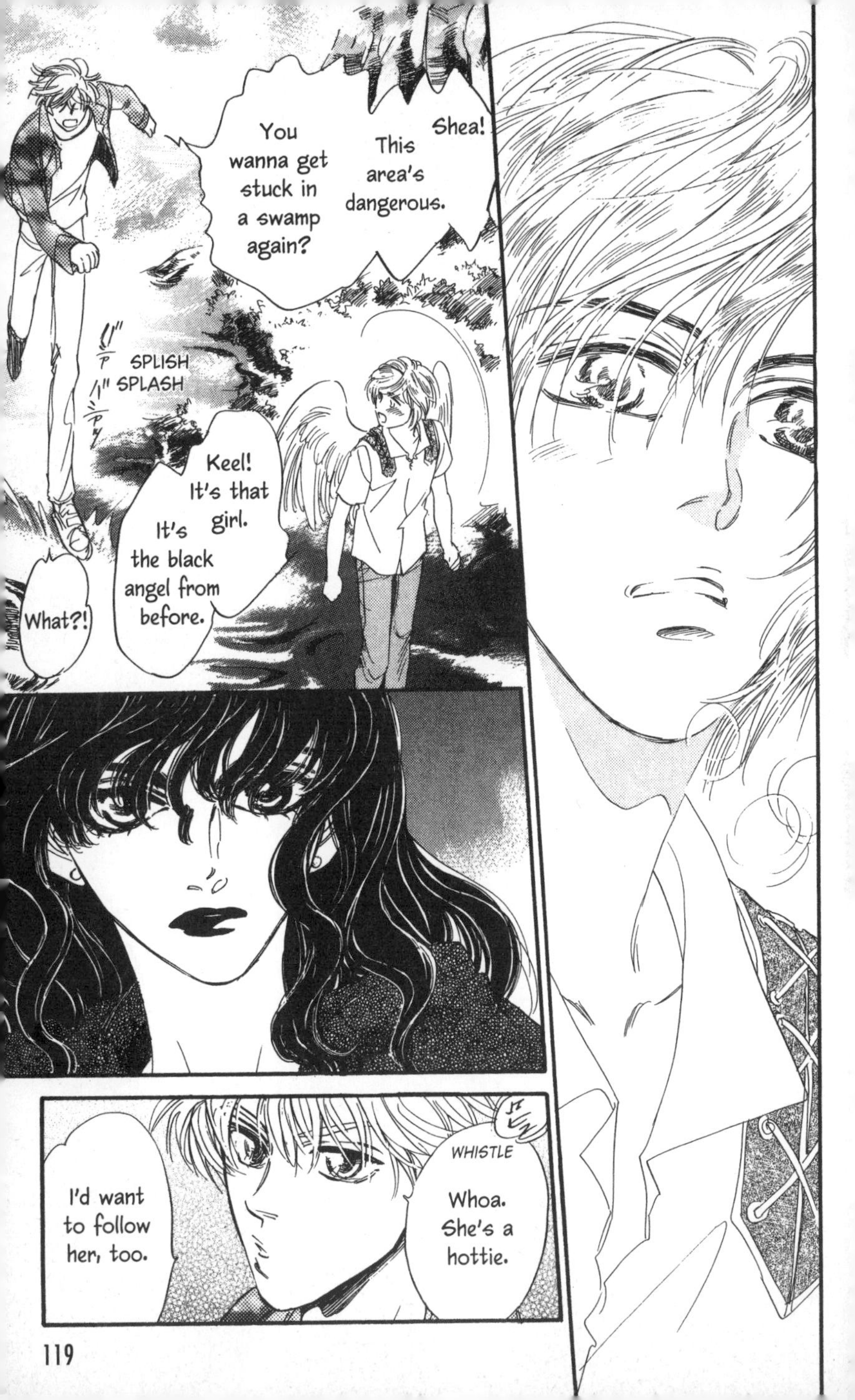
Shea!
This area's dangerous.
You wanna get stuck in a swamp again?
SPLISH SPLASH
Keel! It's that girl.
It's the black angel from before.
What?!
WHISTLE
Whoa. She's a hottie.
I'd want to follow her, too.

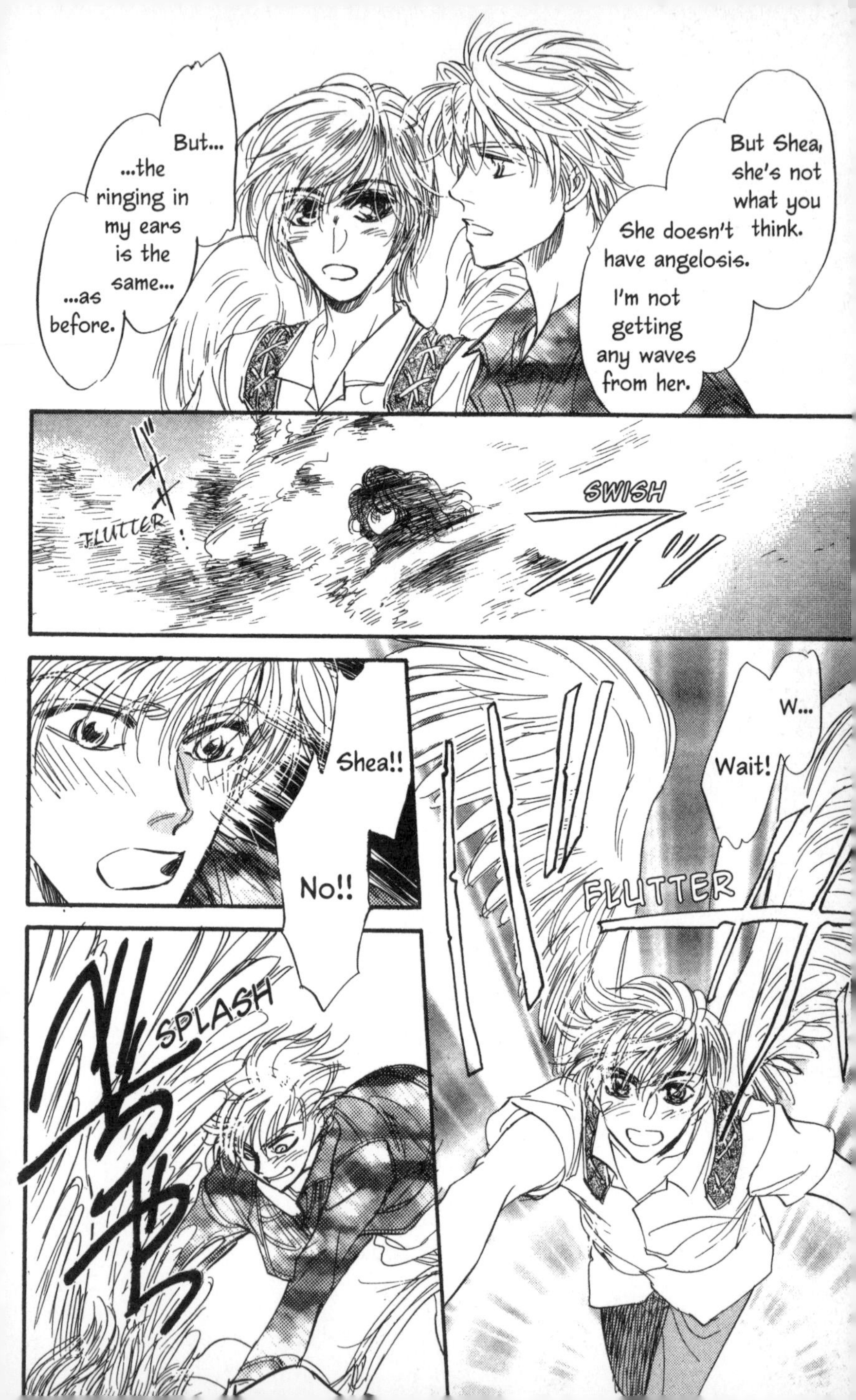
But Shea, she's not what you think.
She doesn't have angelosis.
I'm not getting any waves from her.
But...
...the ringing in my ears is the same...
...as before.
SWISH
FLUTTER
W...
Wait!
FLUTTER
Shea!!
No!!
SPLASH

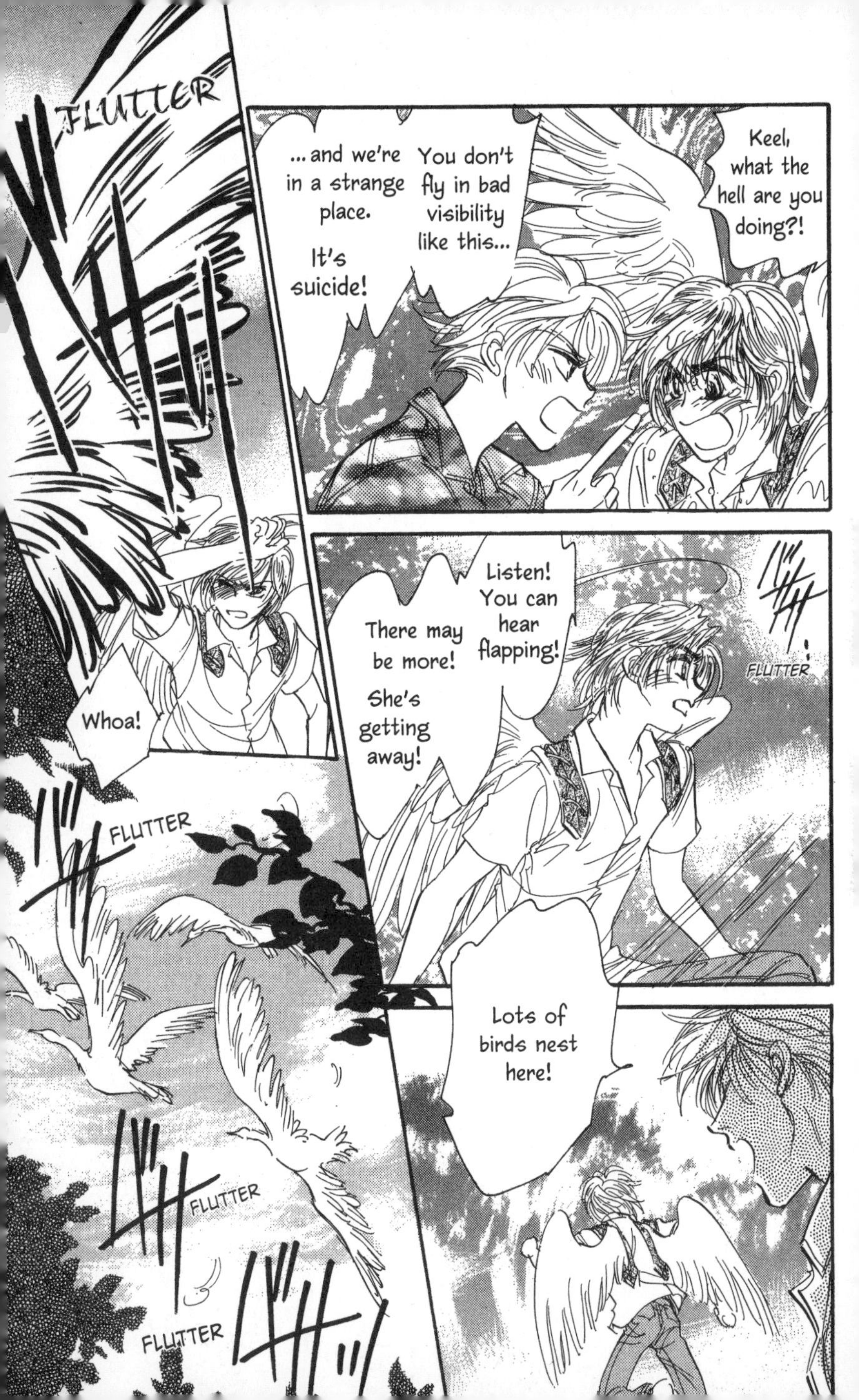
Keel, what the hell are you doing?!
You don't fly in bad visibility like this...
...and we're in a strange place.
It's suicide!
FLUTTER
Listen! You can hear flapping!
There may be more!
She's getting away!
Lots of birds nest here!
FLUTTER
Whoa!
FLUTTER
FLUTTER
FLUTTER

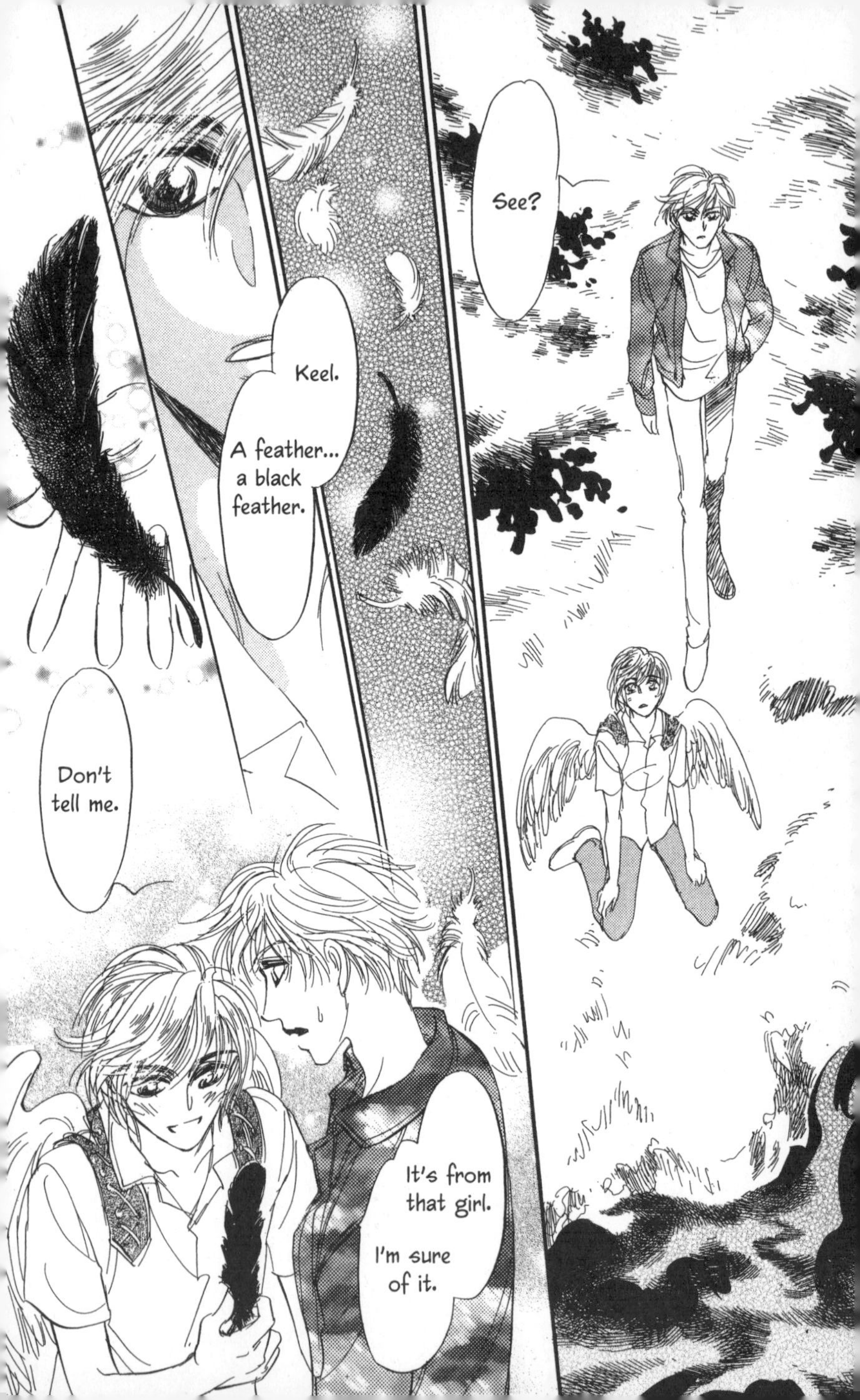
See?
Keel.
A feather... a black feather.
Don't tell me.
It's from that girl.
I'm sure of it.

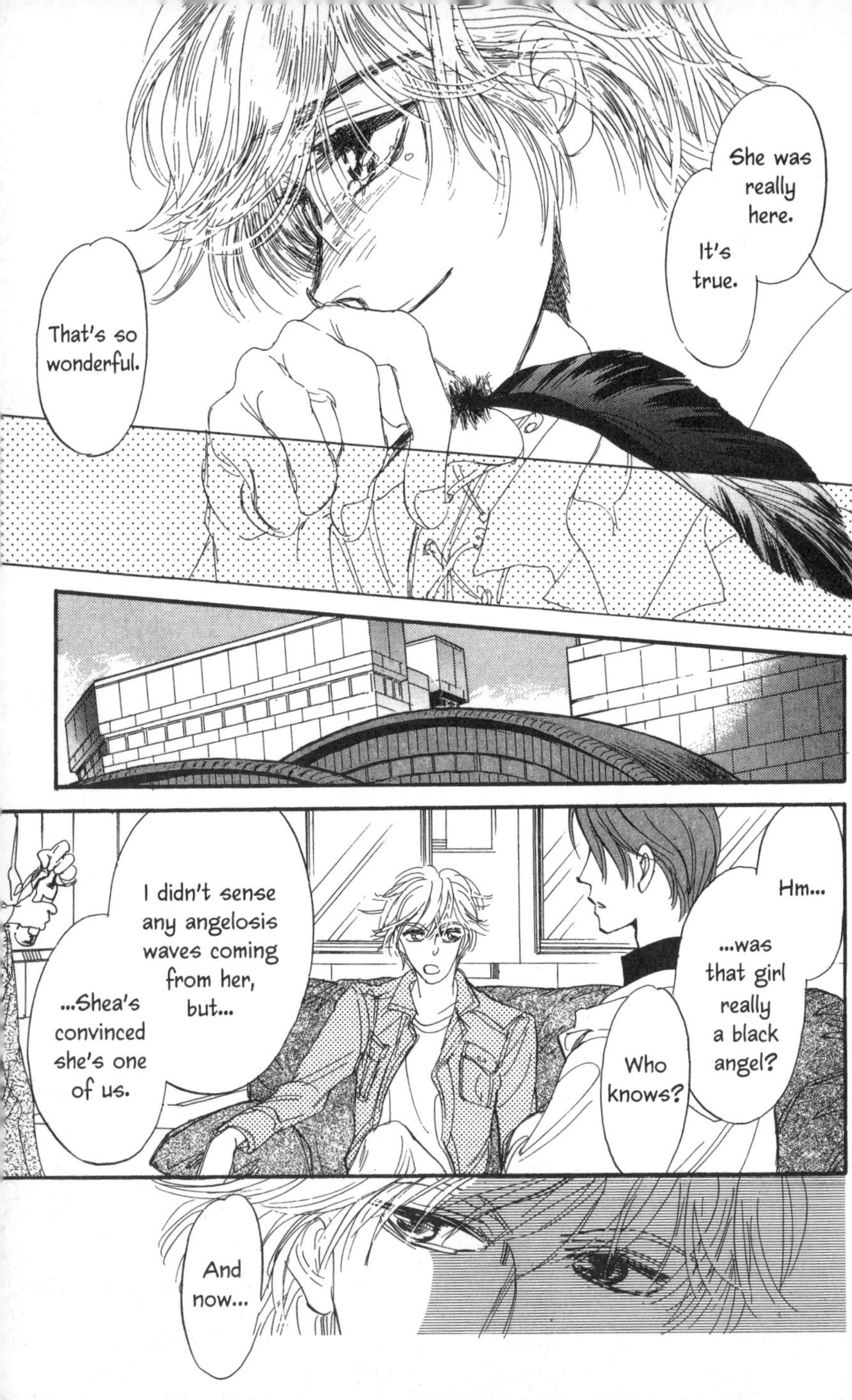
She was really here.
It's true.
That's so wonderful.
Hm...
...was that girl really a black angel?
Who knows?
I didn't sense any angelosis waves coming from her, but...
...Shea's convinced she's one of us.
And now...

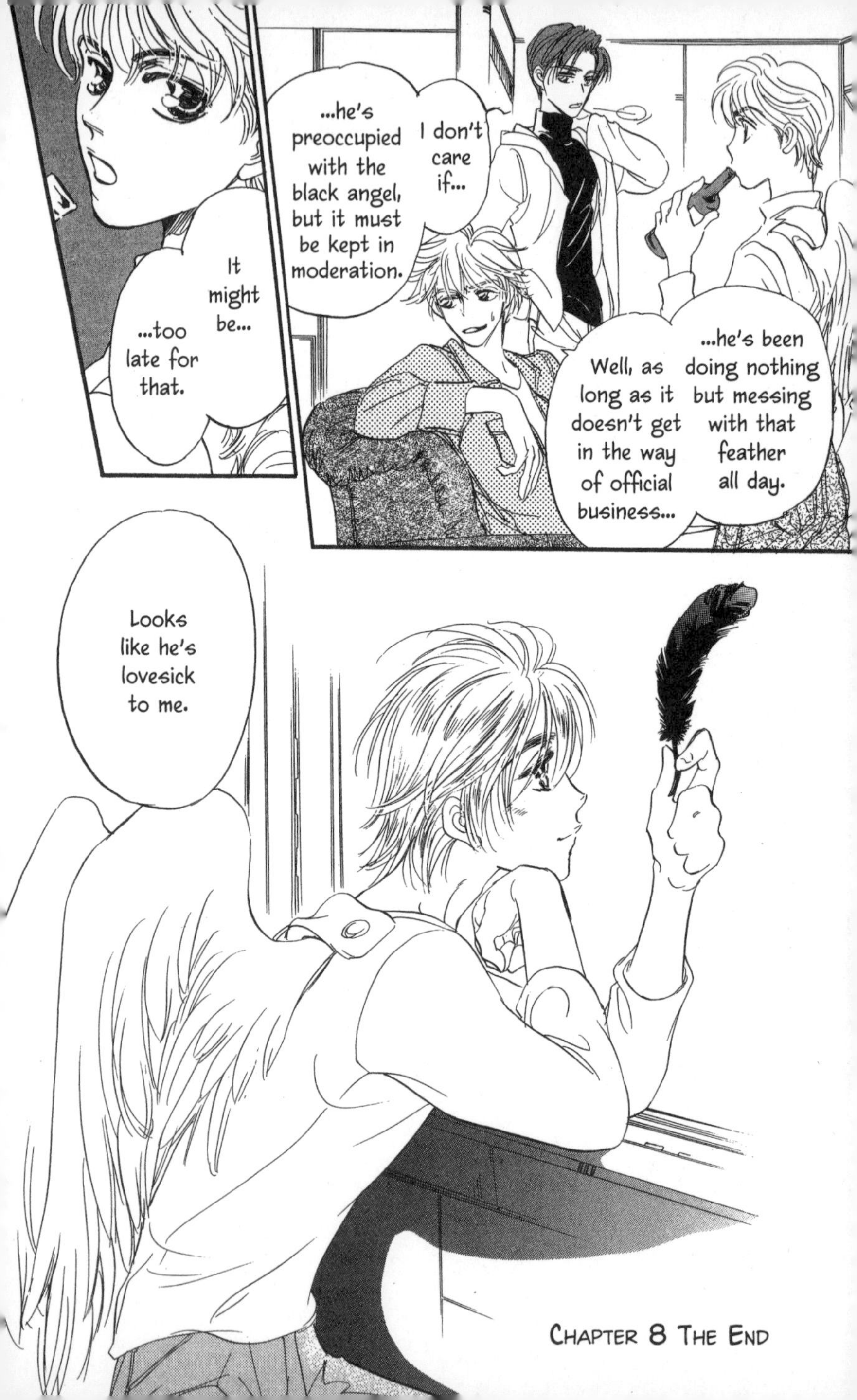
I don't care if...
...he's preoccupied with the black angel, but it must be kept in moderation.
...he's been doing nothing but messing with that feather all day.
Well, as long as it doesn't get in the way of official business...
It might be...
...too late for that.
Looks like he's lovesick to me.
Chapter 8 The End

Chapter 9

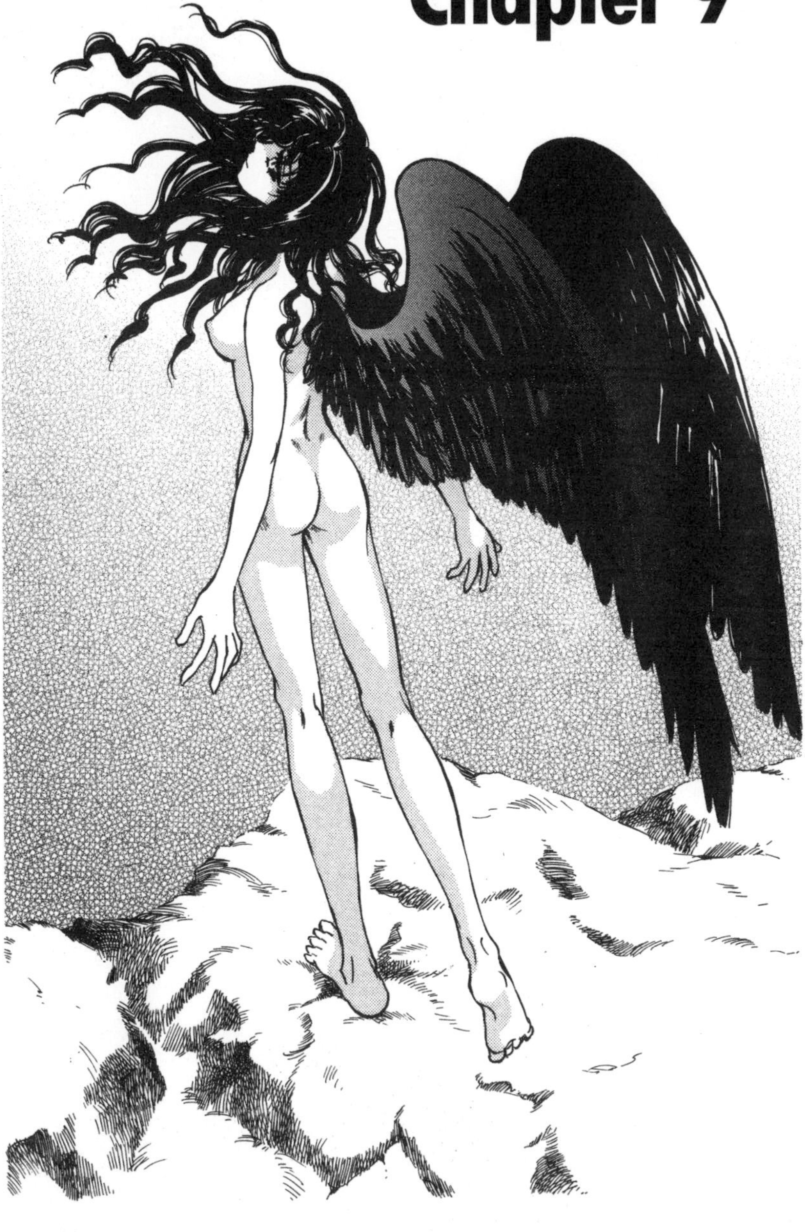

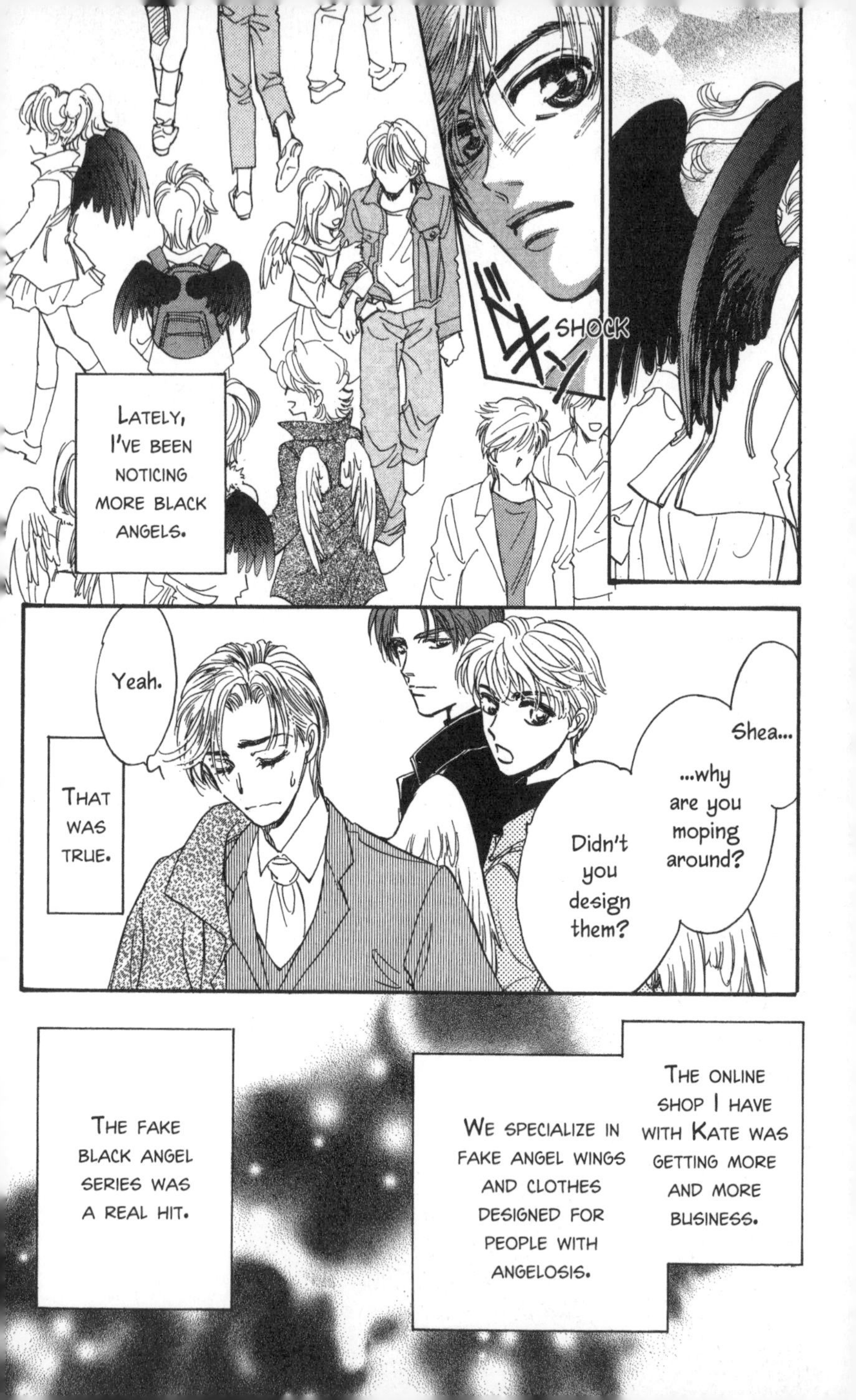
SHOCK
Lately, I've been noticing more black angels.
Shea...
...why are you moping around?
Didn't you design them?
Yeah.
That was true.
The online shop I have with Kate was getting more and more business.
We specialize in fake angel wings and clothes designed for people with angelosis.
The fake black angel series was a real hit.

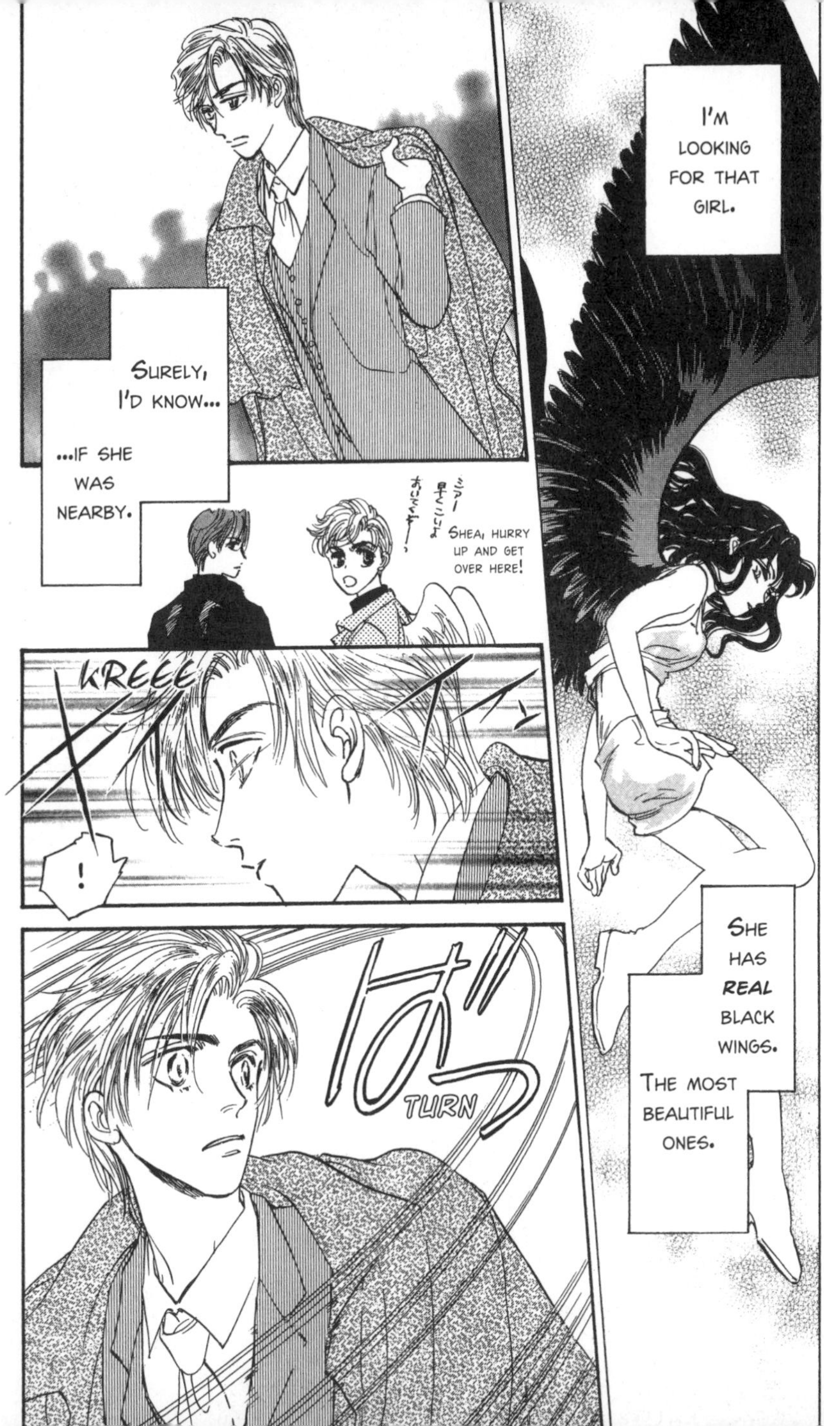
I'M LOOKING FOR THAT GIRL.
SHE HAS **REAL** BLACK WINGS.
THE MOST BEAUTIFUL ONES.
SURELY, I'D KNOW...
...IF SHE WAS NEARBY.
SHEA, HURRY UP AND GET OVER HERE!
KREEE
!
TURN

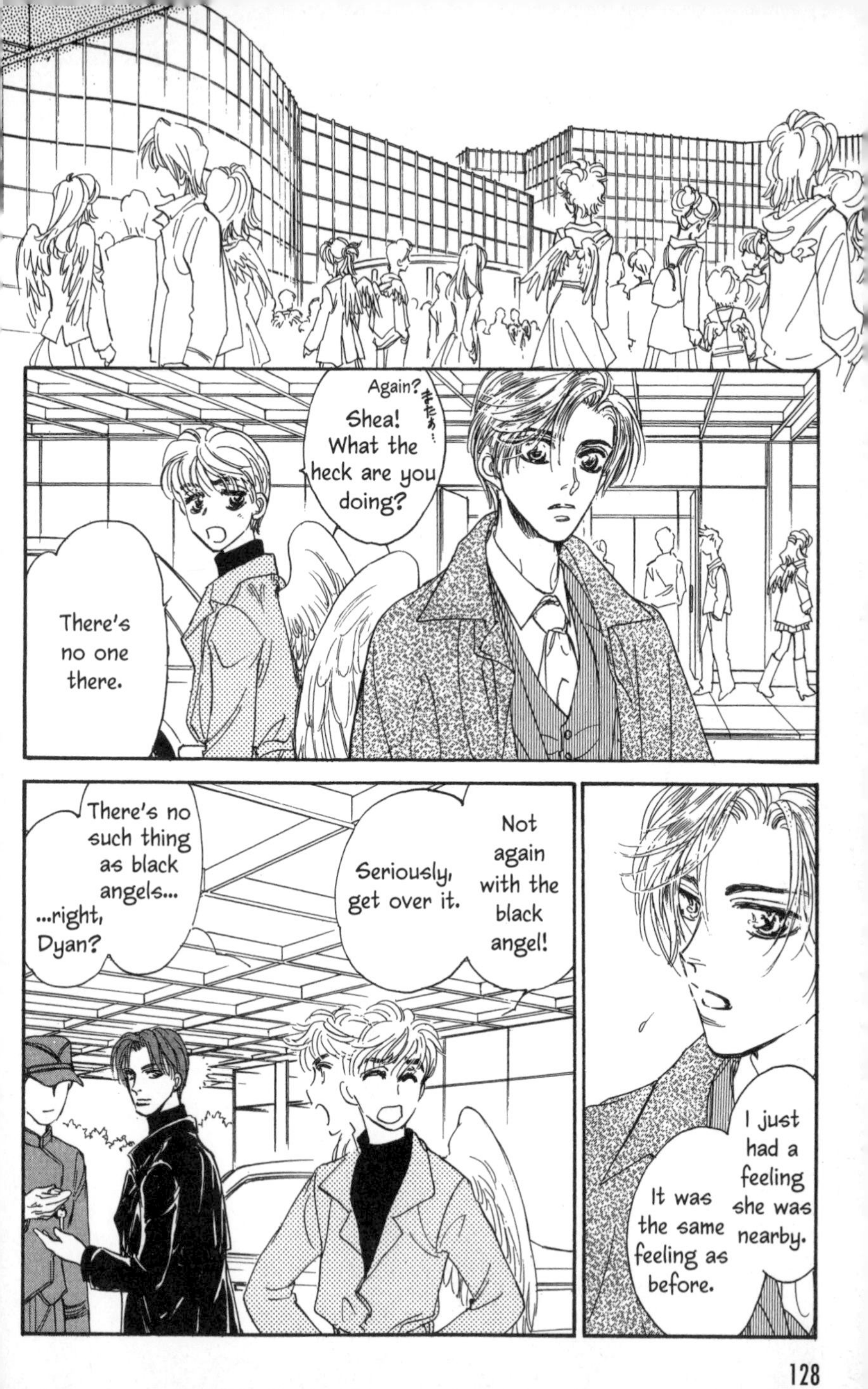
Again? またぁ…
Shea! What the heck are you doing?
There's no one there.
I just had a feeling she was nearby.
It was the same feeling as before.
Not again with the black angel!
Seriously, get over it.
There's no such thing as black angels... ...right, Dyan?

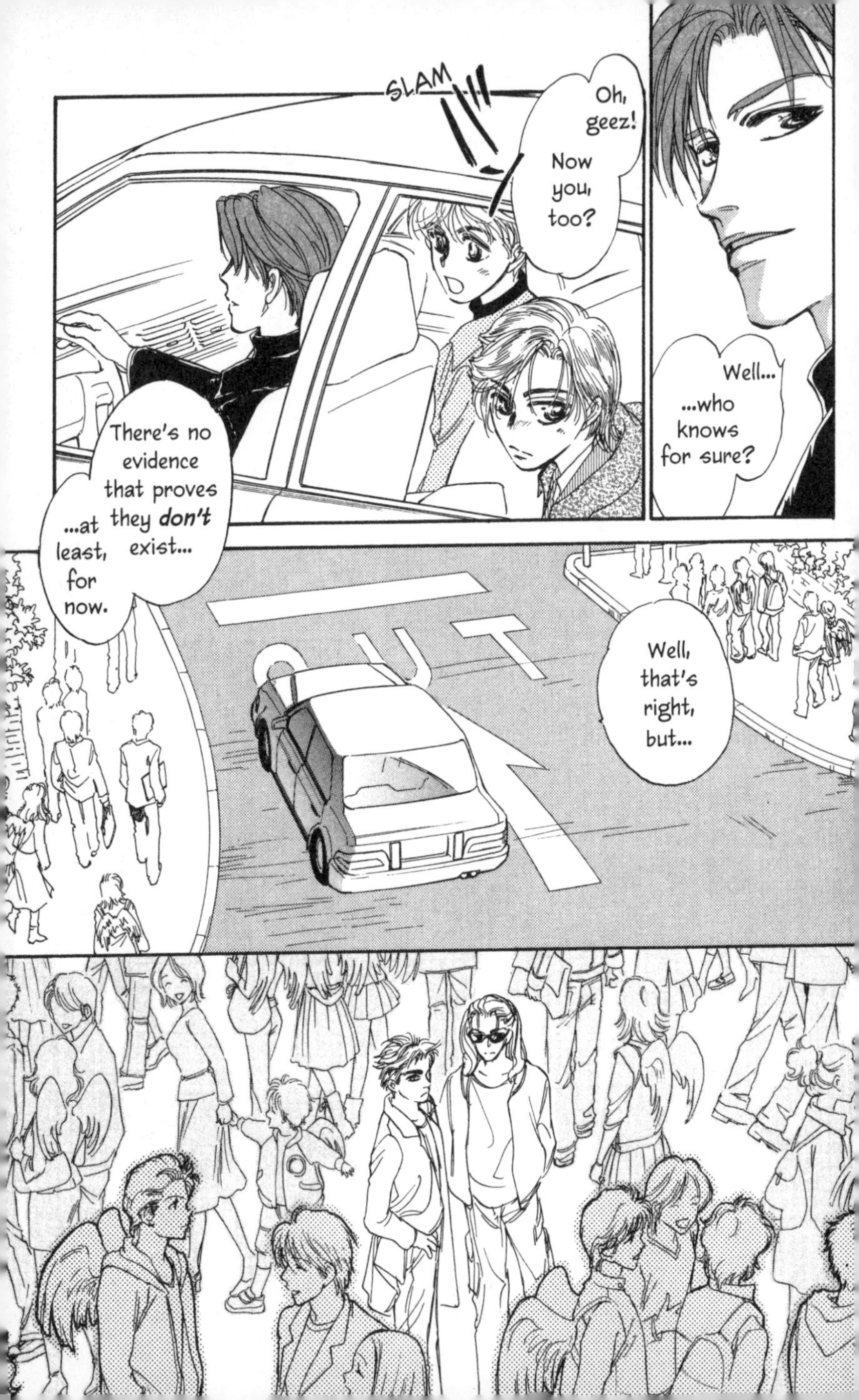
Well...
...who knows for sure?
SLAM
Oh, geez!
Now you, too?
There's no evidence that proves they *don't* exist...
...at least, for now.
Well, that's right, but...

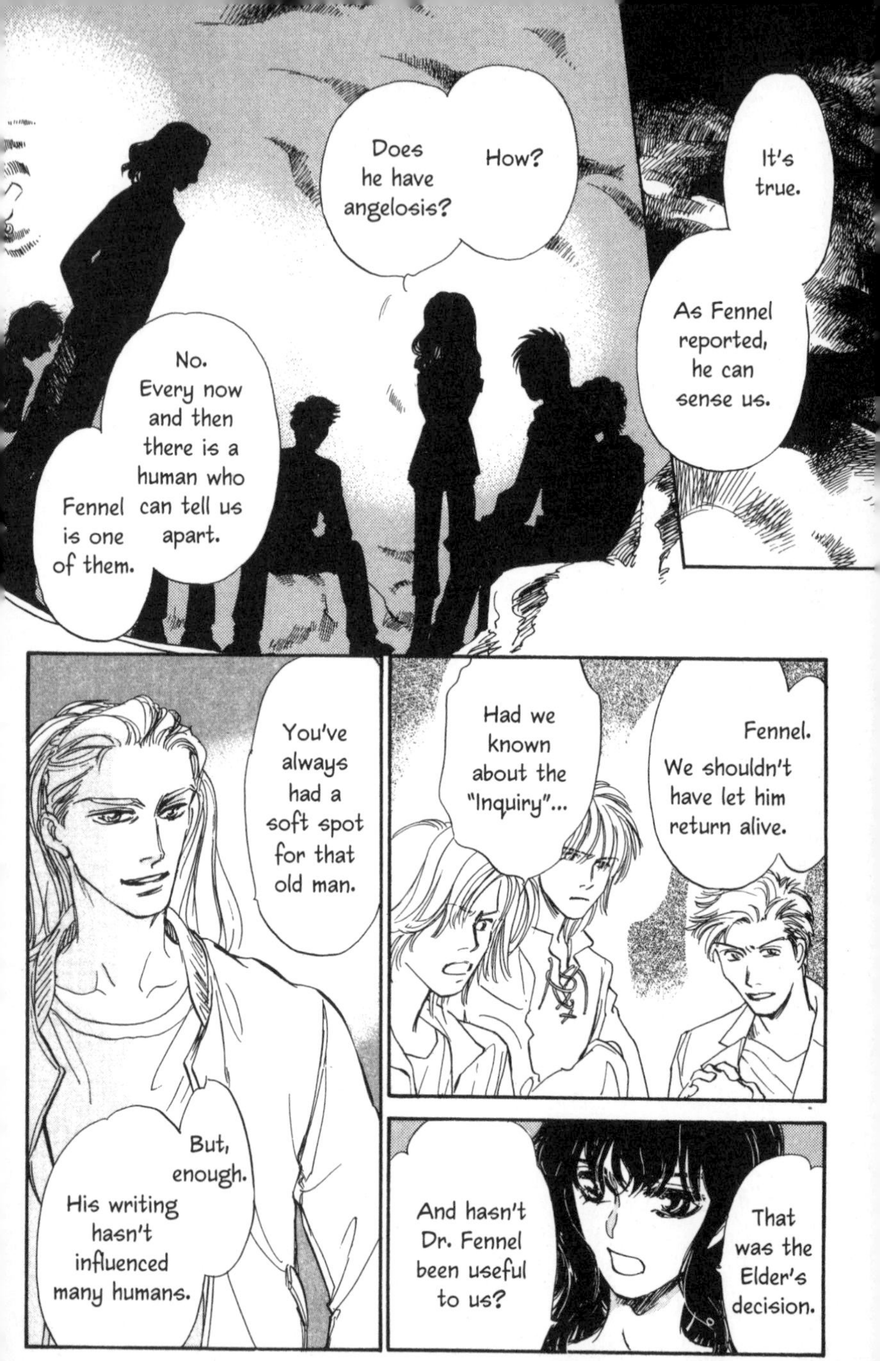
It's true.
As Fennel reported, he can sense us.
How?
Does he have angelosis?
No. Every now and then there is a human who can tell us apart.
Fennel is one of them.
Fennel. We shouldn't have let him return alive.
Had we known about the "Inquiry"...
That was the Elder's decision.
And hasn't Dr. Fennel been useful to us?
You've always had a soft spot for that old man.
But, enough.
His writing hasn't influenced many humans.

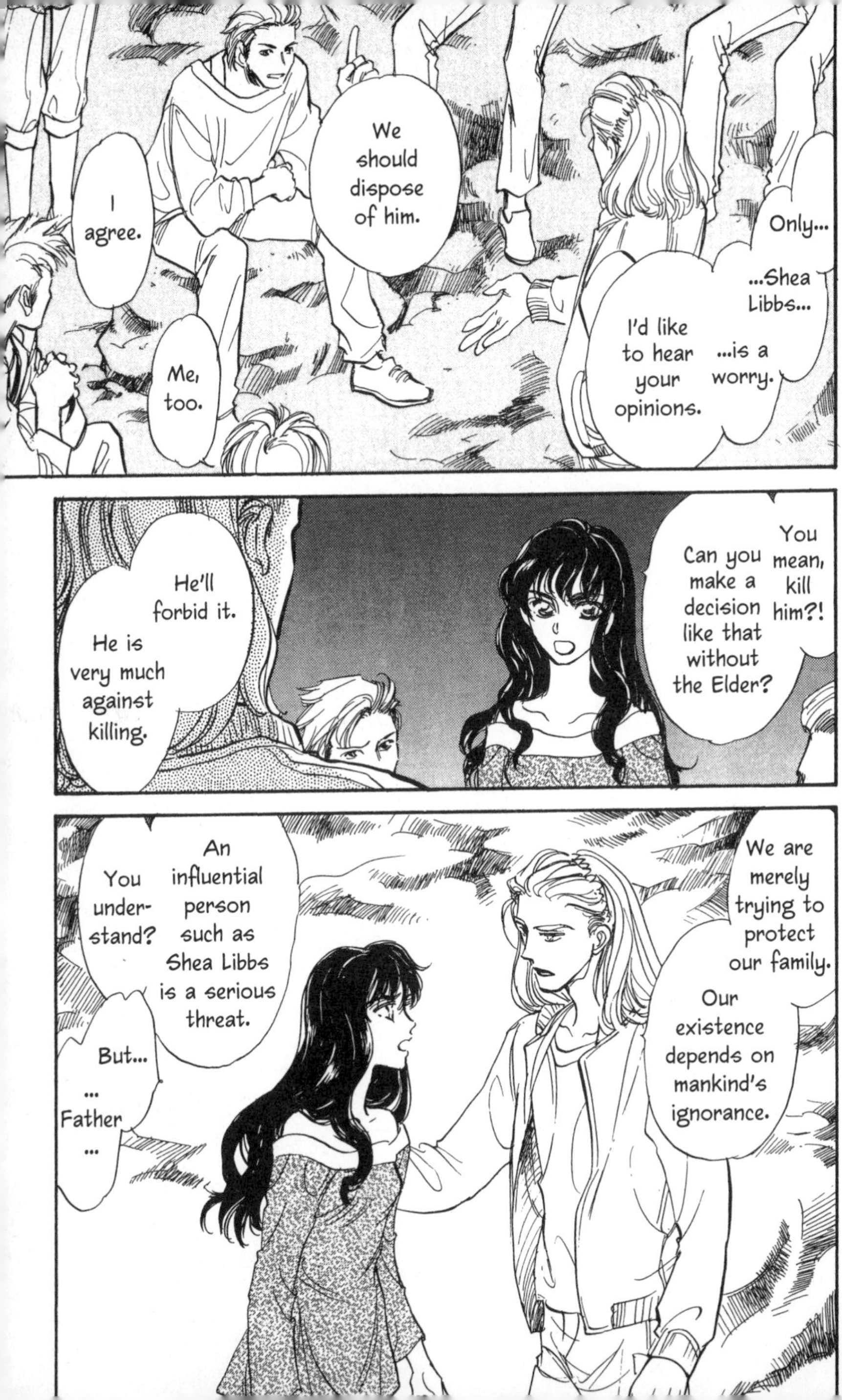
Only...
...Shea Libbs...
...is a worry.
I'd like to hear your opinions.
We should dispose of him.
I agree.
Me, too.
You mean, kill him?!
Can you make a decision like that without the Elder?
He'll forbid it.
He is very much against killing.
We are merely trying to protect our family.
Our existence depends on mankind's ignorance.
An influential person such as Shea Libbs is a serious threat.
You under-stand?
But...
...Father...

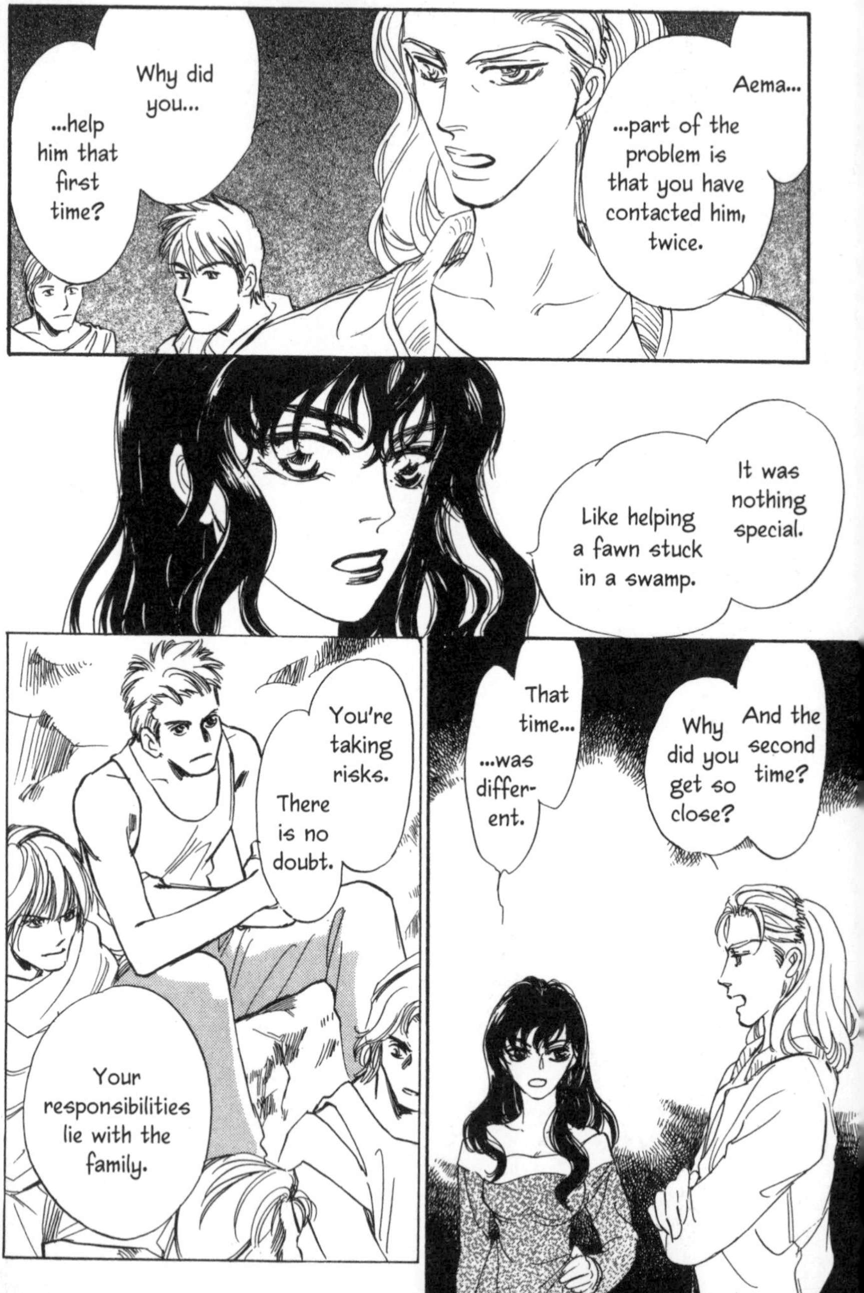
Aema...
...part of the problem is that you have contacted him, twice.
Why did you...
...help him that first time?
It was nothing special.
Like helping a fawn stuck in a swamp.
And the second time?
Why did you get so close?
That time...
...was differ-ent.
You're taking risks.
There is no doubt.
Your responsibilities lie with the family.

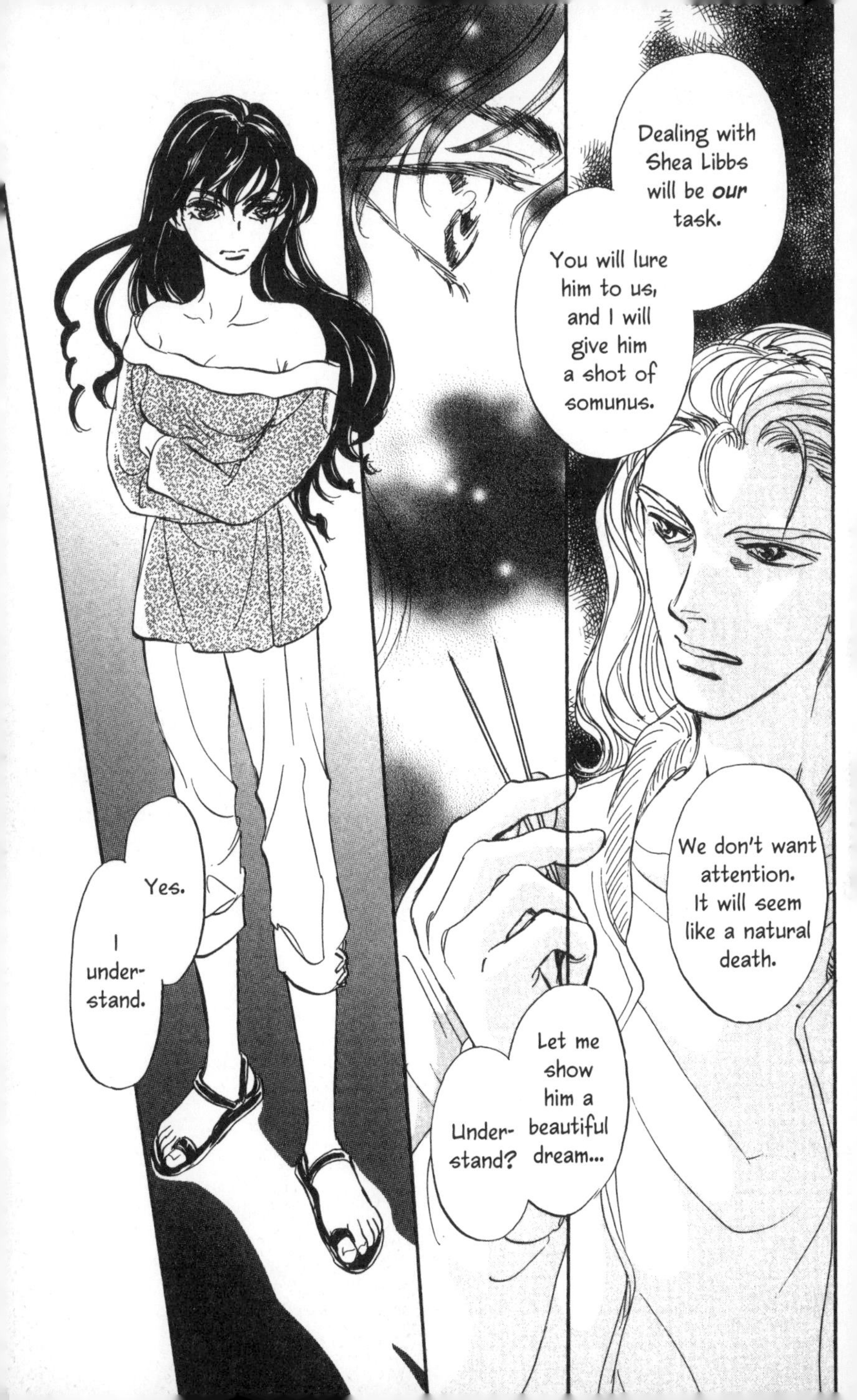
Dealing with Shea Libbs will be ***our*** task.
You will lure him to us, and I will give him a shot of somunus.
We don't want attention. It will seem like a natural death.
Let me show him a beautiful dream...
Under-stand?
Yes.
I under-stand.

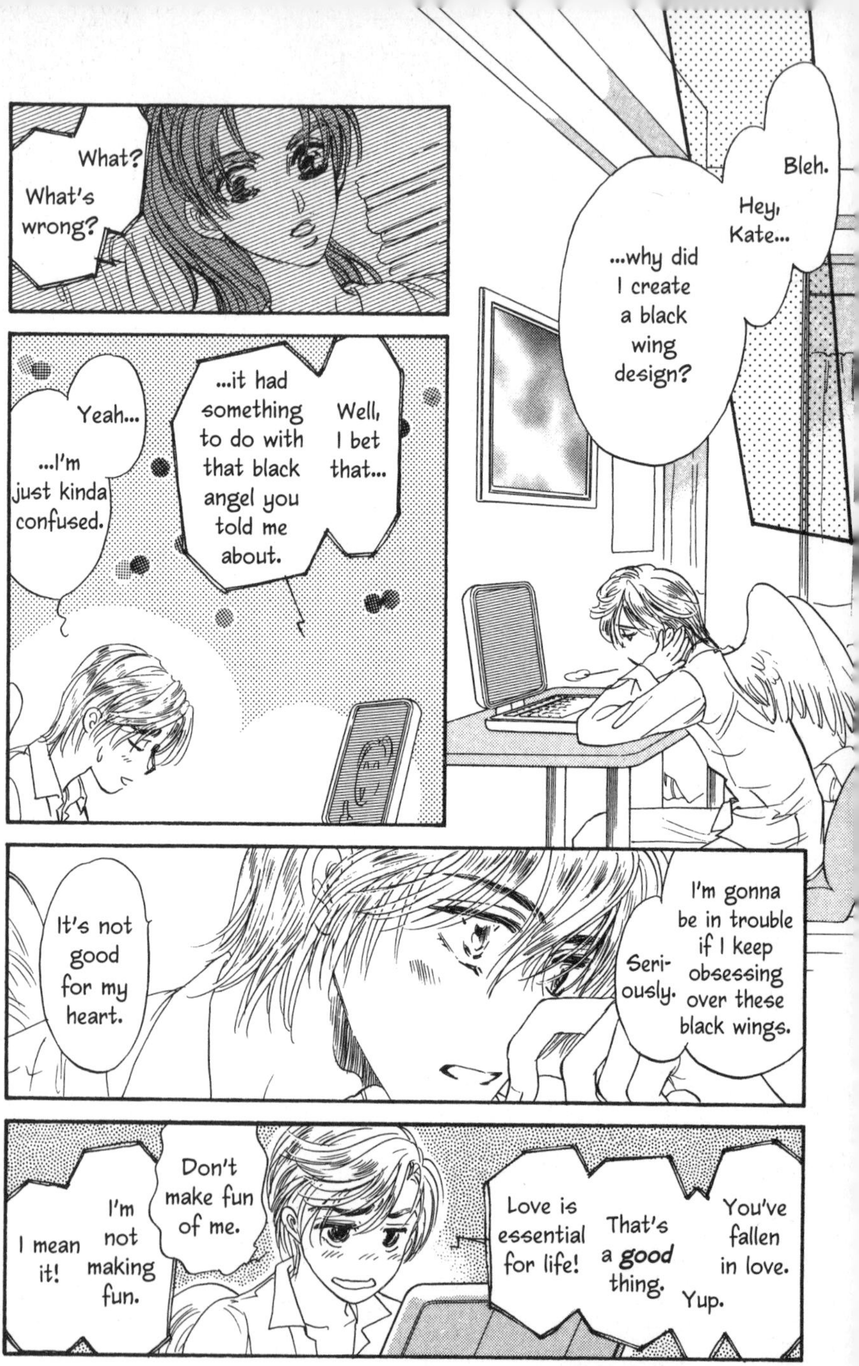
Bleh.
Hey, Kate...
...why did I create a black wing design?
What? What's wrong?
Well, I bet that...
...it had something to do with that black angel you told me about.
Yeah...
...I'm just kinda confused.
I'm gonna be in trouble if I keep obsessing over these black wings.
Seriously.
It's not good for my heart.
You've fallen in love.
Yup.
That's a **good** thing.
Love is essential for life!
Don't make fun of me.
I'm not making fun.
I mean it!

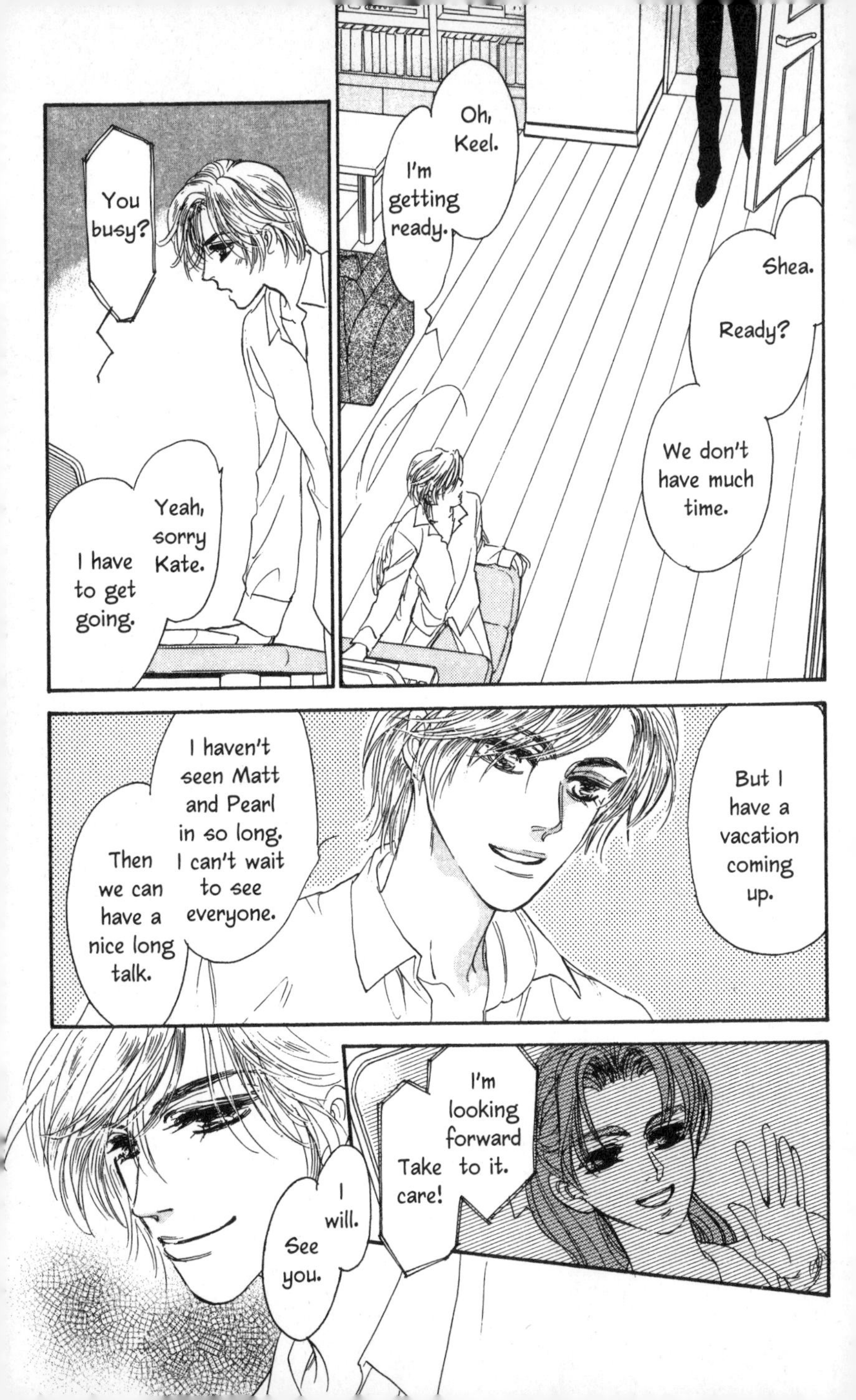
Shea.
Ready?
We don't have much time.
Oh, Keel. I'm getting ready.
You busy?
Yeah, sorry Kate. I have to get going.
But I have a vacation coming up.
I haven't seen Matt and Pearl in so long. I can't wait to see everyone.
Then we can have a nice long talk.
I'm looking forward to it. Take care!
I will. See you.

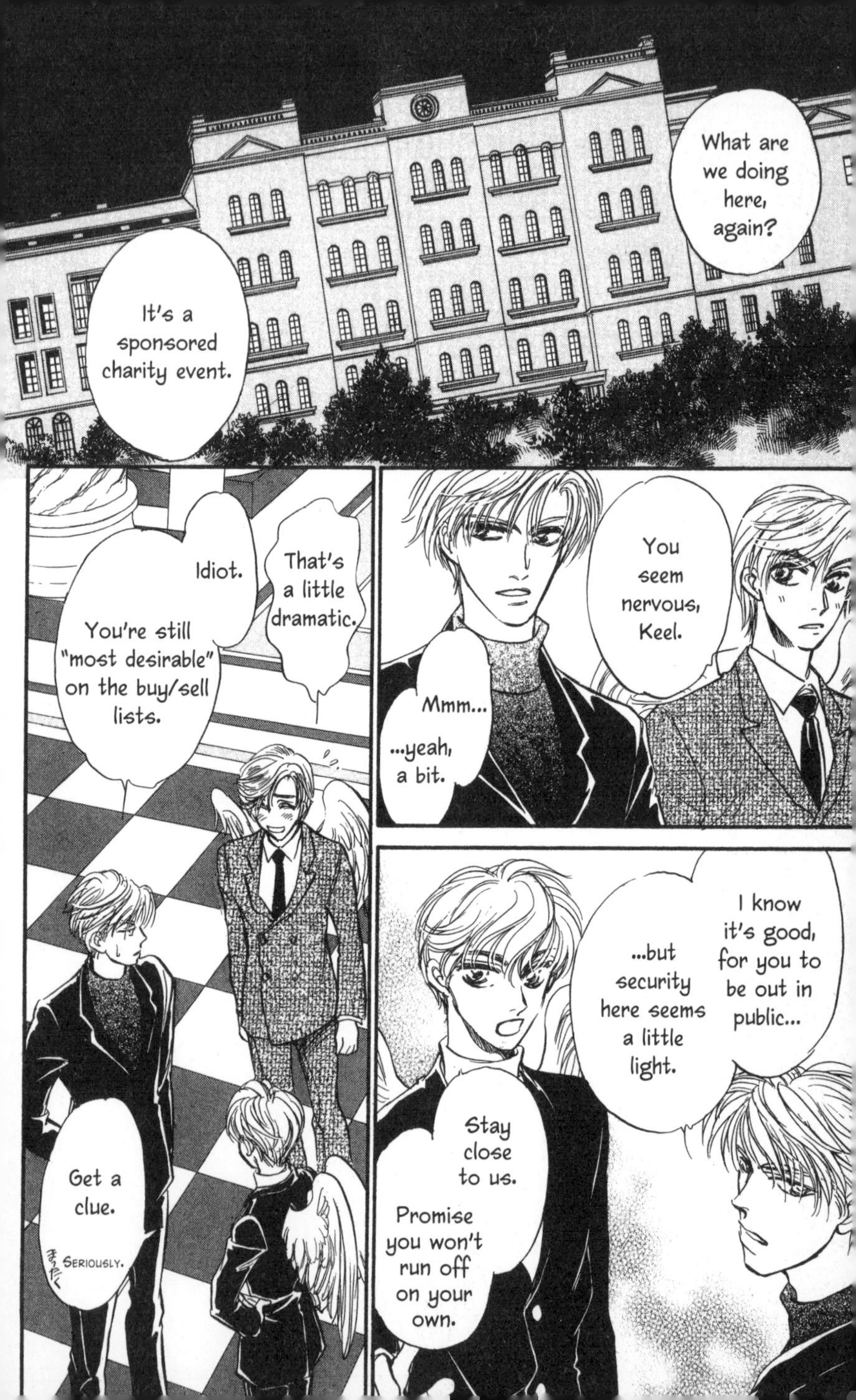

What are we doing here, again?
It's a sponsored charity event.
You seem nervous, Keel.
Mmm...
...yeah, a bit.
I know it's good, for you to be out in public...
...but security here seems a little light.
Stay close to us.
Promise you won't run off on your own.
That's a little dramatic.
Idiot.
You're still "most desirable" on the buy/sell lists.
Get a clue.
まったく
Seriously.

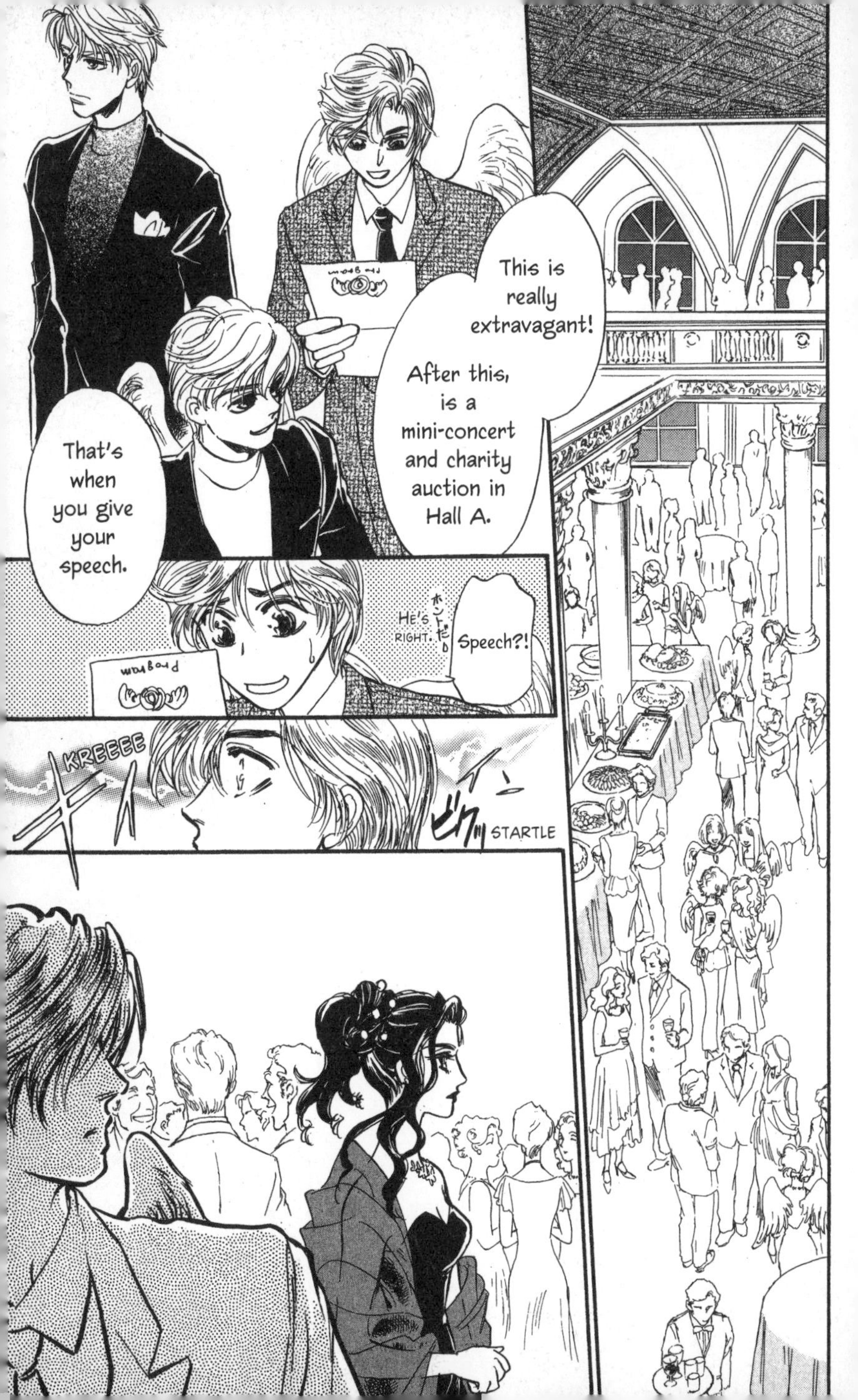
This is really extravagant!
After this, is a mini-concert and charity auction in Hall A.
That's when you give your speech.
Speech?!
HE'S RIGHT.
KREEEE
STARTLE

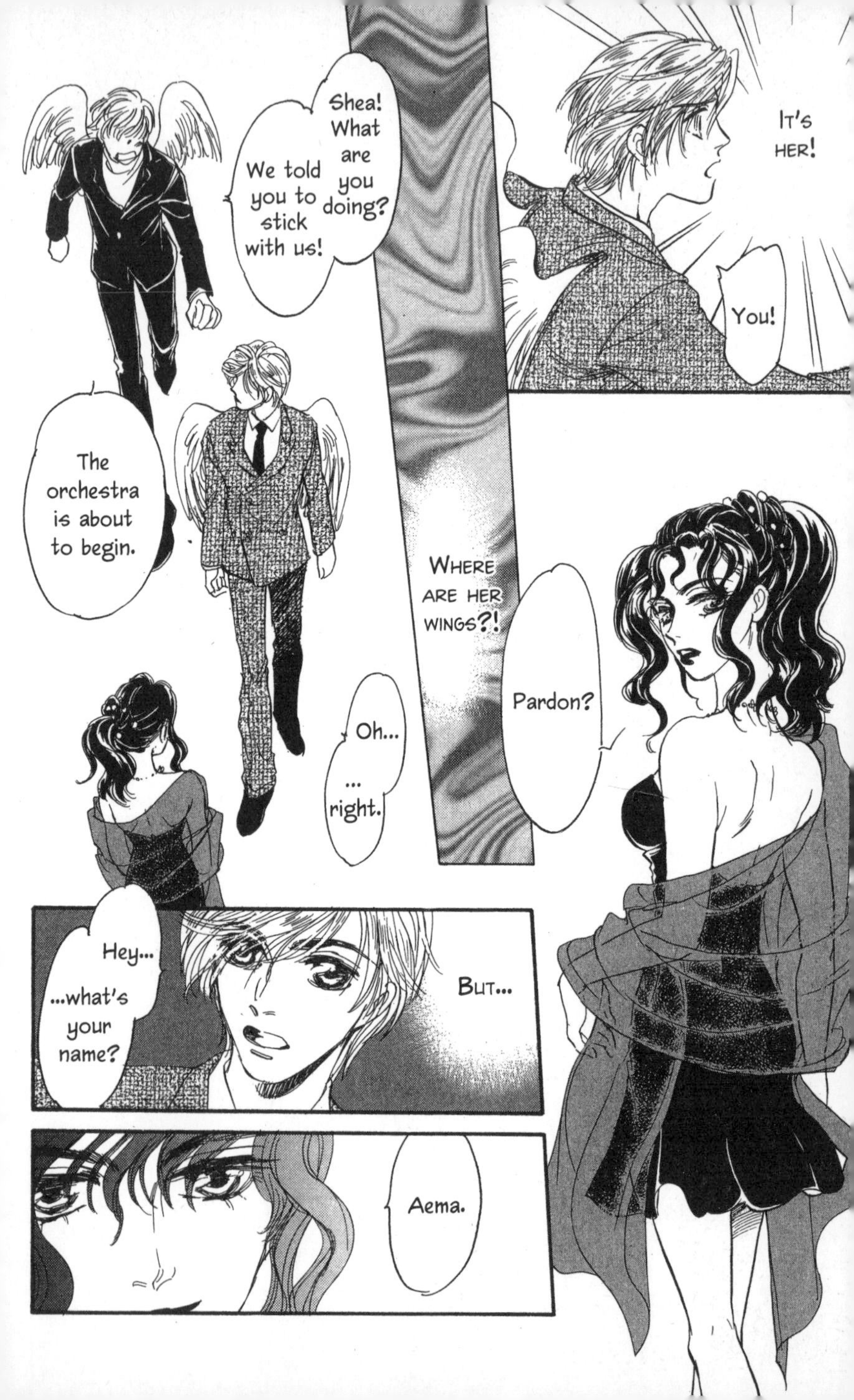
It's her!
You!
Shea! What are you doing?
We told you to stick with us!
The orchestra is about to begin.
Pardon?
Where are her wings?!
Oh...
... right.
But...
Hey...
...what's your name?
Aema.

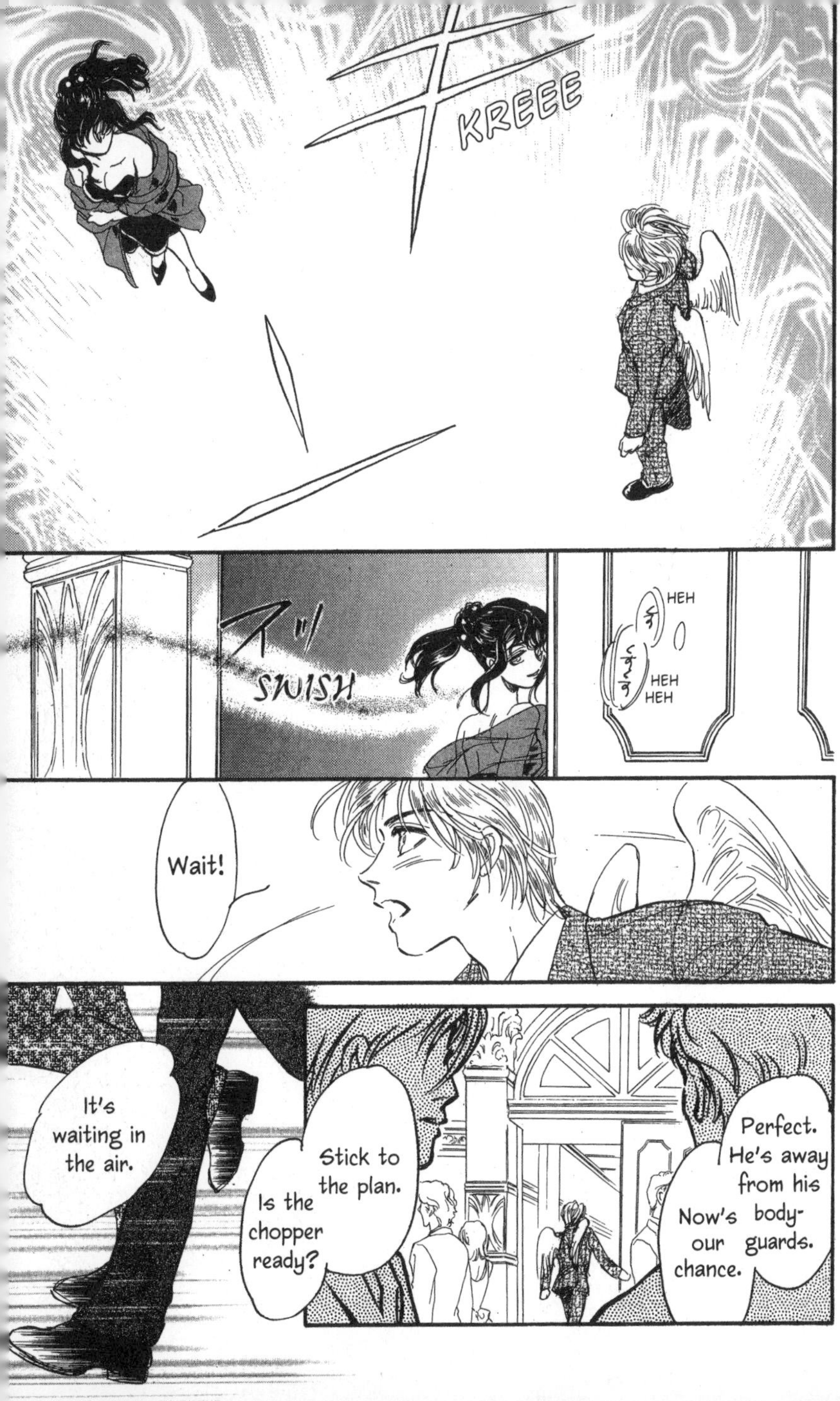
KREEE
HEH
HEH HEH
SWISH
Wait!
Perfect. He's away from his body-guards.
Now's our chance.
Stick to the plan.
Is the chopper ready?
It's waiting in the air.

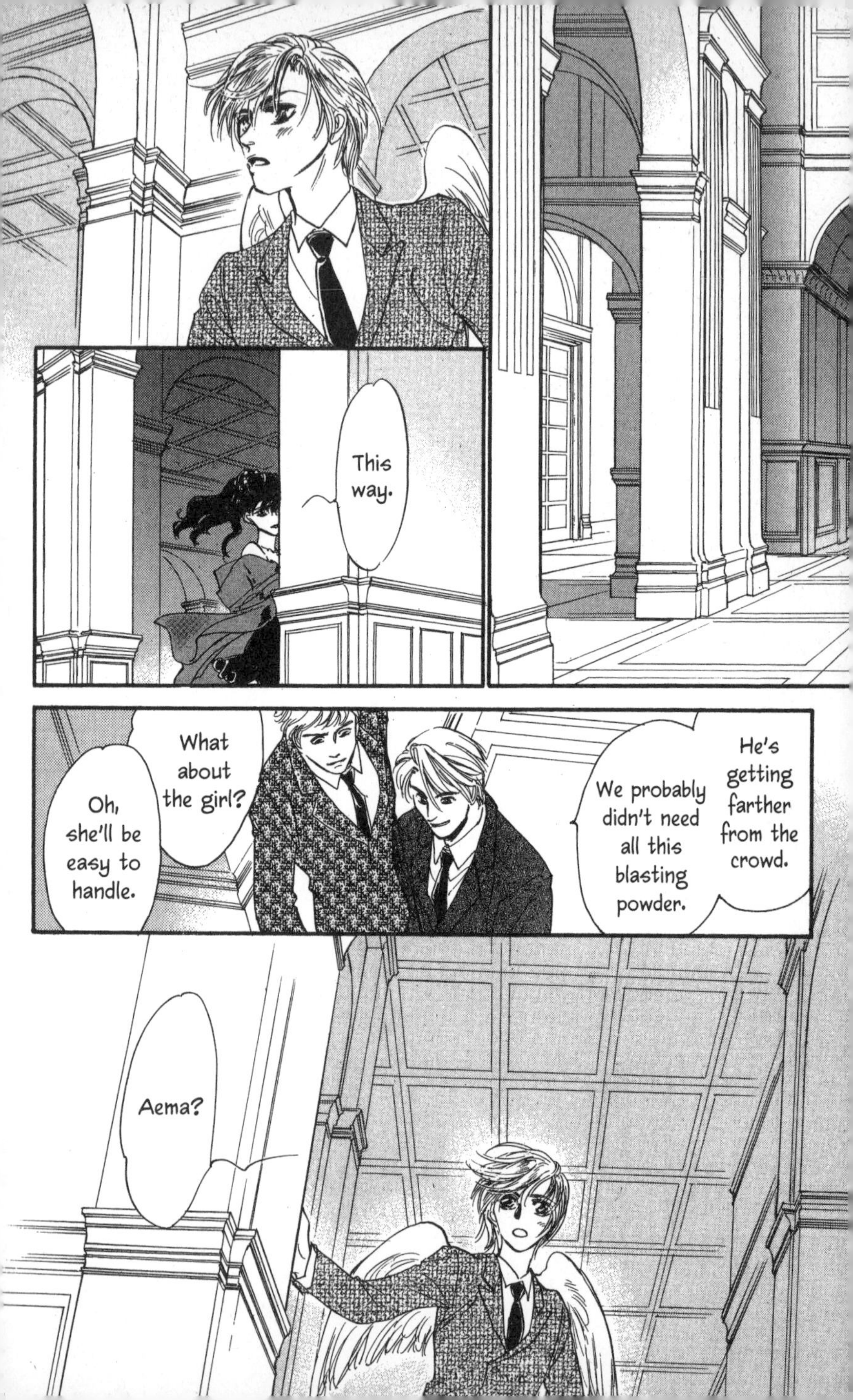
This way.
He's getting farther from the crowd.
We probably didn't need all this blasting powder.
What about the girl?
Oh, she'll be easy to handle.
Aema?

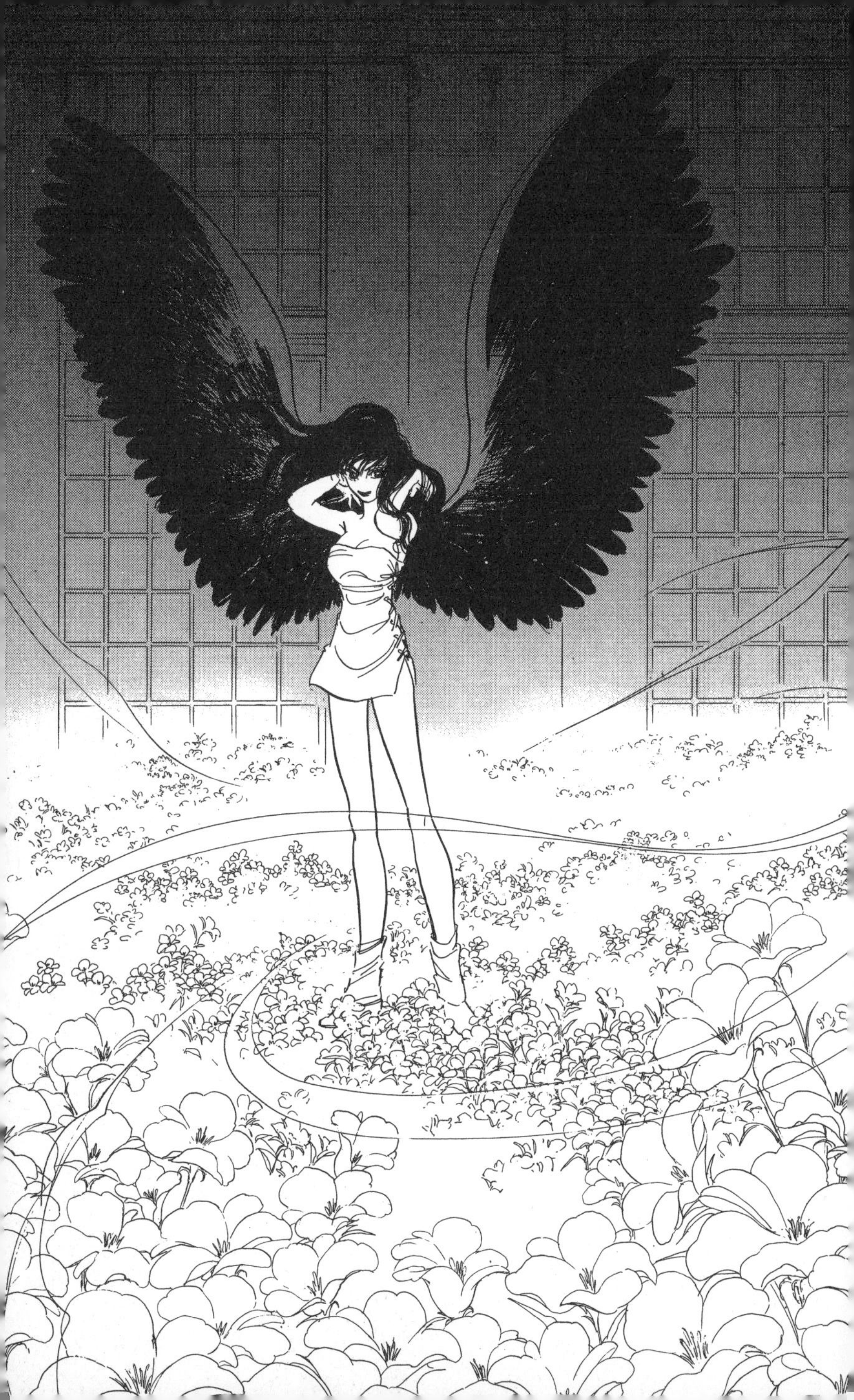

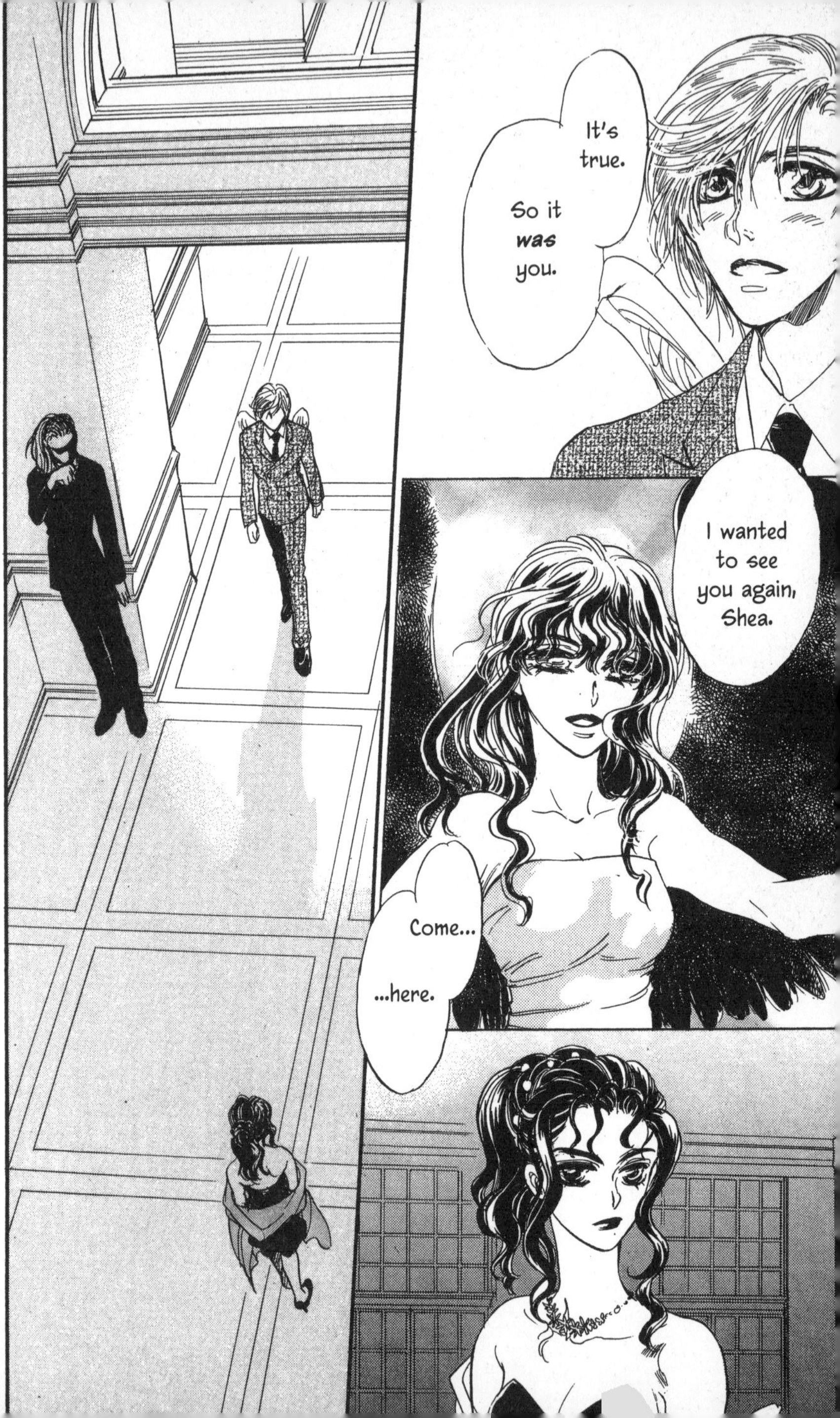
It's true.
So it was you.
I wanted to see you again, Shea.
Come...
...here.

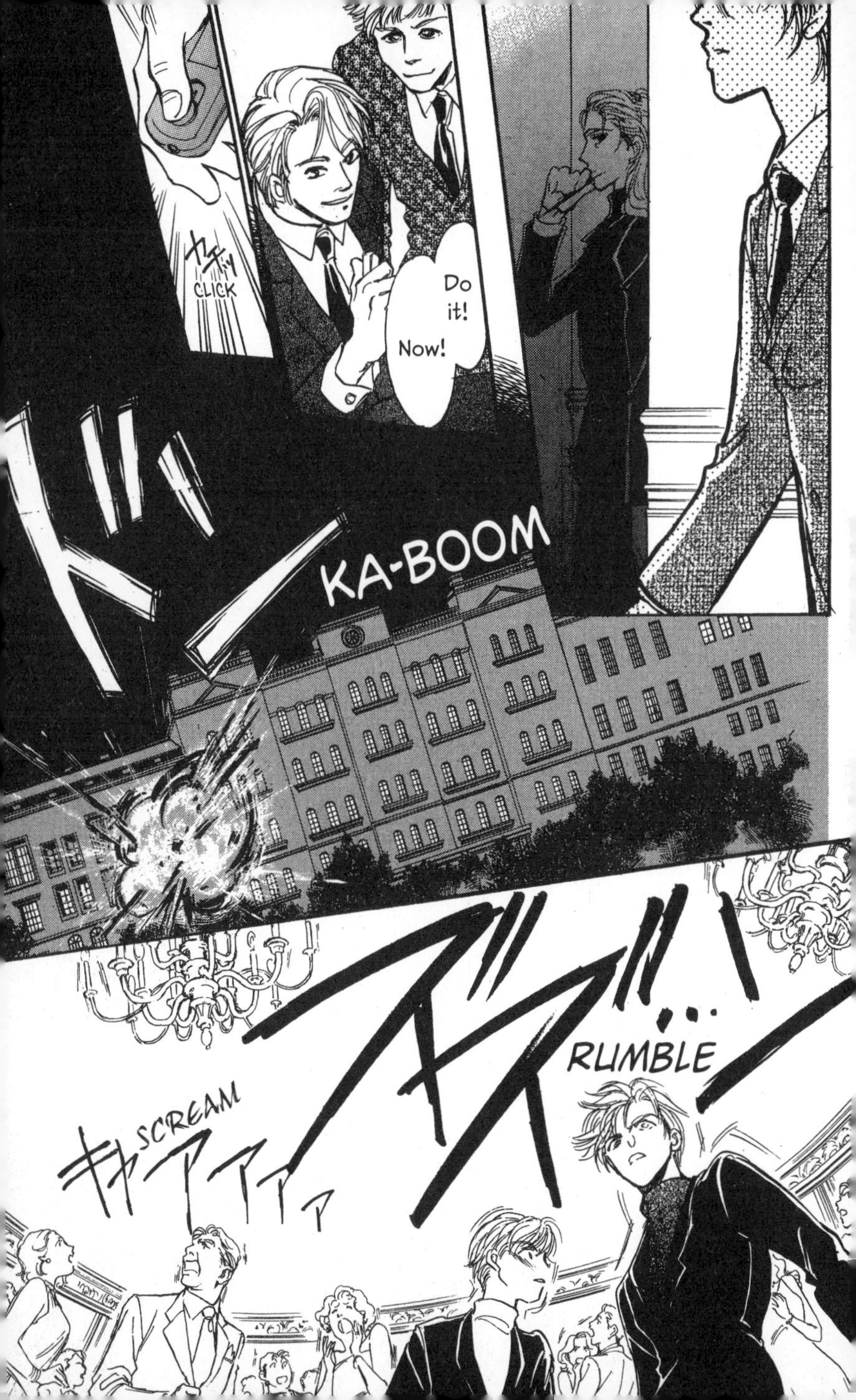
Do it! Now!
CLICK
KA-BOOM
RUMBLE
SCREAM

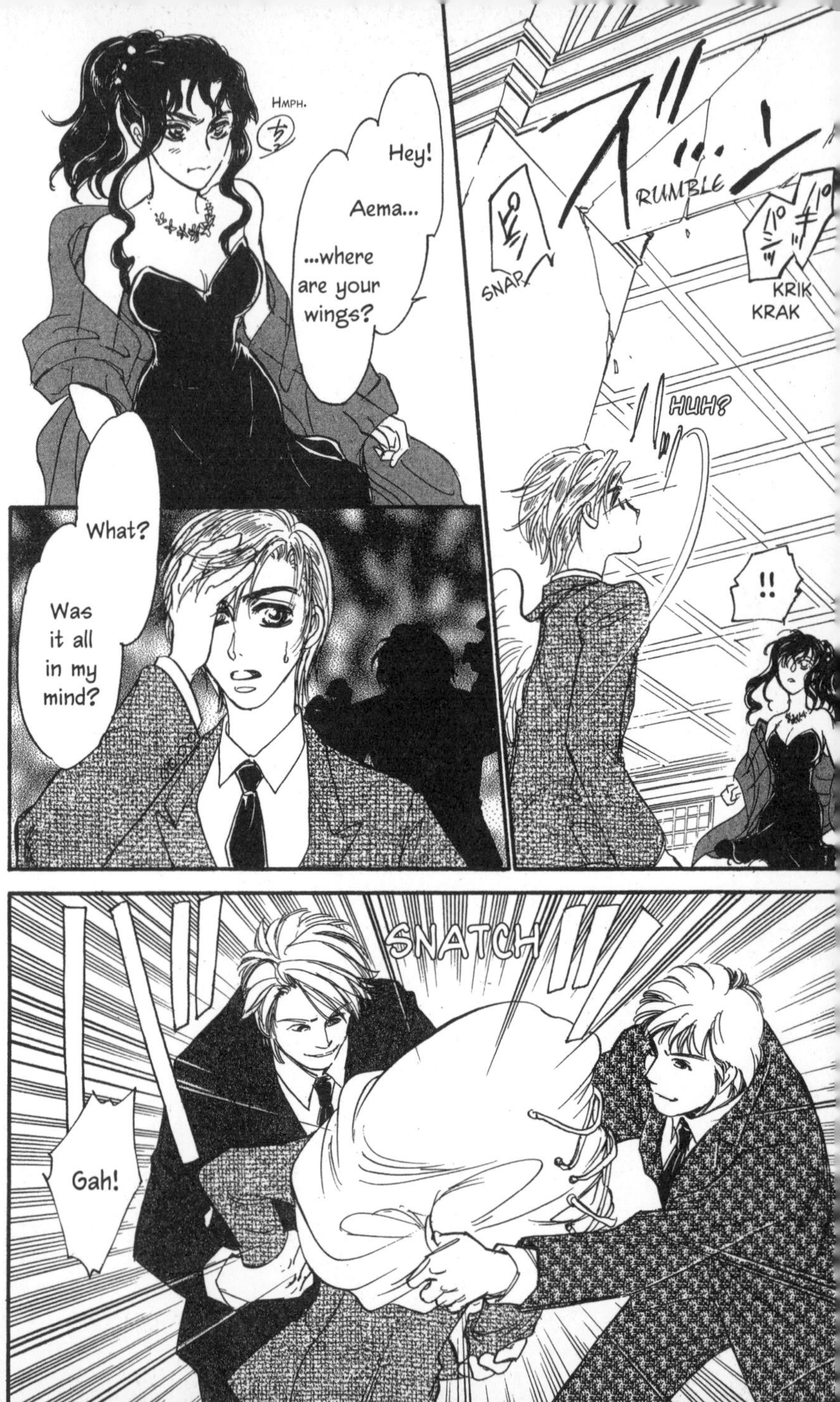
RUMBLE
SNAP
KRIK KRAK
HUH?
!!
Hmph.
Hey!
Aema...
...where are your wings?
What?
Was it all in my mind?
SNATCH
Gah!

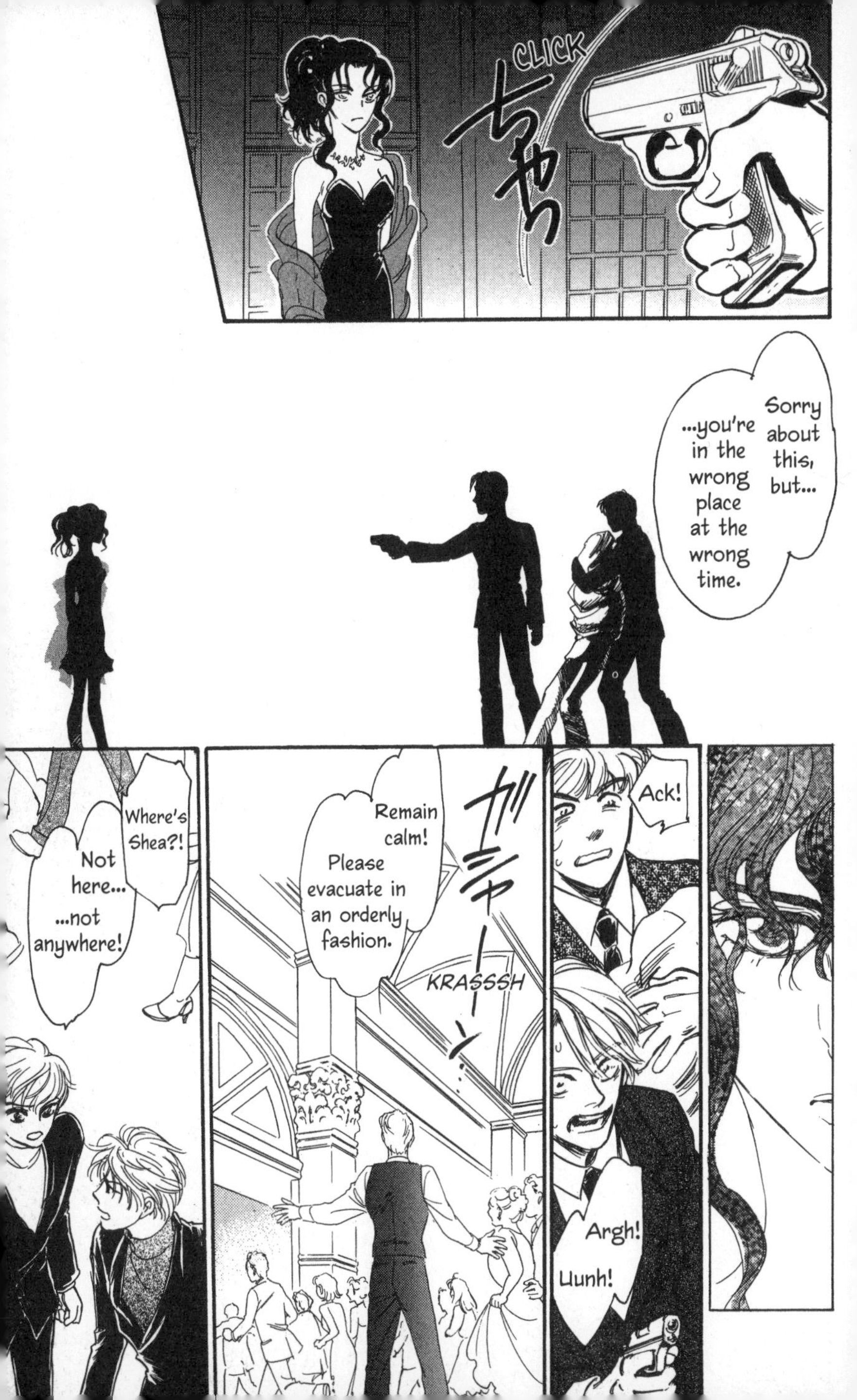
CLICK
ちゃ
Sorry about this, but...
...you're in the wrong place at the wrong time.
Ack!
Argh!
Uunh!
ガシャーン
KRASSSH
Remain calm! Please evacuate in an orderly fashion.
Where's Shea?!
Not here... ...not anywhere!

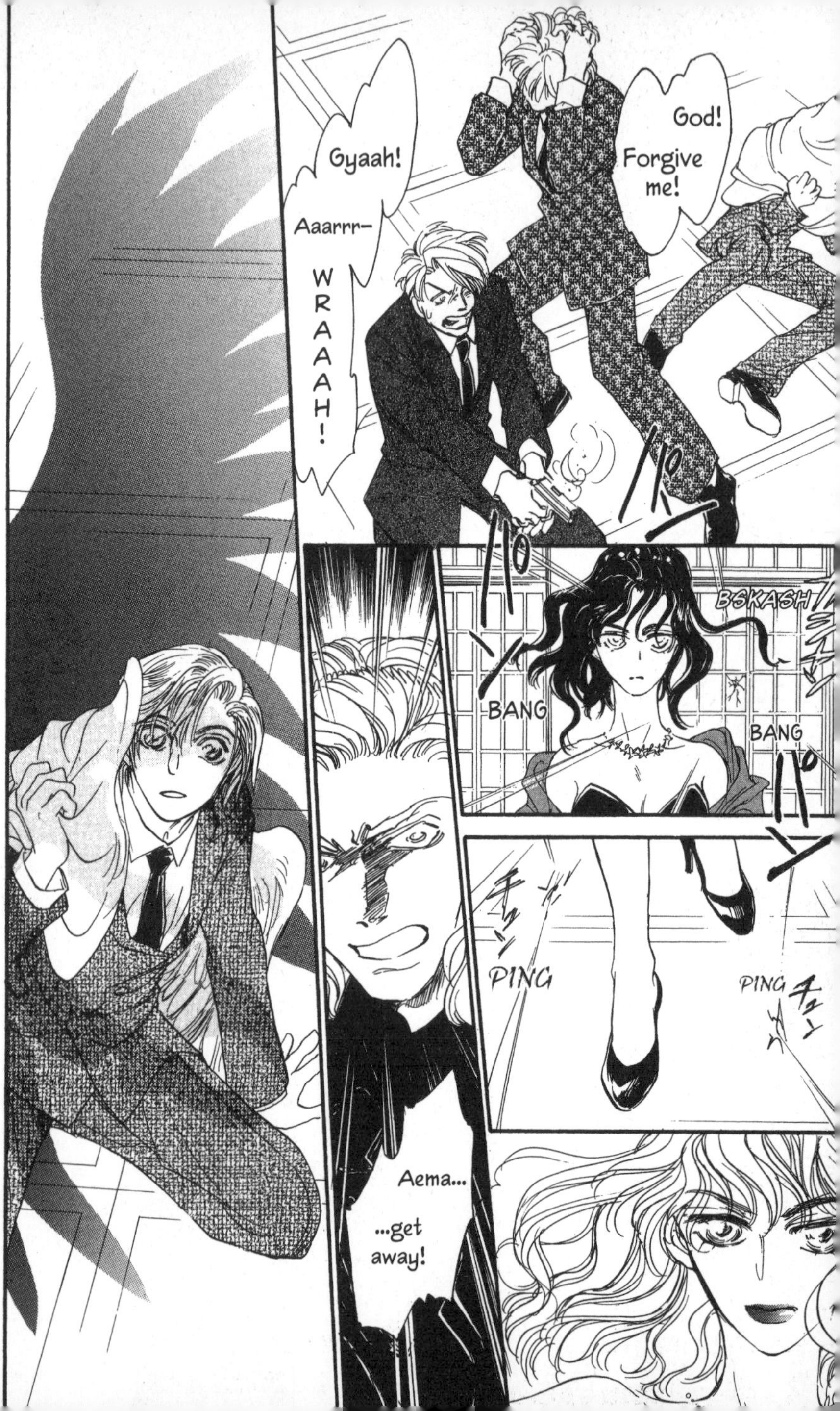
God!
Forgive me!
Gyaah!
Aaarrr-
WRAAAAH!
BSKASH
BANG
BANG
PING
PING
Aema...
...get away!

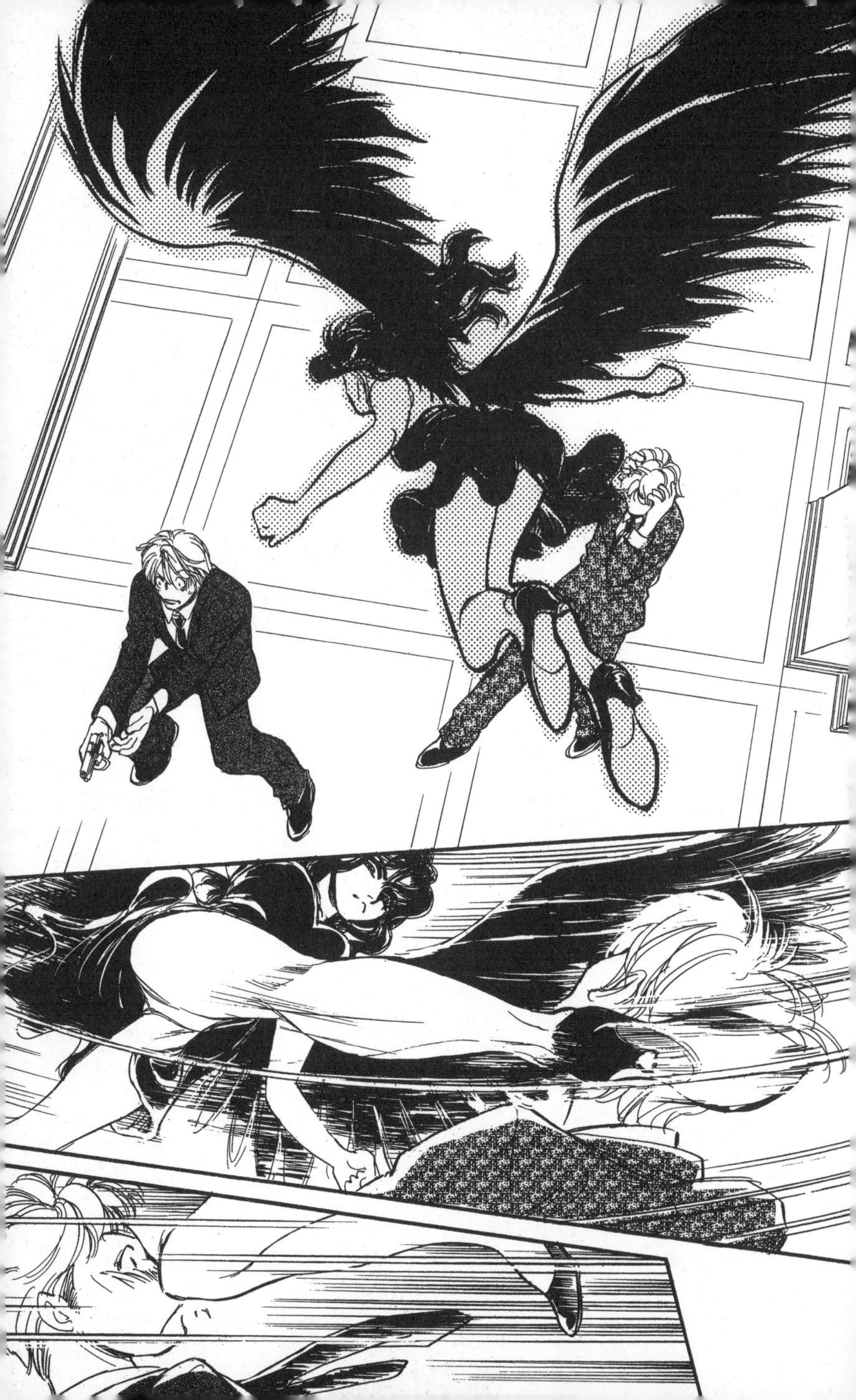

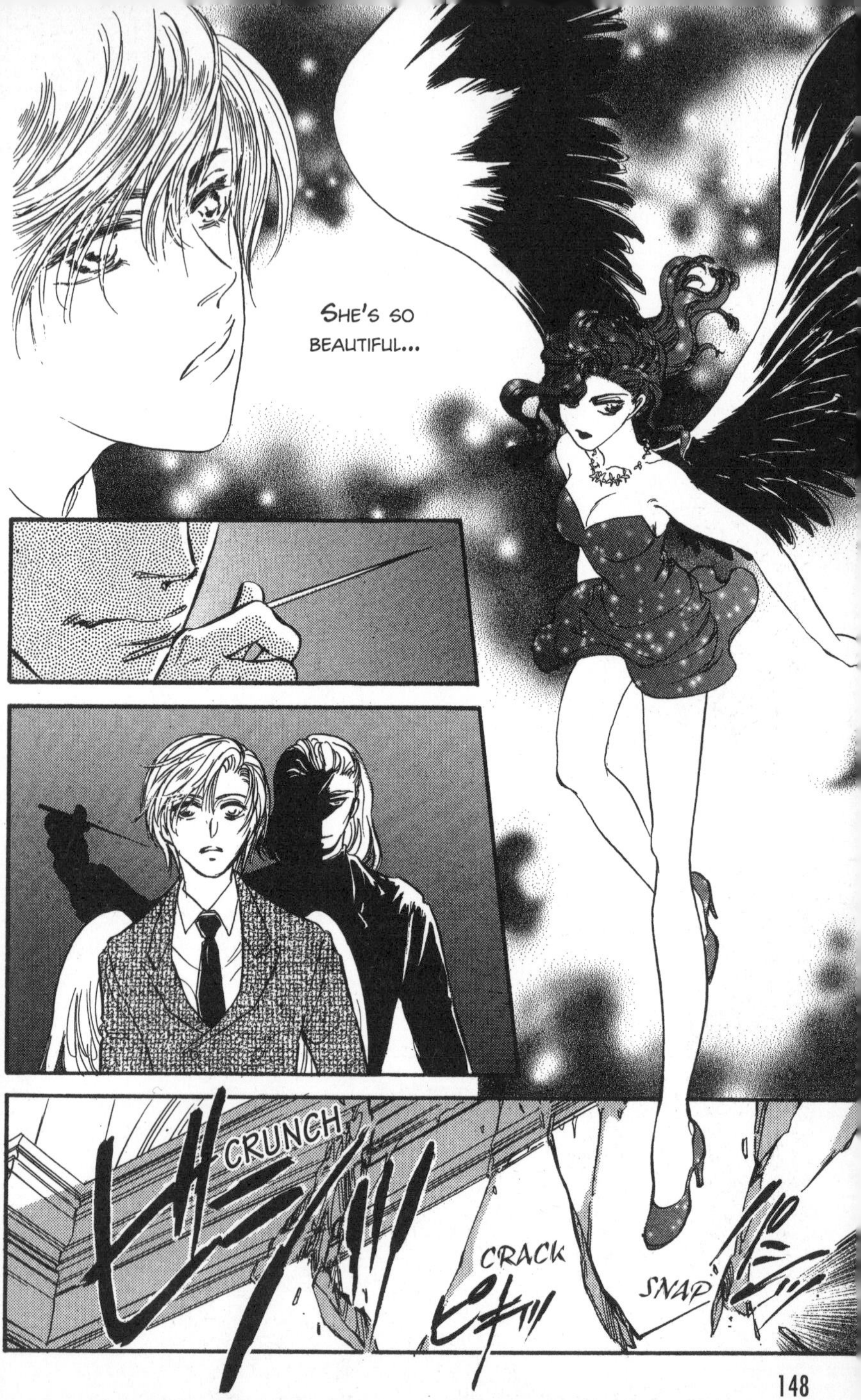
She's so beautiful...
Snap
Crack
Crunch

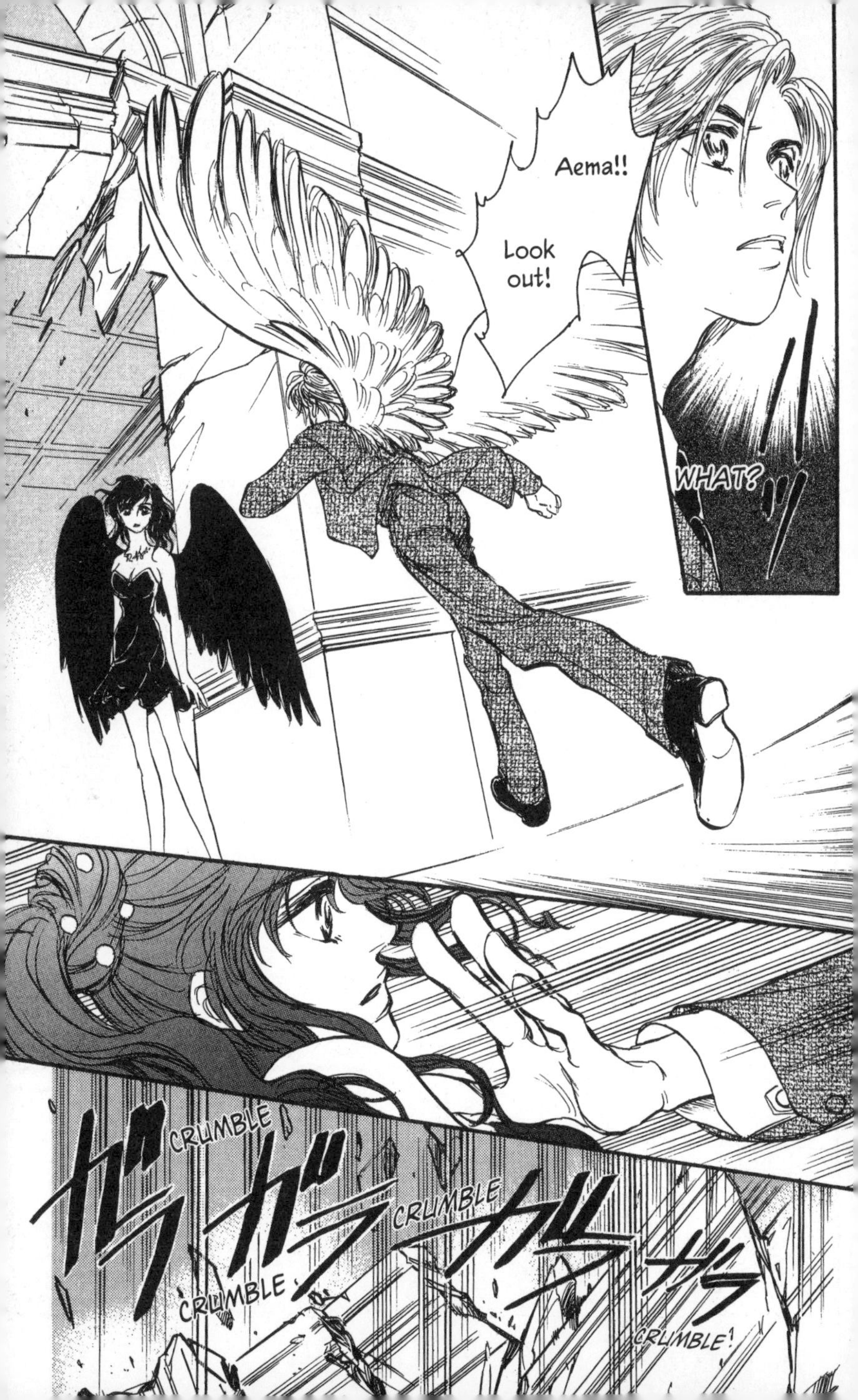
Aema!!
Look out!
WHAT?
CRUMBLE
CRUMBLE
CRUMBLE
CRUMBLE!

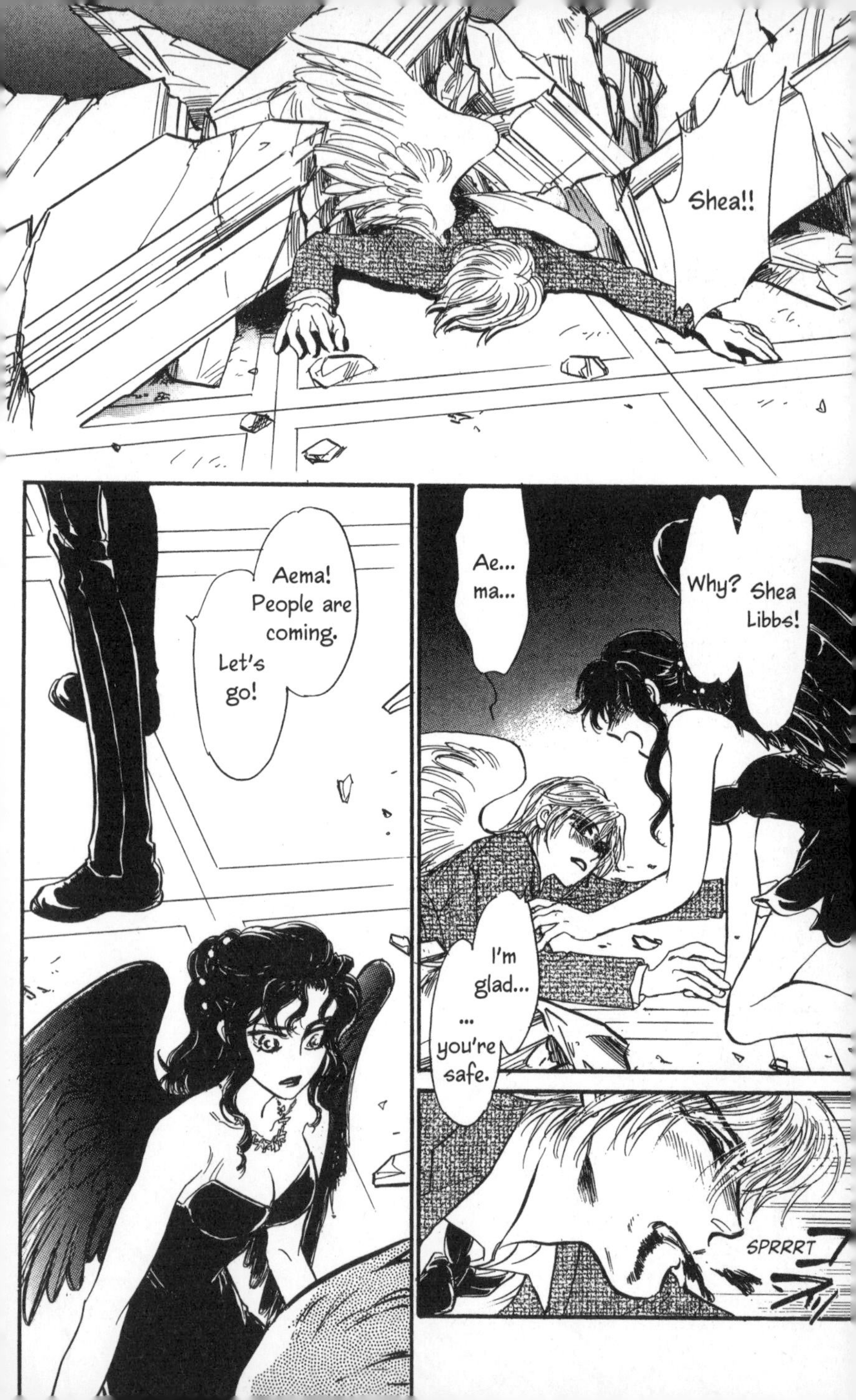
Shea!!
Why? Shea Libbs!
Ae... ma...
I'm glad... ... you're safe.
SPRRRT
Aema! People are coming. Let's go!

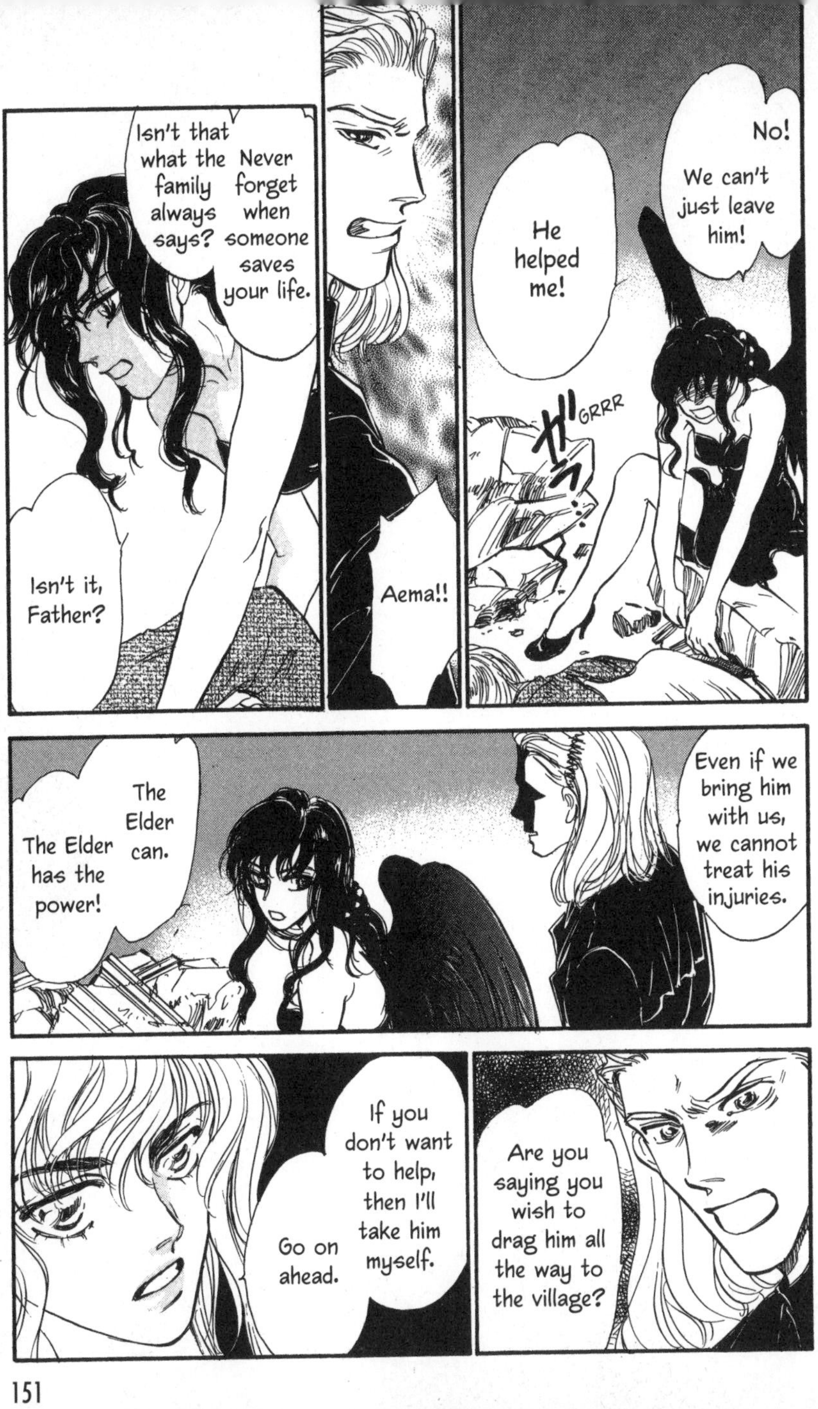
No!
We can't just leave him!
He helped me!
GRRR
Aema!!
Never forget when someone saves your life.
Isn't that what the family always says?
Isn't it, Father?
Even if we bring him with us, we cannot treat his injuries.
The Elder can.
The Elder has the power!
Are you saying you wish to drag him all the way to the village?
If you don't want to help, then I'll take him myself.
Go on ahead.

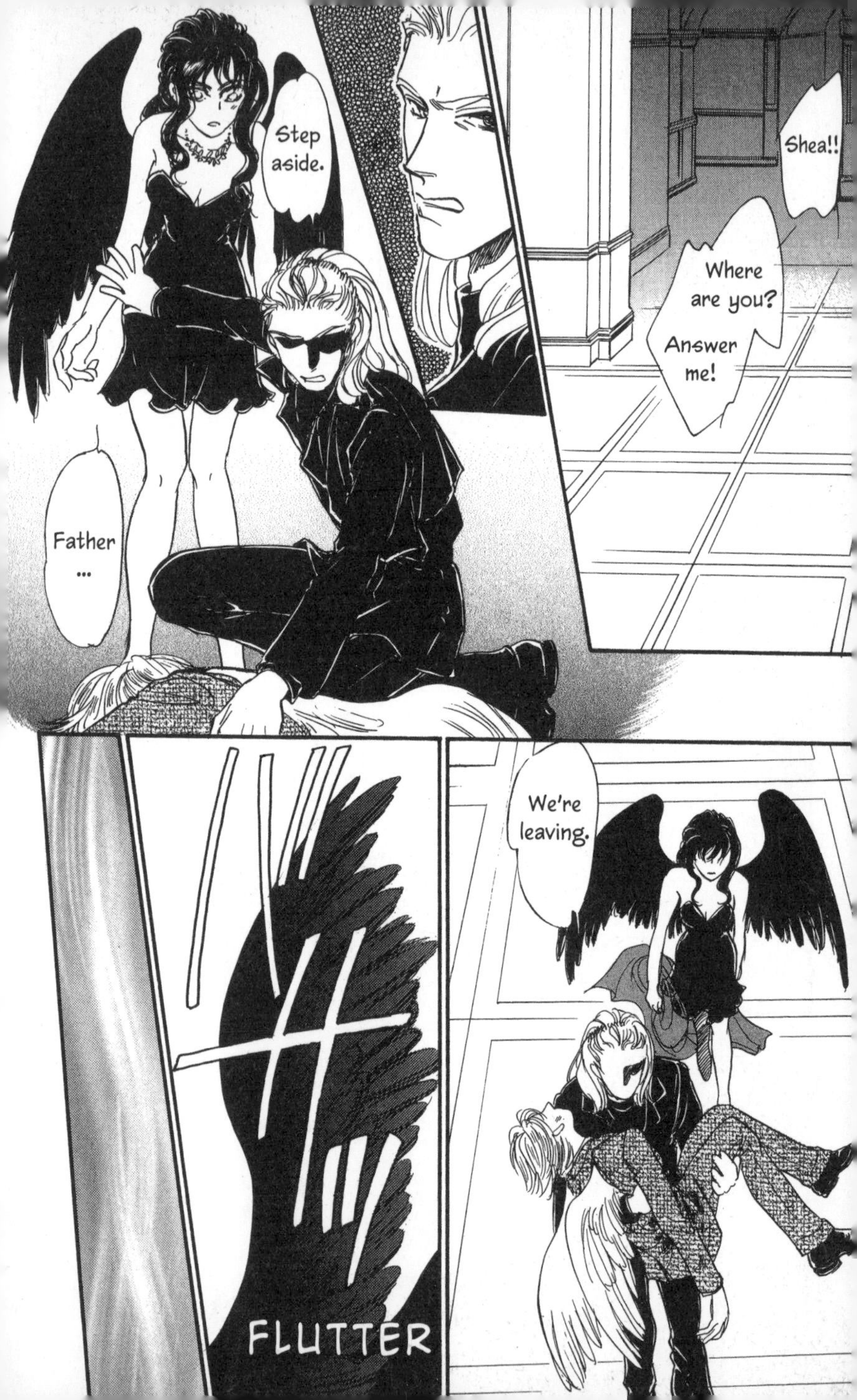
Shea!!
Where are you?
Answer me!
Step aside.
Father ...
We're leaving.
FLUTTER

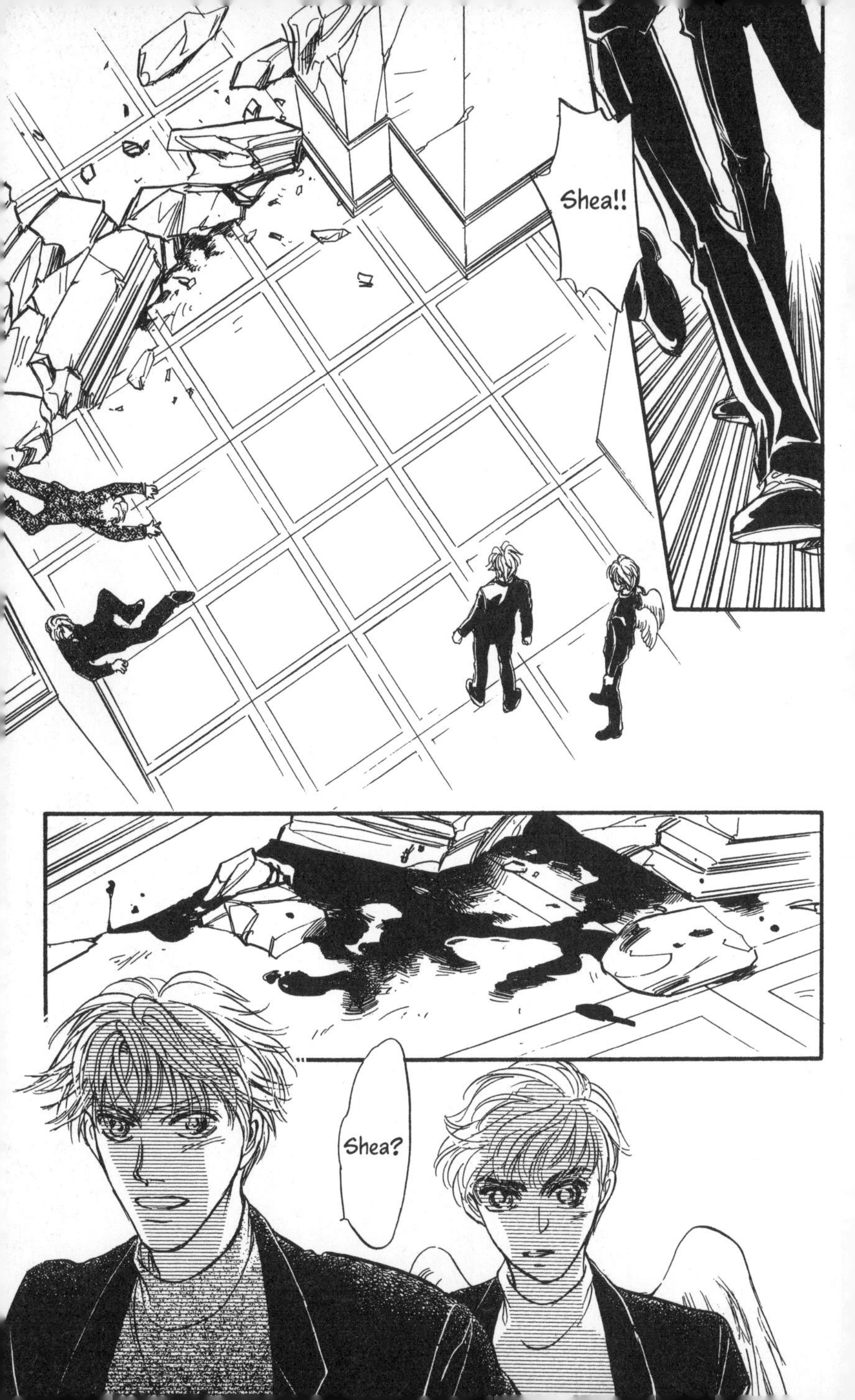
Shea!!
Shea?

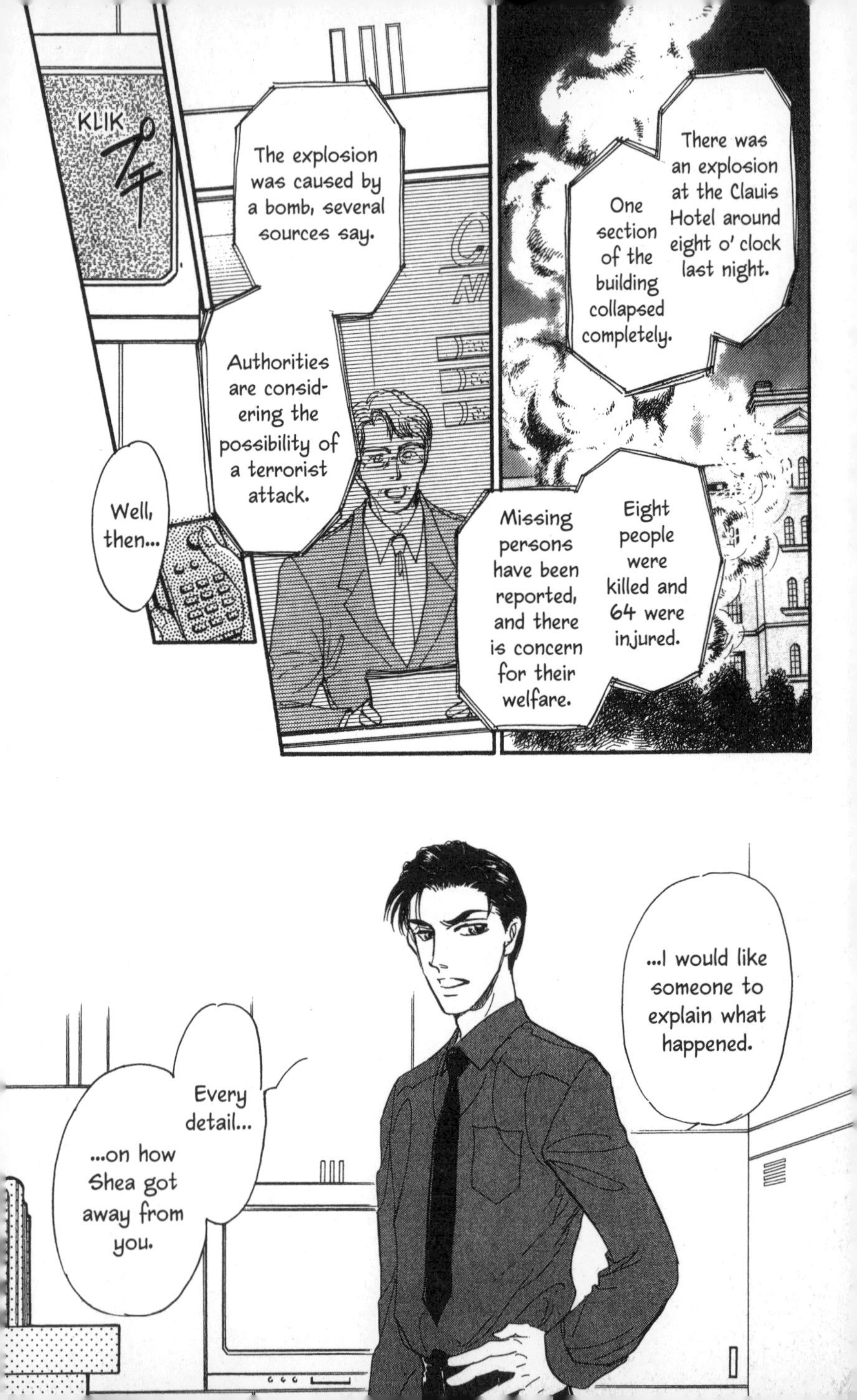
There was an explosion at the Clauis Hotel around eight o' clock last night.
One section of the building collapsed completely.
Eight people were killed and 64 were injured.
Missing persons have been reported, and there is concern for their welfare.
The explosion was caused by a bomb, several sources say.
Authorities are consid-ering the possibility of a terrorist attack.
KLIK
Well, then...
...I would like someone to explain what happened.
Every detail...
...on how Shea got away from you.

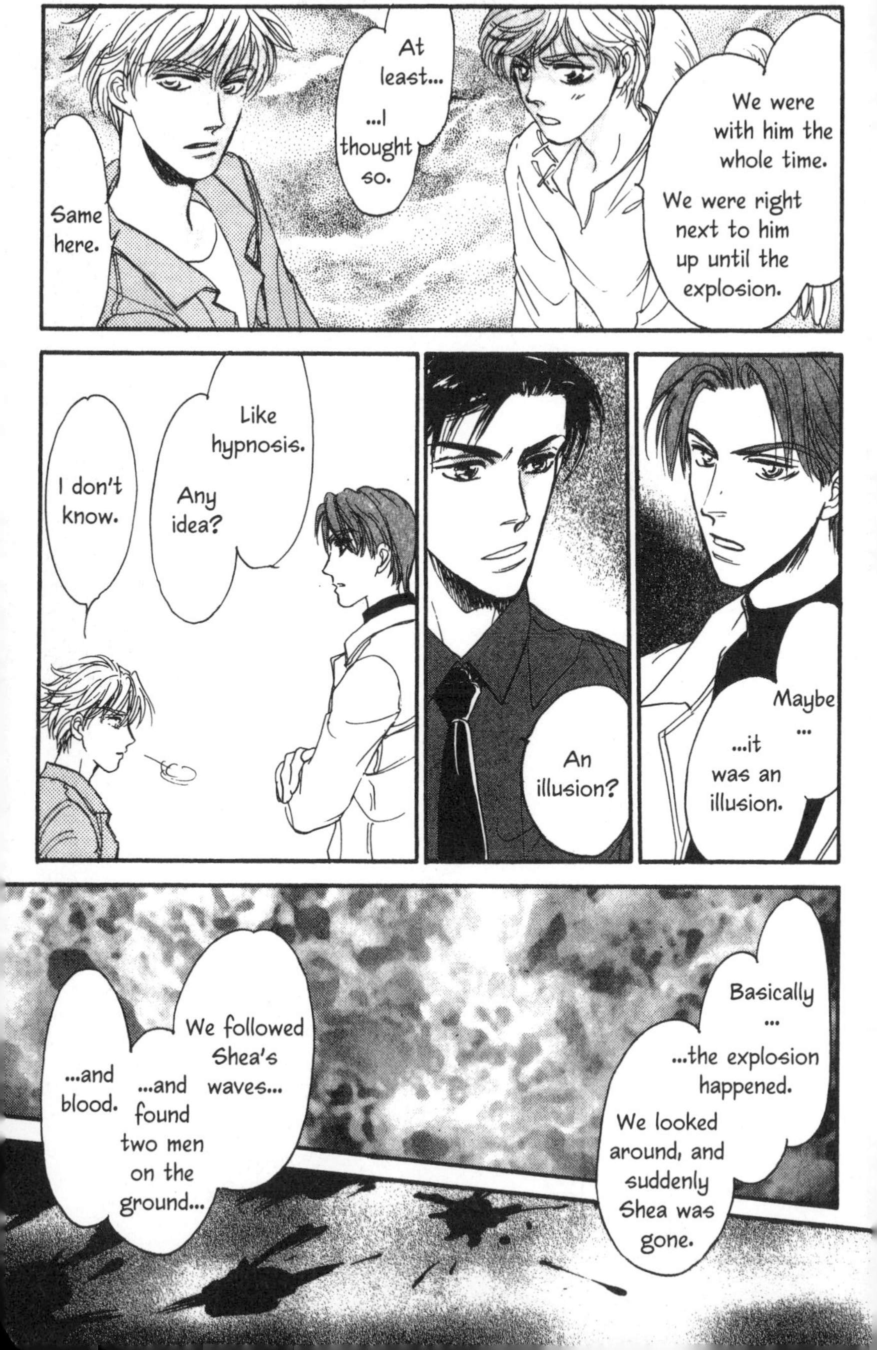
We were with him the whole time.
We were right next to him up until the explosion.
At least...
...I thought so.
Same here.
Maybe...
...it was an illusion.
An illusion?
Like hypnosis.
Any idea?
I don't know.
Basically...
...the explosion happened.
We looked around, and suddenly Shea was gone.
We followed Shea's waves...
...and found two men on the ground...
...and blood.

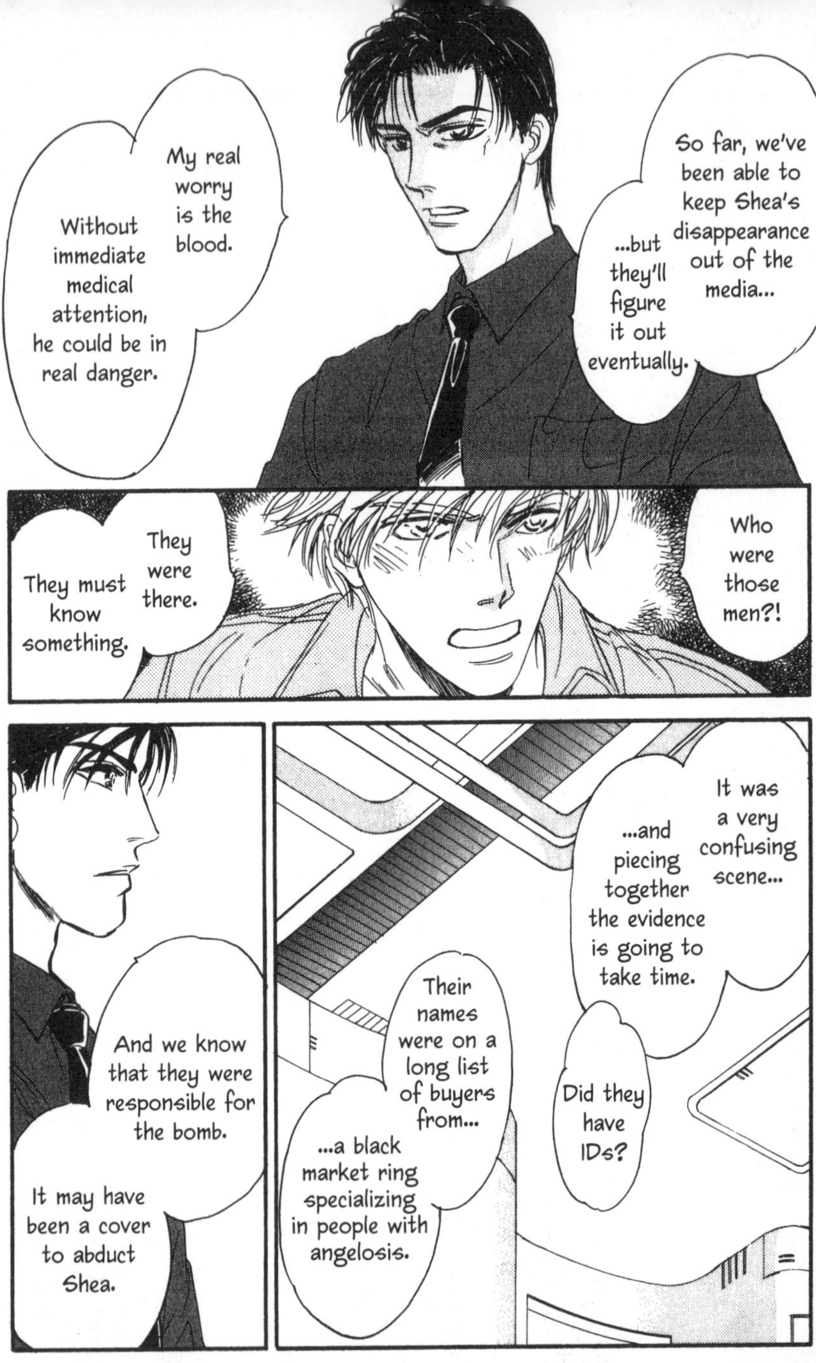
So far, we've been able to keep Shea's disappearance out of the media...
...but they'll figure it out eventually.
My real worry is the blood.
Without immediate medical attention, he could be in real danger.
Who were those men?!
They were there.
They must know something.
It was a very confusing scene...
...and piecing together the evidence is going to take time.
Did they have IDs?
Their names were on a long list of buyers from...
...a black market ring specializing in people with angelosis.
And we know that they were responsible for the bomb.
It may have been a cover to abduct Shea.

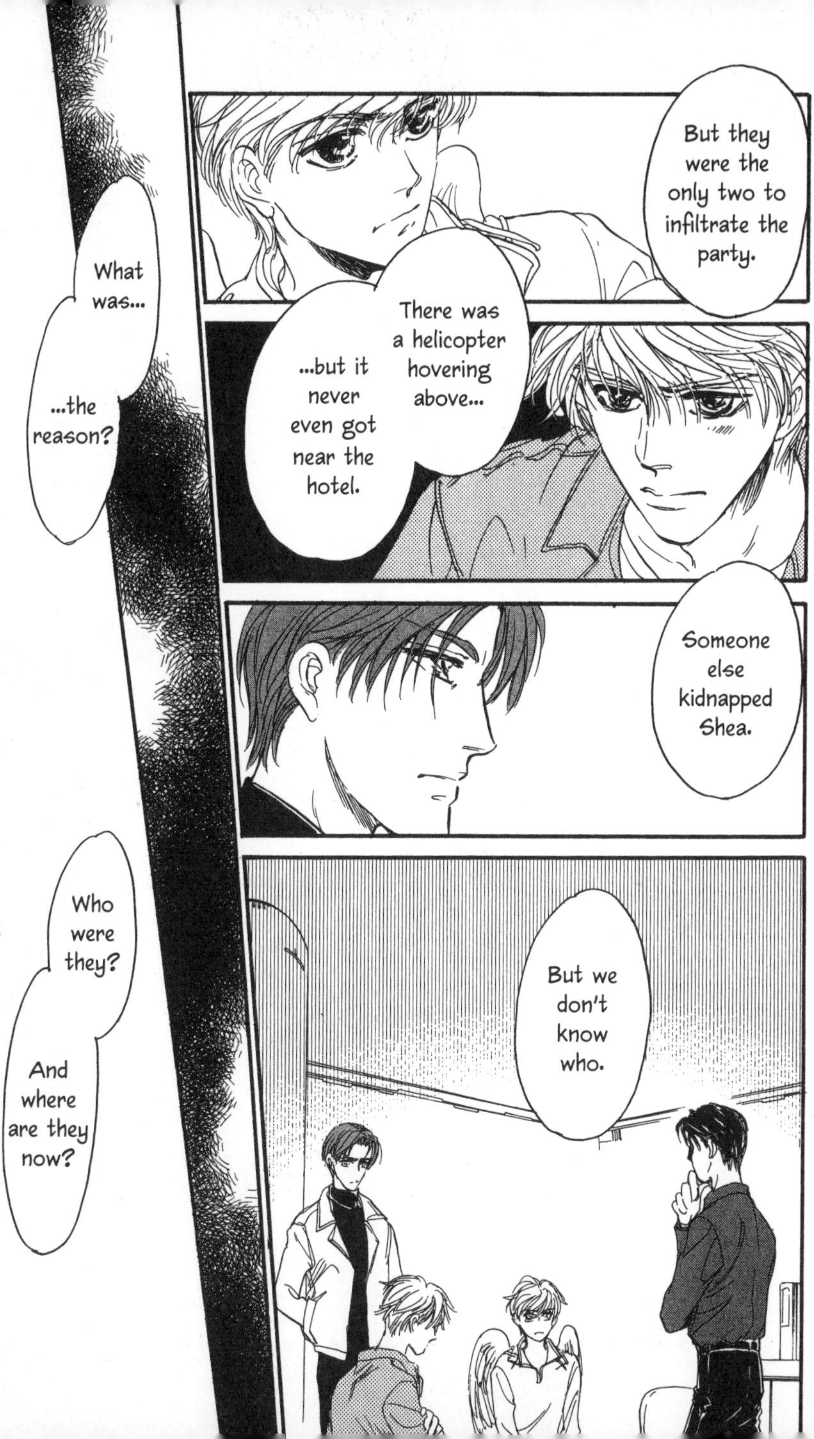

But they were the only two to infiltrate the party.
There was a helicopter hovering above...
...but it never even got near the hotel.
Someone else kidnapped Shea.
But we don't know who.
What was...
...the reason?
Who were they?
And where are they now?

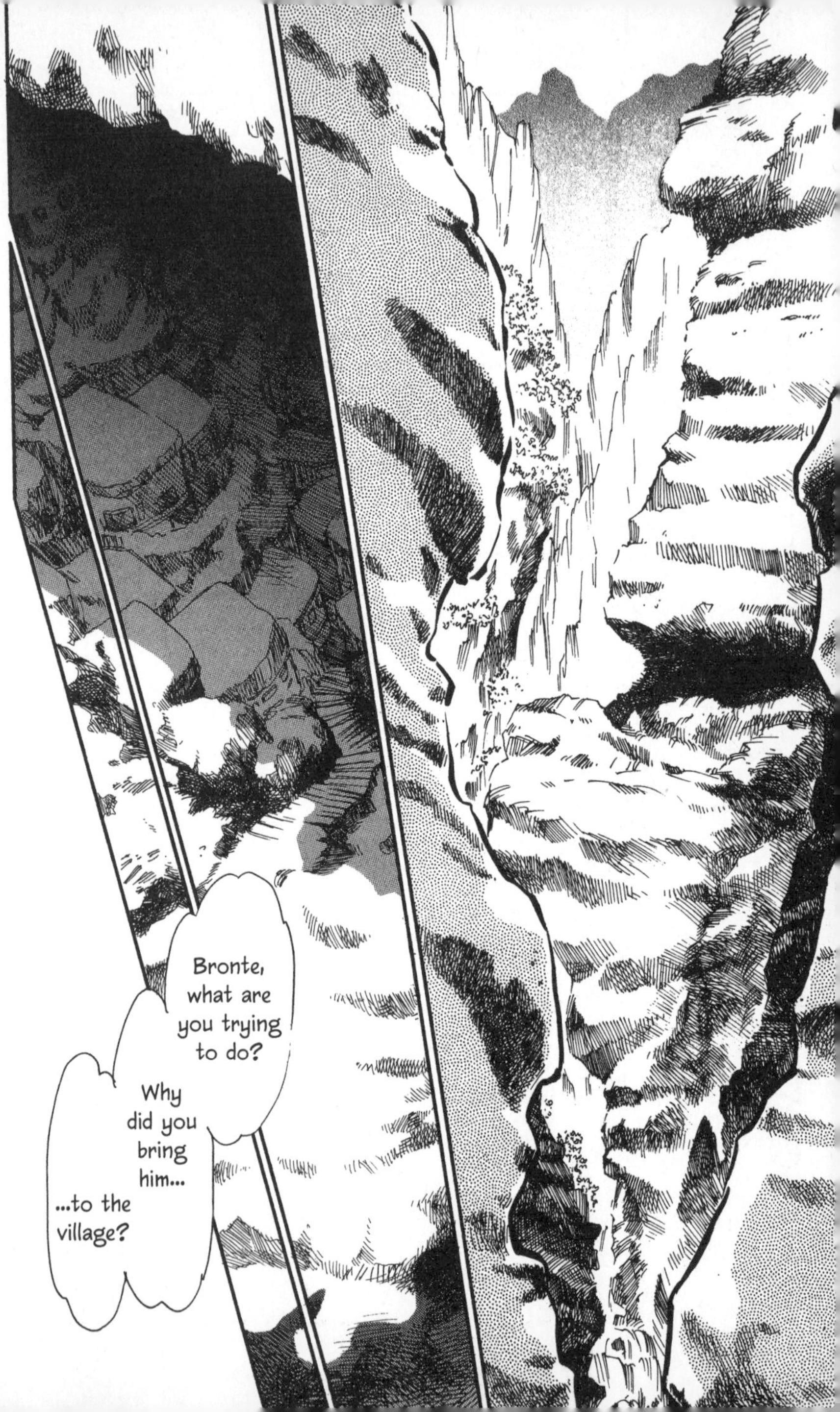
Bronte, what are you trying to do?
Why did you bring him... ...to the village?

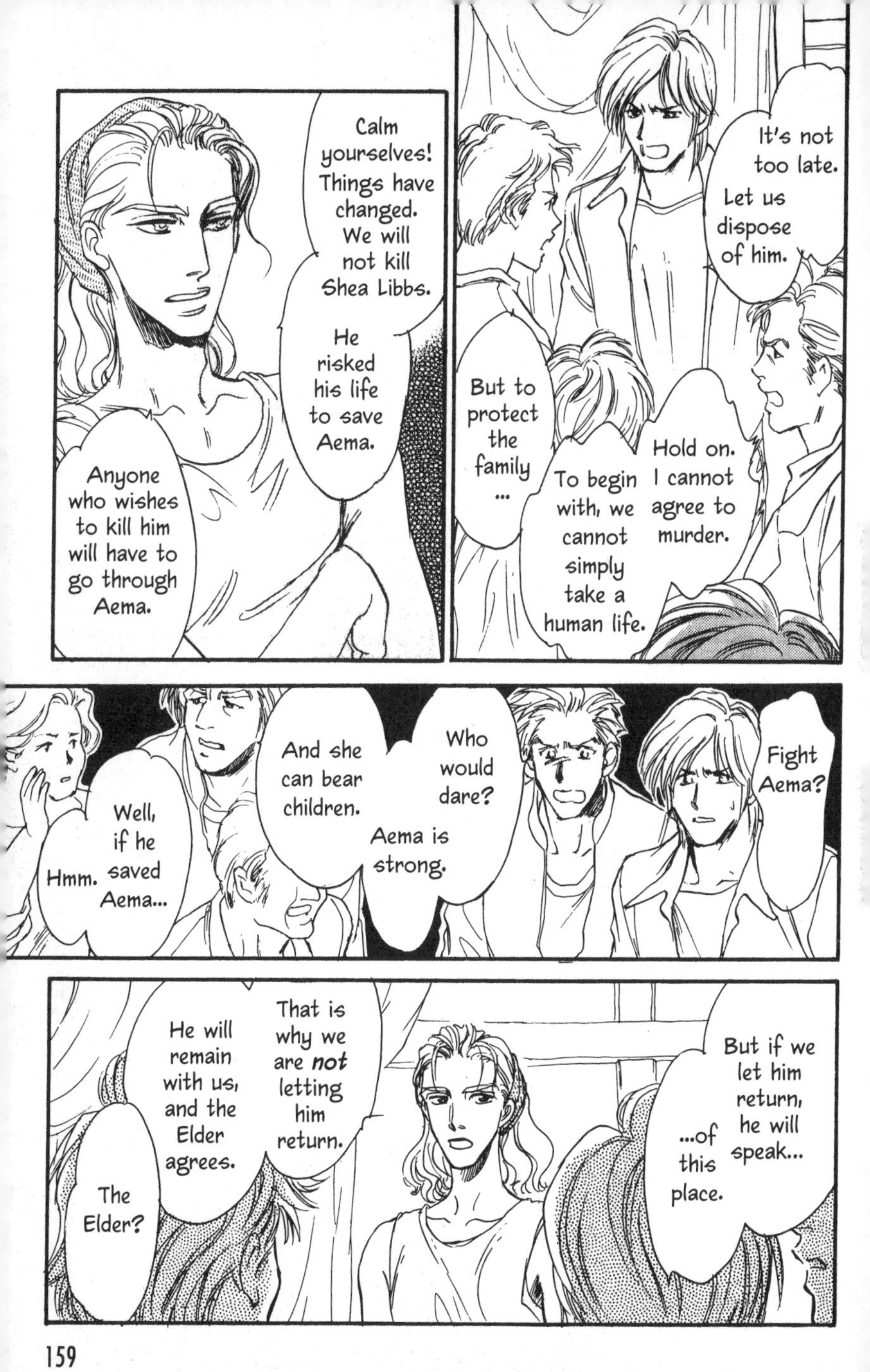
It's not too late.
Let us dispose of him.
But to protect the family ...
Hold on. I cannot agree to murder.
To begin with, we cannot simply take a human life.
Calm yourselves! Things have changed. We will not kill Shea Libbs.
He risked his life to save Aema.
Anyone who wishes to kill him will have to go through Aema.
Fight Aema?
Who would dare?
Aema is strong.
And she can bear children.
Well, if he saved Aema...
Hmm.
But if we let him return, he will speak...
...of this place.
That is why we are *not* letting him return.
He will remain with us, and the Elder agrees.
The Elder?

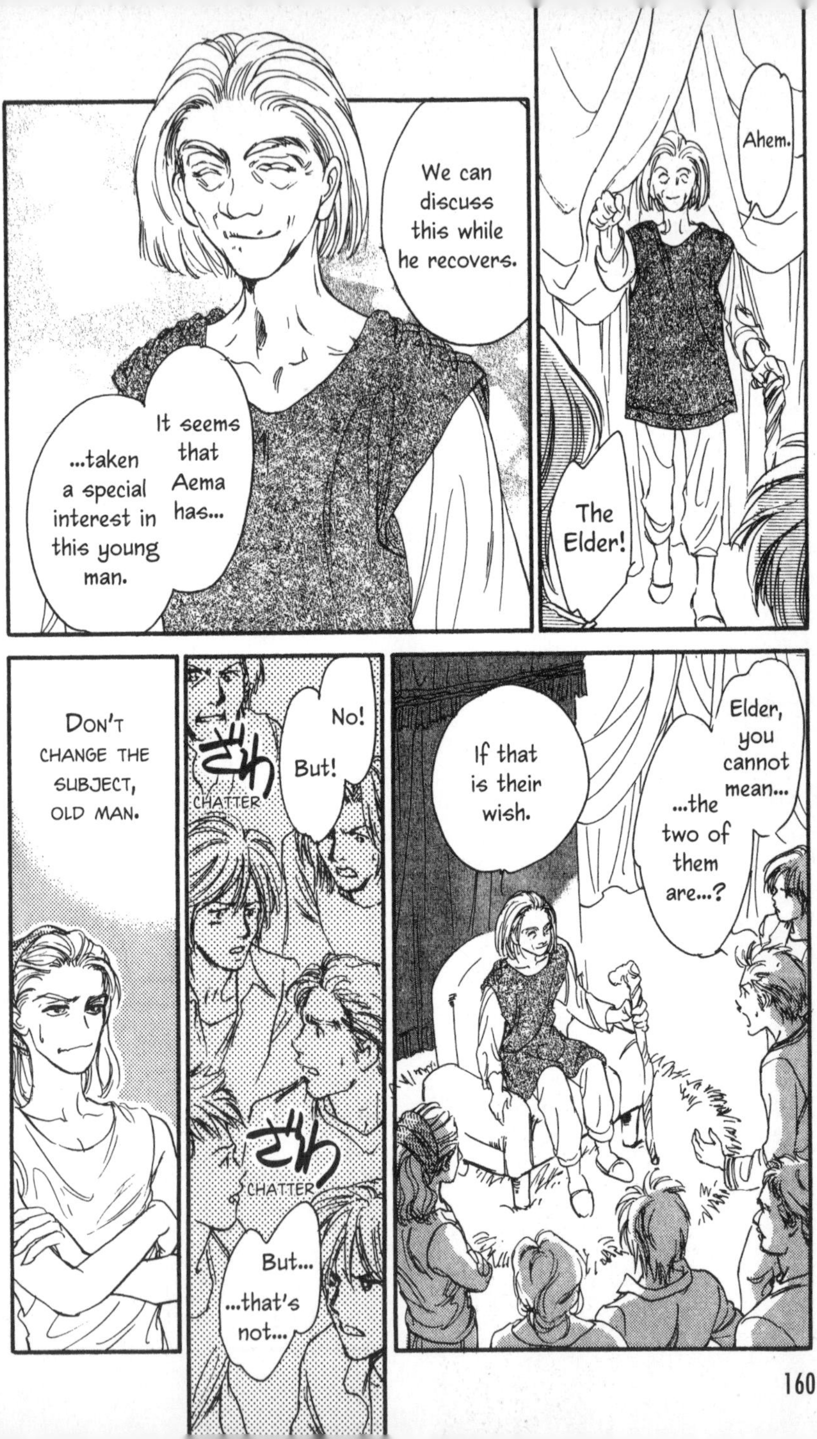
Ahem.
The Elder!
We can discuss this while he recovers.
It seems that Aema has...
...taken a special interest in this young man.
Elder, you cannot mean...
...the two of them are...?
If that is their wish.
No!
But!
ざわ
CHATTER
ざわ
CHATTER
But...
...that's not...
DON'T CHANGE THE SUBJECT, OLD MAN.

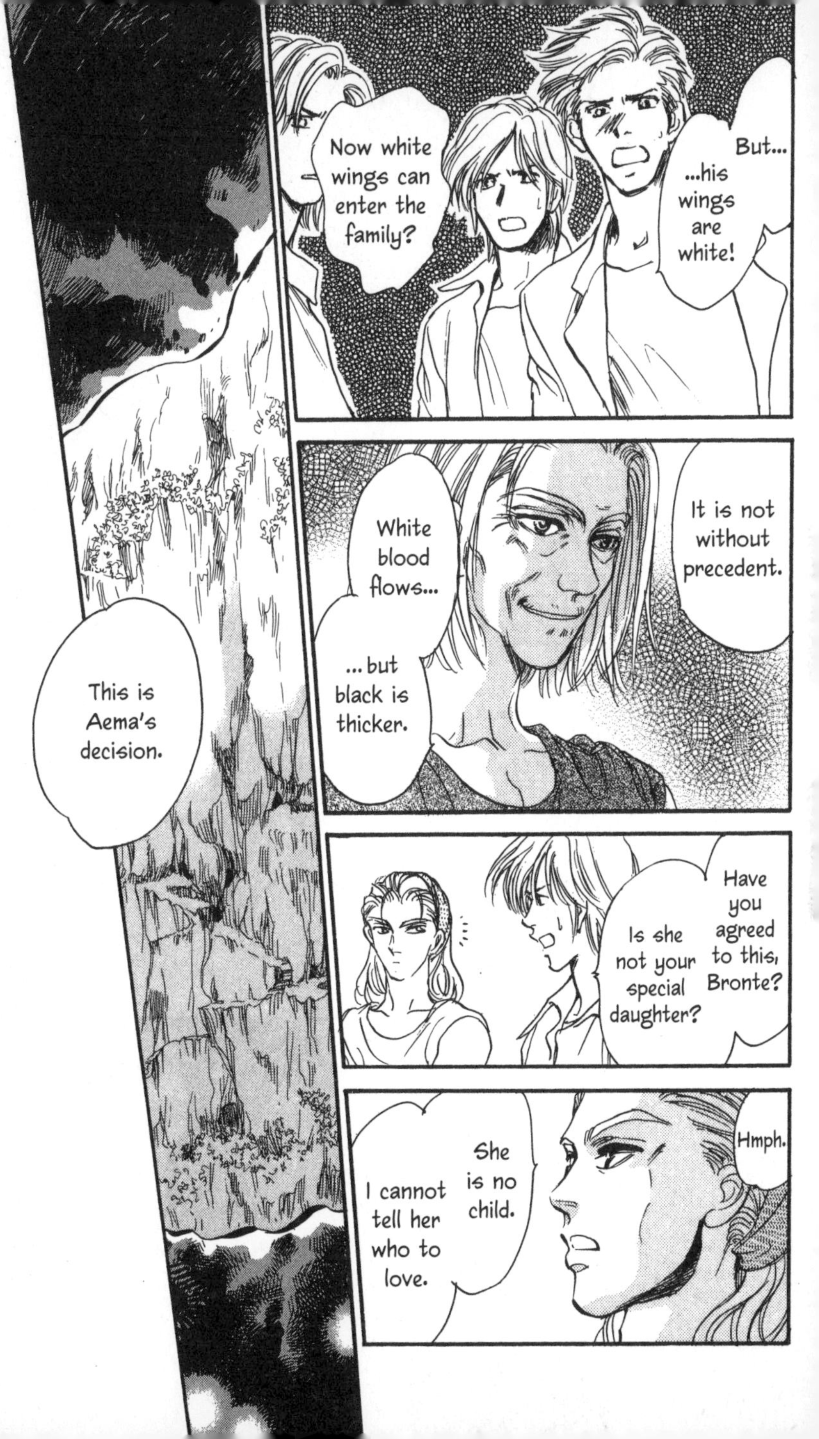
But... ...his wings are white!
Now white wings can enter the family?
It is not without precedent.
White blood flows...
... but black is thicker.
Have you agreed to this, Bronte?
Is she not your special daughter?
Hmph.
She is no child.
I cannot tell her who to love.
This is Aema's decision.

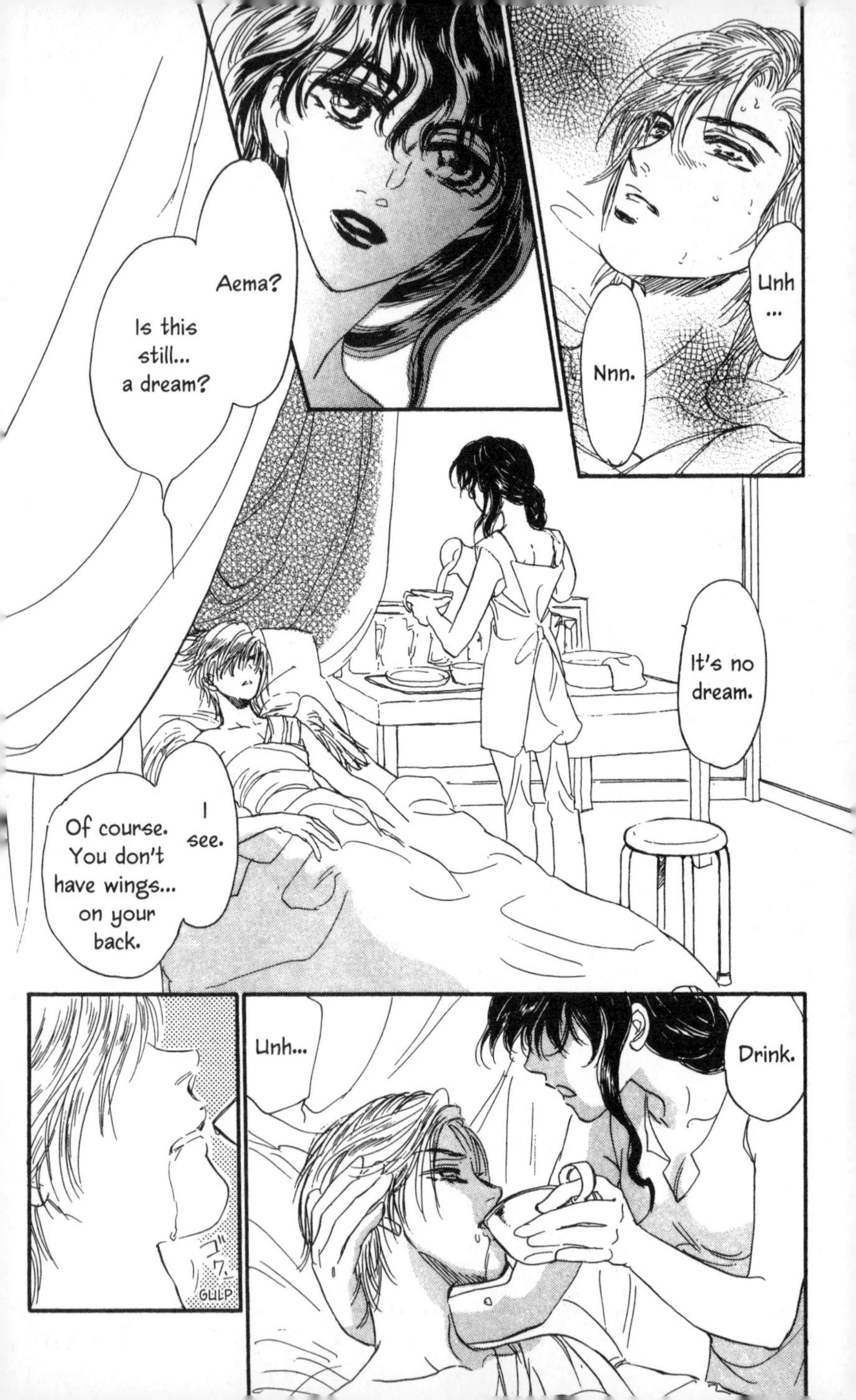

Unh ...
Nnn.
Aema? Is this still... a dream?
It's no dream.
I see.
Of course. You don't have wings... on your back.
Drink.
Unh...
ゴクッ
GULP

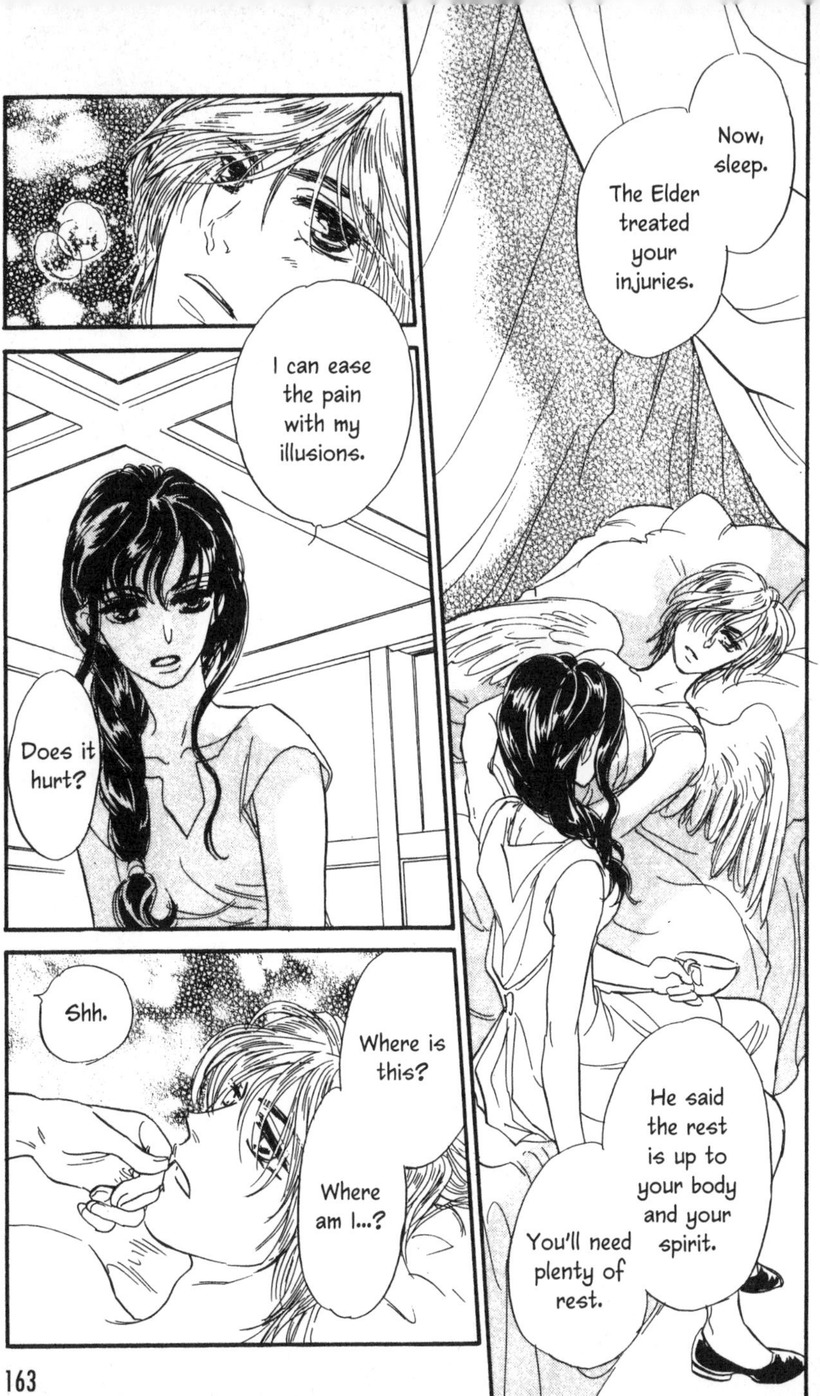
Now, sleep.
The Elder treated your injuries.
He said the rest is up to your body and your spirit.
You'll need plenty of rest.
I can ease the pain with my illusions.
Does it hurt?
Where is this?
Where am I...?
Shh.

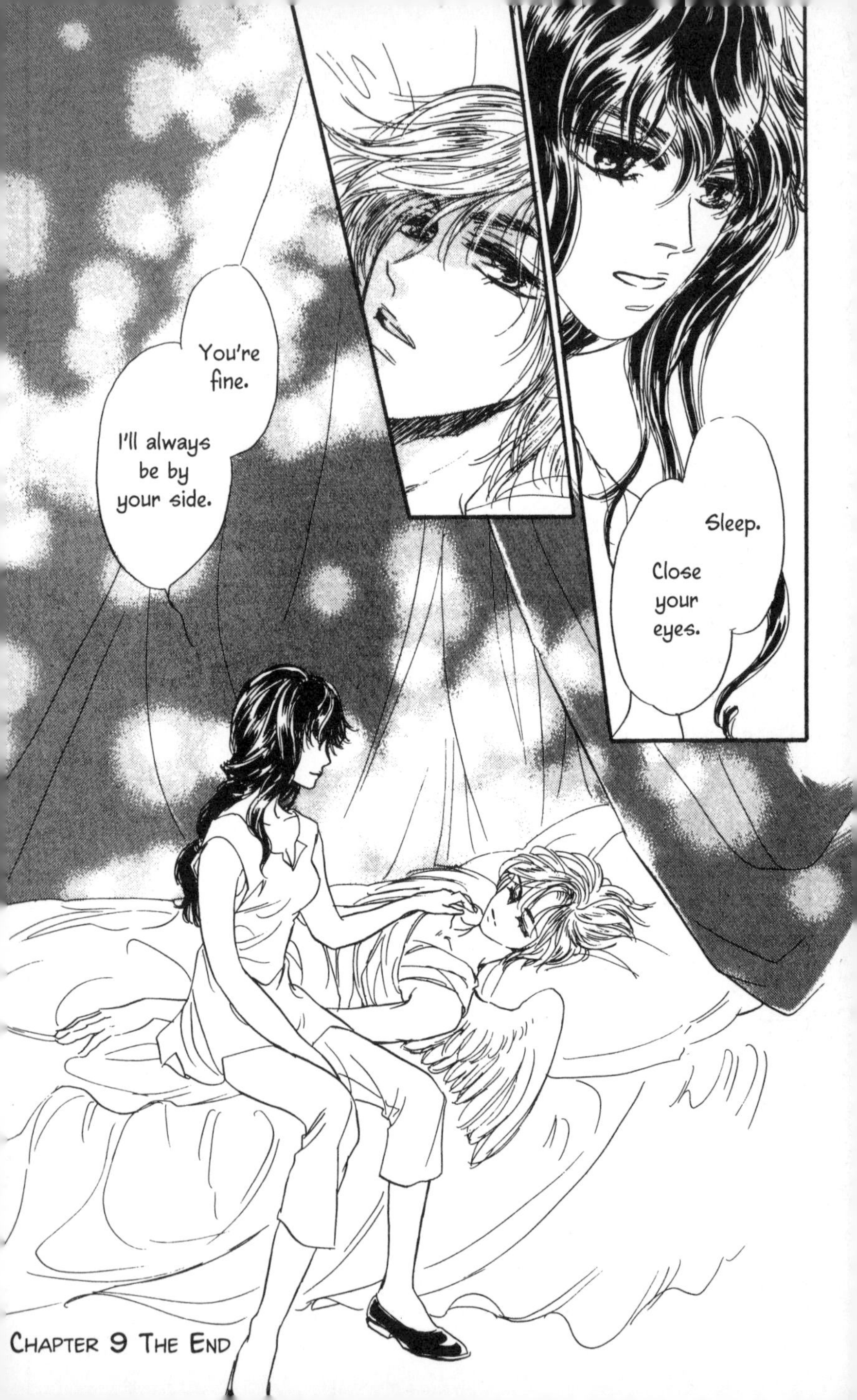
Sleep.
Close your eyes.
You're fine.
I'll always be by your side.
Chapter 9 The End

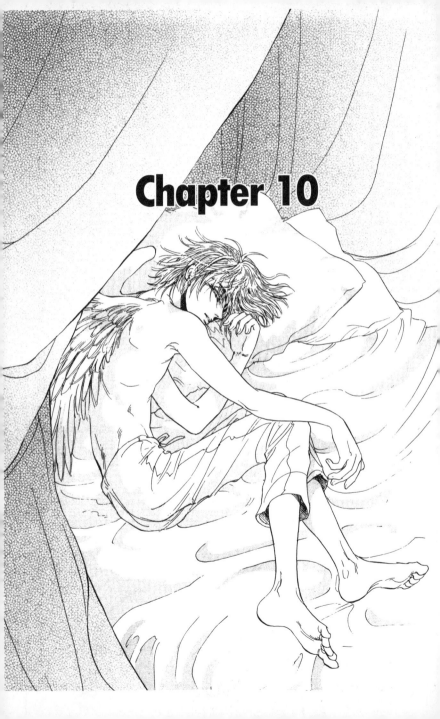

Chapter 10

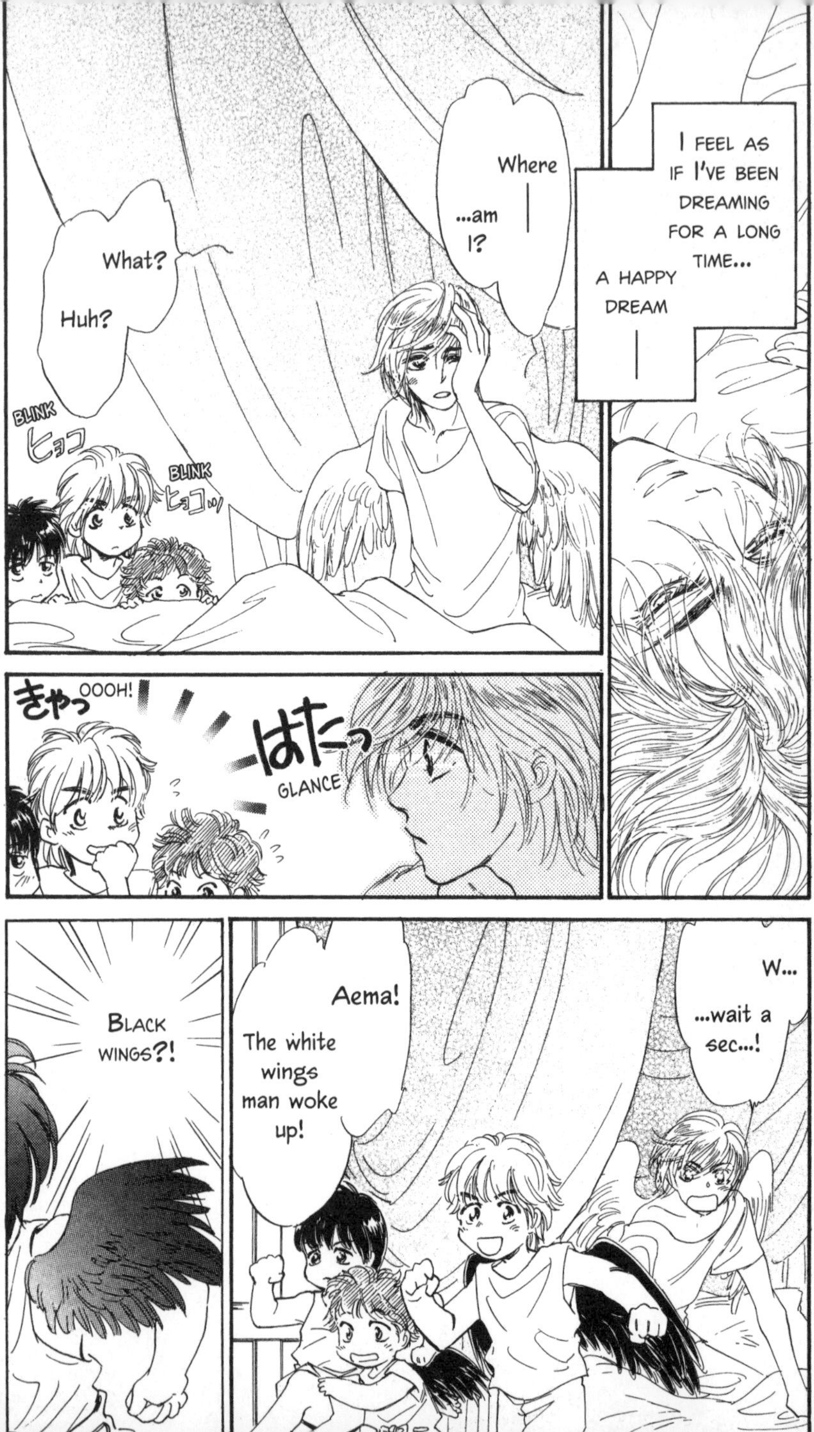
I FEEL AS IF I'VE BEEN DREAMING FOR A LONG TIME...
A HAPPY DREAM —
Where — ...am I?
What? Huh?
BLINK ヒョコ
BLINK ヒョコッ
はたっ GLANCE
きゃっ OOOH!
W... ...wait a sec...!
Aema! The white wings man woke up!
BLACK WINGS?!

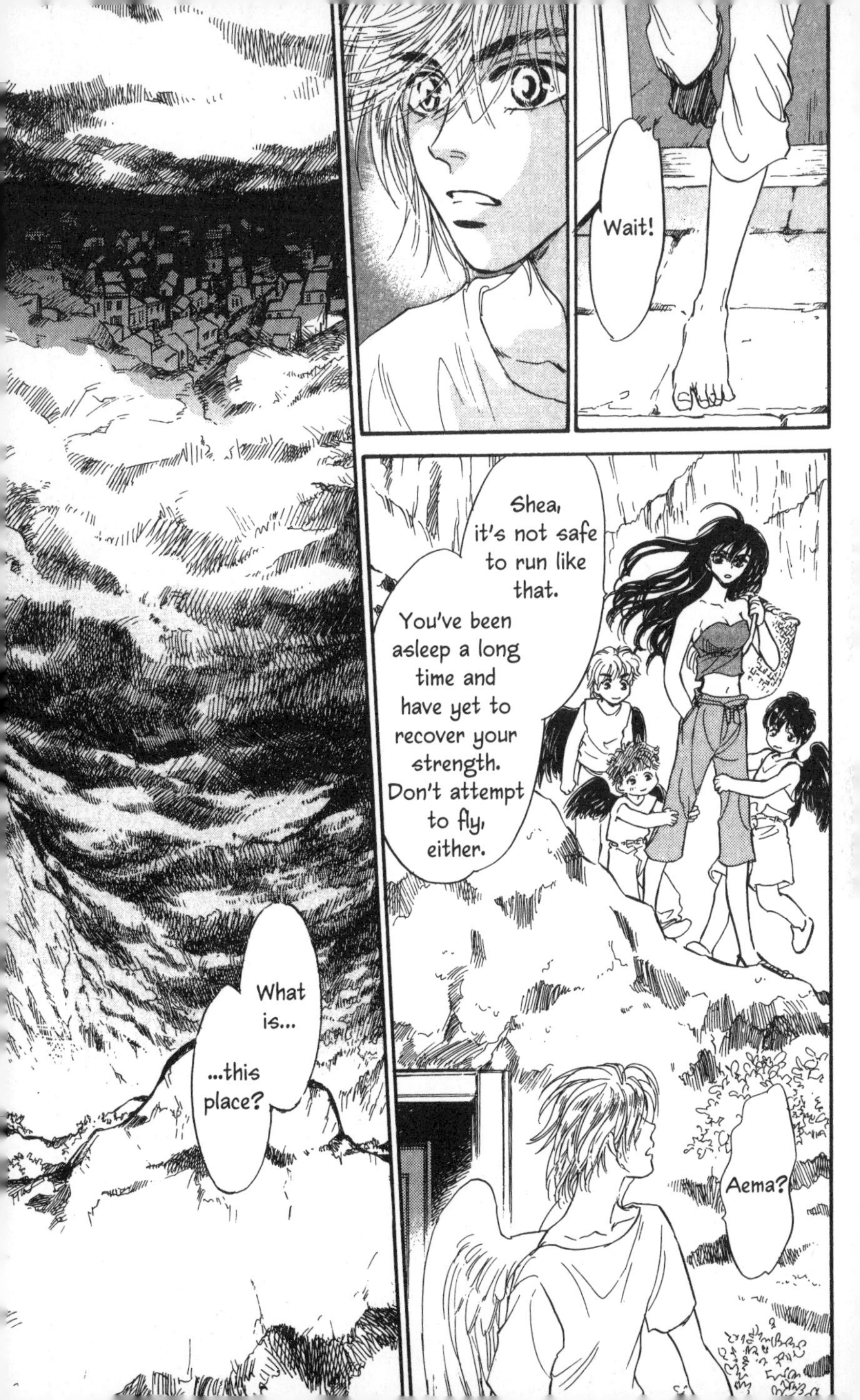
Wait!
Shea, it's not safe to run like that.
You've been asleep a long time and have yet to recover your strength. Don't attempt to fly, either.
Aema?
What is...
...this place?

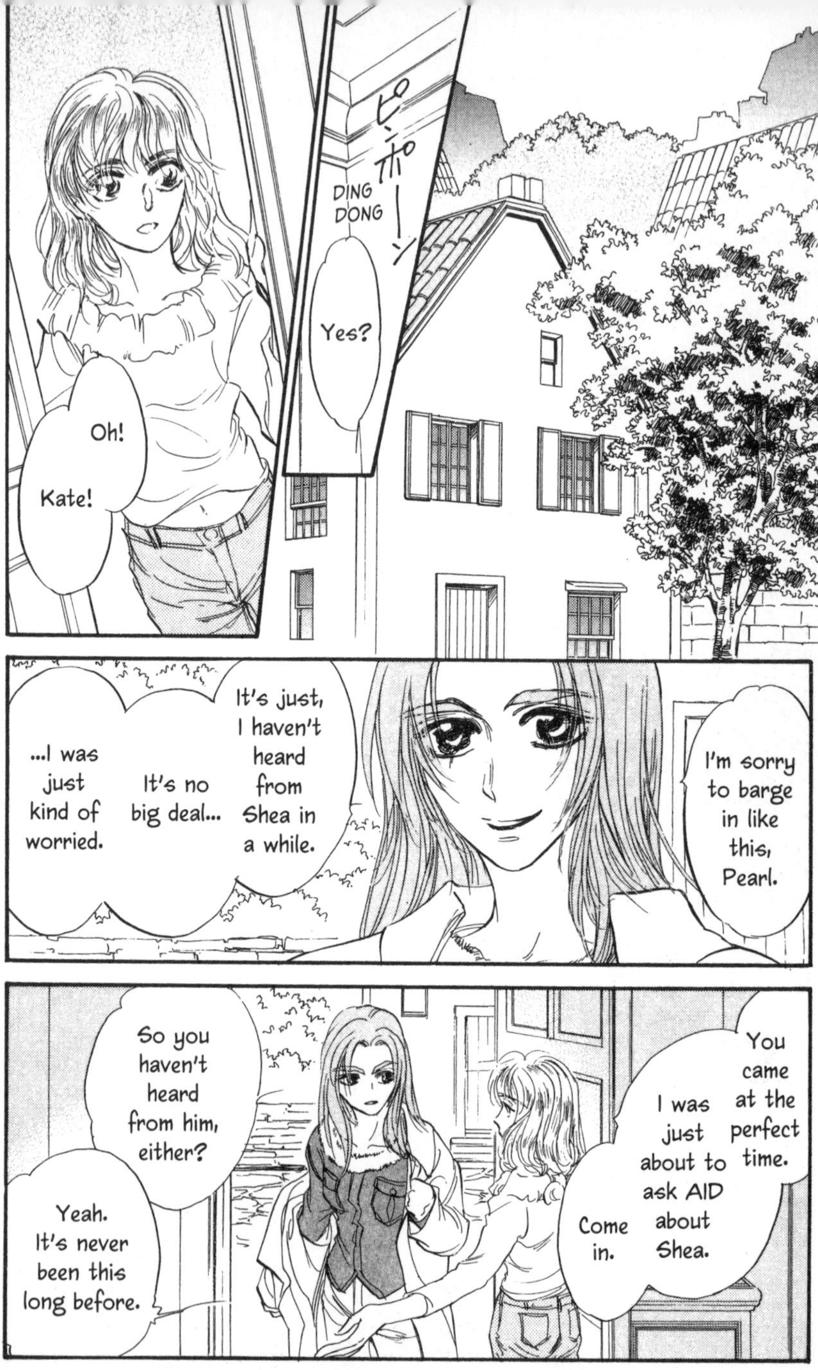
DING DONG
Yes?
Oh! Kate!
I'm sorry to barge in like this, Pearl.
It's just, I haven't heard from Shea in a while.
It's no big deal...
...I was just kind of worried.
You came at the perfect time.
I was just about to ask AID about Shea.
Come in.
So you haven't heard from him, either?
Yeah. It's never been this long before.

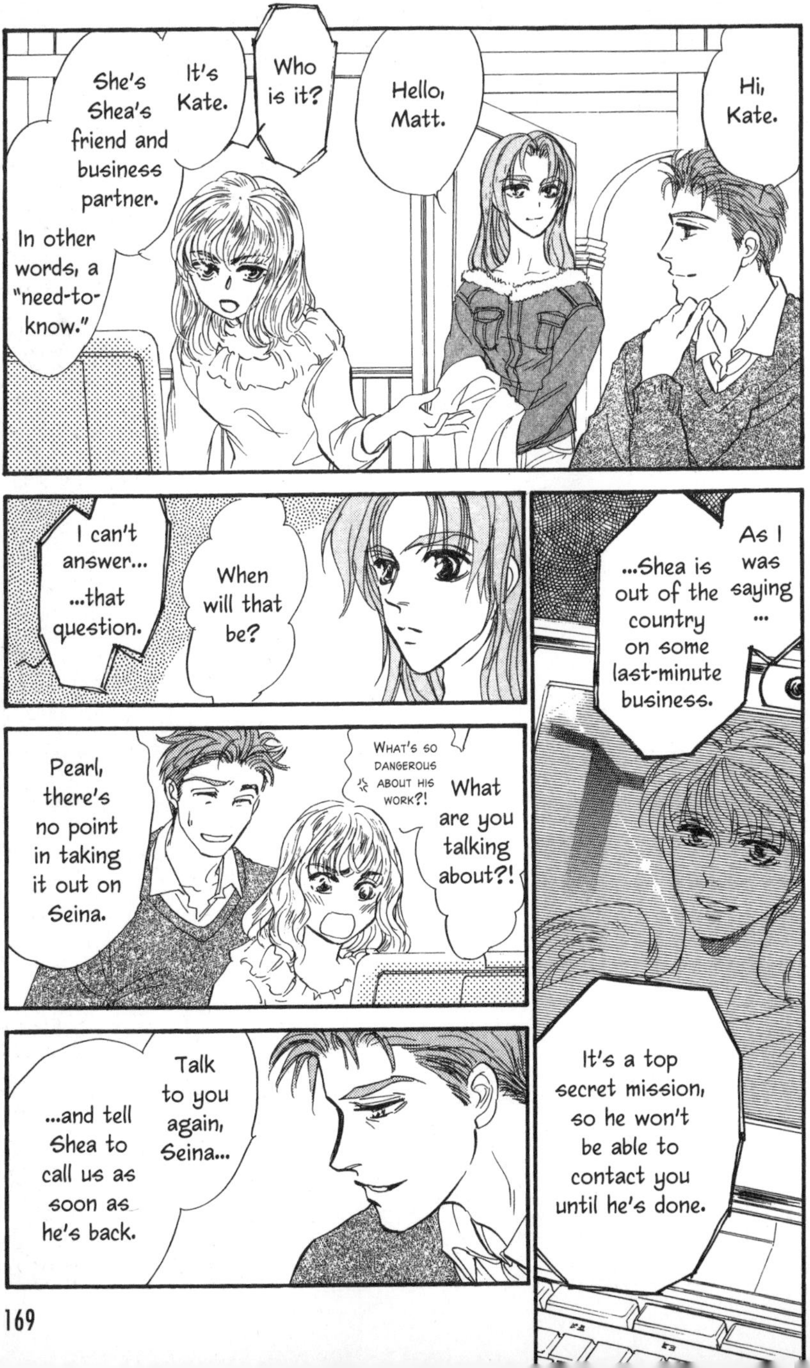
Hi, Kate.
Hello, Matt.
Who is it?
It's Kate.
She's Shea's friend and business partner.
In other words, a "need-to-know."
As I was saying...
...Shea is out of the country on some last-minute business.
It's a top secret mission, so he won't be able to contact you until he's done.
When will that be?
I can't answer... ...that question.
What are you talking about?!
WHAT'S SO DANGEROUS ABOUT HIS WORK?!
Pearl, there's no point in taking it out on Seina.
Talk to you again, Seina...
...and tell Shea to call us as soon as he's back.

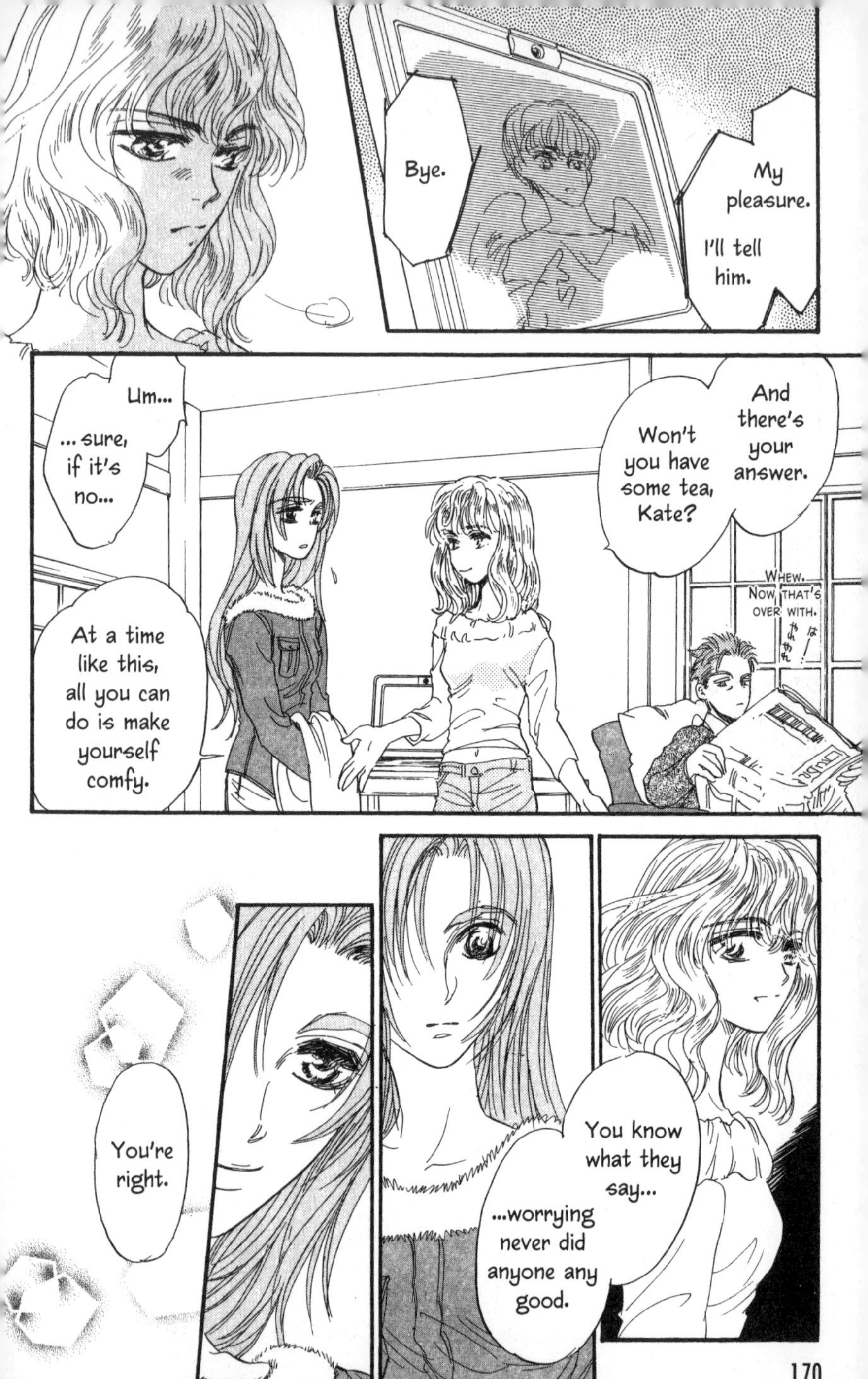
My pleasure.
I'll tell him.
Bye.
And there's your answer.
Won't you have some tea, Kate?
Whew. Now that's over with.
Um...
... sure, if it's no...
At a time like this, all you can do is make yourself comfy.
You know what they say...
...worrying never did anyone any good.
You're right.

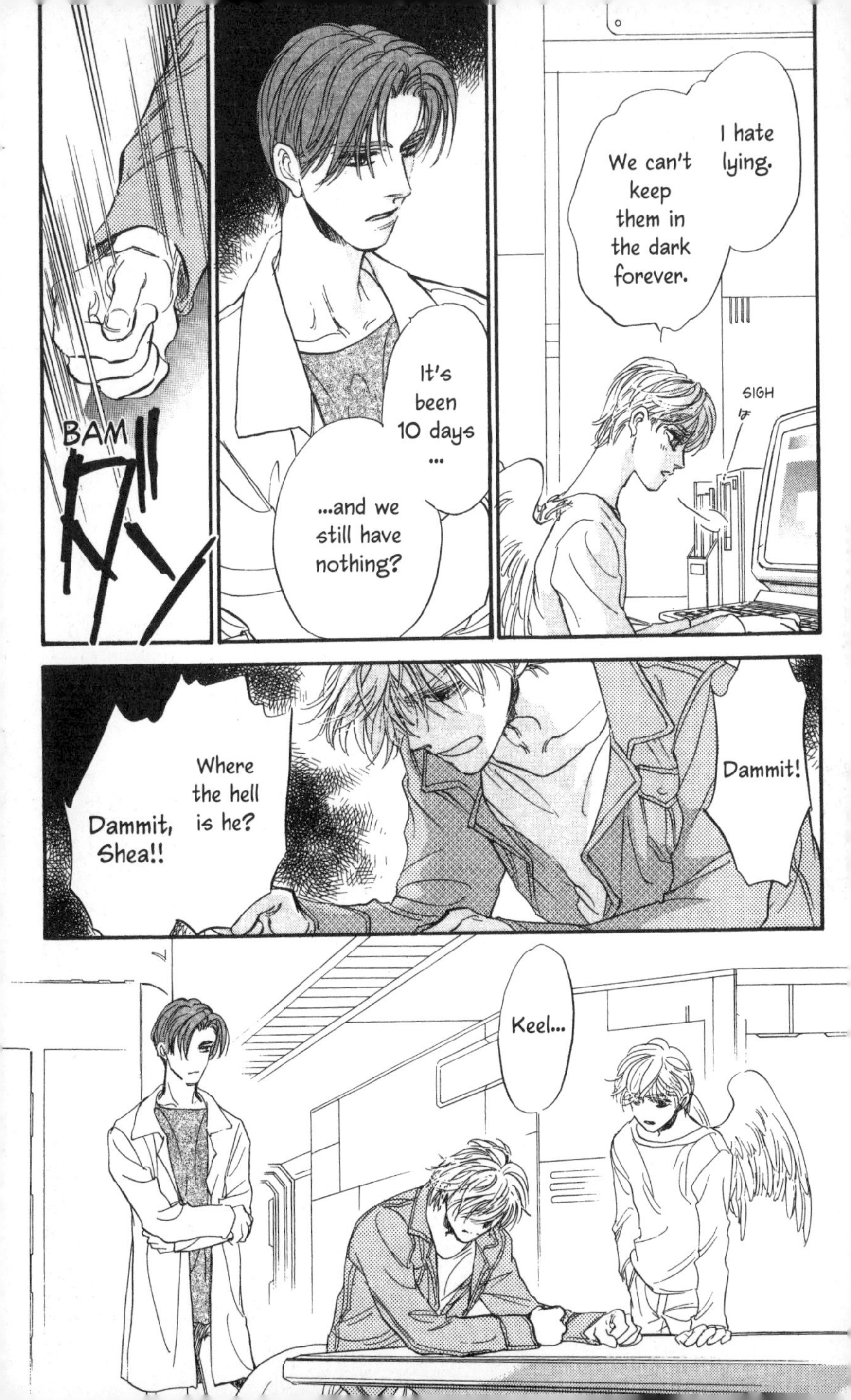
I hate lying.
We can't keep them in the dark forever.
SIGH
は
It's been 10 days ...
...and we still have nothing?
BAM
Dammit!
Where the hell is he?
Dammit, Shea!!
Keel...

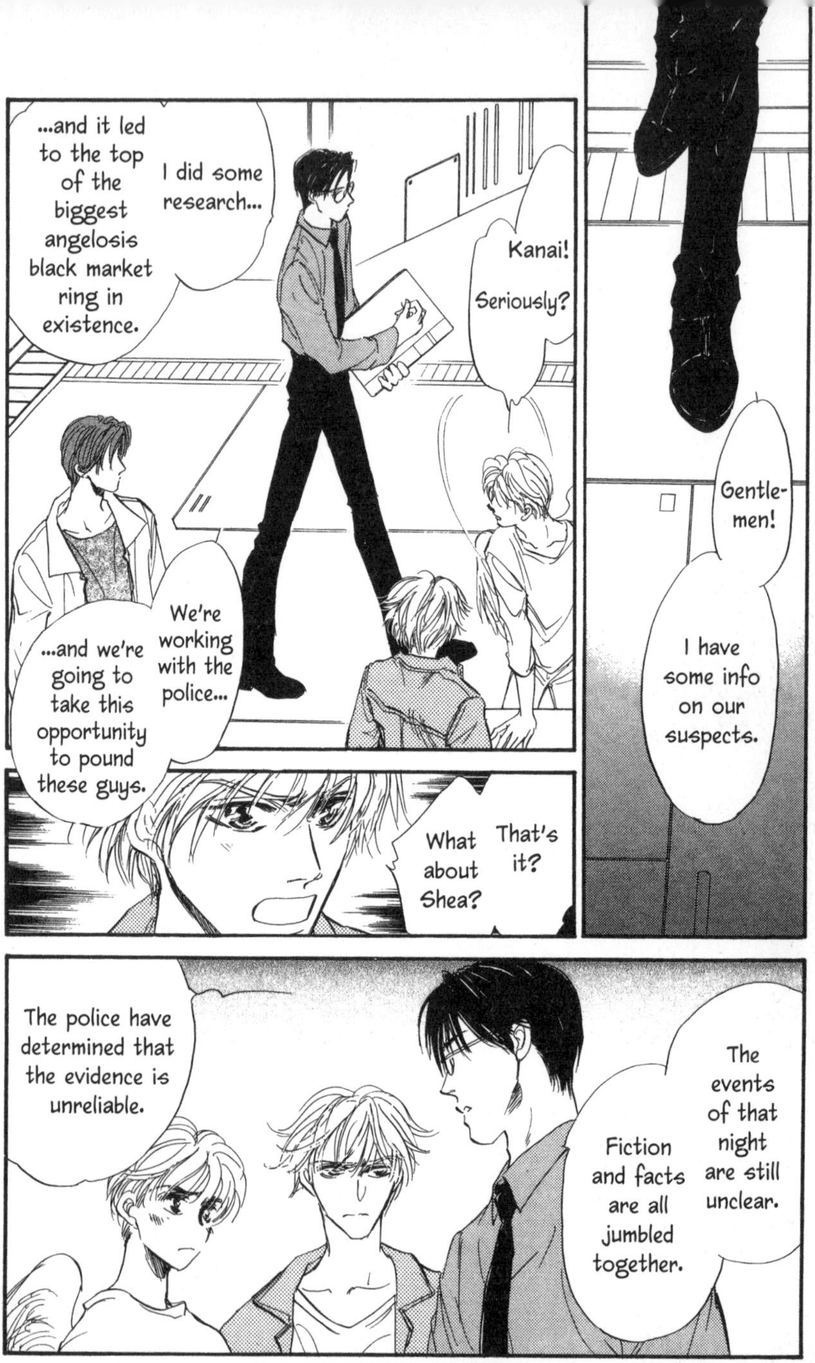
Gentle-men!
I have some info on our suspects.
Kanai!
Seriously?
I did some research...
...and it led to the top of the biggest angelosis black market ring in existence.
We're working with the police...
...and we're going to take this opportunity to pound these guys.
That's it?
What about Shea?
The events of that night are still unclear.
Fiction and facts are all jumbled together.
The police have determined that the evidence is unreliable.

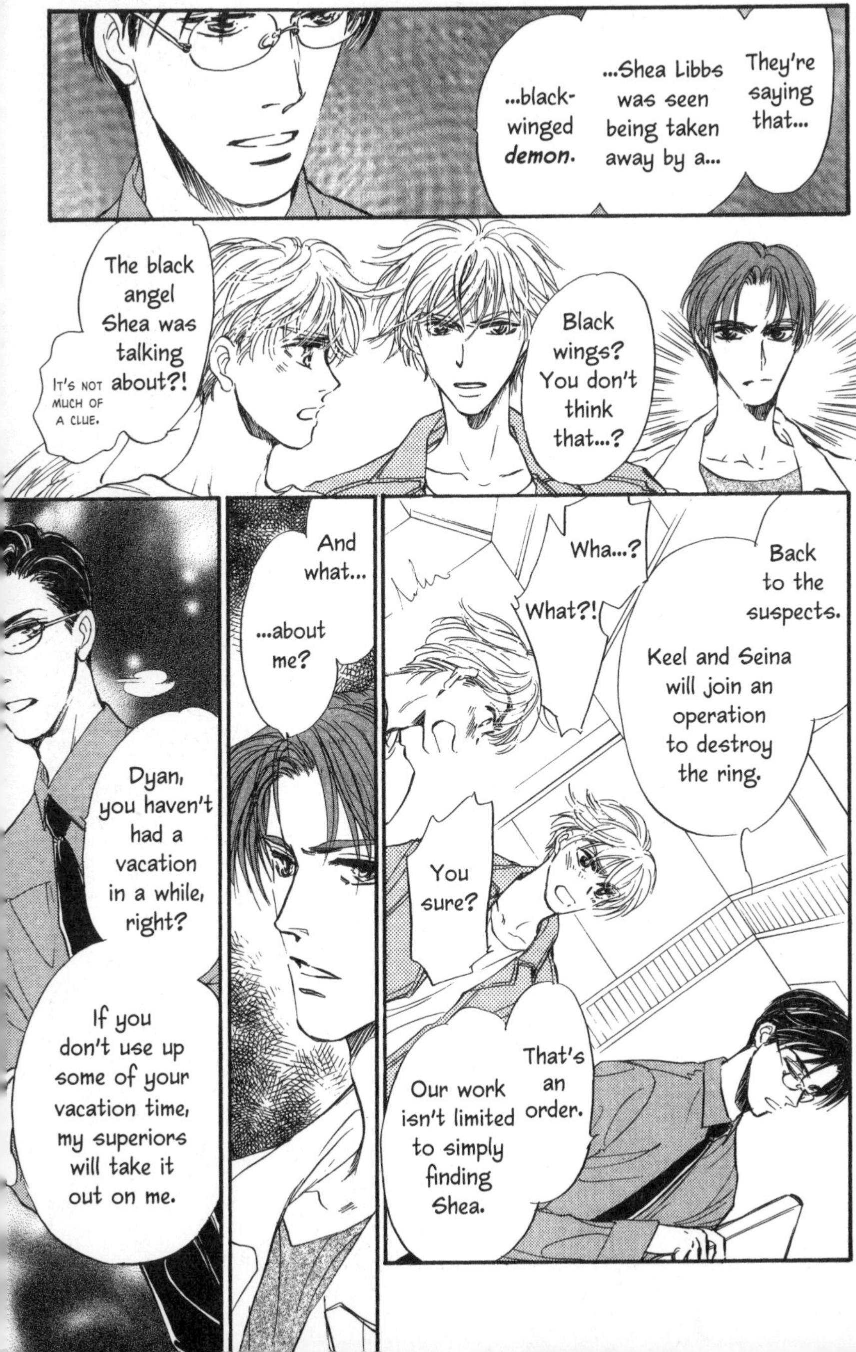

They're saying that...
...Shea Libbs was seen being taken away by a...
...black-winged **demon**.
Black wings? You don't think that...?
The black angel Shea was talking about?!
It's not much of a clue.
Back to the suspects.
Keel and Seina will join an operation to destroy the ring.
Wha...?
What?!
You sure?
That's an order.
Our work isn't limited to simply finding Shea.
And what...
...about me?
Dyan, you haven't had a vacation in a while, right?
If you don't use up some of your vacation time, my superiors will take it out on me.

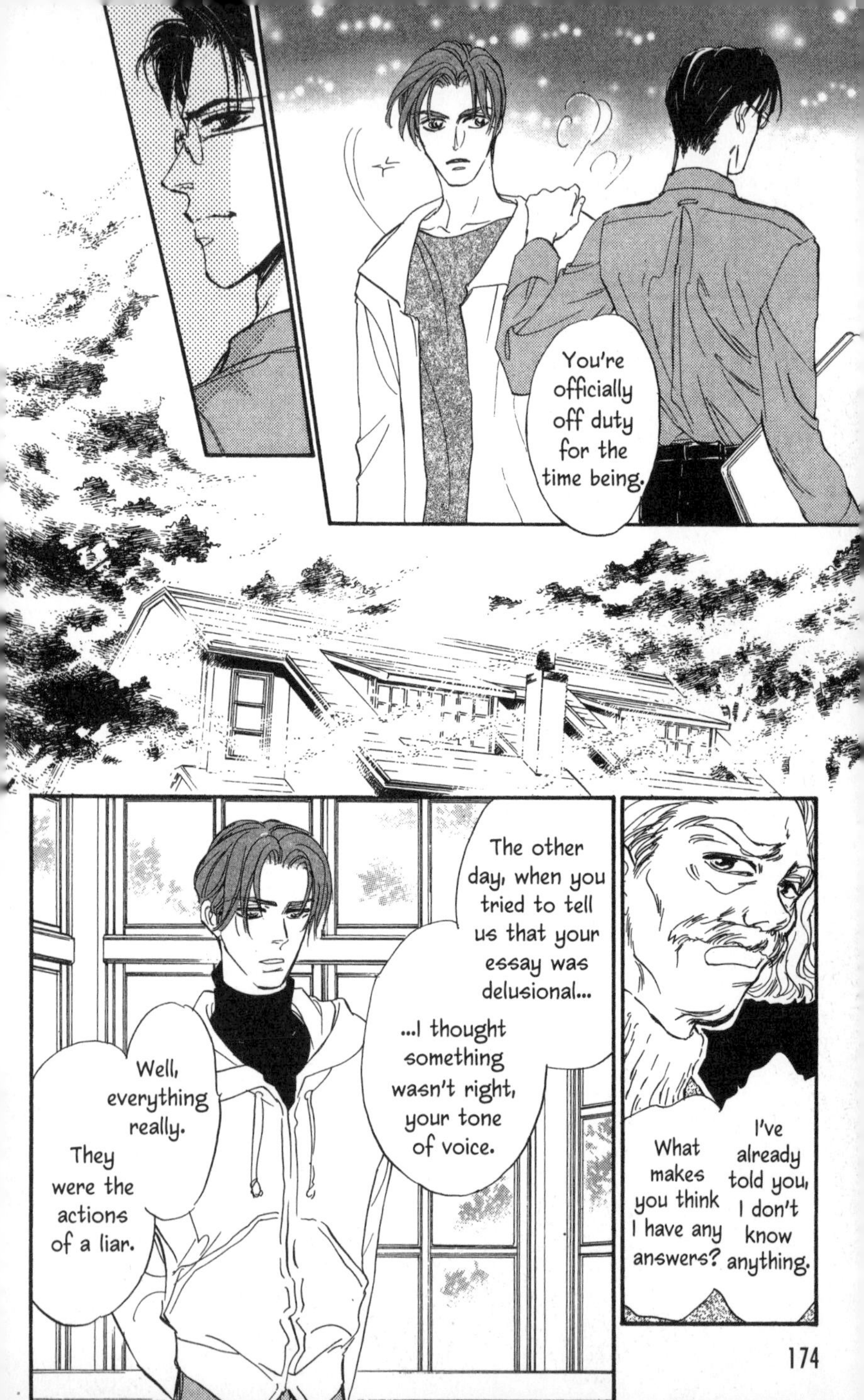
You're officially off duty for the time being.
The other day, when you tried to tell us that your essay was delusional...
...I thought something wasn't right, your tone of voice.
What makes you think I have any answers?
I've already told you, I don't know anything.
Well, everything really.
They were the actions of a liar.

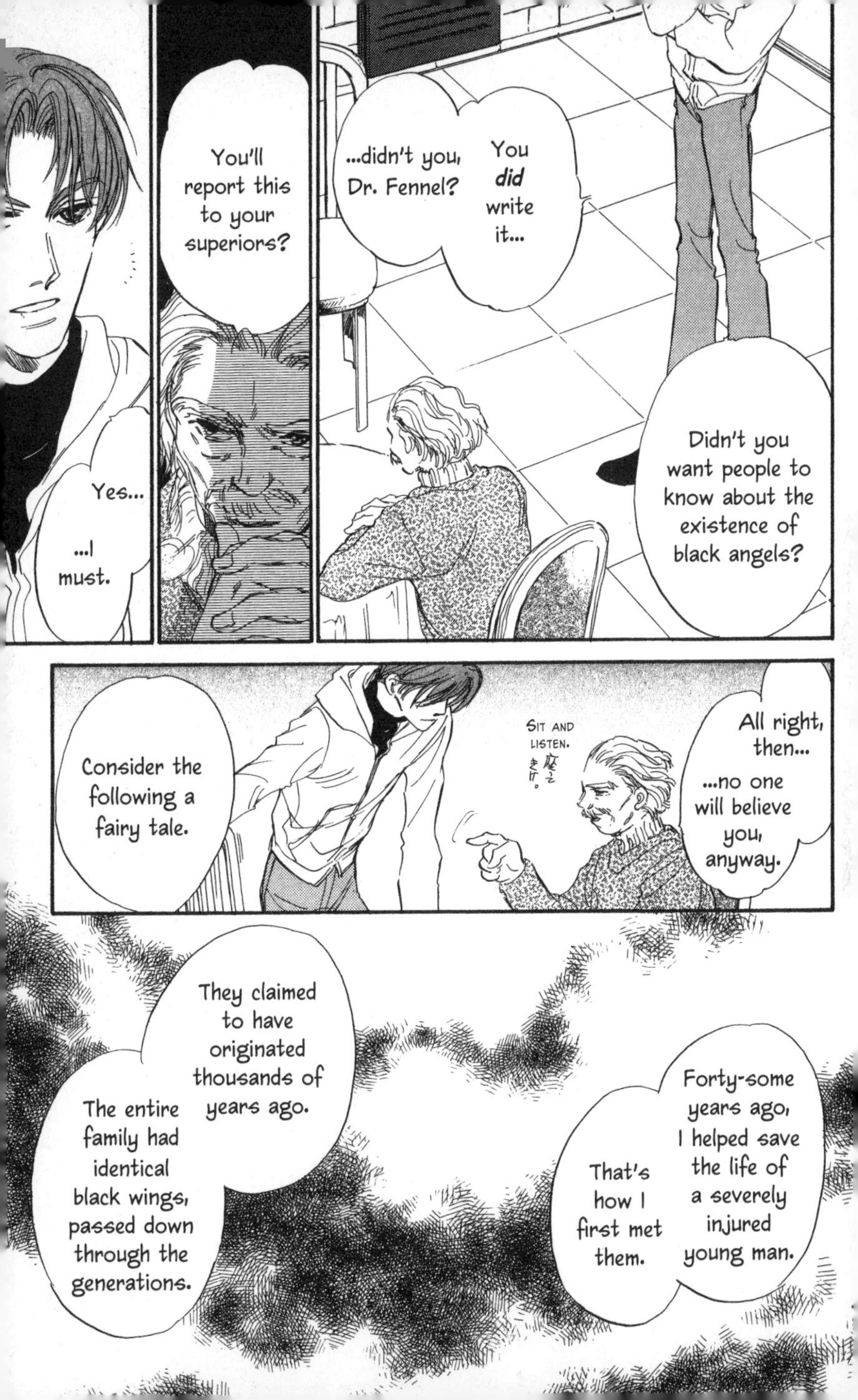
You did write it...
...didn't you, Dr. Fennel?
Didn't you want people to know about the existence of black angels?
You'll report this to your superiors?
Yes...
...I must.
All right, then...
...no one will believe you, anyway.
SIT AND LISTEN.
座ってきけ。
Consider the following a fairy tale.
Forty-some years ago, I helped save the life of a severely injured young man.
That's how I first met them.
They claimed to have originated thousands of years ago.
The entire family had identical black wings, passed down through the generations.

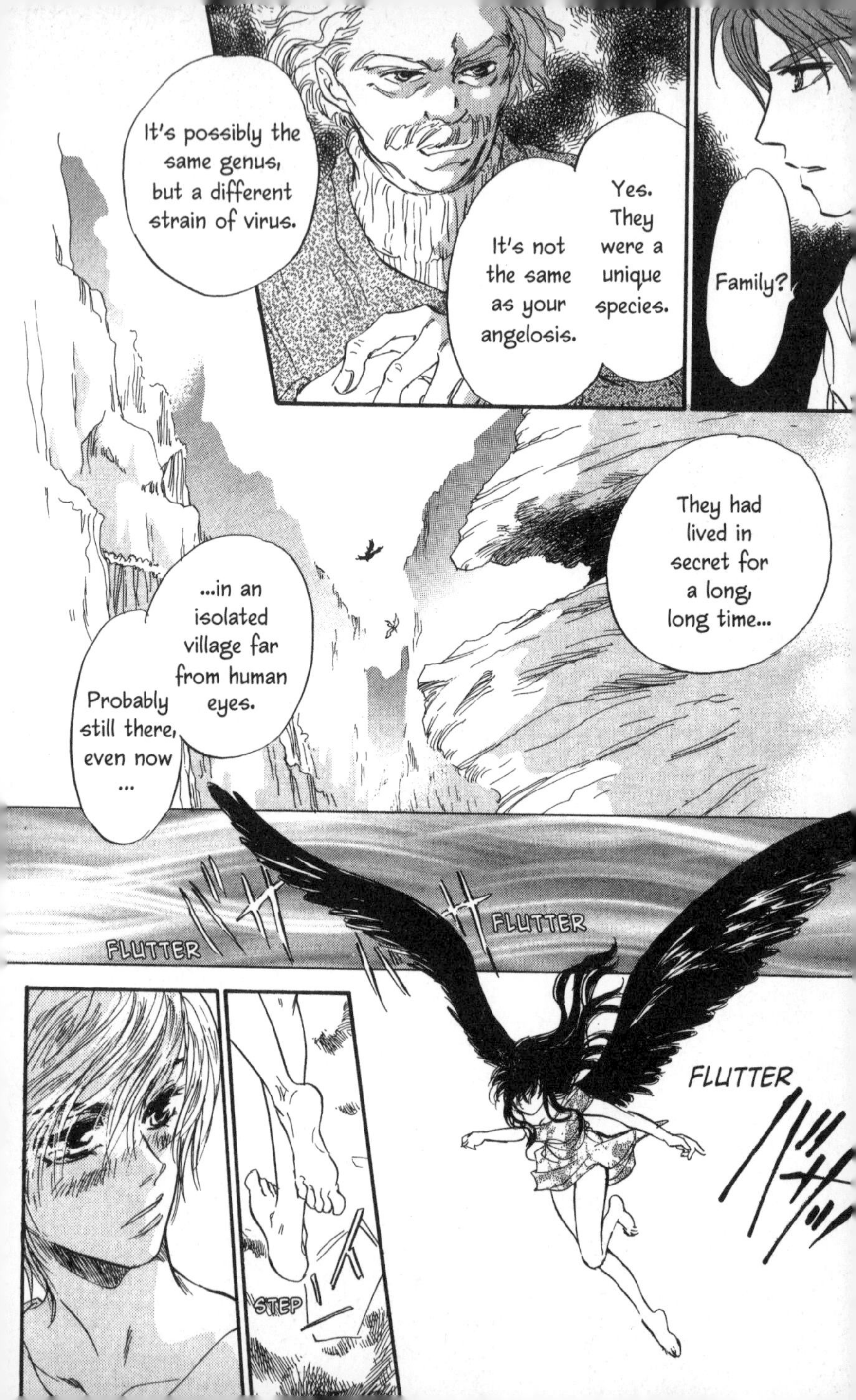
Family?
Yes. They were a unique species.
It's not the same as your angelosis.
It's possibly the same genus, but a different strain of virus.
They had lived in secret for a long, long time...
...in an isolated village far from human eyes.
Probably still there, even now ...
FLUTTER
FLUTTER
FLUTTER
STEP

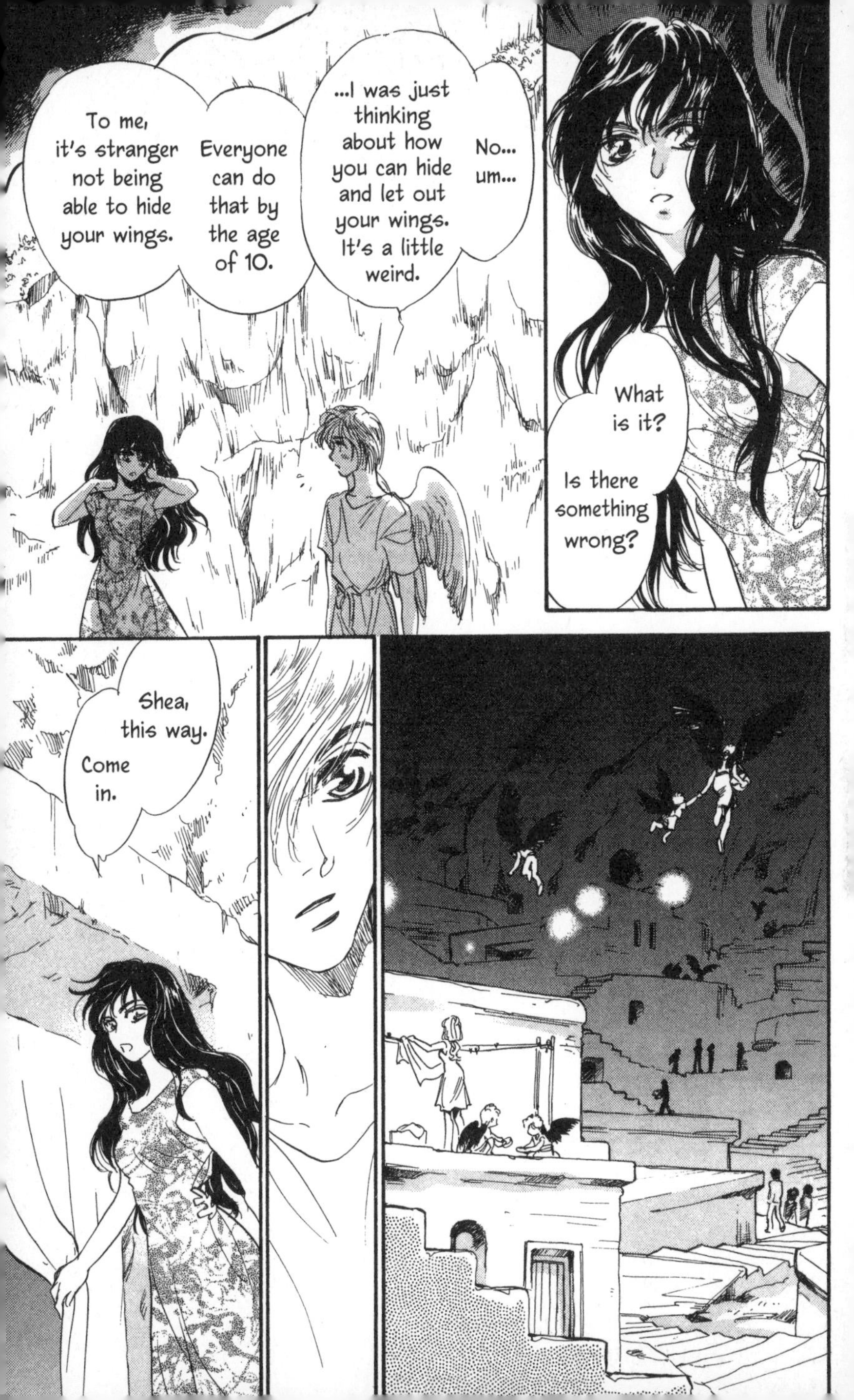
What is it?
Is there something wrong?
No... um...
...I was just thinking about how you can hide and let out your wings. It's a little weird.
Everyone can do that by the age of 10.
To me, it's stranger not being able to hide your wings.
Shea, this way.
Come in.

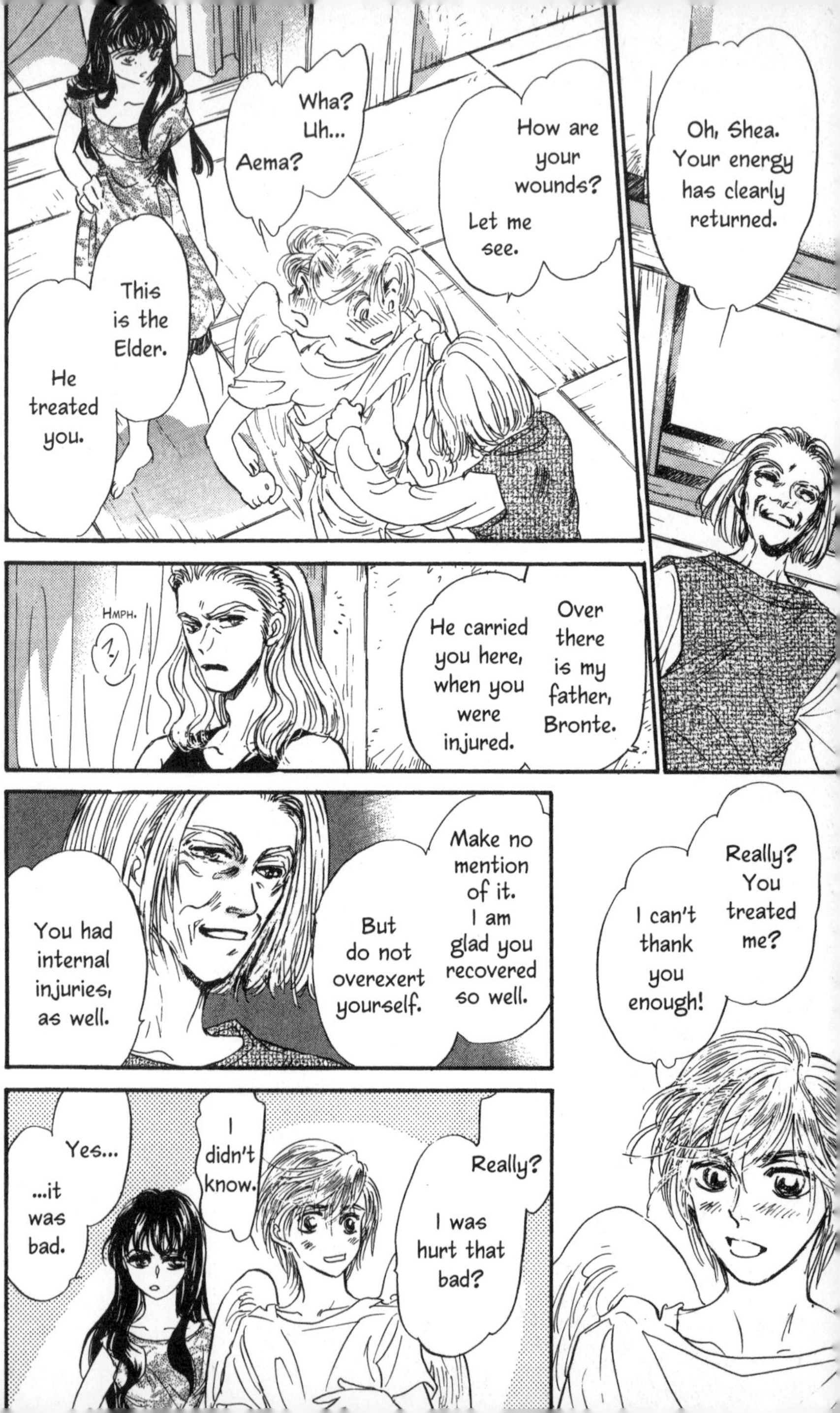
Oh, Shea. Your energy has clearly returned.
How are your wounds? Let me see.
Wha? Uh... Aema?
This is the Elder. He treated you.
Over there is my father, Bronte.
He carried you here, when you were injured.
HMPH.
Really? You treated me?
I can't thank you enough!
Make no mention of it. I am glad you recovered so well.
But do not overexert yourself.
You had internal injuries, as well.
Really? I was hurt that bad?
I didn't know.
Yes... ...it was bad.

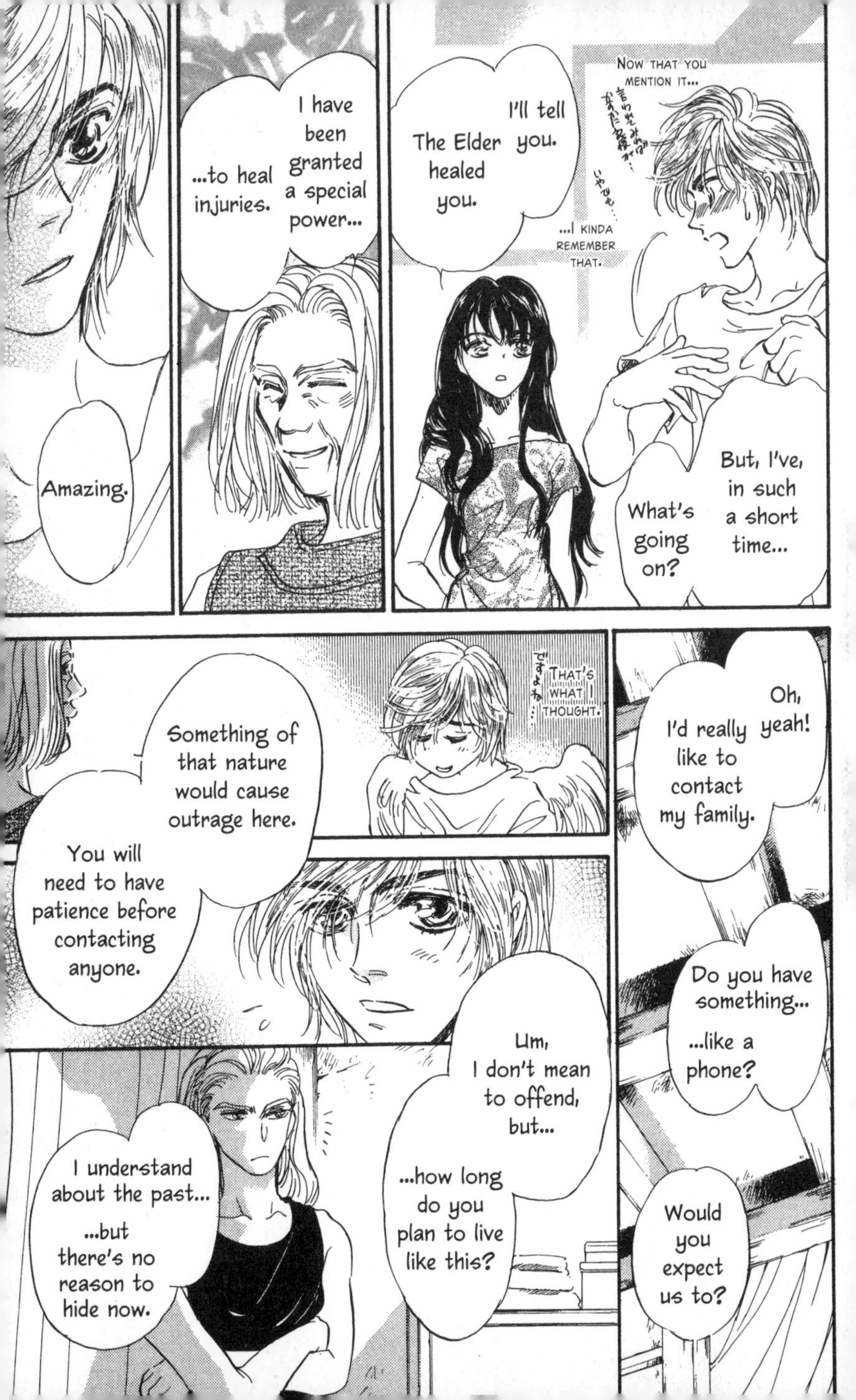

Now that you mention it...
I'll tell you.
The Elder healed you.
...I kinda remember that.
But, I've, in such a short time...
What's going on?
I have been granted a special power...
...to heal injuries.
Amazing.
Oh, yeah!
I'd really like to contact my family.
Do you have something...
...like a phone?
Would you expect us to?
That's what I thought.
Something of that nature would cause outrage here.
You will need to have patience before contacting anyone.
Um, I don't mean to offend, but...
...how long do you plan to live like this?
I understand about the past...
...but there's no reason to hide now.

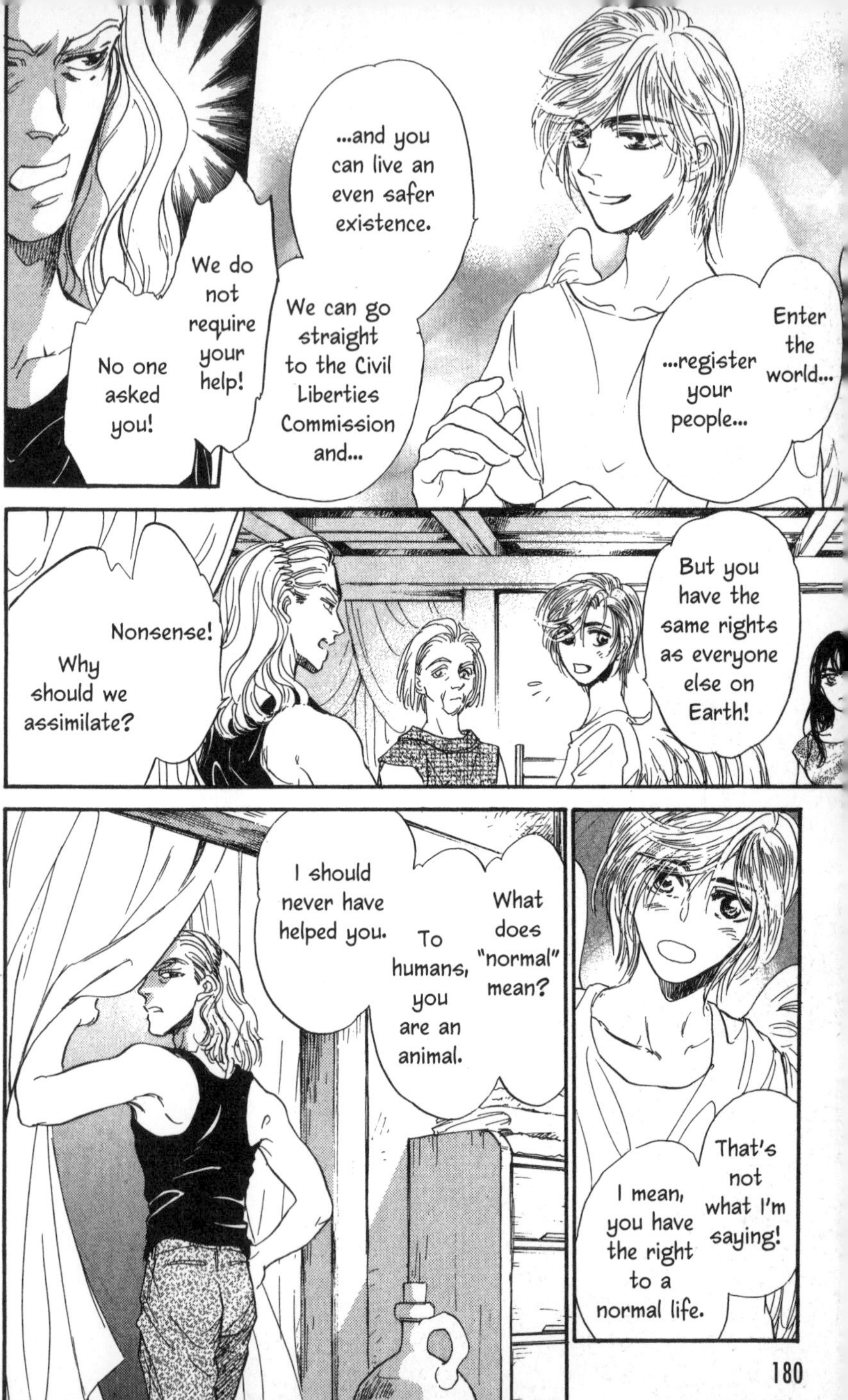
Enter the world...
...register your people...
We can go straight to the Civil Liberties Commission and...
...and you can live an even safer existence.
We do not require your help!
No one asked you!
But you have the same rights as everyone else on Earth!
Nonsense!
Why should we assimilate?
That's not what I'm saying!
I mean, you have the right to a normal life.
What does "normal" mean?
To humans, you are an animal.
I should never have helped you.

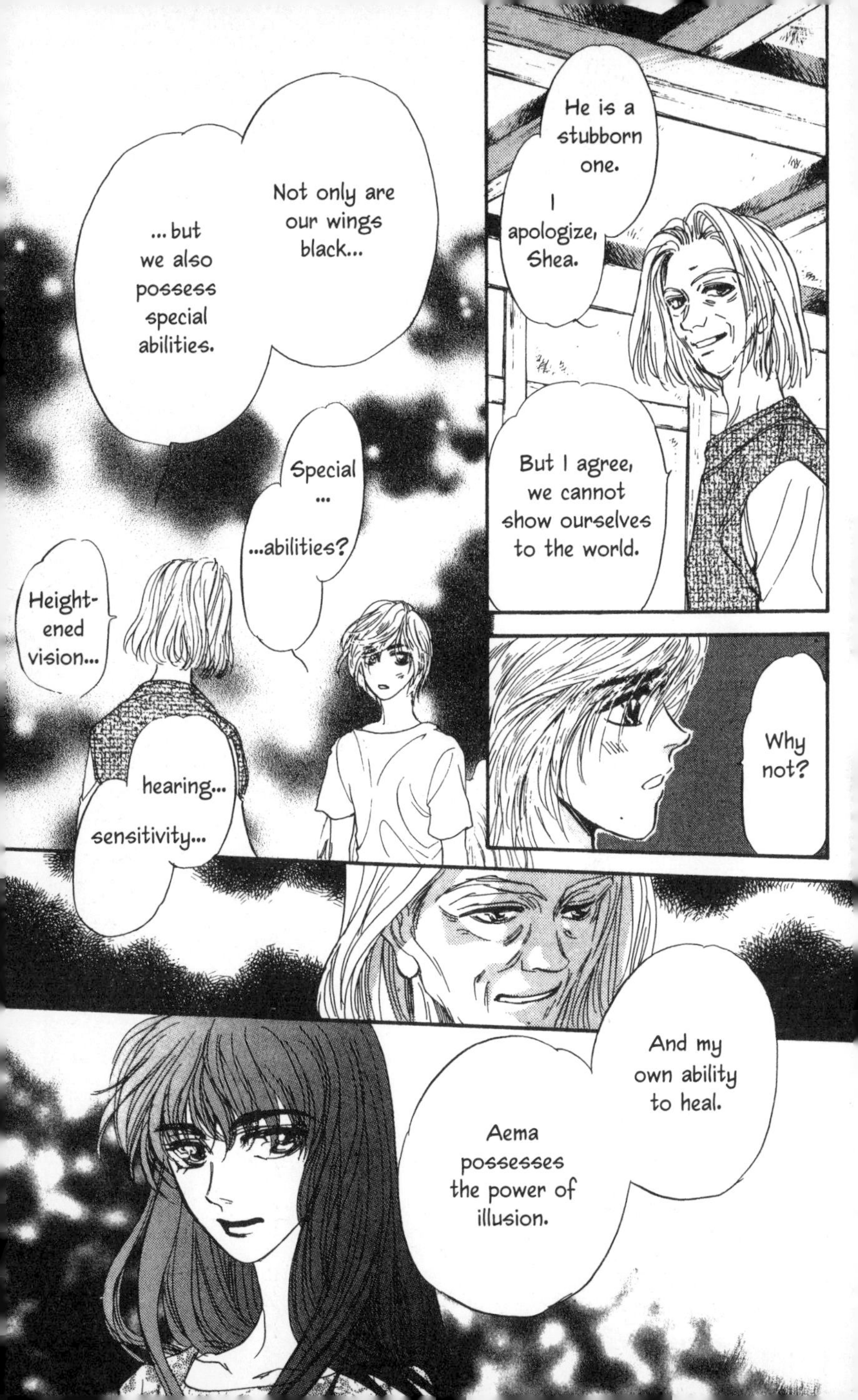
He is a stubborn one.
I apologize, Shea.
But I agree, we cannot show ourselves to the world.
Why not?
Not only are our wings black...
...but we also possess special abilities.
Special...
...abilities?
Height-ened vision...
hearing...
sensitivity...
And my own ability to heal.
Aema possesses the power of illusion.

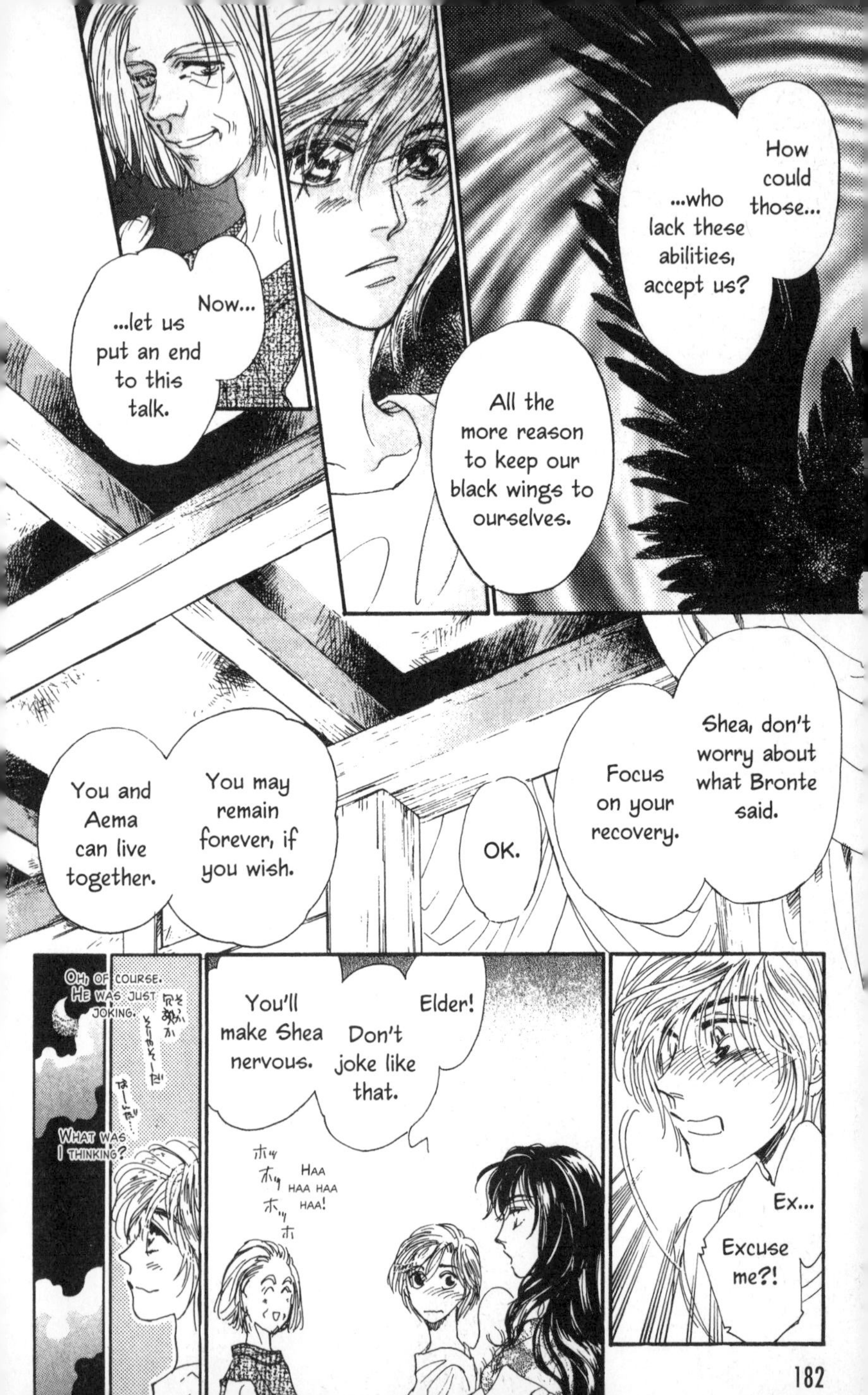
How could those...
...who lack these abilities, accept us?
All the more reason to keep our black wings to ourselves.
Now...
...let us put an end to this talk.
Shea, don't worry about what Bronte said.
Focus on your recovery.
OK.
You may remain forever, if you wish.
You and Aema can live together.
Ex...
Excuse me?!
Elder!
Don't joke like that.
You'll make Shea nervous.
Haa haa haa haa!
Oh, of course. He was just joking.
What was I thinking?

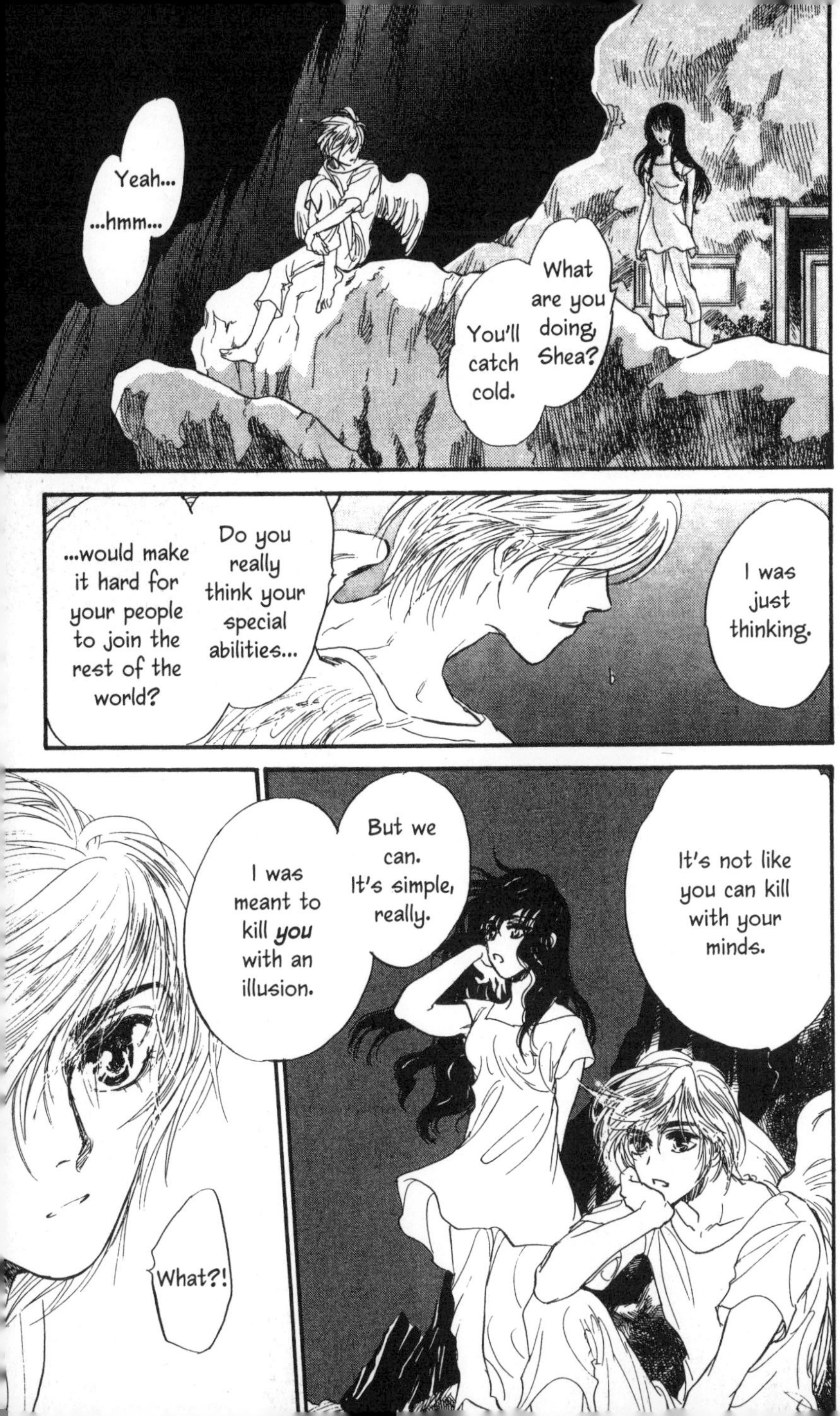
What are you doing, Shea?
You'll catch cold.
Yeah... ...hmm...
I was just thinking.
Do you really think your special abilities...
...would make it hard for your people to join the rest of the world?
It's not like you can kill with your minds.
But we can. It's simple, really.
I was meant to kill *you* with an illusion.
What?!

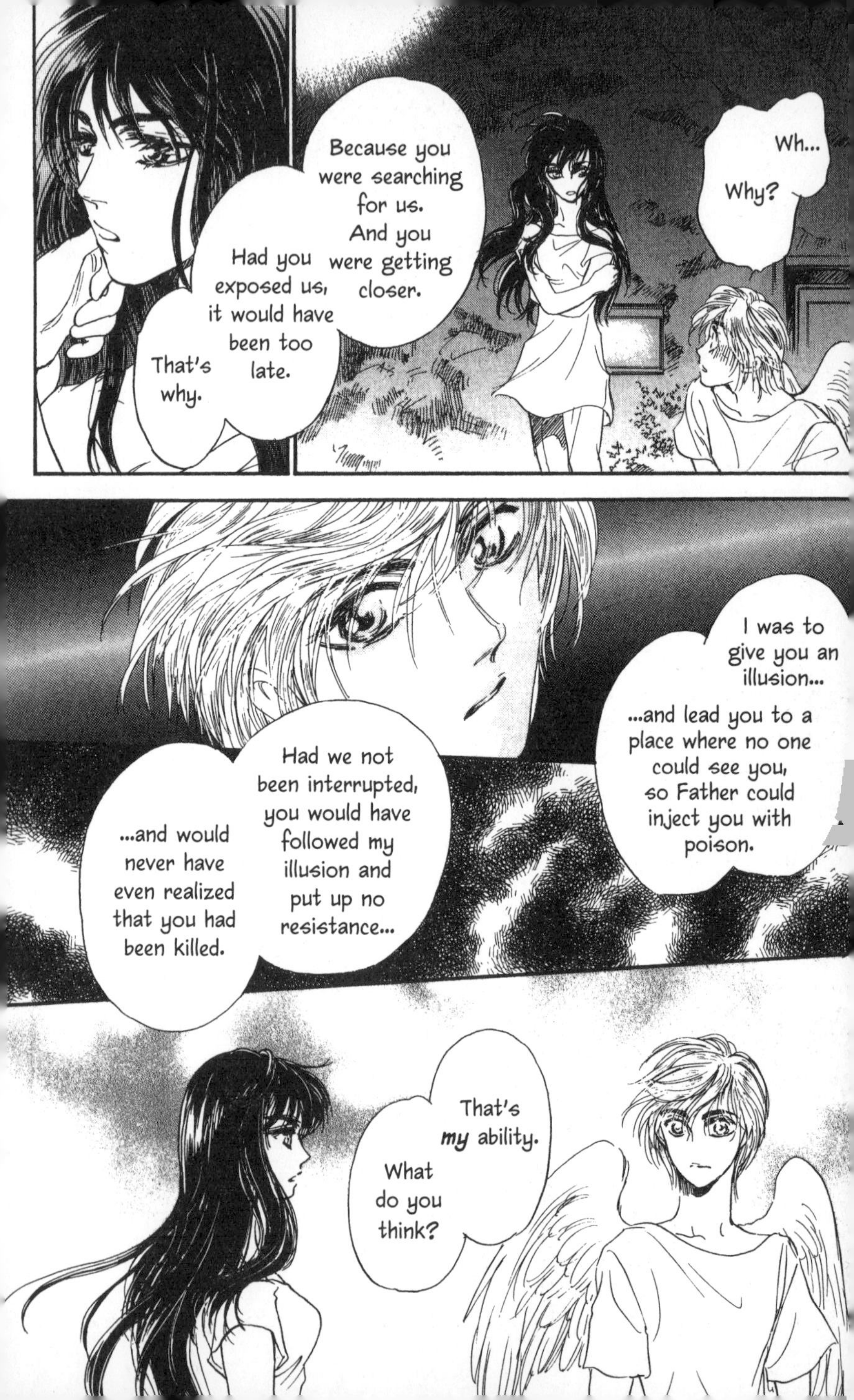
Wh...
Why?
Because you were searching for us. And you were getting closer.
Had you exposed us, it would have been too late.
That's why.
I was to give you an illusion...
...and lead you to a place where no one could see you, so Father could inject you with poison.
Had we not been interrupted, you would have followed my illusion and put up no resistance...
...and would never have even realized that you had been killed.
That's *my* ability.
What do you think?

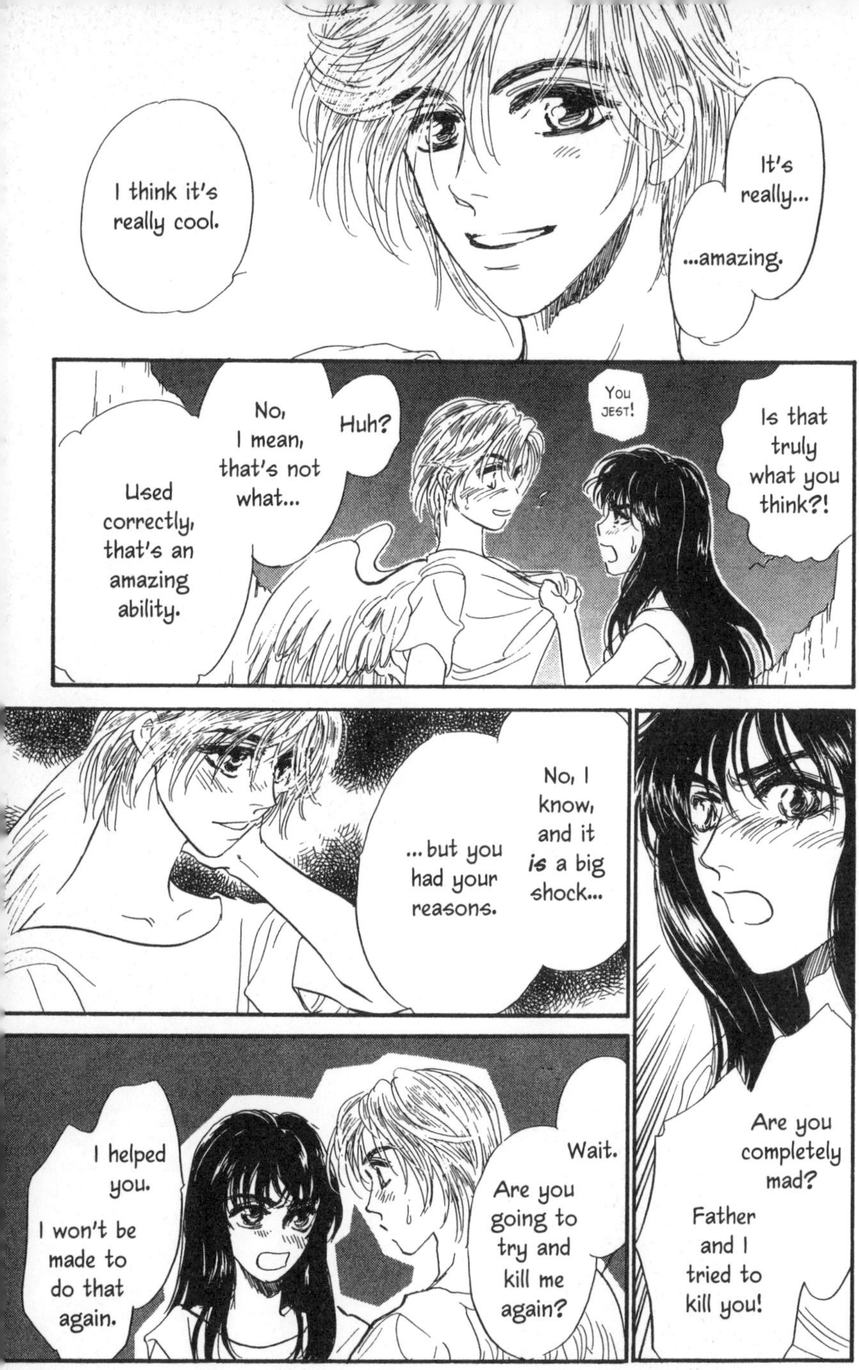

It's really... ...amazing.
I think it's really cool.
Is that truly what you think?!
You jest!
Huh?
No, I mean, that's not what...
Used correctly, that's an amazing ability.
Are you completely mad?
Father and I tried to kill you!
No, I know, and it *is* a big shock...
...but you had your reasons.
Wait.
Are you going to try and kill me again?
I helped you.
I won't be made to do that again.

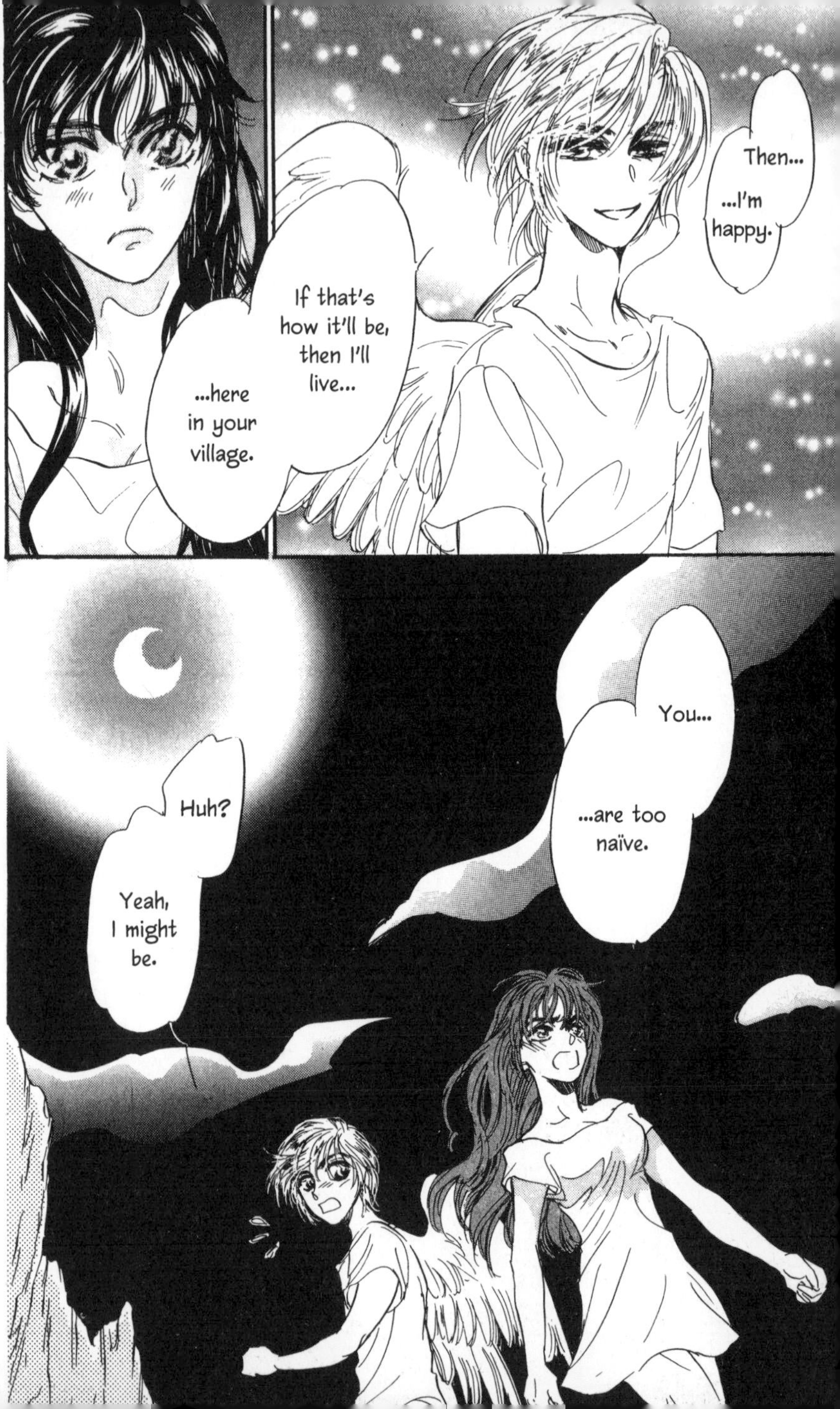
Then...
...I'm happy.
If that's how it'll be, then I'll live...
...here in your village.
You...
...are too naïve.
Huh?
Yeah, I might be.

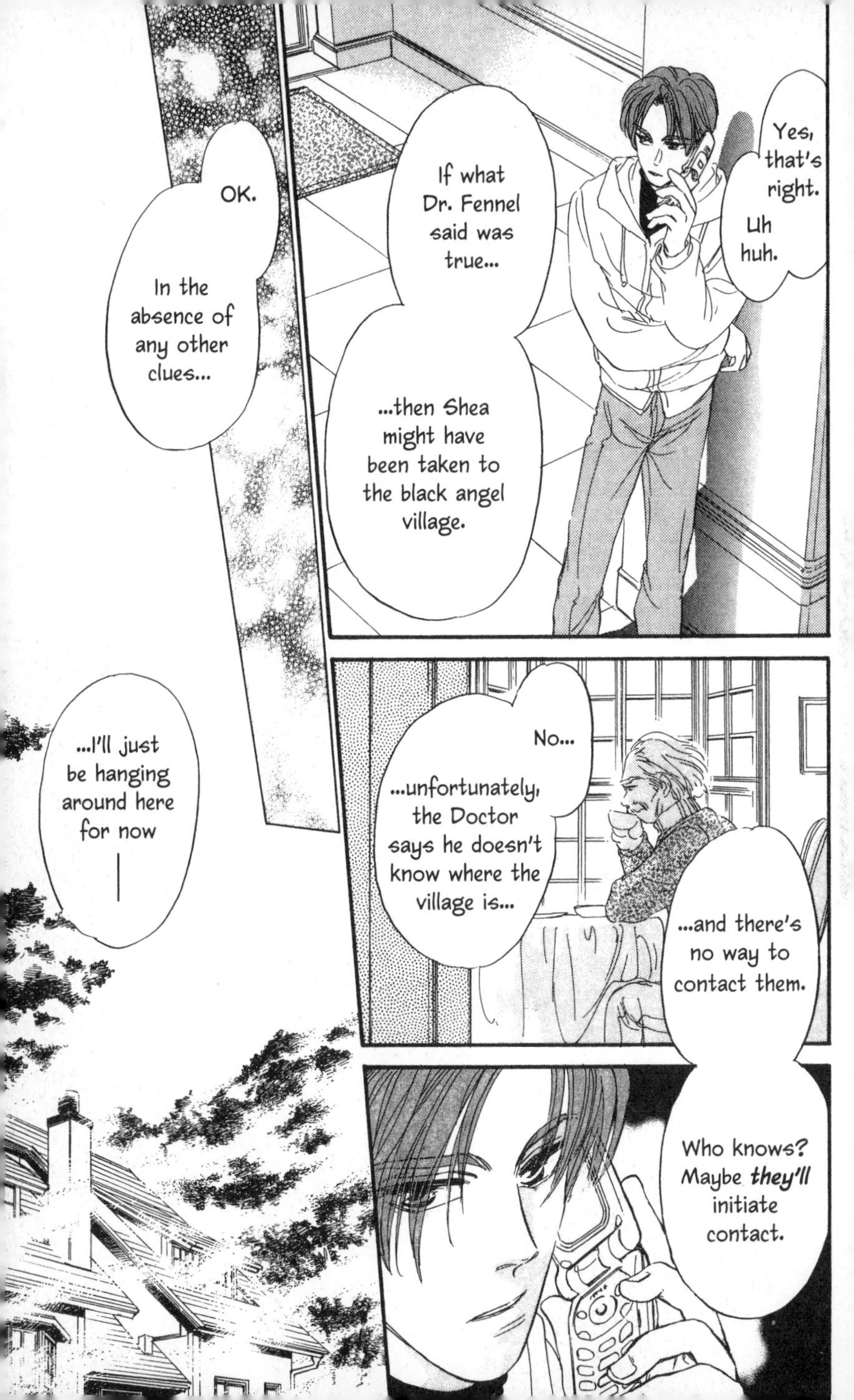
Yes, that's right.
Uh huh.
If what Dr. Fennel said was true...
...then Shea might have been taken to the black angel village.
No...
...unfortunately, the Doctor says he doesn't know where the village is...
...and there's no way to contact them.
Who knows? Maybe *they'll* initiate contact.
OK.
In the absence of any other clues...
...I'll just be hanging around here for now
|

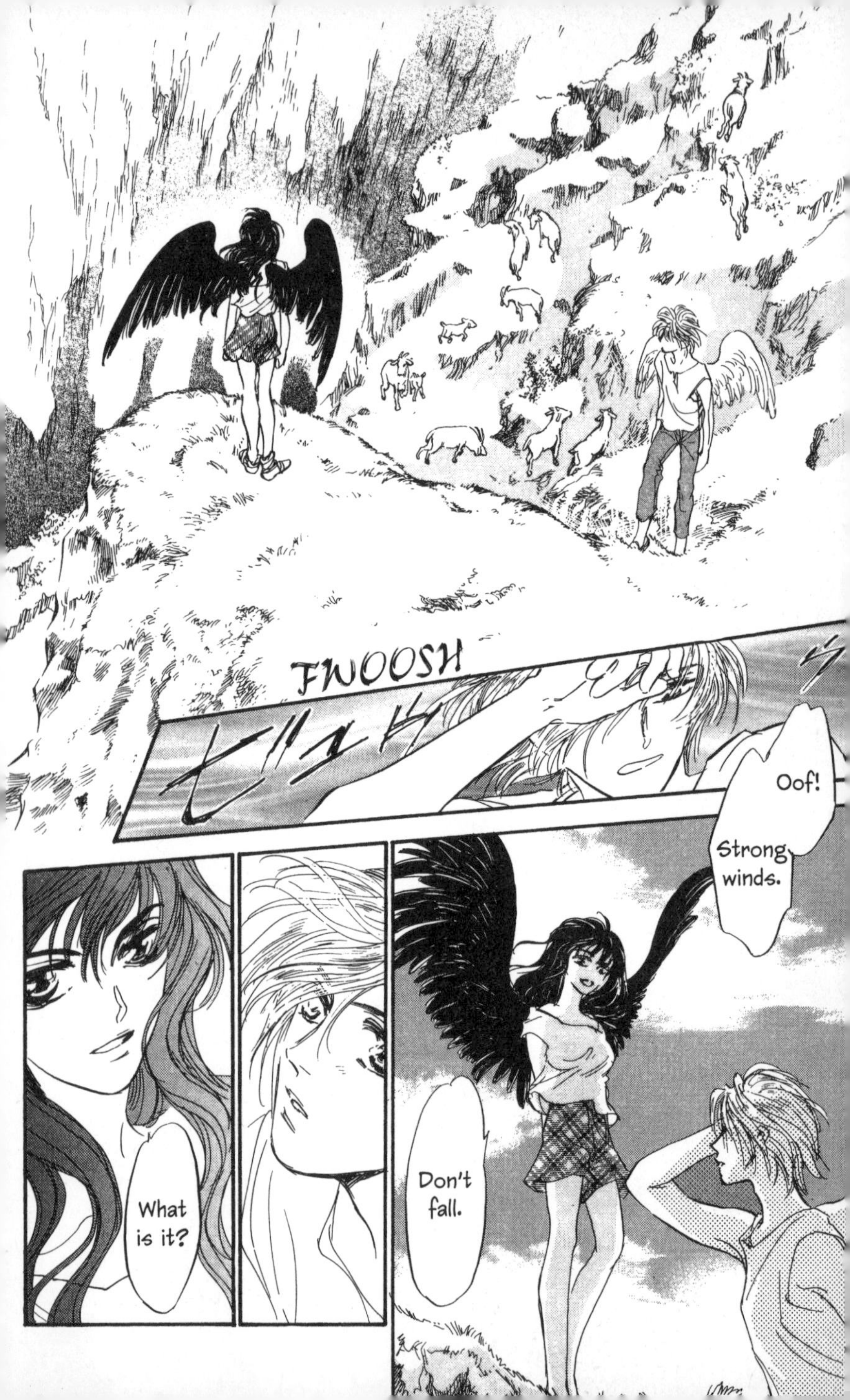
FWOOSH
Oof!
Strong winds.
Don't fall.
What is it?

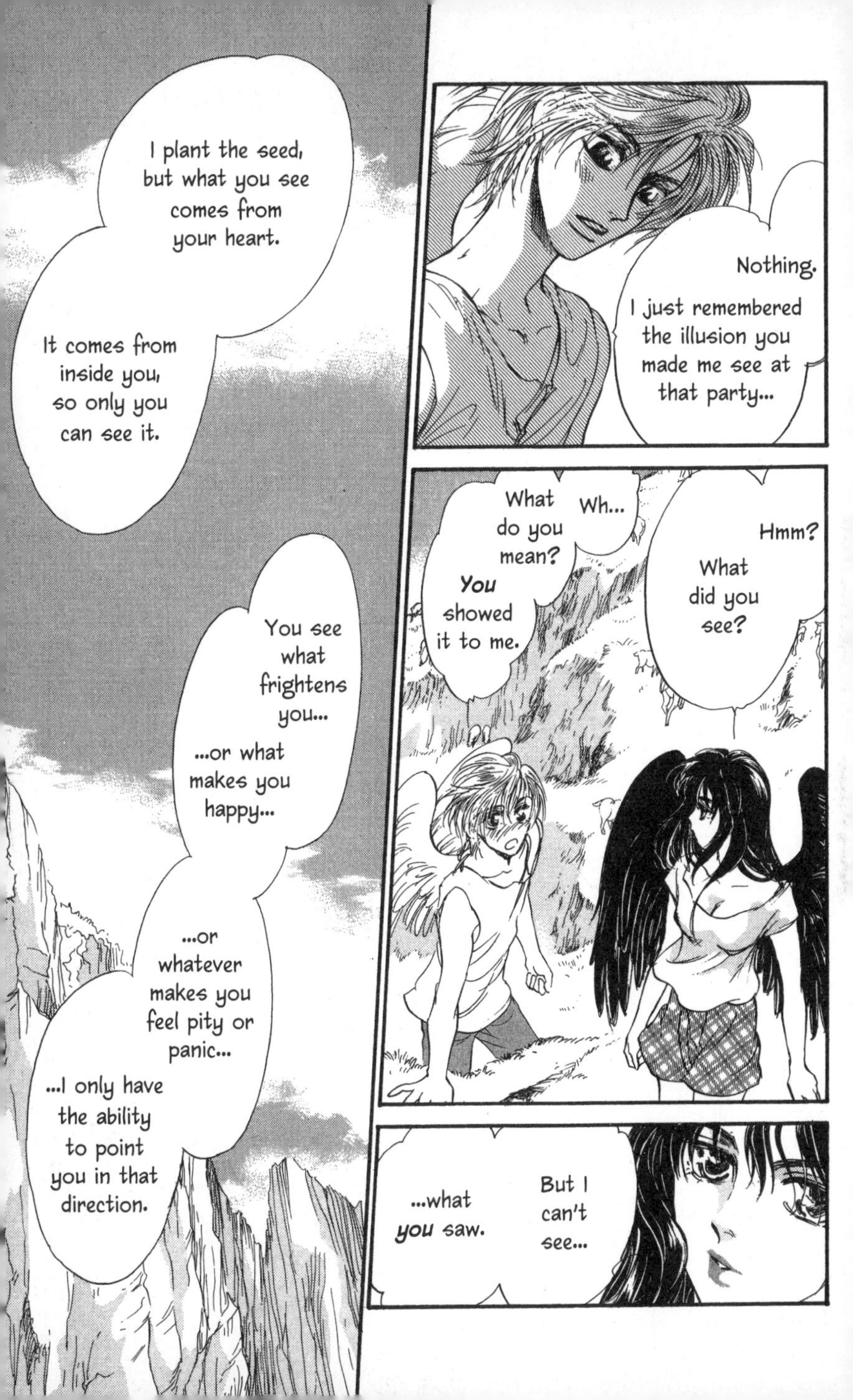
Nothing.
I just remembered the illusion you made me see at that party...
Hmm? What did you see?
Wh...
What do you mean? *You* showed it to me.
But I can't see...
...what *you* saw.
I plant the seed, but what you see comes from your heart.
It comes from inside you, so only you can see it.
You see what frightens you...
...or what makes you happy...
...or whatever makes you feel pity or panic...
...I only have the ability to point you in that direction.

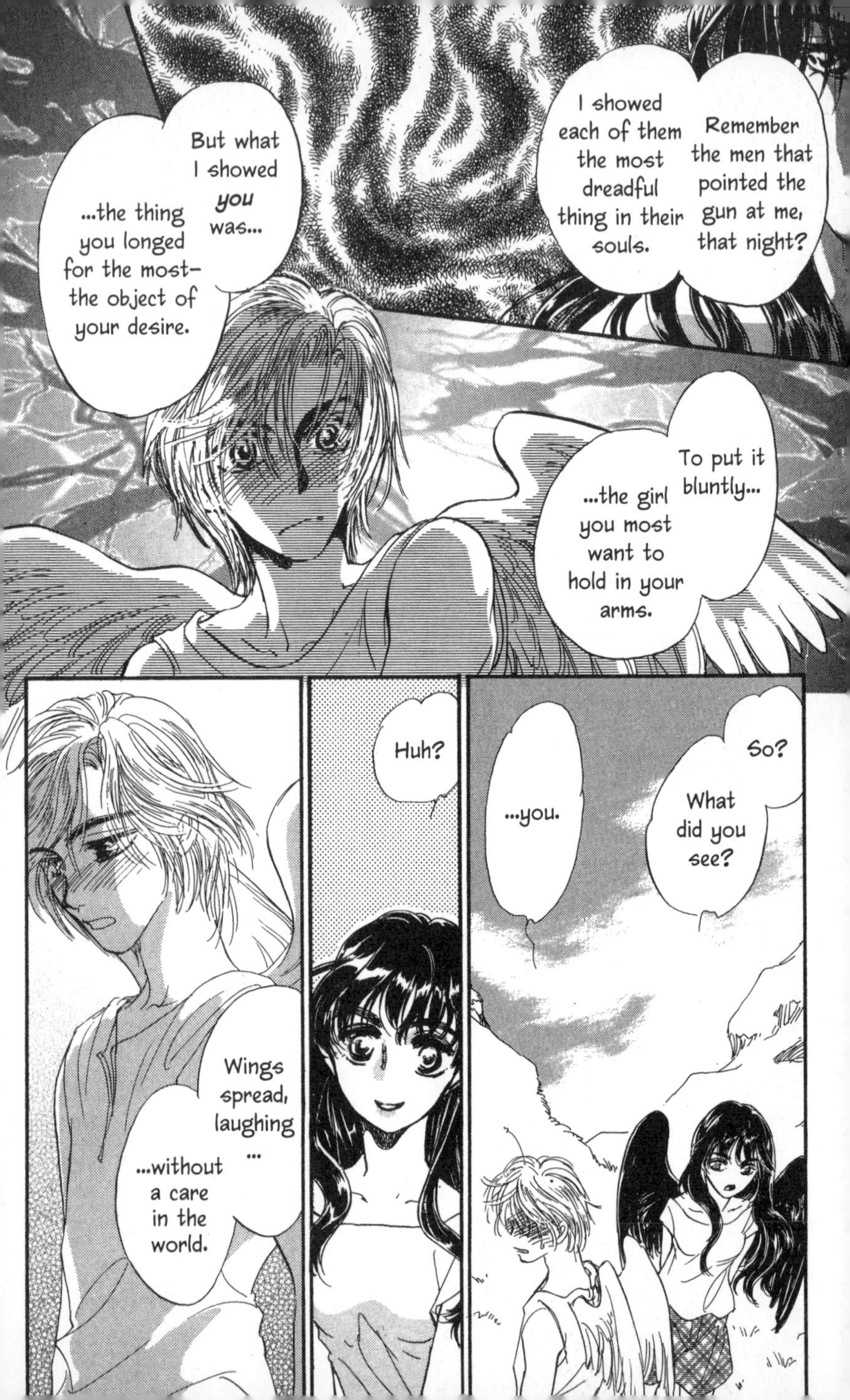

Remember the men that pointed the gun at me, that night?
I showed each of them the most dreadful thing in their souls.
But what I showed *you* was...
...the thing you longed for the most— the object of your desire.
To put it bluntly...
...the girl you most want to hold in your arms.
So?
What did you see?
...you.
Huh?
Wings spread, laughing ...
...without a care in the world.

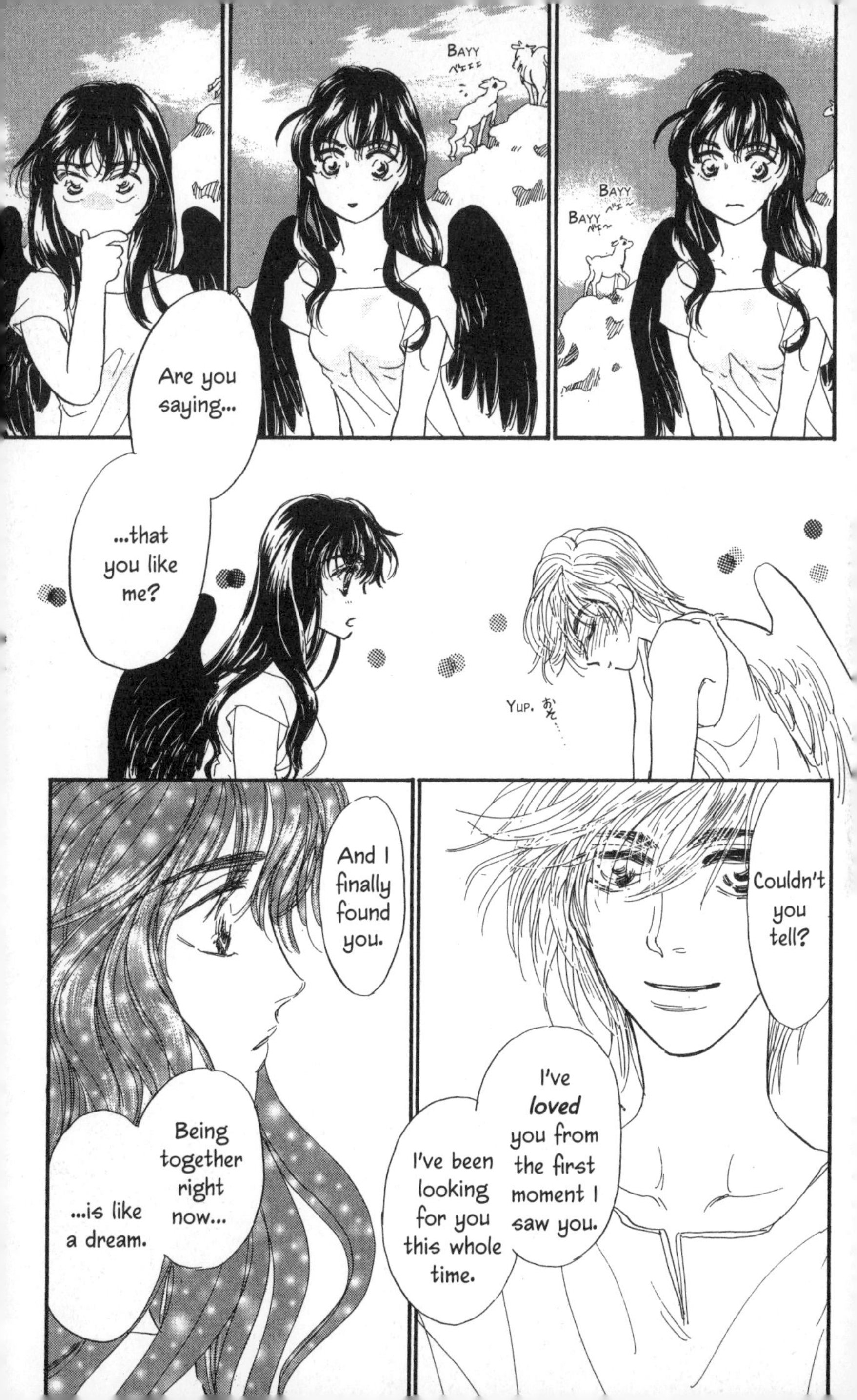
Bayy
Bayy
Bayy
Are you saying...
...that you like me?
Yup.
Couldn't you tell?
I've *loved* you from the first moment I saw you.
I've been looking for you this whole time.
And I finally found you.
Being together right now...
...is like a dream.

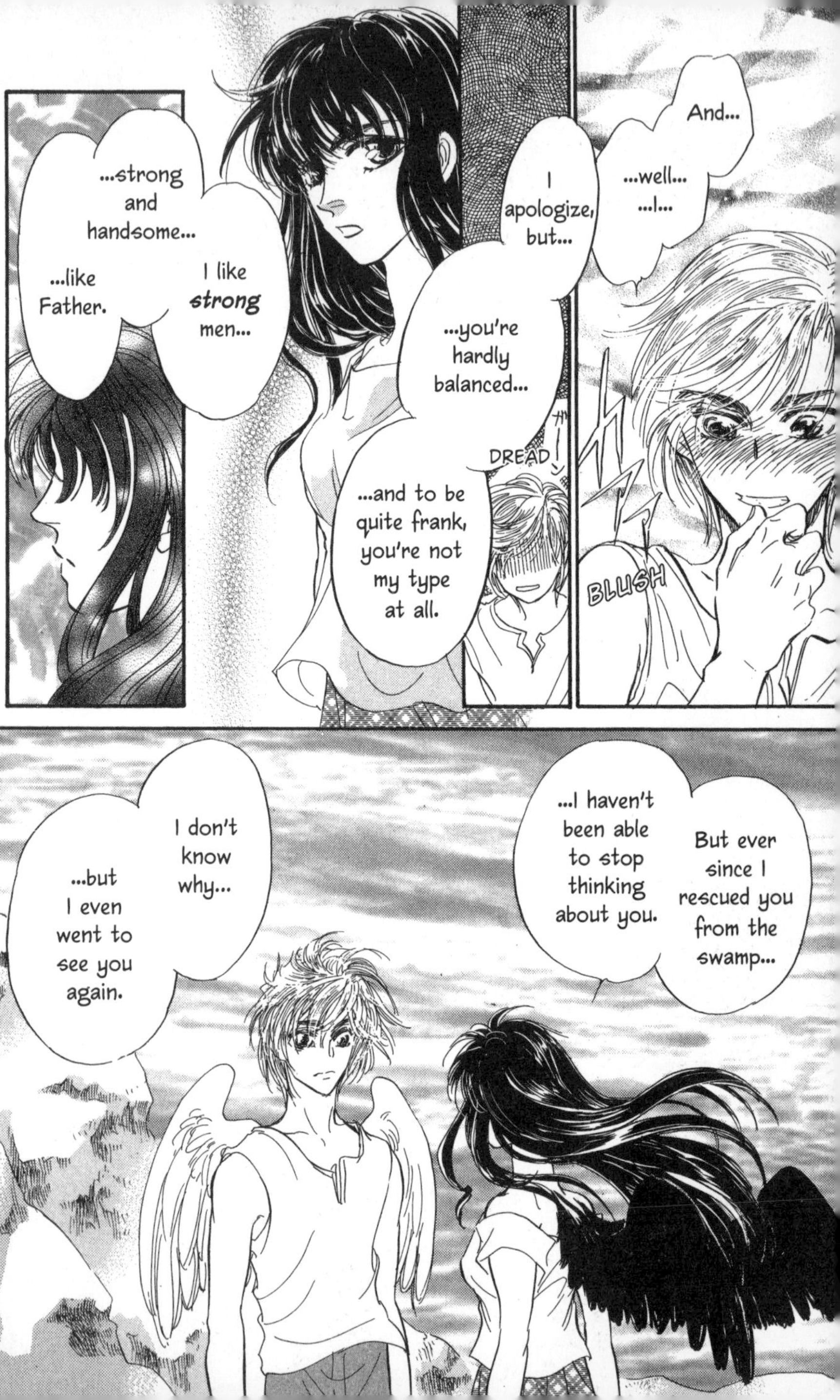
And...
...well... ...I...
BLUSH
I apologize, but...
...you're hardly balanced...
DREAD
...and to be quite frank, you're not my type at all.
I like **strong** men...
...strong and handsome...
...like Father.
But ever since I rescued you from the swamp...
...I haven't been able to stop thinking about you.
I don't know why...
...but I even went to see you again.

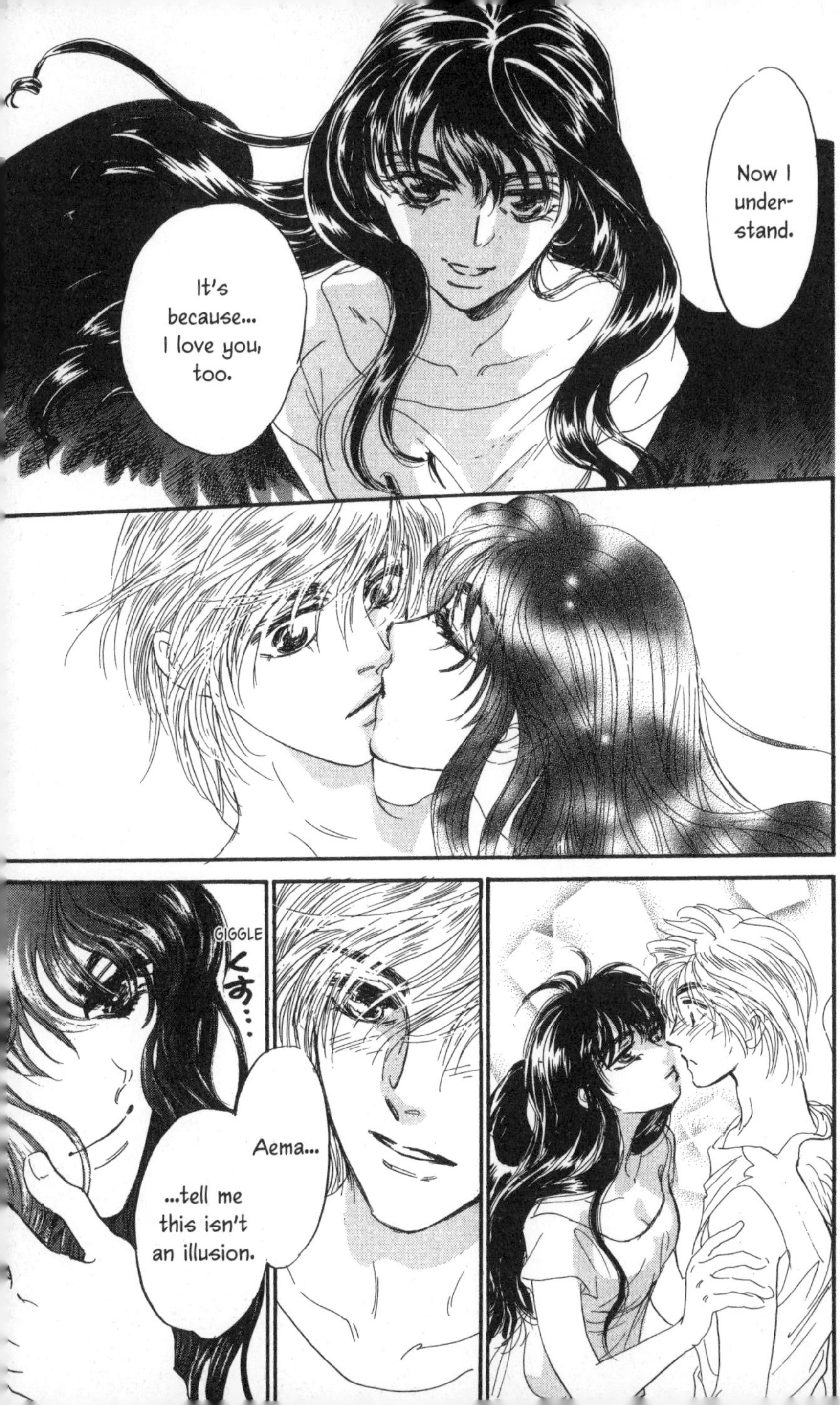
Now I understand.
It's because... I love you, too.
Aema...
...tell me this isn't an illusion.
GIGGLE
くす…

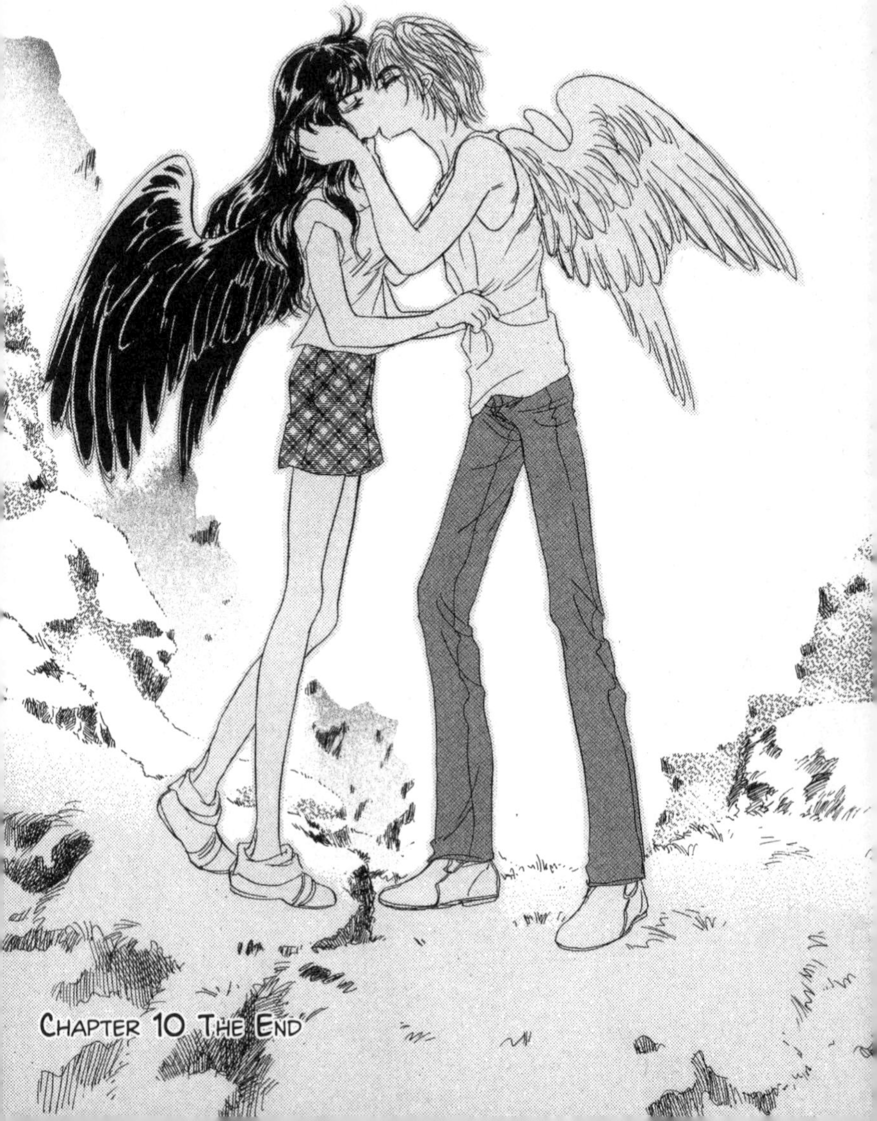

Chapter 10 The End

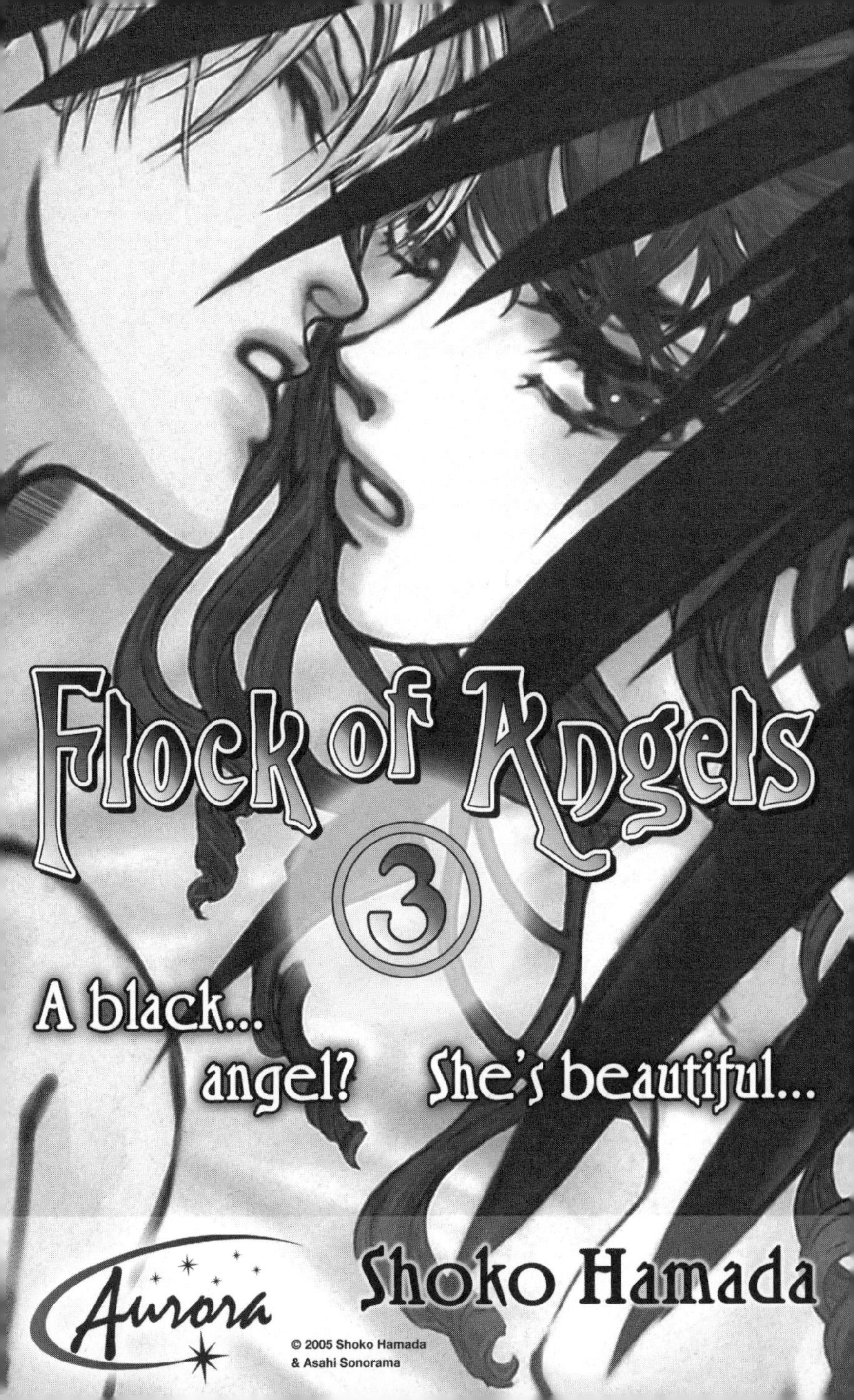
Flock of Angels
3
A black...
angel? She's beautiful...
Aurora
Shoko Hamada
© 2005 Shoko Hamada
& Asahi Sonorama

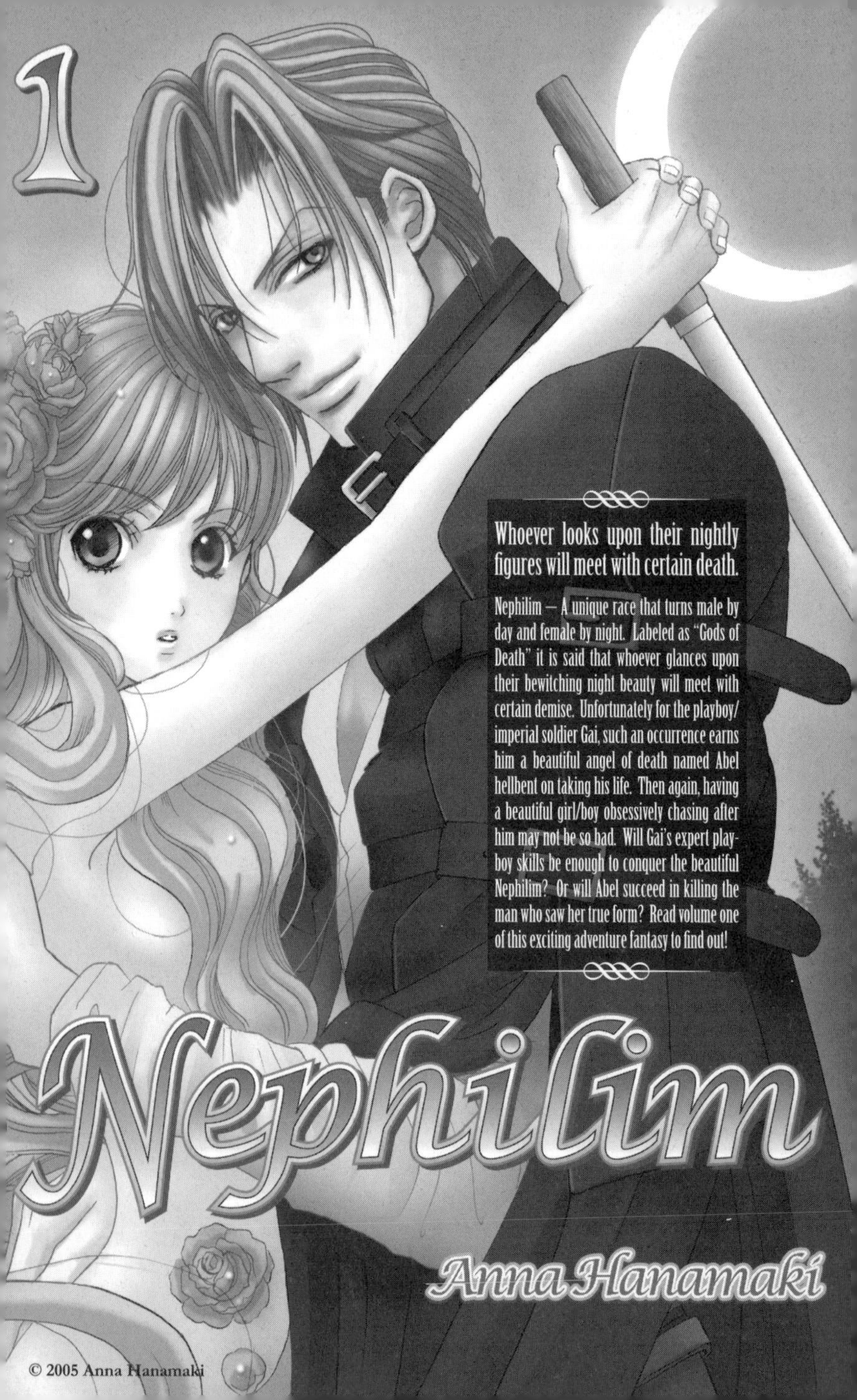
1
Whoever looks upon their nightly figures will meet with certain death.
Nephilim — A unique race that turns male by day and female by night. Labeled as "Gods of Death" it is said that whoever glances upon their bewitching night beauty will meet with certain demise. Unfortunately for the playboy/imperial soldier Gai, such an occurrence earns him a beautiful angel of death named Abel hellbent on taking his life. Then again, having a beautiful girl/boy obsessively chasing after him may not be so bad. Will Gai's expert playboy skills be enough to conquer the beautiful Nephilim? Or will Abel succeed in killing the man who saw her true form? Read volume one of this exciting adventure fantasy to find out!
Nephilim
Anna Hanamaki
© 2005 Anna Hanamaki

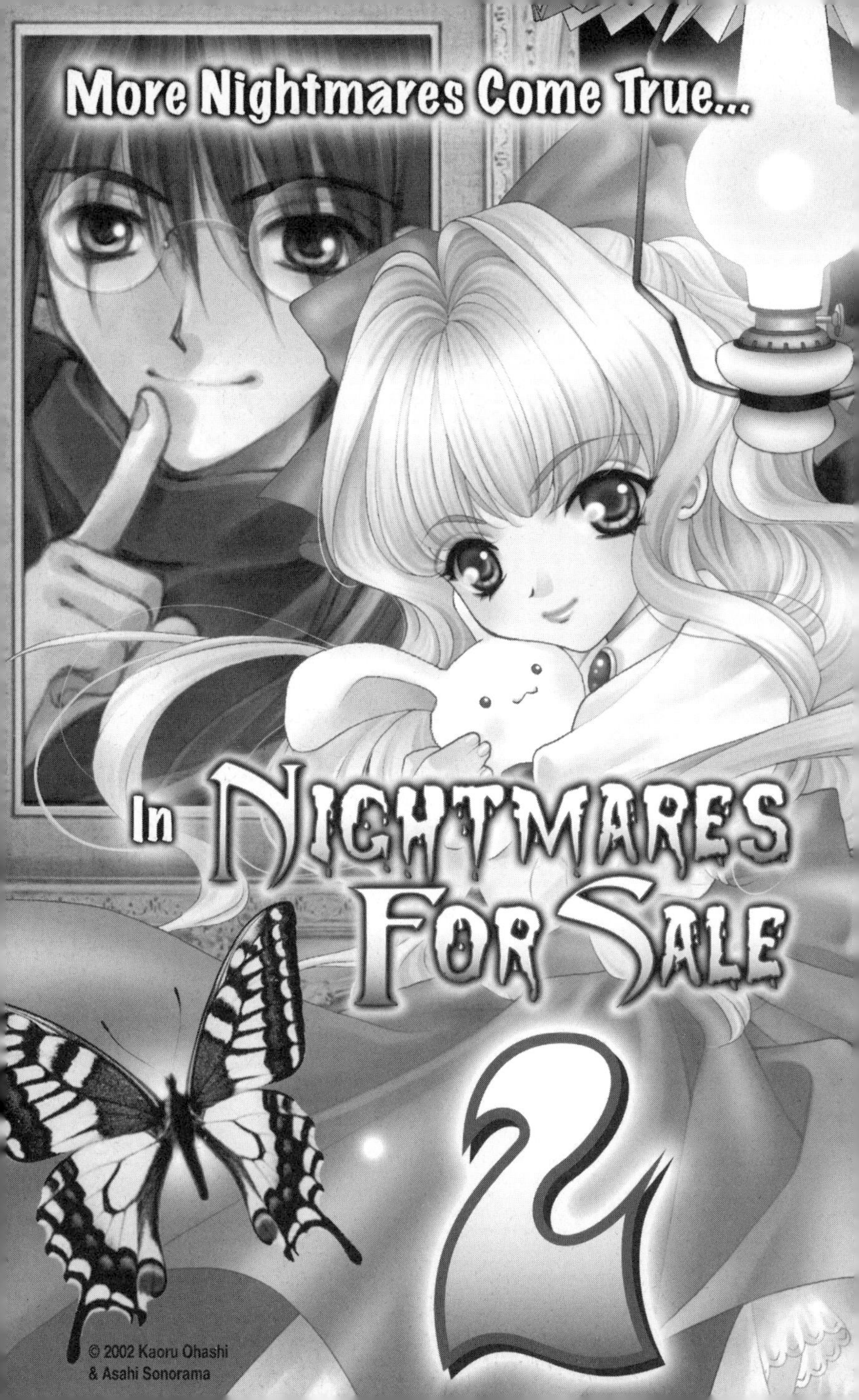
More Nightmares Come True...
In Nightmares For Sale
2
© 2002 Kaoru Ohashi
& Asahi Sonorama

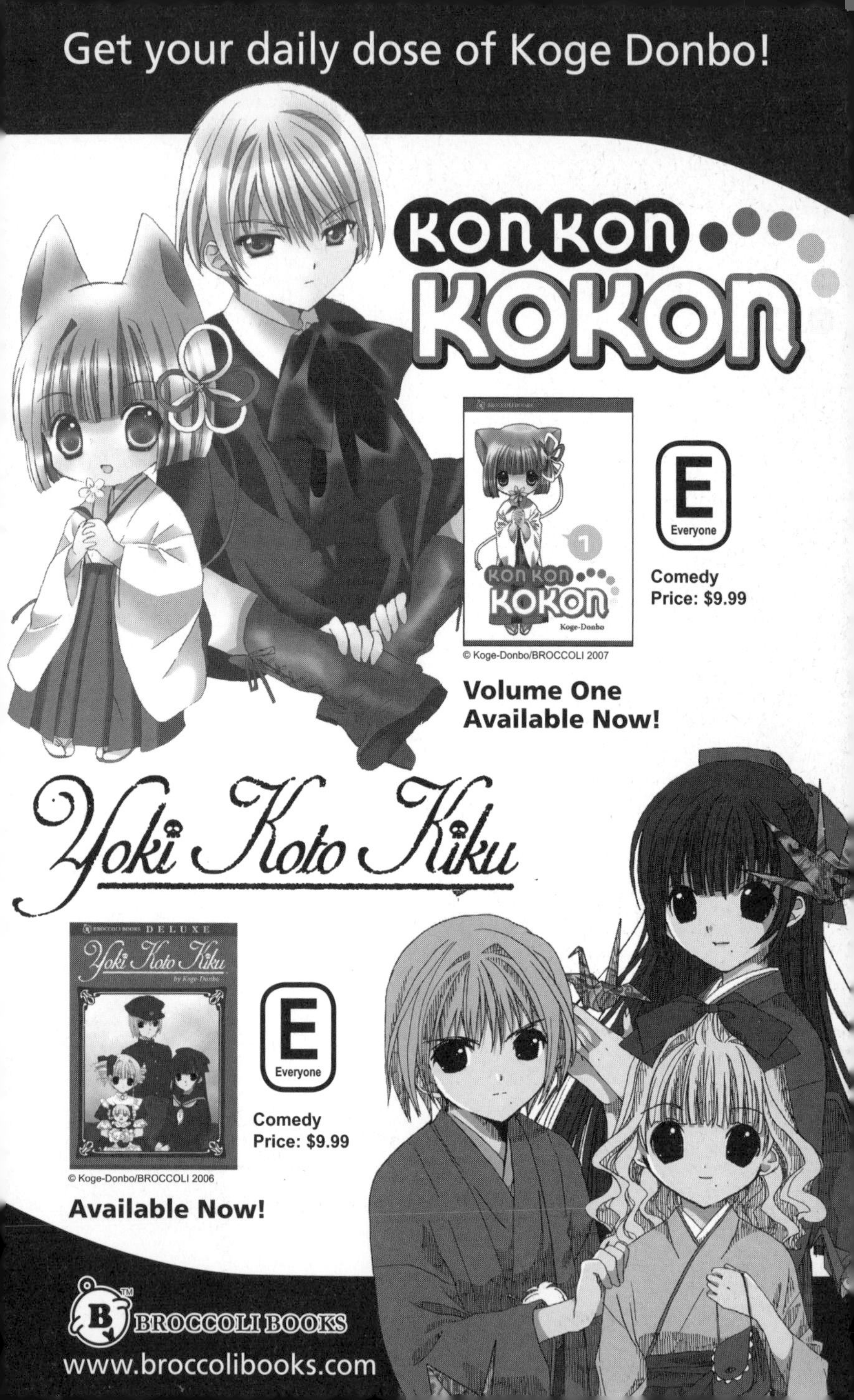
Get your daily dose of Koge Donbo!
KON KON KOKON
BROCCOLI BOOKS
KON KON KOKON
Koge-Donbo
E
Everyone
Comedy
Price: $9.99
© Koge-Donbo/BROCCOLI 2007
Volume One
Available Now!
Yoki Koto Kiku
BROCCOLI BOOKS DELUXE
Yoki Koto Kiku
by Koge-Donbo
E
Everyone
Comedy
Price: $9.99
© Koge-Donbo/BROCCOLI 2006
Available Now!
BROCCOLI BOOKS
www.broccolibooks.com

www.aurora-publishing.com

Aurora

Experience the Allure of Manga

Flock of Angels

2

Flock of Angels • Volume 2
Story and Art by Shoko Hamada

© 2004 by Shoko Hamada. First published in Japan in 2004
by Asahi Sonorama Co. Ltd., Tokyo as *Tenshi no Mure*.
English translation rights arranged with Asahi Sonorama Co. Ltd., Tokyo.

Translation: John Thomas, HC Language Solutions, Inc.
English Adaptation: Michelle Ma, HC Language Solutions, Inc.
Lettering: Thea Willis

Producer: Rod Sampson

Publisher: Nobuo Kitawaki

Published by Aurora Publishing, Inc.
www.aurora-publishing.com

This book is a work of fiction. Names, characters, places, and incidents
are the products of the author's imagination or are used fictitiously.

Printed in Japan